***TM 1-1520-236-10**

AH-1 COBRA
Attack Helicopter
Pilot's Flight Operating
Instructions

by HEADQUARTERS, DEPARTMENT OF THE ARMY

©2011 Periscope Film LLC
ISBN #978-1-935700-64-7
www.PeriscopeFilm.com

NOTICE:

This manual is sold for historic research purposes only, as an entertainment. It is not intended to be used as part of an actual flight training program. No book can substitute for flight training by an authorized instructor. The licensing of pilots is overseen by organizations and authorities such as the FAA and CAA. Operating an aircraft without the proper license is a federal crime.

*TM 1-1520-236-10

TECHNICAL MANUAL
OPERATORS MANUAL
FOR
ARMY MODEL
AH-1F
ATTACK HELICOPTER

- WARNING DATA
- TABLE OF CONTENTS
- INTRODUCTION
- DESCRIPTION AND OPERATION
- AVIONICS
- MISSION EQUIPMENT
- OPERATING LIMITS AND RESTRICTIONS
- WEIGHT/BALANCE AND LOADING
- **B540** PERFORMANCE DATA
- **K747** PERFORMANCE DATA
- NORMAL PROCEDURES
- EMERGENCY PROCEDURES
- REFERENCES
- ABBREVIATIONS AND TERMS
- ALPHABETICAL INDEX

DISTRIBUTION STATEMENT A: Approved for public release; distribution is unlimited.

HEADQUARTERS, DEPARTMENT OF THE ARMY
26 JANUARY 2001

*This manual supersedes TM 55-1520-236-10, dated 11 January 1980 including all changes.

TM 1-1520-236-10

INSERT LATEST CHANGED PAGES: DESTROY SUPERCEDED PAGES.

LIST OF EFFECTIVE PAGES

NOTE: The portion of the text affected by the changes is indicated by a vertical line in the outer margins of the page. Changes to illustrations are indicated by miniature pointing hands. Changes to wiring diagrams are indicated by shaded areas.

Date of issue for original and change pages are: 26 January 2001

Original .... 0 ...... 26 January 2001

TOTAL NUMBER OF PAGES IN THIS PUBLICATION IS 372, CONSISTING OF THE FOLLOWING:

Page No.	*Change No.
Cover	0
a thru e	0
f blank	0
A	0
B blank	0
i thru iii	0
iv blank	0
1-1 and 1-2	0
2-1 thru 2-47	0
2-48 blank	0
3-1 thru 3-45	0
3-46 blank	0
4-1 thru 4-54	0
5-1 thru 5-7	0
5-8 blank	0
6-1 thru 6-33	0
6-34 blank	0
7-1 thru 7-47	0
7-48 blank	0
7.1-1 thru 7.1-47	0
7.1-48 blank	0
8-1 thru 8-21	0
8-22 blank	0
9-1 thru 9-13	0
9-14 blank	0
A-1 thru A-3	0
A-4 blank	0
B-1 thru B-4	0
Index-1 thru Index-9	0
Index-10 blank	0

*Zero in this column indicates an original page.

*TM 1-1520-236-10

TECHNICAL MANUAL
No. 1-1520-236-10

HEADQUARTERS
DEPARTMENT OF THE ARMY
WASHINGTON, D.C., 26 January 2001

TECHNICAL MANUAL

OPERATORS MANUAL
FOR
ARMY MODEL
AH-1F
ATTACK HELICOPTER

REPORTING ERRORS AND RECOMMENDING IMPROVEMENTS

You can help improve this manual. If you find any mistakes, or if you know of a way to improve these procedures, please let us know. Mail your letter, DA Form 2028 (Recommended Changes to Publications and Blank Forms) or DA Form 2028-2 located in the back of this manual directly to: Commander, U.S. Army Aviation and Missile Command, ATTN: AMSAM-MMC-LS-LP, Redstone Arsenal, AL 35898-5000. A reply will be furnished directly to you.

You may also submit your recommended changes by E-mail directly to ls-lp@redstone.army.mil or by fax (256) 842-6546/DSN 788-6546. Instructions for sending an electronic 2028 may be found at the end of this manual immediately preceding the hard copy 2028s.

DISTRIBUTION STATEMENT A: Approved for public release; distribution is unlimited.

TABLE OF CONTENTS

			Page
CHAPTER	1	INTRODUCTION	1-1
CHAPTER	2	HELICOPTER AND SYSTEMS DESCRIPTION AND OPERATION	
Section	I	Helicopter	2-1
	II	Emergency Equipment	2-10
	III	Engine and Related Systems	2-12
	IV	Helicopter Fuel System	2-19
	V	Flight Controls	2-20
	VI	Hydraulic Systems	2-22
	VII	Power Train System	2-23
	VIII	Main and Tail Rotors	2-24
	IX	Utility System	2-24
	X	Heating, Ventilation, Cooling and Environmental Control Unit	2-26
	XI	Electrical Power Supply and Distribution System	2-26
	XII	Lighting	2-30

*This manual supersedes TM 55-1520-236-10, dated 11 January 1980, including all changes:

i

TABLE OF CONTENTS (Continued)

	XIII	Flight Instruments	2-35
	XIV	Servicing, Parking, and Mooring	2-39
CHAPTER 3		AVIONICS	
Section	I	General	3-1
	II	Communications	3-1
	III	Navigation	3-21
	IV	Transponder and Radar	3-34
CHAPTER 4		MISSION EQUIPMENT	
Section	I	Mission Avionics	4-1
	II	Armament	4-2
	III	Active and Passive Defense Equipment	4-51
CHAPTER 5		OPERATING LIMITS AND RESTRICTIONS	
Section	I	General	5-1
	II	System Limits	5-1
	III	Power Limits	5-4
	IV	Loading Limits	5-5
	V	Airspeed Limits	5-5
	VI	Maneuvering Limits	5-7
	VII	Environmental Restrictions	5-7
	VIII	Height Velocity	5-7
CHAPTER 6		WEIGHT/BALANCE AND LOADING	
Section	I	General	6-1
	II	Weight and Balance	6-3
	III	Personnel	6-3
	IV	Mission Equipment	6-5
	V	Cargo Loading (Not Applicable)	6-29
	VI	Fuel/Oil	6-29
	VII	Allowable Loading	6-31
CHAPTER 7		PERFORMANCE DATA B540	
Section	I	Introduction	7-1
	II	Performance Planning	7-5
	III	Torque Available	7-7
	IV	Hover	7-12
	V	Cruise	7-18

*TM 1-1520-236-10

TABLE OF CONTENTS (Continued)

	VI	Drag	7-42
	VII	Climb - Descent	7-44
	VIII	Idle Fuel Flow	7-46
CHAPTER 7.1		PERFORMANCE DATA K747	
Section	I	Introduction	7.1-1
	II	Performance Planning	7.1-5
	III	Torque Available	7.1-7
	IV	Hover	7.1-12
	V	Cruise	7.1-18
	VI	Drag	7.1-42
	VII	Climb - Descent	7.1-44
	VIII	Idle Fuel Flow	7.1-46
CHAPTER 8		NORMAL PROCEDURES	
Section	I	Crew Duties	8-1
	II	Operating Procedures and Maneuvers	8-4
	III	Instrument Flight	8-13
	IV	Flight Characteristics	8-13
	V	Adverse Environmental Conditions	8-19
CHAPTER 9		EMERGENCY PROCEDURES	
Section	I	Helicopter Systems	9-1
	II	Mission Equipment	9-11
APPENDIX A		REFERENCE	A-1
APPENDIX B		ABBREVIATIONS AND TERMS	B-1
INDEX			Index 1

iii/(iv blank)

CHAPTER 1
INTRODUCTION

2-1. GENERAL.

These instructions are for use by the operator of the AH-1F helicopter.

2-2. WARNING, CAUTIONS, AND NOTES DEFINITION.

Warnings, cautions, and notes are used to emphasize important and critical instructions and are used for the following conditions:

WARNING

An operating procedure, practice, etc., which, if not correctly followed, could result in personal injury or loss of life.

CAUTION

An operating procedure, practice, etc., which, if not strictly observed could result in damage to or destruction of equipment.

NOTE

An operating procedure, condition, etc., which it is essential to highlight.

2-3. DESCRIPTION.

This manual contains the best operating instructions and procedures for the AH-1F helicopter under most circumstances. The observance of limitations, performance and weight balance data provided is mandatory. The observance of procedure is mandatory except when modification is required because of multiple emergencies, adverse weather, terrain, etc. Your flying experience is recognized, and therefore, basic flight principles are not included. **THIS MANUAL SHALL BE CARRIED IN THE HELICOPTER AT ALL TIMES.**

2-4. APPENDIX A. REFERENCES.

Appendix A is a listing of official publications cited within the manual applicable to and available for flight crews.

2-5. APPENDIX B. ABBREVIATIONS AND TERMS.

Appendix B provides a glossary of abbreviations and terms used throughout the text.

2-6. INDEX.

The index lists, in alphabetical order, every titled paragraph, figure and table contained in this manual. Chapters 7 and 7.1 performance data have an additional index within each chapter.

2-7. ARMY AVIATION SAFETY PROGRAM

Reports necessary to comply with the safety program are prescribed in AR 385-40.

2-8. DESTRUCTION OF ARMY MATERIAL TO PREVENT ENEMY USE.

For information concerning destruction of Army material to prevent enemy use, refer to TM 750-244-1-5.

2-9. FORMS AND RECORDS.

Army aviators flight record and helicopter maintenance records which are to be used by crewmembers are prescribed in DA PAM 738-751 and TM 55-1500-342-23.

2-10. EXPLANATION OF CHANGE SYMBOLS.

Changes, except as noted below, to the text and tables, including new material on added pages, are indicated by a vertical line in the outer margin extending close to the entire area of the material affected; exception: pages with emergency markings, which consist of black diagonal lines around three edges, may have the vertical line or change symbol placed along the inner margins. Symbols show current changes only. A miniature pointing hand symbol is used to denote a change to an illustration. However, a vertical line in the outer margin, rather than miniature pointing hands, is utilized when there have been extensive changes to an illustration. Change symbols are utilized to indicate changes in the following:

a. Introductory material.

b. Indexes and tabular data where the change cannot be identified.

c. Blank space resulting from the deletion of text, an illustration, or a table.

d. Correction of minor inaccuracies, such as spelling, punctuation, relocation of material, etc., unless such correction changes the meaning of instructive information and procedures.

2-11. HELICOPTER DESIGNATION SYSTEM.

The designation system prescribed by AR 70-50 is used in helicopter designations as follows:

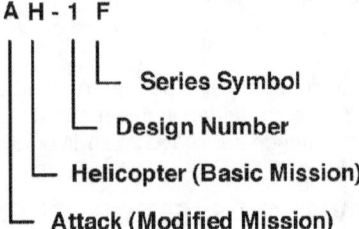

2-12. SERIES AND EFFECTIVITY CODES.

Designator symbols are used in conjunction with text contents, text headings and illustration titles to show limited effectivity of the material. One or more designator symbols may follow a text heading or illustration title to indicate proper effectivity, unless the material applies to all series and configurations within the manual. Designator symbol **CN** C-Nite precedes procedural steps in Chapters 4, 8, and 9 and other areas to indicate effectivity. If the material applies to all series and configurations, no designator symbols will be used. Where practical, descriptive information is condensed and combined for all models to avoid duplication.

Designator symbols for different types of main rotor blades are: **B540** for the Bell main rotor blade and **K747** for the Kaman main rotor blade.

2-13. USE OF SHALL, WILL, SHOULD, AND MAY.

Use "shall" whenever it is necessary to express a provision that is binding. Use "should" and "may" whenever it is necessary to express non-mandatory provisions. "Will" may be used to express a declaration of purpose.

CHAPTER 2

HELICOPTER AND SYSTEMS DESCRIPTION AND OPERATION

SECTION I. HELICOPTER

2-1. GENERAL DESCRIPTION.

The AH-1F helicopter is a tandem seat, two place (pilot and gunner), single engine aerial weapon platform.

a. Fuselage. The fuselage (forward section) employs aluminum alloy skins and aluminum, titanium and fiberglass honeycomb panel construction. Honeycomb deck panels and bulkheads attached to two main beams produce a box-beam structure. These beams make up the primary structure and provide support for the cockpit, landing gear, wings, engine, pylon assembly, fuel cells, and tailboom. The nose section incorporates the turret system and telescopic sight unit.

b. Wing. The fixed cantilever wings have a span of 129 inches (including tip) and a mean chord of 30 inches. The wings provide additional lift and support to the wing stores pylon. Each wing has two pylons. The inboard pylons are fixed and the outboard pylons are articulated by hydraulic actuators. An ejector rack is attached to each pylon. Both inboard and outboard pylons will each support 670 pounds of weight.

c. Tailboom. The tailboom (aft section) is a tapered semimonocoque structure attached to the forward section by four bolts. The tailboom supports the cambered fin, tail skid, elevators, tail rotor and tail rotor drive system.

    d. Main Rotor Blades.

       (1) B540 The main rotor blades are metal, bonded assemblies. Each blade is attached in the hub with a retaining bolt assembly and is held in alignment by adjustable drag braces.

       (2) K747 The main rotor blades are glass fiber epoxy resin bonded assemblies with a rubber erosion guard. The skin is basket weave which will not be as smooth as a metal blade. Each blade is attached in the hub with a retaining bolt assembly and is held in alignment by adjustable drag braces.

e. Weight Classification. The weight classification of this helicopter is Class 2. (Refer to Chapter 6.)

f. Controls and Indicators. Refer to applicable system for descriptive information.

2-2. GENERAL ARRANGEMENT.

Figure 2-1 shows the general arrangement of the items which are referred to in the exterior check paragraph of Chapter 8, Section 11.

2-3. PRINCIPAL DIMENSIONS.

Figure 2-2 shows the principal dimensions of the helicopter to the nearest inch.

2-4. TURNING RADIUS.

Figure 2-3 shows the minimum turning radius of the helicopter.

2-5. MAIN DIFFERENCES.

The main differences between the AH-1F and CN is the TSU FLIR Subsystem M65.

2-6. CREW COMPARTMENT DIAGRAMS.

The upper forward portion between the fuselage is the crew compartment. Tandem seating is provided with the pilot elevated in the rear seat.

    a. Pilot Station. Figure 2-4 shows the location.

    b. Gunner Station. Figure 2-5 shows the locations of equipment in the gunner station.

TM 1-1520-236-10

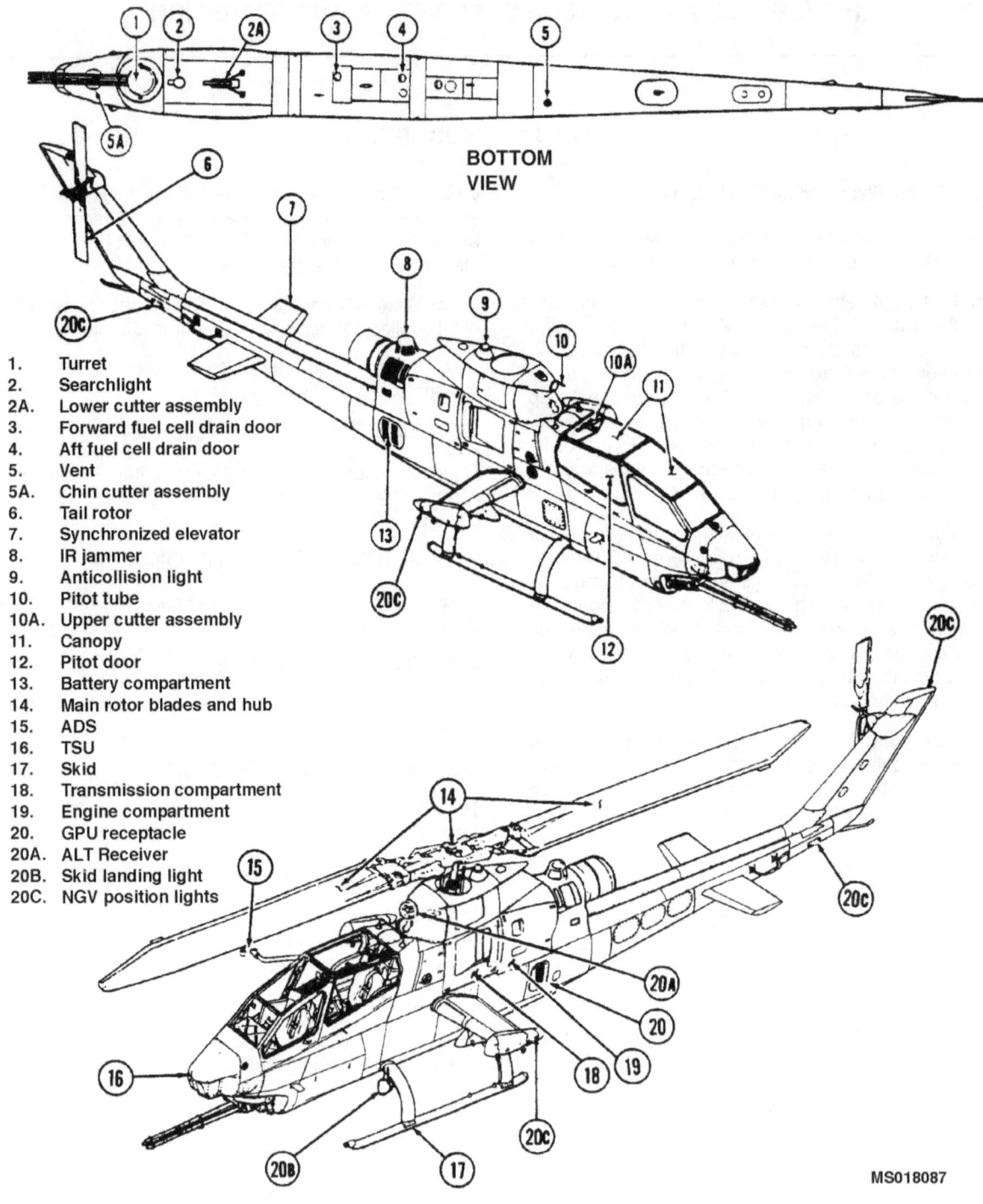

1. Turret
2. Searchlight
2A. Lower cutter assembly
3. Forward fuel cell drain door
4. Aft fuel cell drain door
5. Vent
5A. Chin cutter assembly
6. Tail rotor
7. Synchronized elevator
8. IR jammer
9. Anticollision light
10. Pitot tube
10A. Upper cutter assembly
11. Canopy
12. Pitot door
13. Battery compartment
14. Main rotor blades and hub
15. ADS
16. TSU
17. Skid
18. Transmission compartment
19. Engine compartment
20. GPU receptacle
20A. ALT Receiver
20B. Skid landing light
20C. NGV position lights

Figure 2-1. General Arrangement (Typical) (Sheet 1 of 2)

TM 1-1520-236-10

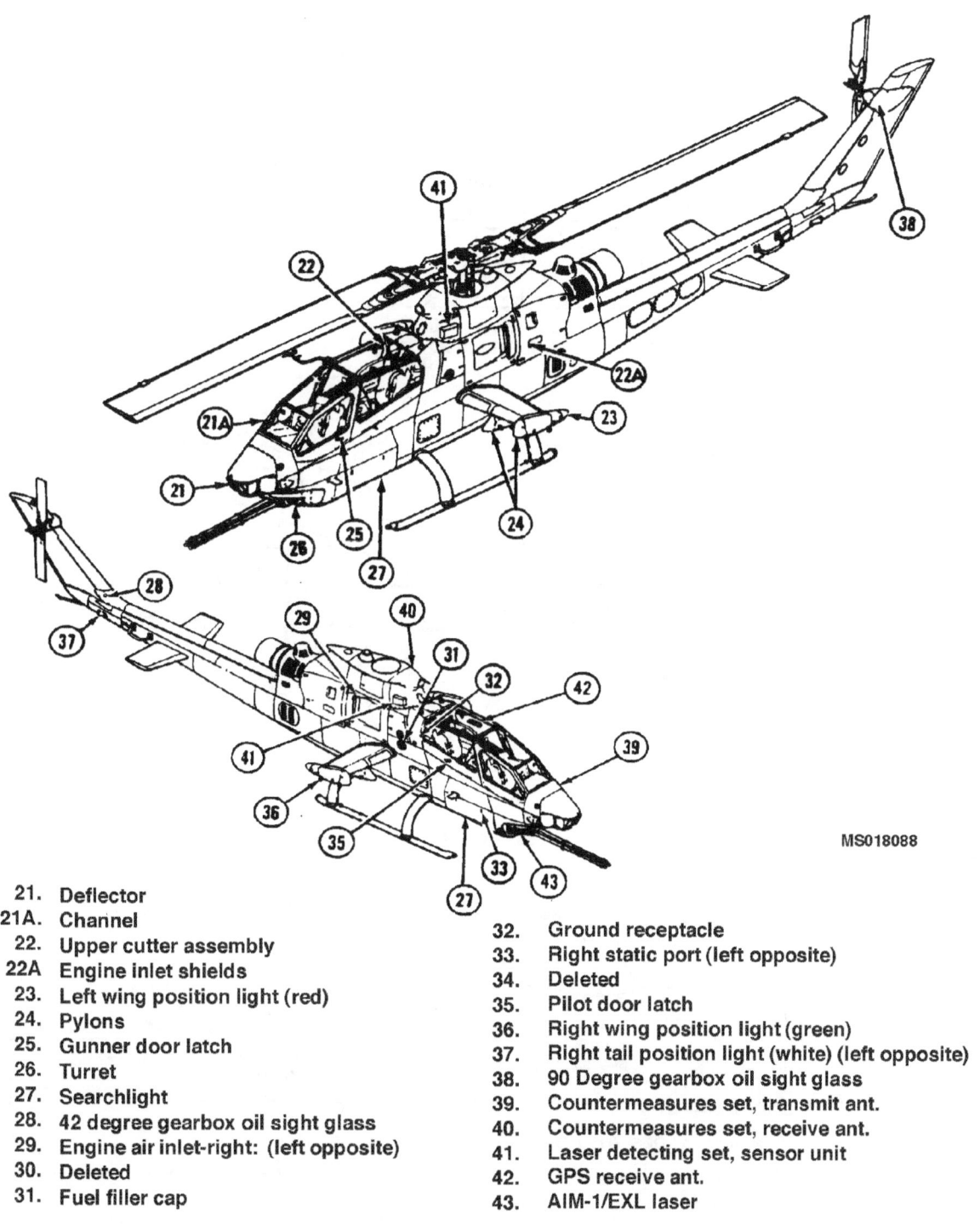

21. Deflector
21A. Channel
22. Upper cutter assembly
22A Engine inlet shields
23. Left wing position light (red)
24. Pylons
25. Gunner door latch
26. Turret
27. Searchlight
28. 42 degree gearbox oil sight glass
29. Engine air inlet-right: (left opposite)
30. Deleted
31. Fuel filler cap
32. Ground receptacle
33. Right static port (left opposite)
34. Deleted
35. Pilot door latch
36. Right wing position light (green)
37. Right tail position light (white) (left opposite)
38. 90 Degree gearbox oil sight glass
39. Countermeasures set, transmit ant.
40. Countermeasures set, receive ant.
41. Laser detecting set, sensor unit
42. GPS receive ant.
43. AIM-1/EXL laser

Figure 2-1. General Arrangement (Typical) (Sheet 2 of 2)

2-3

TM 1-1520-236-10

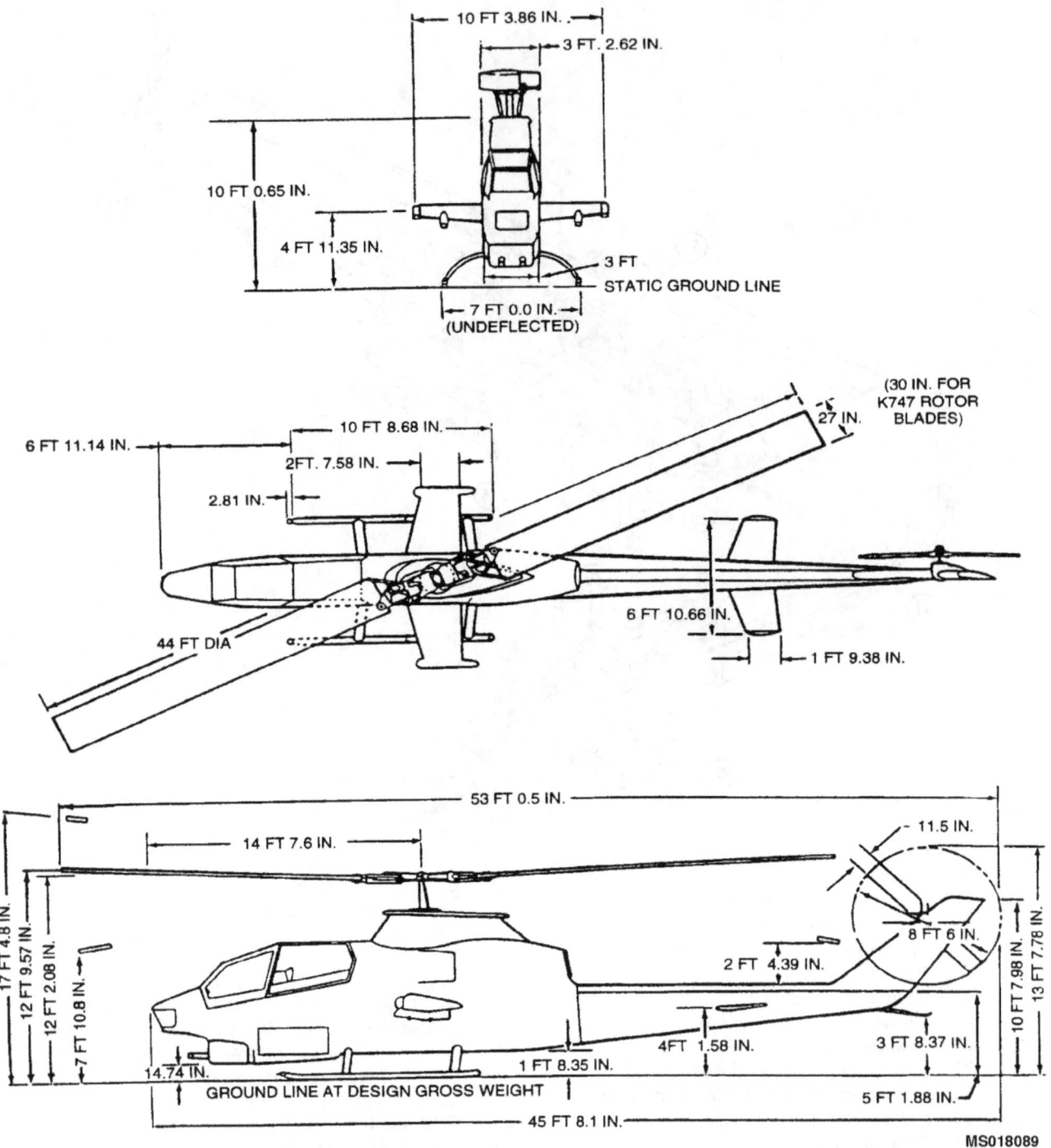

Figure 2-2. Principal Dimensions - Airframe

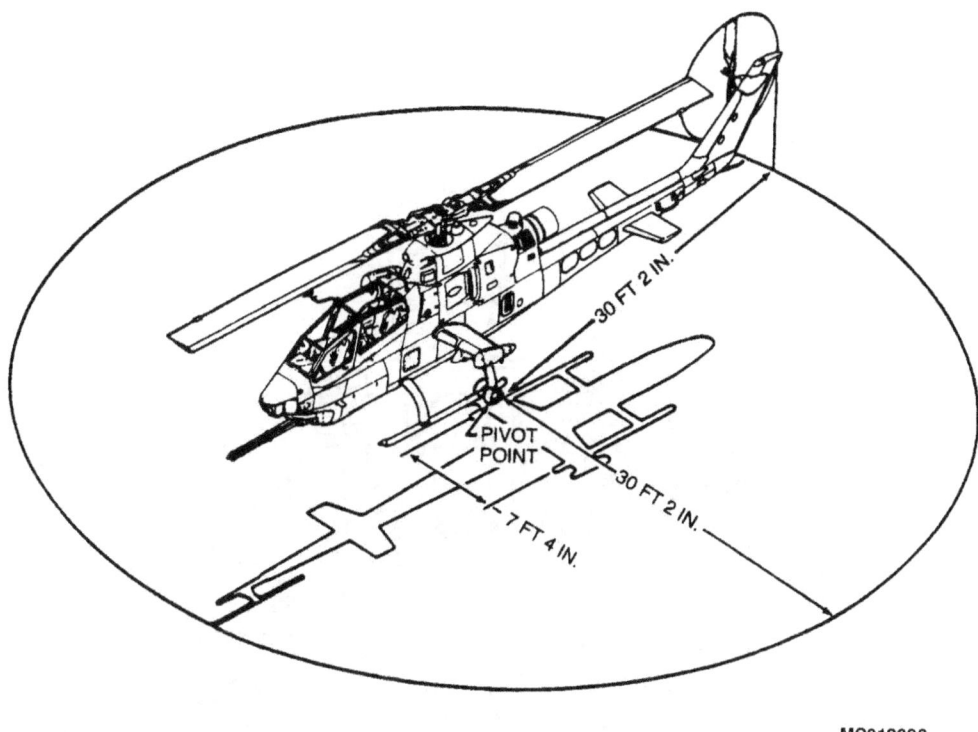

Figure 2-3. Turning Radius (Typical)

2-7. LANDING GEAR.

a. Main Landing Gear. The main landing gear consists of two aluminum lateral mounted arched crosstubes and two aluminum longitudinal skid tubes attached to the cross tubes. Each crosstube is enclosed in a fiberglass fairing for aerodynamic purposes. Each skid tube has a steel skid shoe on the bottom to minimize skid wear.

b. Tail Skid. The steel tubular type tail skid is installed on the aft end of the tailboom to protect the tail rotor blades during tail-low landing.

2-8. INSTRUMENTS AND CONTROLS.

a. Pilot Instrument Panel. Figure 2-6 shows the locations of instruments, switches, panels, and decals in the pilot instrument panel.

b. Gunner Instrument Panel. Figure 2-7 shows the locations of instruments, switches, panels, and decals in the gunner instrument panel.

c. Other Instruments and Controls. These items are shown in the chapter/section which describes their related systems.

2-9. CANOPY.

The canopy is the transparent panels on the upper portion of the fuselage which encloses the crew compartment. The canopy consists of a three piece windshield extending from the nose of the helicopter (over the gunner and pilot heads) to the pylon, the gunner door and pilot window on the left side, and the gunner window and pilot door on the right side. The canopy removal system is used to remove the pilot and gunner windows and doors during emergencies. The system is covered in Chapter 2, Section II.

2-10. PERSONNEL DOORS.

Two access doors are hinged on top and swing outward and up to provide access. The doors have gas operated struts that will hold the doors in the full open position with a force of approximately 70 pounds.

TM 1-1520-236-10

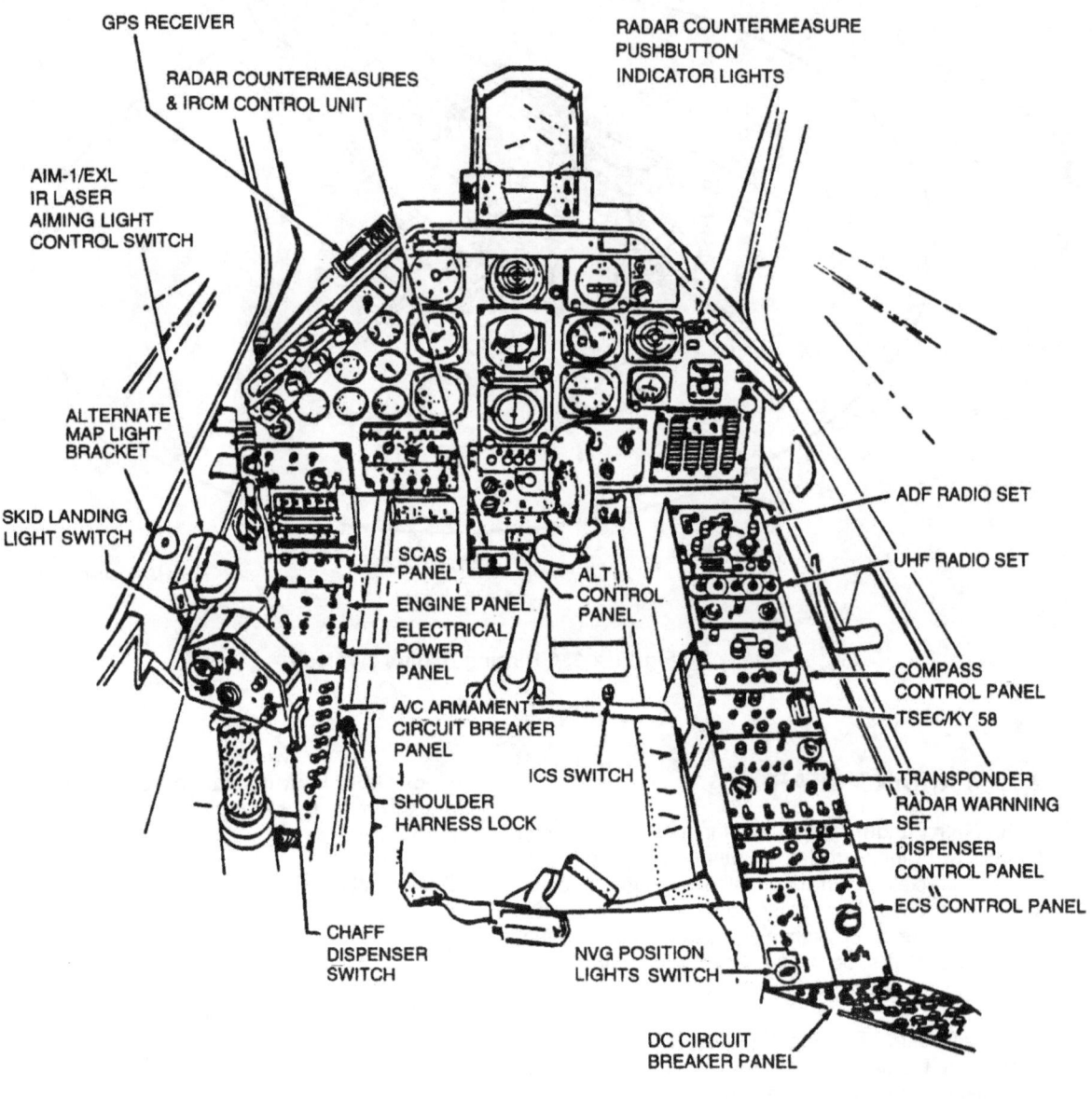

Figure 2-4. Pilot Station Diagram (Typical)

TM 1-1520-236-10

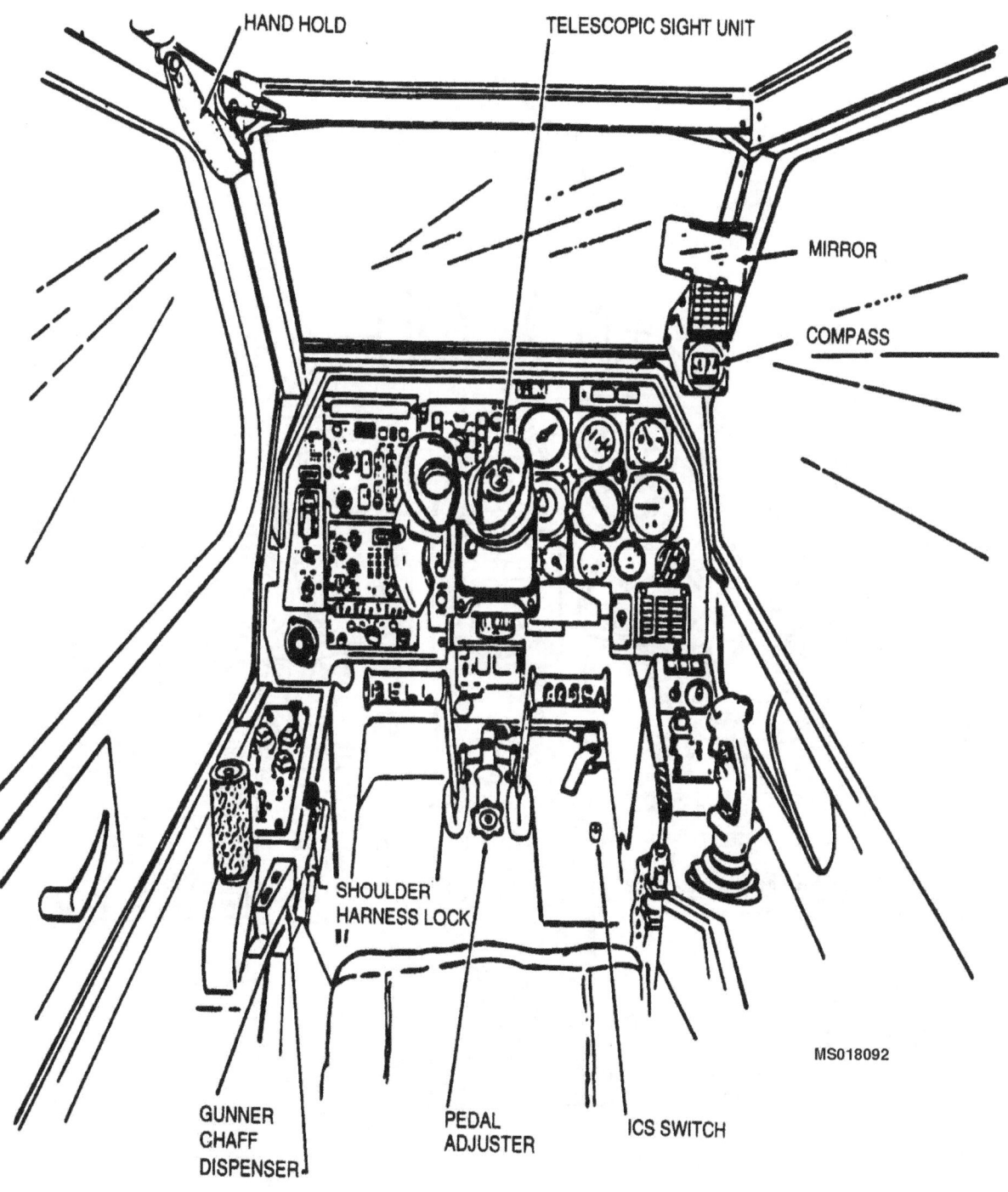

Figure 2-5. Gunner Station Diagram (Typical)

2-7

TM 1-1520-236-10

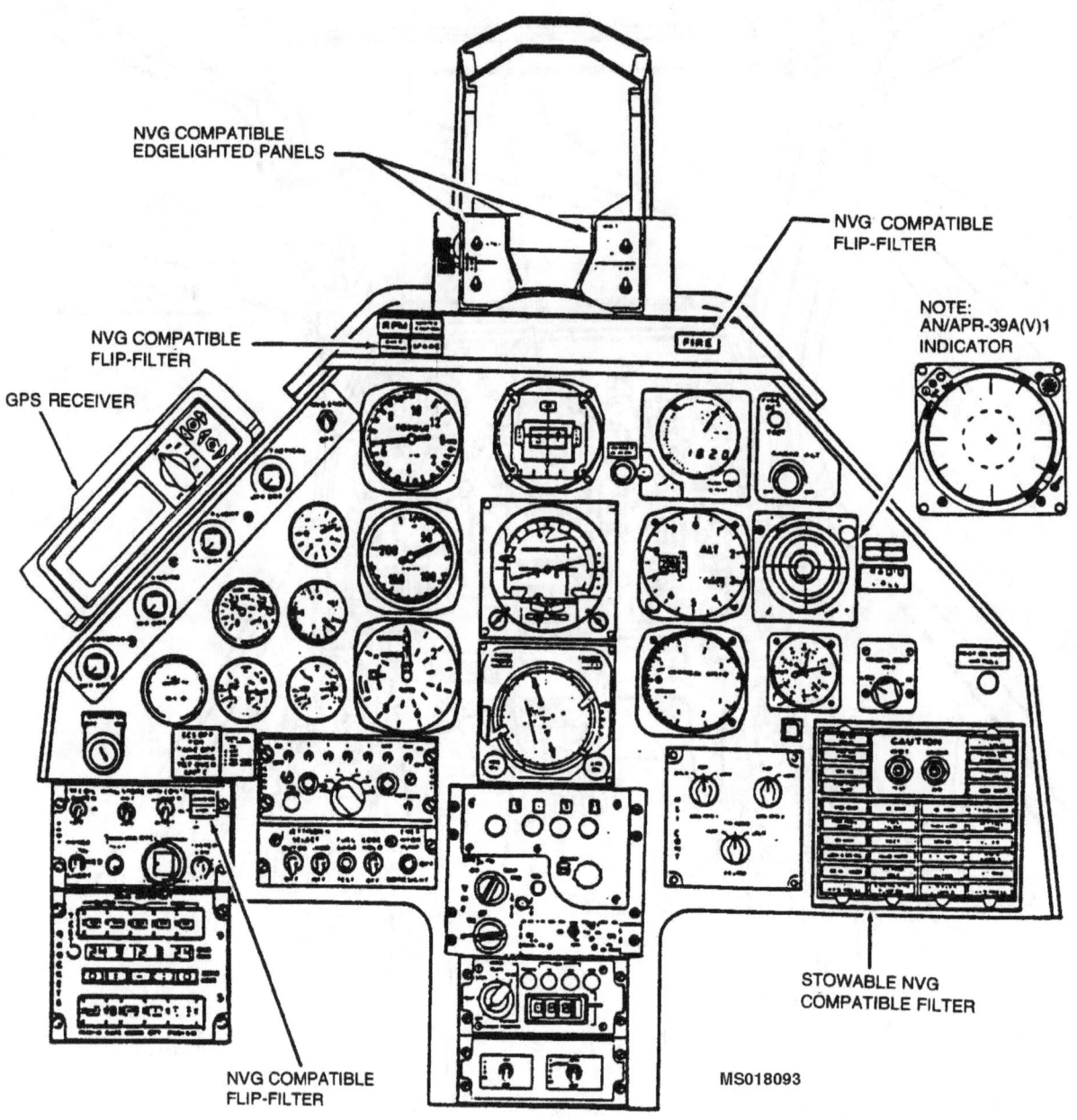

Figure 2-6. Pilot Instrument and Control Panel

TM 1-1520-236-10

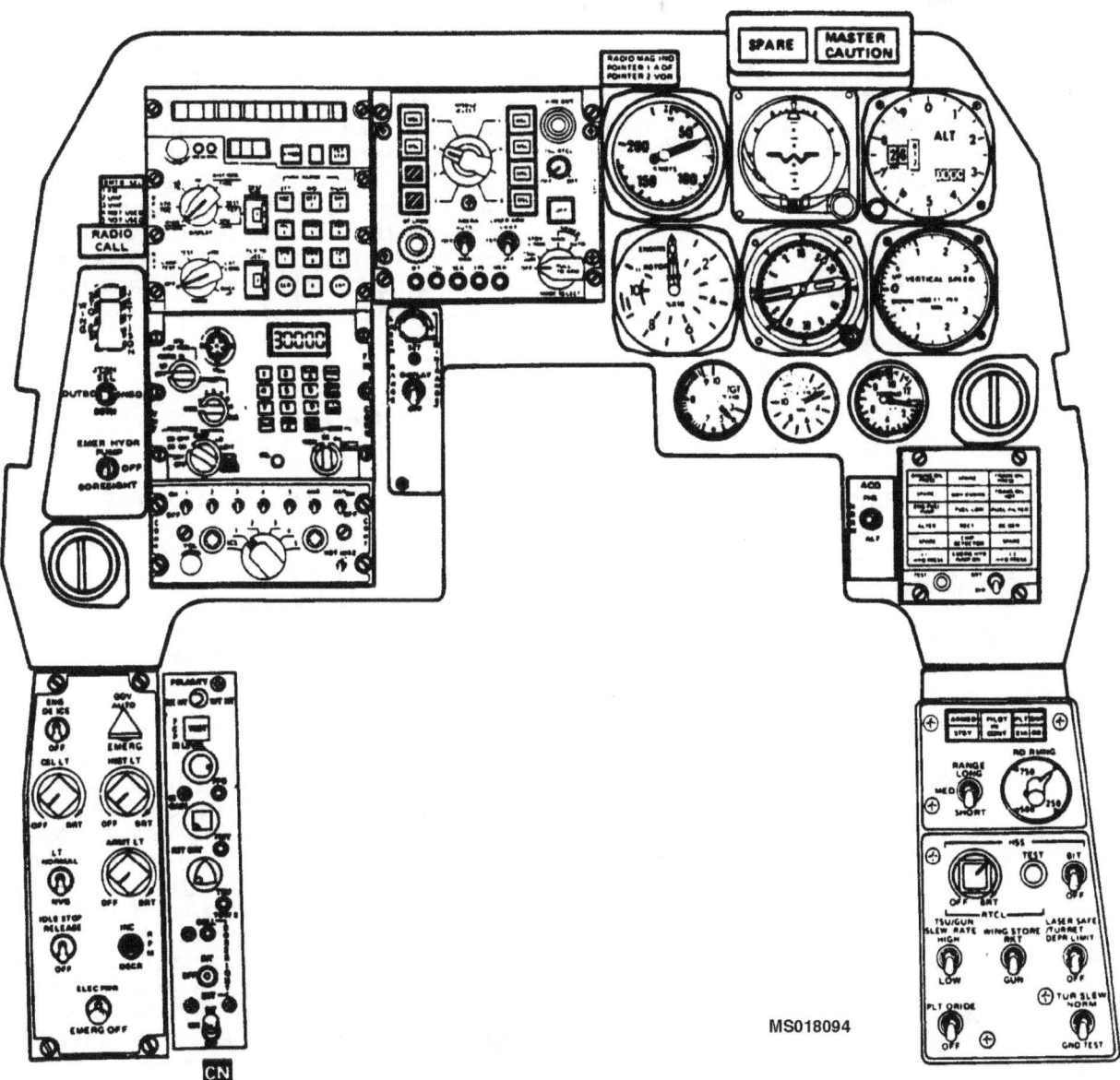

Figure 2-7. Gunner Instrument and Control Panel

2-11. SEATS.

a. Construction. The seats, side-shoulder panels, and head protective panels are of armor material which provides protection. Both seats are equipped with contoured seat cushions and back supports made of foam and open mesh for vibration attenuation and crew comfort.

b. Pilot Seat. The pilot seat is vertically adjustable nonreclining type. The vertical adjustment is reclined at 15 degrees. The vertical height adjustable handle (Figure 2-8) is under the left side of the seat. The seat is equipped with a lap safety belt and inertia reel shoulder harness.

c. Gunner Seat. The gunner seat is a fixed seat (non-adjustable and nonreclining). The seat is equipped with a lap safety belt and inertia reel shoulder harness. The seat also has arm rests.

d. Inertia Reel Shoulder Harness. An inertia reel shoulder harness is incorporated in the pilot and gunner seats with a manual lock-unlock control handle (Figure 2-8). The handles are located to left front of each seat. With the control in the unlocked position, the reel cable will extend allowing the occupant to lean forward; however, the reel will automatically lock when helicopter encounters an impact force of two to three "g" deceleration. Locking of the reel can be accomplished from any position and the reel will automatically take up the slack in the harness. To release the lock, it is necessary to lean back slightly to release tension on the lock and then unlock position. It is possible to have pressure against the seat back whereby no additional movement can be accomplished and the lock cannot be released. If this condition occurs, it will be necessary to loosen shoulder harness. Manual locking of the reel should be accomplished for emergency landings.

SECTION II. EMERGENCY EQUIPMENT

2-12. PORTABLE FIRE EXTINGUISHER.

A portable hand-operated fire extinguisher is located forward of the gunner seat (Figure 9-1).

2-13. FIRST AID KIT.

An aeronautical type first aid kit is located behind the pilot seat (Figure 9-1).

2-14. SURVIVAL KIT.

Aircraft Modular Survival System (AMSS) AH-1 tow tube survival kit can be installed on the aircraft. Refer to TM 1-1680-354-10 for fabrication instructions and limitations.

NOTE

The preferred installation position for the AMSS tow survival kit is the upper right and/or left side outboard position of the tow launcher. However, if these positions are occupied by training devices (i.e., air to ground engagement simulator/air defense (AGES/AD) then the AMSS tow survival kit can be installed in any of the remaining positions of the tow launchers.

2-15. CANOPY REMOVAL SYSTEM.

Debris may be expelled 50 feet outward when system is actuated.

Cutting assemblies are mounted in the pilot and gunner doors and windows frames. The linear explosive is contained with the cutting assemblies. The cutting assemblies are controlled by the pilot or gunner arming/firing mechanisms. Rotating the arming/firing mechanism handle 90 degrees counterclockwise (torque required 6 to 12 inch-pounds) will arm the cutting assemblies. Pulling the handle (20 to 35 pounds tension) will fire the percussion primer causing the cutting assemblies to be detonated. The explosive force will be outward and remove two windows and two doors from the helicopter simultaneously. If handle has been rotated but not pulled, the handle can be rotated clockwise and the safety pin installed DA Form 2408-13-1 entry required. Refer to Chapter 9 for emergency procedure and Figure 9-1 for equipment location.

2-16. WING STORES JETTISON.

Wing stores jettison capability is provided by explosive cartridges installed at each wing stores pylon.

TM 1-1520-236-10

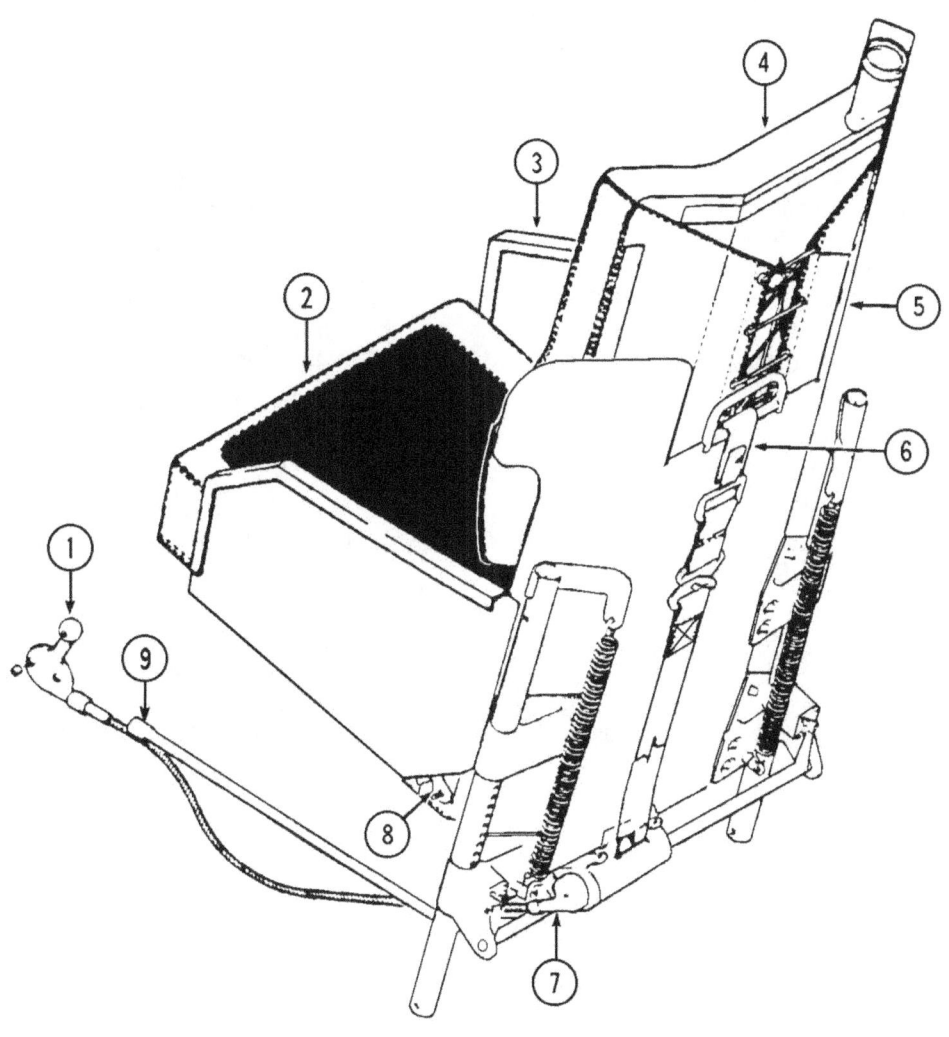

MS018095

1. Shoulder harness lock
2. Seat cushion
3. Side armor panels
4. Seat back cushion
5. Seat assembly
6. Shoulder harness
7. Inertia reel
8. Seat lap belt
9. Height adjustment handle

Figure 2-8. Pilot Seat Installation (Typical)

SECTION III. ENGINE AND RELATED SYSTEMS

2-17. ENGINE.

The helicopter is equipped with a T53-L-703 engine (Figure 2-9). The engine, in this installation, is derated by limitation of the helicopter transmission to 100% (1290 SHP) torque for 30 minutes and 88% (1134 SHP) torque for continuous operation at 100% rpm. The engine compartment is cooled by ram and ambient air.

2-18. ENGINE PROTECTION.

Armor material is located on the left and right engine compartment doors to provide armor protection for the engine compressor, fuel control, oil filter, and fuel filter.

2-19. AIR INDUCTION SYSTEM.

Ambient air enters the transmission compartment door air inlet, then is routed through the improved particle separator. The particle separator prevents debris and dirt particles from entering the engine air inlet and causing ingestion damage to the engine. Bleed air from the engine is used to purge the separator and eject the particle overboard.

2-20. ENGINE INLET ANTI-ICING/DEICING SYSTEM.

WARNING

The system will not deice or prevent icing of the particle separator. A power loss will occur if the formation of ice in the particle separator obstructs the flow of ambient air to the engine.

a. Description. The system prevents ice from forming in the engine air inlet. The system consists of a hot air solenoid valve on the engine, controlled by the pilot or gunner ENG DEICE switch (Figure 2-10 and Figure 2-12) powered by the dc essential bus, and protected by the ENG DEICE circuit breaker.

b. Operation. If ice accumulation is suspected, the pilot or gunner ENG DEICE switch is placed in the DEICE position. This action causes the hot air solenoid valve to route engine bleed air to the engine air inlet. A rise in the turbine gas temperature (TGT) will occur when the pilot or gunner ENG DEICE switch is in the DEICE position. Deice operation will become continuous if the hot air solenoid valve (ENG DEICE) circuit fails or if ENG DEICE circuit breaker is out (extended).

TM 1-1520-236-10

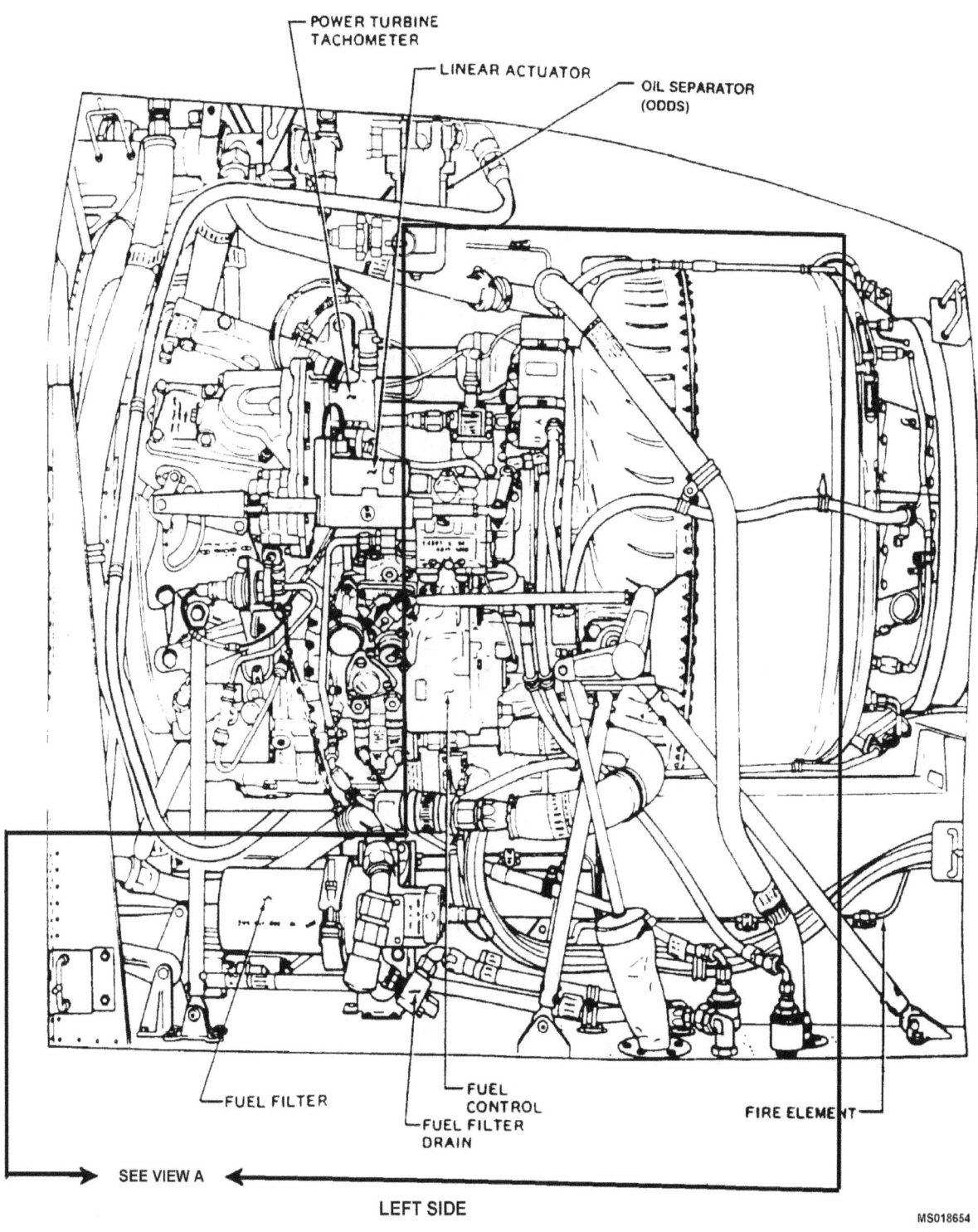

Figure 2-9. Power Plant Installation - (Sheet 1 or 4)

TM 1-1520-236-10

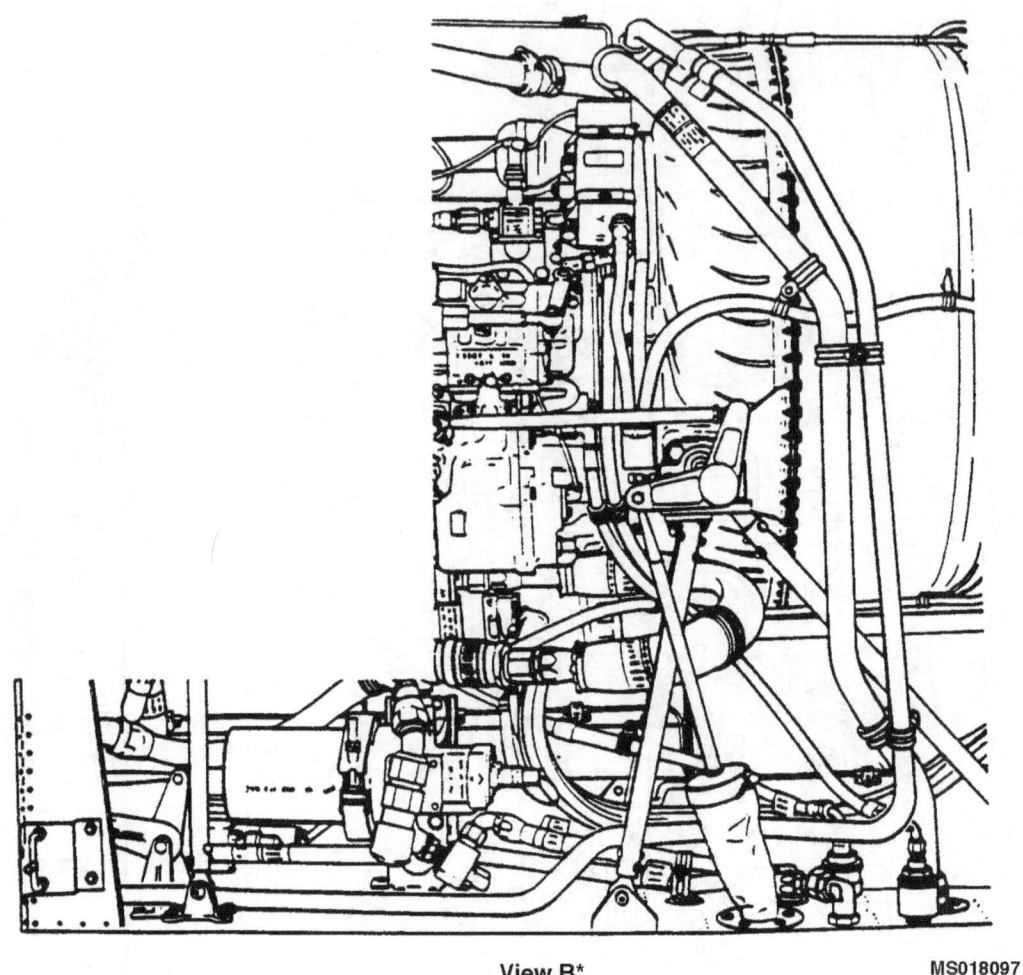

View B*

MS018097

Left Side

*After incorporation of MWO 55-1520-236-50-12.

Figure 2-9. Power Plant Installation - (Sheet 2 of 4)

2-14

TM 1-1520-236-10

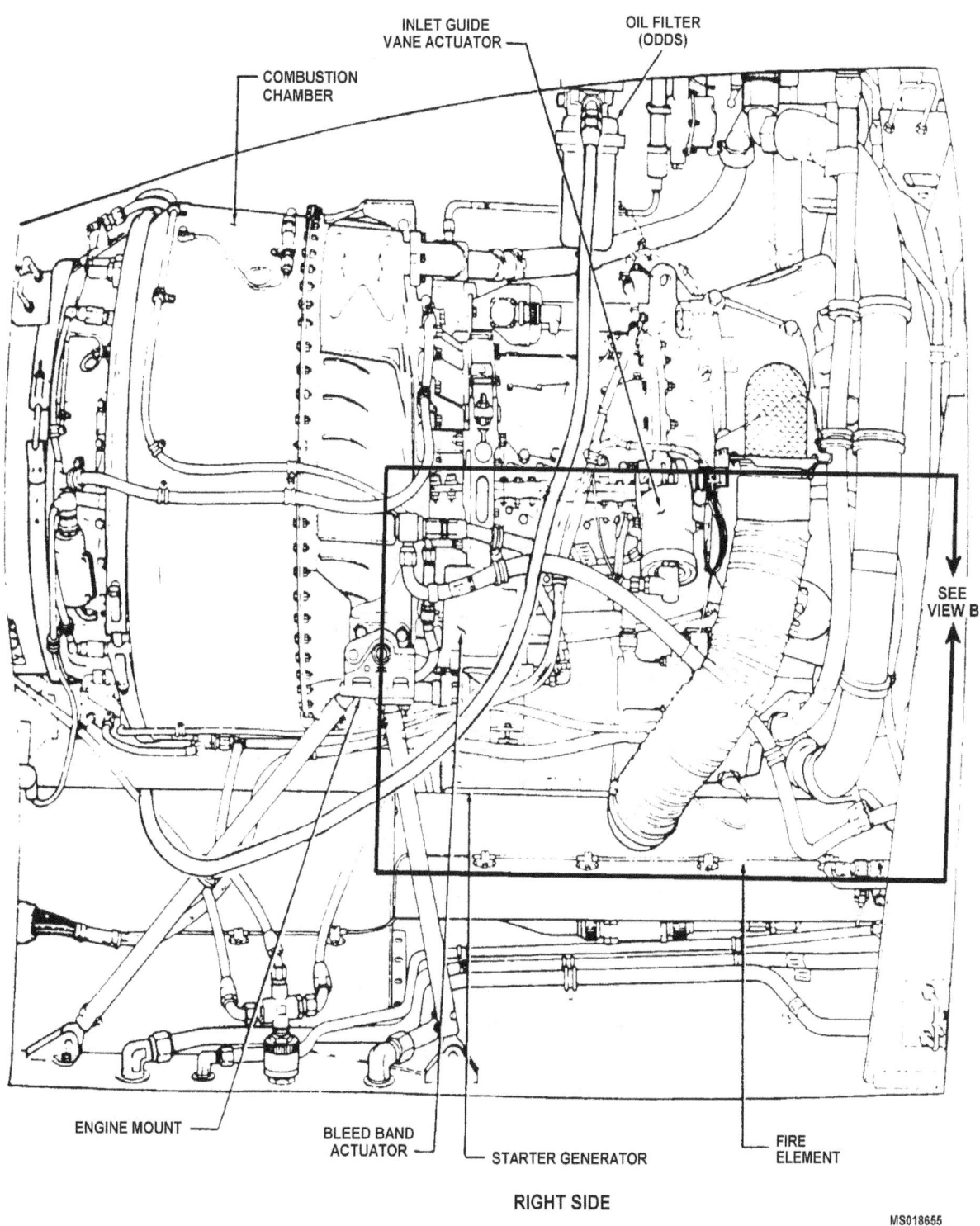

Figure 2-9. Power Plant Installation - (Sheet 3 of 4)

2-15

TM 1-1520-236-10

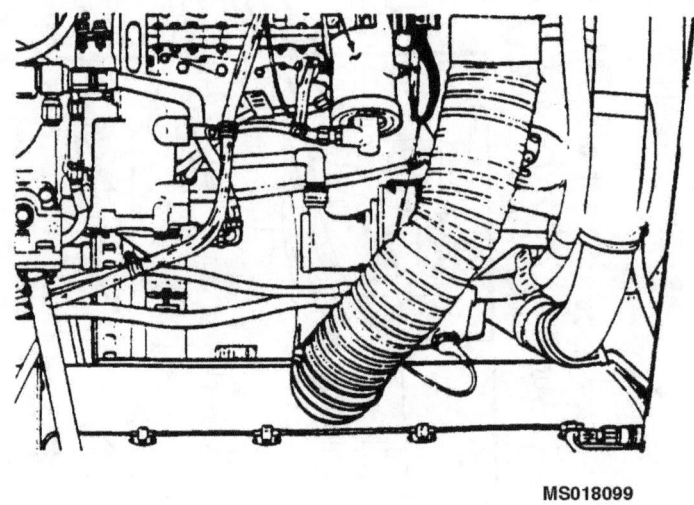

View A*

Right Side

*After incorporation of MWO 55-1520-236-50-12.

Figure 2-9. Power Plant Installation - (Sheet 4 of 4)

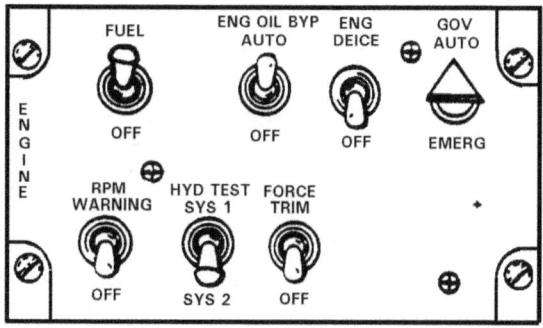

Figure 2-10. Pilot Engine Control Panel

2-21. ENGINE FUEL CONTROL SYSTEM

a. Engine Mounted Component. The fuel control assembly is mounted on the left side of the engine. This unit is controlled by the pilot or gunner throttle and GOV switch. The assembly consists of a metering section, a computer section, and an overspeed governor. The metering section pumps fuel to the engine. The computer section determines the rate of fuel delivery. The overspeed governor maintains a constant N2 rpm.

b. Crew Controls.

(1) **Throttles.** Setting the pilot or gunner throttle to the full open position allows the engine to operate up to full power available. Rotating the throttle back toward idle position decreases the allowable N2 and power which, if below that demanded by collective pitch input, results in proportional N2 speed decrease. Rotating the throttle past the engine idle stop to the fully closed position shuts off fuel flow. A solenoid operated idle stop is incorporated to prevent inadvertent throttle closure. The idle stop is controlled by the pilot IDLE STOP REL switch (Figure 2-15) or the gunner IDLE STOP RELEASE switch (Figure 2-12). The engine idle stop release circuit is powered by the dc essential bus and protected by the IDLE STOP SOL circuit breaker. Friction can be induced into both throttles by rotating the pilot throttle friction (Figure 2-15) counterclockwise.

(2) **Governor Switches.** The pilot or gunner GOV Switches (Figure 2-11 and Figure 2-12) AUTO position, permits the overspeed governor to automatically control fuel metering and engine speeds (N1 and N2). The EMER position permits the pilot and gunner to manually control the engine rpm. The governor circuit is powered by the dc essential bus and protected by the GOV CONTR circuit breaker.

2-22. IGNITION-STARTER SYSTEM.

The pilot ignition-starter trigger switch (Figure 2-15) is pressed and held to start the engine. The switch must be released manually when the engine starts or the time limit expires. The pilot FUEL switch (Figure 2-10) must be in the FUEL position and the pilot ignition keylock switch (Figure 2-6) in the ON position to complete the ignition and start fuel circuit. The GEN switch must be in OFF position for normal starting. The circuits are powered by the dc essential bus and protected by the START RLY and IGN SOL circuit breakers.

2-23. RPM INCREASE-DECREASE (INCR-DECR) SWITCHES.

The pilot RPM INCR-DECR or gunner INC-DECR switch (Figure 2-11 and Figure 2-12) is a three-position, momentary-type switch located in the pilot collective switch box and gunner miscellaneous control panel. The switch is held forward to increase and aft to decrease the power turbine speed. The circuit is powered by the dc essential bus and protected by the GOV CONTR circuit breaker.

2-24. DROOP COMPENSATOR.

A droop compensator maintains engine rpm (N2) as power demand is increased by the pilot. The compensator is a direct mechanical linkage between the collective stick and the speed selector lever on the N2 governor. No crew controls are provided or required. The compensator will hold N2 rpm to ± 0.6% when properly rigged. Droop is defined as the speed change in engine rpm (N2) as power is increased from a no-load condition and is an inherent characteristic of the governor system. Without this characteristic, instability would develop as engine output is increased resulting in N1 speed overshooting or hunting the value necessary to satisfy the new power condition. Design droop of the engine governor system is as much as 4.5 to 6% (flat pitch to full power). If N2 power were allowed to droop, other than momentarily, the reduction in rotor speed could become critical.

TM 1-1520-236-10

M65/C-NITE TSU FLIR INTENSITY LEVEL SETTING

CONTROL/INDICATOR		FUNCTION
ARMT LT RHEOSTAT	NVG SW	M65/C-NITE FLIR
OFF	LT NORM	DAY (HIGH)
ON	LT NORM	NIGHT (MED)
ON	NVG	NVG (LOW)

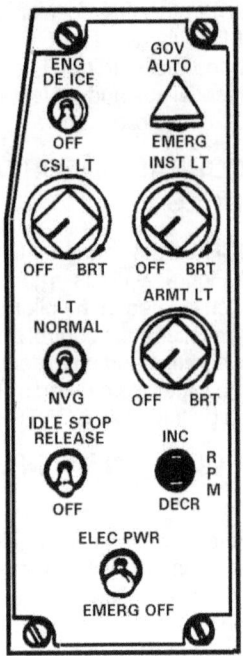

Figure 2-11. Gunner Miscellaneous Control Panel (Typical)

2-25. ENGINE OIL SUPPLY SYSTEM.

a. Description. The engine oil system is a dry sump, pressure type, and completely automatic. The oil tank is located in the upper pylon fairing. It will self-seal a 30 caliber projectile hole and is equipped with deaeration provisions. Oil is gravity fed from tank to engine driven oil pump which provides pressure and scavenging for the system. On helicopters with ODDS, an external oil separator, with integral chip detector, and a 3-micron oil filter are installed downstream of the sump.

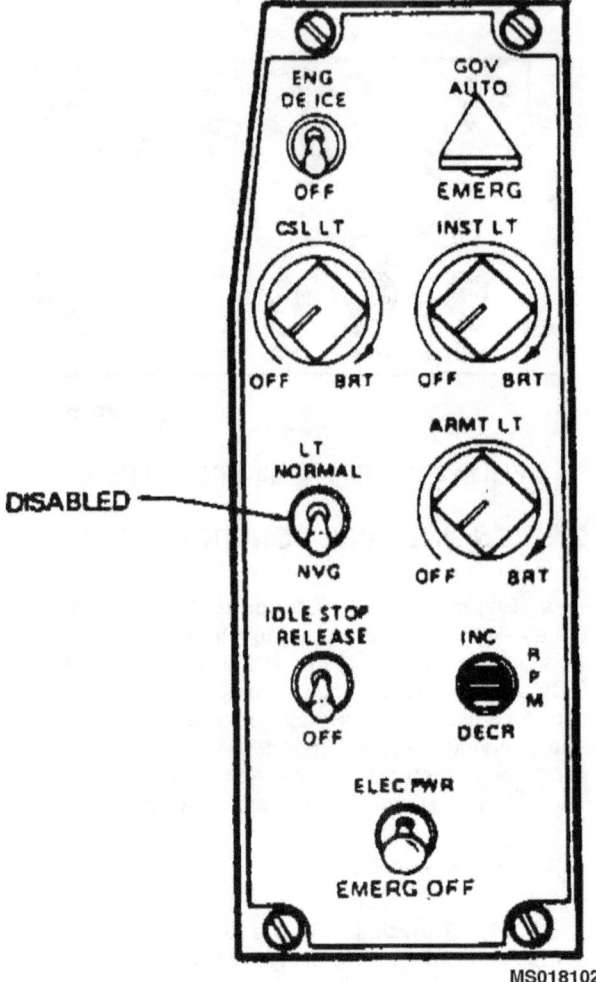

Figure 2-12. Gunner Miscellaneous Control Panel (Typical)

b. Cooling. Engine oil cooling is accomplished by an oil cooler and a bleed air driven turbine fan. The engine and transmission oil coolers use the same fan.

c. Switching Action. The pilot ENG OIL BYP switch (Figure 2-10) AUTO position permits the oil to automatically bypass the oil cooler when the oil tank is approximately 3.8 quarts low. The OFF position deactivates the automatic bypass feature causing the oil to pass through the oil cooler regardless of the oil tank level. The switch circuit is powered by the dc essential bus and protected by the FUEL OIL VALVE circuit breaker.

2-26. ENGINE INSTRUMENTS AND INDICATORS.

a. Torquemeters. The pilot and gunner torquemeters (Figure 2-6 and Figure 2-7) play percent of torque

2-18

imposed upon the engine output shaft. Each torquemeter is powered by a separate transducer. The circuit is powered by the dc essential bus and protected by the TRQ IND circuit breaker.

b. Turbine Gas Temperature (TGT) Indicators. The pilot and gunner indicators (Figure 2-6 and Figure 2-7) display the temperature in degrees Celsius of the air in the first stage N2 nozzle. The circuits are powered by the dc essential bus and protected by the TGT IND circuit breaker.

c. Dual Tachometers. The pilot and gunner tachometers (Figure 2-6 and Figure 2-7) display the rpm of the engine and main rotor speed in percent. The tachometer outer scale is marked ENGINE and the inner scale is marked ROTOR. The ENGINE and ROTOR needles are synchronized during normal helicopter operation. The circuit is powered by the dc essential bus and protected by the TACH DUAL circuit breaker.

d. Gas Producer N1 Tachometers. The pilot and gunner tachometers (Figure 2-6 and Figure 2-7) display the rpm of the gas producer turbine speed in percent. The circuit is powered by the dc essential bus and protected by the GAS PROD circuit breaker.

e. Oil Pressure/Temperature Indicator. The pilot indicator (Figure 2-6) displays the psi pressure of the oil at the pressure side of the oil pump and the temperature as degrees Celsius of the oil at the engine oil inlet. The circuit is powered by the dc essential bus and protected by the TEMP IND ENG XMSN circuit breaker.

f. Oil Pressure Caution Light. The pilot ENG OIL PRESS and gunner ENGINE OIL PRESS (Figure 2-23) will illuminate when the engine oil pressure is below safe limits.

g. Oil Bypass Caution Light. The pilot ENG OIL BYPASS caution light (Figure 2-23) illuminates when oil tank level is approximately 3.8 quarts low.

h. Engine Oil Chip Detector Caution Light. The caution lights, ENG CHIP in pilot caution panel and CHIP DETECTOR in gunner caution panel, illuminate when sufficient metal chips to complete the electrical circuit are collected from the engine oil.

i. Fuel Pump Caution Lights. The pilot and gunner ENG FUEL PUMP caution lights (Figure 2-23) illuminate when either element of the engine driven fuel pump fails.

j. Governor Caution Lights. The pilot and gunner GOV EMERG caution lights (Figure 2-23) illuminate when the pilot GOV switch is in EMER (Figure 2-10) or when the gunner GOV switch is in EMERG (Figure 2-12).

SECTION IV. HELICOPTER FUEL SYSTEM

2-27. FUEL SUPPLY SYSTEM.

The helicopter is equipped with a crashworthy fuel system. The system is designed with the potential of containing fuel during a severe, but survivable, crash impact to reduce the possibility of fire. The system has a 50 caliber ballistic protection level. Fuel grades and specifications are included in Section XIV.

2-28. CONTROLS AND INDICATORS.

a. Fuel Switch. The pilot FUEL switch (Figure 2-10) FUEL position energizes the forward and aft boost pumps, opens the fuel shutoff valve, and completes the ignition and start fuel circuit. The aft fuel boost pump circuit is powered by the dc nonessential bus. The other circuits are powered by the dc essential bus. The circuits are protected by the START RLY, IGN SOL, FUEL/OIL VALVE, FUEL BOOST FWD, and FUEL BOOST AFT circuit breakers.

b. Fuel Quantity Indicator. The pilot indicator (Figure 2-6) displays the pounds of fuel in the fuel cells. The circuit is powered by the ac system and protected by the FUEL QTY circuit breaker.

c. Fuel Quantity Indicator Test Switch. The pilot FUEL GAGE TEST switch (Figure 2-13) is used to test the fuel quantity indicator operation. Pressing the switch causes the indicator pointer to move from the actual reading to a lesser reading. Releasing the switch will cause the pointer to return to the actual reading. The circuit is powered by an ac system and protected by the FUEL QTY circuit breaker.

NOTE

Low fuel caution systems alert the pilot that the fuel level in the tank has reached a specified level (capacity). Differences in fuel densities due to temperature and fuel type will vary the weight of the fuel remaining and the actual time the aircraft engine(s) may operate. Differences in fuel consumption rates, aircraft attitude and operational condition of the fuel subsystem will also affect actual time the aircraft engine(s) may operate.

d. Low Quantity Caution Lights. The pilot and gunner FUEL LOW caution lights (Figure 2-23) illuminate when there is approximately 209 pounds of fuel remaining. The illumination of this light does not mean a fixed time period remains before fuel exhaustion, but is an indication that a low fuel condition exists.

e. Low Fuel Pressure Caution Lights. The pilot FWD FUEL BOOST and AFT FUEL BOOST caution lights (Figure 2-23) illuminate when the boost pumps in the forward/aft fuel cell fail.

f. Fuel Filter Caution Lights. The pilot and gunner FUEL FILTER caution lights (Figure 2-23) illuminate when the filter in the fuel supply line becomes partially obstructed.

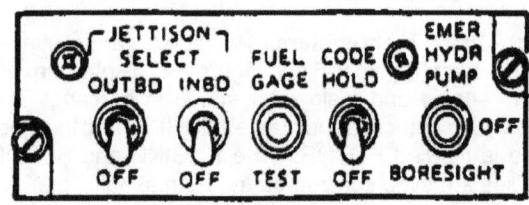

Figure 2-13. Pilot Miscellaneous Control Panel

SECTION V. FLIGHT CONTROLS

2-29. DESCRIPTION.

The flight control system is a positive mechanical type, actuated by cyclic, collective, and tail rotor controls. Complete controls are provided for both pilot and gunner. The gunner controls are slaved to the pilot controls. The system includes a cyclic system, a collective control system, a tail rotor system, a force trim system, and a stability and control augmentation system (SCAS).

2-30. CYCLIC CONTROL SYSTEM.

The pilot and gunner cyclic sticks (Figure 2-14) have a built-in operating friction. The cyclic control movements are not mixed, but are transmitted directly to the swashplate. The longitudinal cyclic control linkage is routed from the cyclic stick through the SCAS actuator, the dual boost hydraulic actuator to the right horn of the fixed swashplate ring. The lateral is similarly routed to the left horn. Control "feel" is provided by the force trim units. The fore and aft movement also changes the synchronized elevator (Figure 2-1) attitude to assist controllability and lengthen c.g. range.

2-33. FORCE TRIM SYSTEM.

The system incorporates a magnetic brake and force gradient in the cyclic and directional control systems to provide artificial feel into the systems. Also, it provides a means to trim the controls. Placing the FORCE TRIM switch (Figure 2-10) in the FORCE TRIM position will induce artificial feel into the systems. Depressing the cyclic stick force trim switch (Figure 2-14) will cause the magnetic brake and force gradient to be repositioned to correspond to the positions of the cyclic stick and pedals thus providing trim. The system is powered by the dc essential bus and protected by the FORCE TRIM circuit breaker.

2-34. STABILITY AND CONTROL AUGMENTATION SYSTEM (SCAS).

a. Description. The SCAS is a three-axis, limited authority rate reference augmentation system. The SCAS cancels undesired motion of the helicopter during flight. This is accomplished by inducing an electrical input into the flight control system to augment the pilot mechanical input.

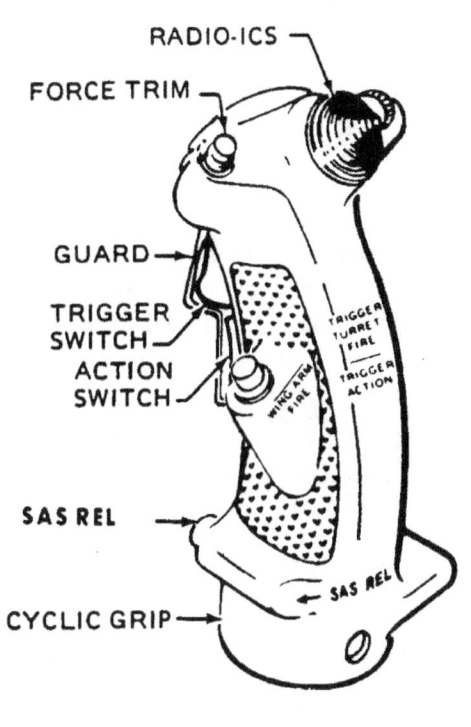

Figure 2-14. Pilot and Gunner Cyclic Control Stick

2-31. COLLECTIVE CONTROL SYSTEM.

The pilot and gunner collective pitch controls (Figure 2-15) are located on the left side of the pilot and gunner seats and control vertical mode of flight. Moving the stick up or down changes the angle of attack and lift developed by the main rotor resulting in the ascent or descent of the helicopter. The collective assembly consists of a collective stick, with adjustable friction system (pilot only), twist grip-type throttle with friction adjuster, and switch box assembly (pilot only). The switch box assembly incorporates the ignition starter switch, rpm increase-decrease switch, jettison, searchlight switches, wire cut switch, and idle stop release switch. A collective hold down strap is provided for the pilot collective.

2-32. TAIL ROTOR CONTROL SYSTEM.

Pushing a pedal changes the pitch of the tail rotor resulting in directional control and is used to pivot the helicopter on its own vertical axis and trim the helicopter in flight. A pedal adjuster is provided to adjust the pedal distance for individual comfort. Heel rests are provided for the gunner to prevent inadvertent pedal operation.

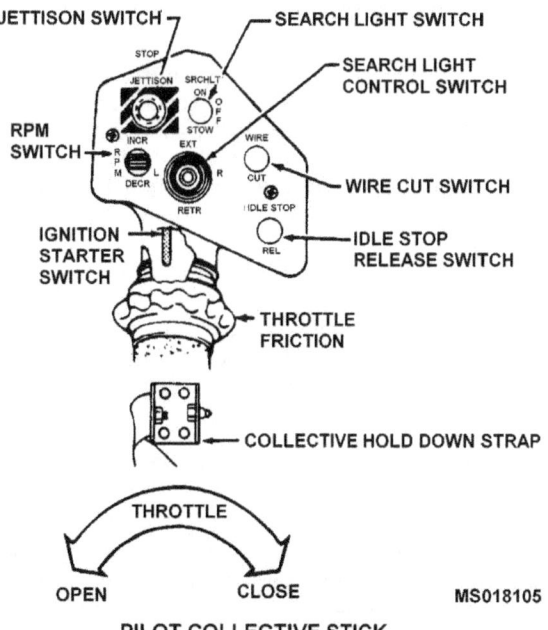

Figure 2-15. Pilot Collective Control Stick

b. Control Panel. The SCAS control panel (Figure 2-16) contains a POWER switch for applying dc (essential bus) and ac power to the system. The circuits are protected by the SCAS POWER dc and SCAS PWR ac circuit breakers. The panel also contains three channel engage switches which energize electric solenoid valves controlling hydraulic pressure to the system. The panel has three amber colored NO-GO lights, one associated with each PITCH, ROLL, and YAW channel engage switch. These lights are illuminated during the warmup to indicate the presence of current in each associated channel actuator. Should an engagement be attempted during this warmup period, the actuator may make an abrupt input to the flight controls at the moment of engagement. When engagement is made, the NO-GO lights are locked out of the circuit and do not operate as malfunction indicators. Disengaging a channel, however, restores the associated light to operation. The NO-GO lights have a built-in press-to-test feature for ensuring that the indicator is operational, but this feature works only prior to channel engagement.

c. SCAS (SAS) Release Switch. The cyclic grip mounted switch (Figure 2-14) is used to disengage the pitch, roll, and yaw channels simultaneously. The channels are re-engaged by the PITCH, ROLL, and YAW switches on the SCAS control panel.

d. RECOIL COMP Switch. The RECOIL COMP switch is a three position switch (LO-MED-HI) located on the right side of the pilot instrument panel. It may be used to vary the magnitude of the signals from the Armament Compensation Unit to the SCAS to compensate for a lower/higher than average M197 firing rate.

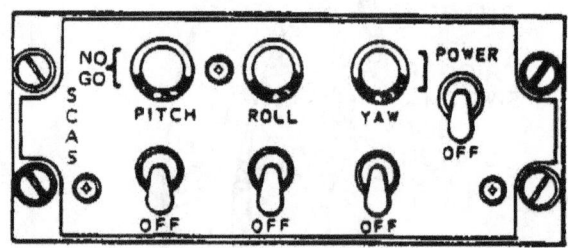

Figure 2-16. Pilot SCAS Control Panel

SECTION VI. HYDRAULIC SYSTEMS

2-35. DESCRIPTION.

The hydraulic system is a dual system (No.1 and No. 2 system) used to minimize the force required by the pilot to move the cyclic, collective, and pedal controls. The No. 1 and No. 2 systems are installed to provide maximum separation to reduce the probability of a single projectile from incapacitating both systems.

2-36. HYDRAULIC SYSTEM NO. 1.

The No. 1 system provides hydraulic power to the cyclic controls, collective controls, pedal controls, and SCAS yaw controls. The No. 1 system is located on the left side of the helicopter.

2-37. HYDRAULIC SYSTEM NO. 2.

The No. 2 system provides hydraulic power to the cyclic controls, collective controls, SCAS pitch and roll controls, articulated wing pylons. The No. 2 system is located on the right side of the helicopter.

2-38. TEST SWITCH.

The pilot HYD TEST switch (Figure 2-10) is used to test the No. 1 and No. 2 hydraulic systems. Holding the switch in the SYS 1 position will cause the No. 1 system to be the only system supplying hydraulic pressure. Similar action occurs when the switch is held in the SYS 2 position.

2-39. RESERVOIR FLUID SIGHT GASSES.

The No. 1 and No. 2 reservoirs are provided with a fluid sight glass. Both sight glasses can be seen only from the left hydraulic compartment door.

2-40. FILTER INDICATORS.

The No. 1 and No. 2 pressure and return filters are provided with a differential pressure indicator. The red indicator pops out when the filter needs changing or during cold weather operation.

2-41. LOW PRESSURE CAUTION LIGHTS.

The pilot NO. 1 HYD PRESS and NO. 2 HYD PRESS, and gunner #1 HYD PRESS and #2 HYD PRESS caution lights (Figure 2-23) will illuminate when hydraulic pressure is below safe limits.

2-42. ELECTRICAL CIRCUIT.

The hydraulic electrical circuit is powered by the dc essential bus and protected by the HYD CONTR circuit breaker.

2-43. EMERGENCY HYDRAULIC SYSTEM.

The emergency hydraulic system serves two functions. It provides hydraulic power to outboard pylons for boresighting, or to the collective pitch control if both hydraulic systems fail. The system is controlled by the EMER HYD PUMP switches (Figure 2-7 and Figure 2-13) powered by the dc essential bus and protected by the EMER HYD PUMP circuit breaker.

2-44. ARMAMENT HYDRAULIC SYSTEM.

The TOW missile system is powered by the No. 2 system and is used to position the outboard articulated wing pylons during TOW missile operations. The system is controlled by the TOW missile controls. The system electrical circuits are powered by the dc essential bus and the ac system. The circuits are protected by the HYD CONTR, ac TMS PWR, and SECU PWR circuit breakers.

SECTION VII. POWER TRAIN SYSTEM

2-45. TRANSMISSION.

The transmission transfers engine power to the main rotor through the mast assembly and to the tail rotor through a series of driveshafts and gearboxes. The transmission has a self-contained pressure oil system. The oil is cooled by an oil cooler and bleed air turbine fan. The transmission and engine oil coolers use the same fan. The oil system has an automatic bypass system which causes the oil to bypass the cooler when a leak is sensed in the oil cooler circuit. Two oil level sight glasses, an oil fill cap, and a magnetic chip detector are provided. On helicopters with ODDS, a full-flow debris monitor with integral chip detector replaces an integral oil filter and a 3-micron filter replaces a 25-micron external filter.

2-46. GEAR BOXES.

a. Intermediate Gearbox - 42 Degree. The gearbox is located at the base of the vertical fin (Figure 2-1). It provides a 42 degree change of direction of the tail rotor driveshaft. The gearbox has a self-contained wet sump oil system. An oil level sight glass, a filler cap, and a magnetic chip detector are provided.

b. Tail Rotor Gearbox - 90 Degree. The gearbox is located near the top of the vertical fin (Figure 2-1). It provides a 90 degree change of direction of the tail rotor driveshaft. The gearbox has a self-contained wet sump oil system. An oil level sight glass, a filler cap, and a magnetic chip detector are provided.

2-47. DRIVESHAFTS.

a. Main Driveshaft. The main driveshaft connects the engine output shaft to the transmission input drive quill.

b. Tail Rotor Driveshaft. The tail rotor driveshaft consists of five driveshafts and three hanger bearing assemblies. The assemblies and the 42 and 90 degree gearboxes connect the transmission tail rotor drive quill to the tail rotor.

2-48. INDICATORS AND CAUTION LIGHTS.

a. Transmission Oil Pressure/Temperature Indicator (Figure 2-6). The pilot indictor displays the pressure in psi and temperature in degrees Celsius of the transmission oil. The electrical circuit is powered by the dc essential bus and protected by the INDTEMP ENG/XMSN circuit breaker.

b. Transmission Oil Low Pressure Caution Lights. The TRANS OIL PRESS caution lights (Figure 2-23) illuminate when the transmission oil pressure drops below safe limits.

c. Transmission Oil Hot Caution Lights. The TRANS OIL HOT caution lights (figure 2-23) illuminate when the transmission oil temperature exceeds the safe limits.

d. Transmission and Gearboxes Chip Detectors.

(1) The pilot chip detector caution lights (Figure 2-23) illuminate when sufficient metal chips are detected in the 42 degree gearbox, 90 degree gearbox, or the transmission oil. On aircraft equipped with Oil Debris Detection System (ODDS), when a chip gap is bridged by conductive particles, a power module provides an electrical pulse which burns away normal wear particles.

(2) The pilot caution lights are worded: 42° CHIP, 90° CHIP, and TRANS CHIP for the respective unit.

(3) The gunner chip detector caution light (Figure 2-23) will only illuminate CHIP DETECTOR. This caution light does not identify the contaminated component.

SECTION VIII. MAIN AND TAIL ROTORS

2-49. MAIN ROTOR.

a. Description.

(1) `B540` The main rotor blades are metal, bonded assemblies. Each blade is attached in the hub with a retaining bolt assembly and is held in alignment by adjustable drag braces.

(2) `K747` The main rotor blades are glass fiber epoxy resin bonded assemblies with a rubber erosion guard. The skin is basket weave which will not be as smooth as a metal blade. Each blade is attached in the hub with a retaining bolt assembly and is held in alignment by adjustable drag braces.

(3) The main rotor is driven by the mast which is connected to the transmission. The rotor rpm is governed by the engine rpm during powered flight. The rotor tip path plane is controlled by the cyclic stick. The rotor pitch is controlled by the collective stick.

b. Hub Moment Spring. As an aid in controlling rotor flapping, a hub moment spring kit has been installed in the rotor system. Two nonlinear elastomeric springs are attached to a support affixed to the mast. The hub moment springs provide an additional margin of safety in the event of an inadvertent excursion of the helicopter beyond the approved flight envelope.

c. RPM Indicators. The pilot and gunner indicators are part of the dual tachometers (Figure 2-6 and Figure 2-7). The tachometer inner scale displays percent rotor rpm.

2-50. TAIL ROTOR.

The tail rotor is driven by the 90 degree gearbox which is connected to the transmission by the tail rotor driveshaft assemblies and the 42 degree gearbox. The rotor rpm is governed by the transmission rpm. The rotor blade pitch is controlled by the pedals.

SECTION IX. UTILITY SYSTEM

2-51. PITOT TUBE/AIR DATA SYSTEM HEATER.

a. Pitot Tube Heater. The pitot tube (Figure 2-1) is equipped with an electrical heater. The PITOT/ADS switch (Figure 2-17) in HTR position activates the heater in the tube and prevents ice from accumulating in the pitot tube. The OFF position deactivates the heater. The electrical circuit is powered by the dc nonessential bus and protected by the PITOT HTR circuit breaker.

b. Air Data System (ADS) Heater. The air data system sensing head contains an electrical heater. The pilot PITOT/ADS switch (Figure 2-17) in the HTR position activates the ADS heater, in addition to the pitot tube heater, and prevents ice from accumulating in the pitot tube and air data system. The OFF position deactivates the heater. The system is powered by the dc nonessential bus, ac system, and protected by the ADS PWR and ADS ANTI-ICE circuit breaker.

2-52. CANOPY DEFROSTING, DEICING AND RAIN REMOVAL SYSTEMS.

These systems are considered to be part of the environmental control system. See Section X of this chapter.

TM 1-1520-236-10

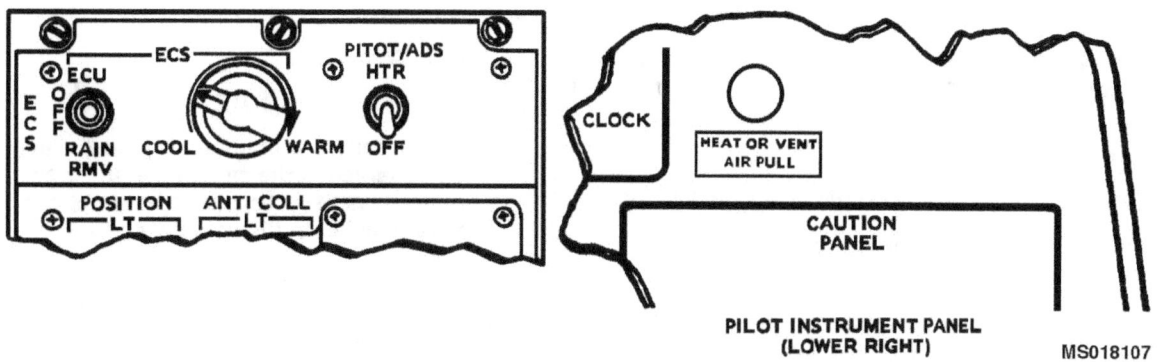

SWITCH/CONTROL	POSITION	FUNCTION
COOL/WARM	COOL to WARM	Controls temperature (35°F - 180°F) in the crew compartment when the ECU/RAIN RMV switch is in the ECU position.
ECU/RAIN RMV	RAIN RMV	Removes rain from canopy. Only ambient air ventilation enters the crew compartment.
		May be used to defrost, defog, or deice the forward area of the canopy.
	ECU	Heats or cools the crew compartment.
	OFF	Ambient air ventilation enters the crew compartment.
HEAT OR VENT AIR PULL	OUT	Directs maximum air to the defrost slots, air vents, and pilot/gunner seat cushions.
	IN	Directs maximum air to the pilot seat cushion.
Air Vent	Open/Closed	Controls the volume/direction of air to the crew compartment.
Defrost Slot Lever	Aft (Open)/Forward (closed)	Controls the volume of air directed to the inner surfaces of the canopy for defogging, defrosting, and deicing.

Figure 2-17. ECS Controls (Typical)

2-25

SECTION X. HEATING, VENTILATION, COOLING, ENVIRONMENTAL CONTROL UNIT

2-53. ENVIRONMENTAL CONTROL SYSTEM (ECS).

    a. **ECS Functions.**

        (1) Heats/cools the crew compartment.

        (2) Removes moisture from the air supplied to the crew compartment.

        (3) Defrosts, defogs, and deices the canopy.

        (4) Rain removal.

        (5) Provides ambient air ventilation to the crew compartment.

    b. **ECS Power Source.** The ECS is electrically controlled and engine bleed air powered. The circuit is powered by the dc nonessential bus and protected by the ECS CONTR circuit breaker.

    c. **ECS Controls.**

NOTE

Under certain conditions a plume may be observed at the air vents in the crew compartment. The plume may appear to be smoke, but is actually condensation.

        (1) The pilot ECS controls and their functions are shown on Figure 2-17.

        (2) Adjustable air vents are provided for the pilot and gunner to control the volume and direction of the air entering the crew compartment.

        (3) Air entering the pilot and gunner seat cushions is controlled by a valve at the top of each seat.

        (4) Rain removal. The rain removal does not remove rain in flight.

SECTION XI. ELECTRICAL POWER SUPPLY AND DISTRIBUTION SYSTEM

2-54. DC AND AC POWER DISTRIBUTION.

Figure 2-18 depicts the general schematic of the dc and ac power distribution system. The dc power is supplied by the battery, starter-generator, alternator through the transformer rectifier unit (TRU), or an external power source through the external power receptacle. The 115 vac power is supplied by the alternator or inverter. The 26 vac power is supplied by the 28 vac transformer.

2-55. BATTERY.

The battery (Figure 2-18) supplies 24 vdc power to the power distribution system when the starter-generator, TRU and the external power receptacle are not in operation.

2-56. STARTER-GENERATOR.

The starter-generator is mounted on and driven by the engine. The starter-generator supplies 28 vdc power to the power distribution system and recharges the battery.

2-57. ALTERNATOR.

A 10kVA alternator is mounted on and driven by the transmission. The alternator supplies 115 vac 3-phase power to the ac buses and transformer rectifier unit (TRU).

2-58. TRANSFORMER RECTIFIER UNIT (TRU).

The transformer rectifier unit converts ac (from alternator) to 28 vdc, thereby powering the TRU bus.

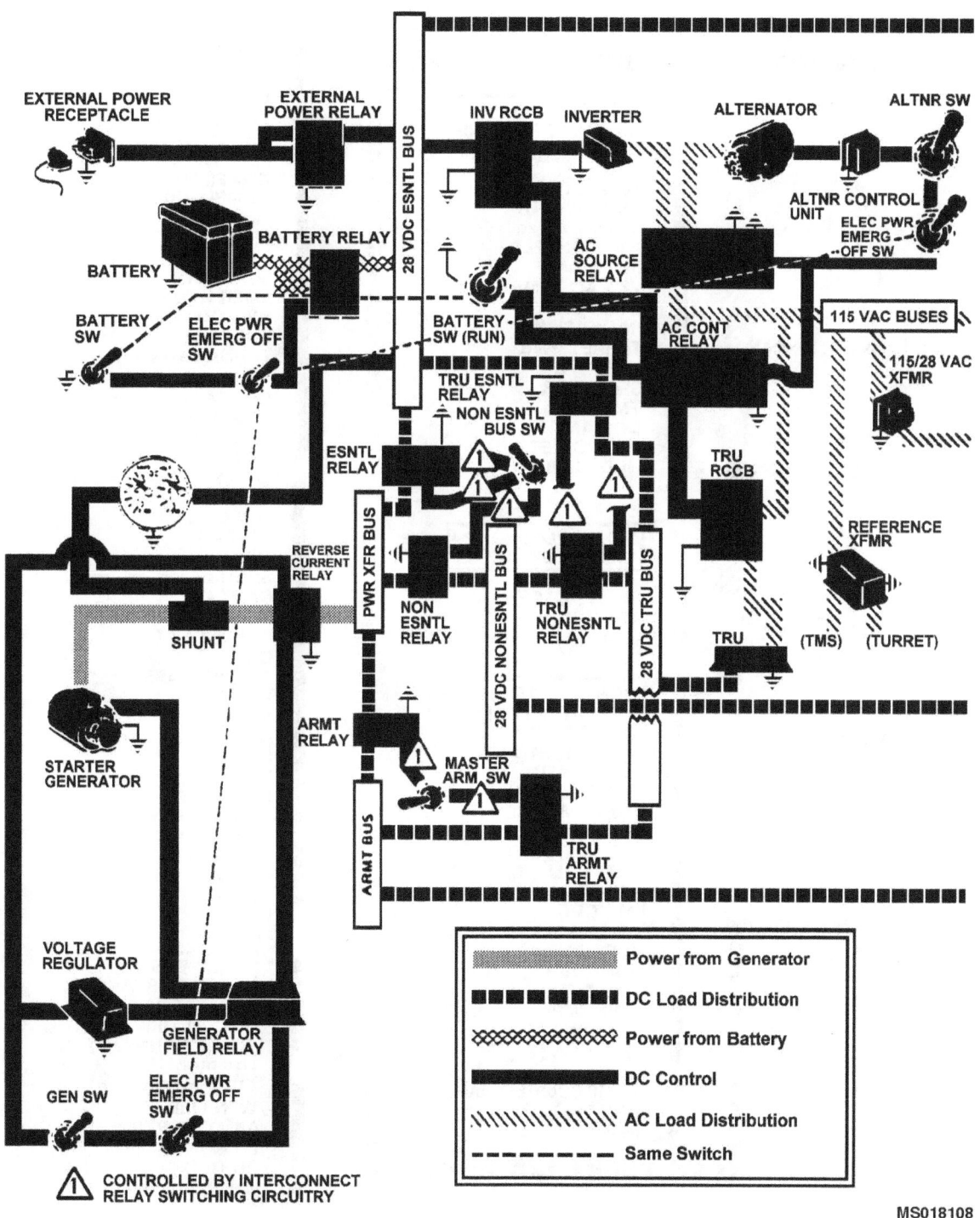

Figure 2-18. DC and AC Power Distribution Schematic (Sheet 1 of 2)

TM 1-1520-236-10

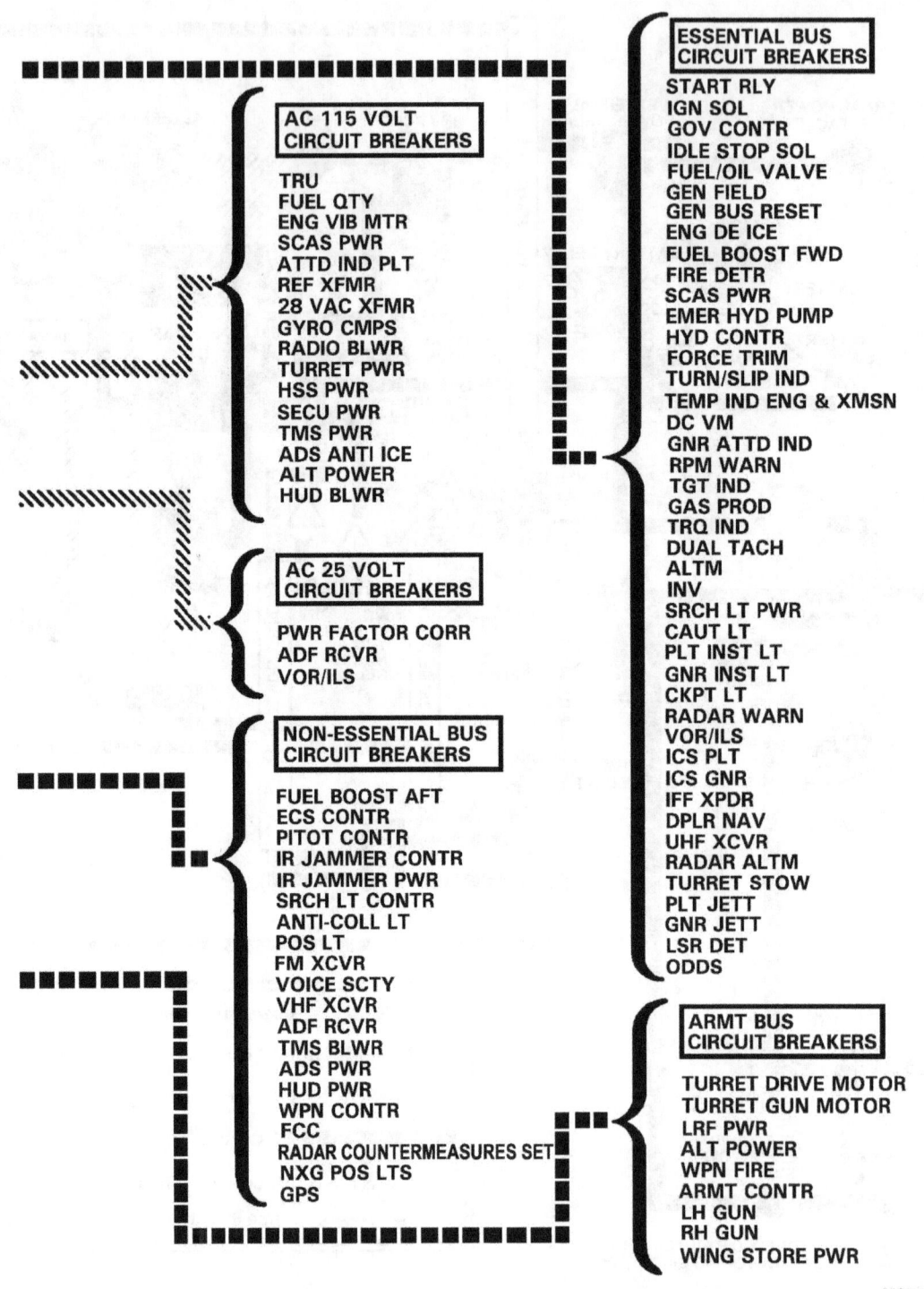

Figure 2-18. DC and AC Power Distribution Schematic (Sheet 2 of 2)

2-59. EXTERNAL POWER RECEPTACLE.

This external power receptacle (Figure 2-1) transmits the ground power unit 28 VDC power to the power distribution system. A 7.5 KW GPU is recommended for external starts.

2-60. GUNNER ELECTRICAL POWER CONTROL.

The gunner ELEC PWR - EMERG OFF switch (Figure 2-12) in the ELEC PWR position permits the pilot to control the electrical system. The switch in EMERG OFF position removes all power from the electrical system.

2-61. PILOT DC POWER INDICATORS AND CONTROLS.

a. Battery Switch. The BATTERY switch (Figure 2-19) START or RUN position permits the battery to supply DC power to the power distribution system or permits the battery to be charged by the starter/generator. The RUN position also activates the inverter. The OFF position isolates the battery and inverter from the systems.

b. Generator Switch. The GEN switch (Figure 2-19) ON position permits the starter-generator to supply DC power to the PWR XFR BUS. The RESET position will reset the starter-generator. When the switch is released, it will return to OFF. The OFF position isolates the generator from the system and allows the starter-generator to function as a starter. The circuit is protected by the GEN BUS RESET and GEN FIELD circuit breakers.

c. Nonessential Bus Switch. The NONESNTL BUS switch (Figure 2-19) functions only when the battery is the sole source of DC power to the helicopter. The NORMAL position supplies DC power to the essential DC bus. The manual position supplies DC power to both the essential and non-essential buses. When either the generator or TRU are operating, the essential and non-essential buses both receive DC power regardless of the position of the non-essential bus switch.

d. DC Circuit Breaker Panel. The DC circuit breakers (Figure 2-20) in the closed position provide circuit protection for the 28 VDC operated equipment. The breakers in the open position deactivates the circuit. The breakers will open automatically in the event of a circuit overload. Each breaker is labeled for the particular circuit it protects. Each applicable breaker is listed in the paragraph describing the equipment it protects.

e. Armament DC Circuit Breakers. The armament DC circuit breakers (Figure 2-20) in the closed position provide circuit protection for the DC operated equipment. The breaker in the open position deactivate the circuit. The breakers will open automatically in the event of a circuit overload. Each breaker is labeled for the particular circuit it protects. Each applicable breaker is listed in the paragraph describing the equipment it protects.

f. Volt-Ammeter Indicator. The pilot indicator (Figure 2-26) displays the DC power voltage being supplied to the power distribution system. Simultaneous display of DC amperage is displayed only when the starter-generator is supplying power to the distribution system. The indicator right scale displays the voltage. The left scale displays the amperage. The circuit is powered by the DC essential bus and protected by the DCVM circuit breaker. There is no means of monitoring amperage load when DC power is supplied by the TRU. Overcharging of the battery or a thermal runaway condition could occur with no indication to the pilot.

g. Generator Caution Lights. The pilot and gunner DC GEN caution lights (Figure 2-23) illuminate when the DC generator fails or when the GEN switch is OFF.

h. External Power Receptacle Caution Light. The pilot EXT PWR caution light (figure 2-23) illuminates when the external power receptacle door is open.

2-62. AC POWER INDICATORS AND CONTROLS.

a. Alternator Switch. The ALTNR switch (Figure 2-19) energizes the alternator to supply power to the AC buses and transformer rectifier unit (TRU) when in ON position. It deactivates and/or resets the alternator when in the OFF RESET position. Any time the alternator is inoperative or the ALTNR switch is in OFF RESET position, the inverter supplies AC power.

b. AC Circuit Breaker Panel. The AC circuit breakers (Figure 2-20) in the closed position provides circuit protection for the AC operated equipment. The breakers in the open position deactivate the circuit. The breakers will open automatically in the event of a circuit overload. Each breaker is labeled for the particular circuit it protects. Each applicable breaker is listed in the paragraph describing the equipment it protects.

c. Alternator Caution Light. The pilot and gunner ALTER caution light (Figure 2-23) will illuminate when rotor rpm is below 91 percent, the ALTNR switch is in the OFF RESET position, or when the alternator has failed.

TM 1-1520-236-10

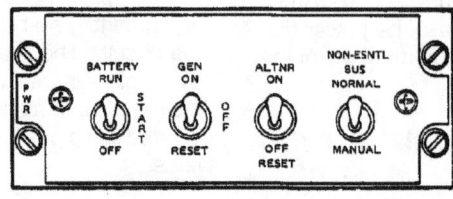

Figure 2-19. Pilot Electrical Power Panel

SECTION XII. LIGHTING

2-63. POSITION LIGHTS.

a. Standard Position Lights.

(1) General. The position lights consist of the right wing green light, left wing red light, and two tailboom white lights (Figure 2-1). The lights are powered by the DC nonessential bus and protected by the POS LT circuit breaker.

(2) Operation. The pilot POSITION LT (FLASH/OFF/STEADY) switch (Figure 2-21) FLASH position flashes the four lights off and on. The STEADY position illuminates the four lights continuously. The OFF position deactivates the four lights. The pilot POSITION LT (BRT/DIM) switch (Figure 2-21) controls the four lights brightness.

b. NVG Position Lights.

(1) General. A covert lighting system, consisting of five infrared NVG position lights, has been provided for use during multi-ship night vision goggle (NVG) operations. The lights are mounted adjacent to the standard position lights and at the top of the vertical fin (Figure 2-1). The lights are powered by the DC nonessential bus and protected by the NVG POS LTS circuit breaker (Figure 2-18 and Figure 2-20).

(2) Operation. The NVG POS LTS (OFF/five position) rotary switch (Figure 2-21) controls the operation of the NVG position lights. Position I activates the lights at minimum intensity. The intensity may be increased incrementally by rotating the switch toward BRT. The OFF position deactivates the five NVG position lights.

2-64. ANTI-COLLISION LIGHT.

a. General. The anti-collision light (Figure 2-1) is powered by the DC nonessential bus and protected by the ANTI-COLL LT circuit breaker.

b. Operation. The pilot ANTI-COLL LT switch (Figure 2-21) ON position illuminates the anti-collision light. The OFF position deactivates the light.

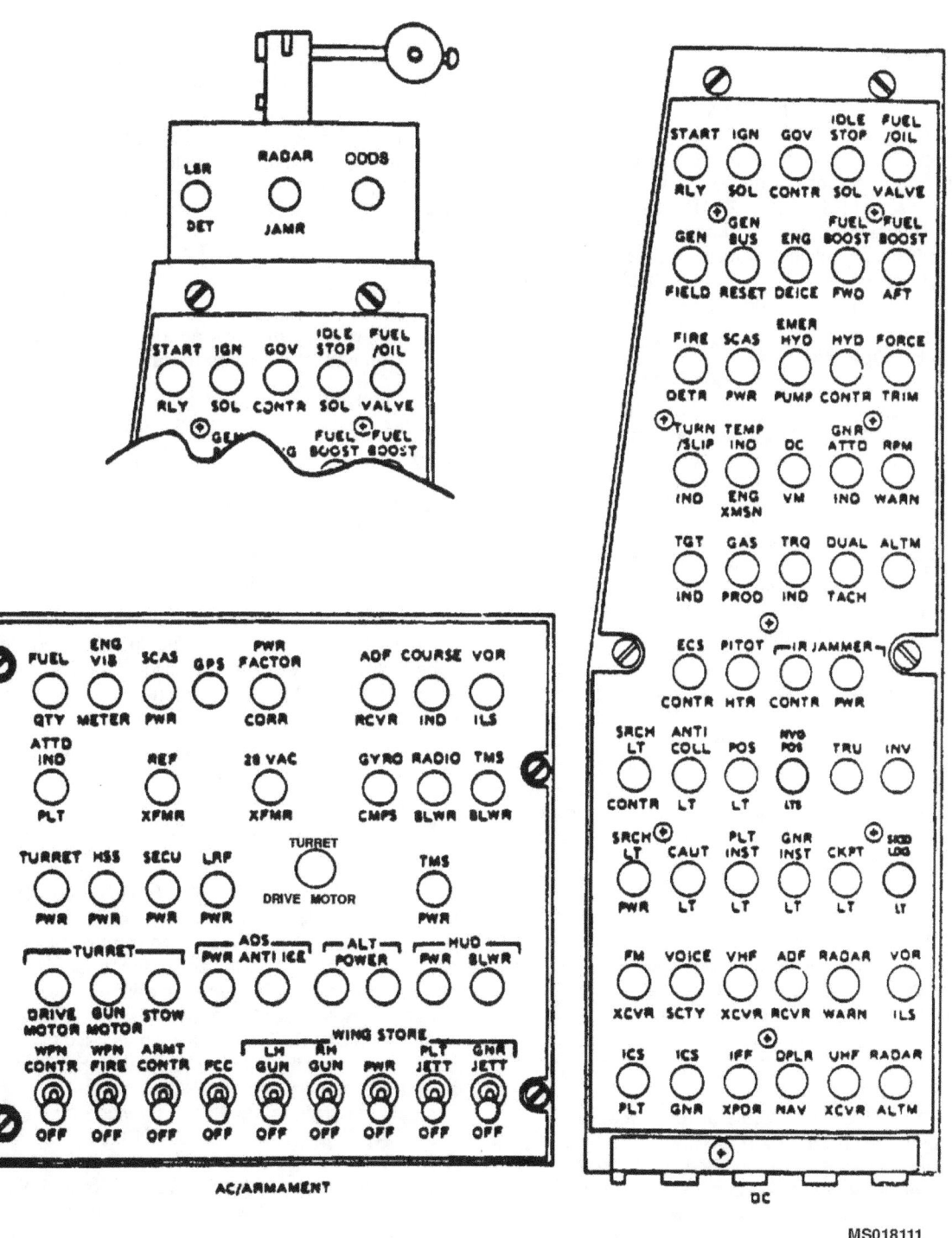

Figure 2-20. Circuit Breaker Panels

2-65. SEARCH LIGHT/LANDING LIGHT.

a. Searchlight.

(1) General. The searchlight consists of an IR bypass filter and 150 watt sealed beam lamp installed on the standard search light housing to provide illumination during NVG operations under low ambient light conditions. The searchlight (Figure 2-1) is powered by the DC essential bus and protected by the SRCH LT PWR circuit breaker. The searchlight control is powered by the nonessential bus and protected by the SRCH LT CONTR circuit breaker (Figure 2-18 and Figure 2-20).

(2) Operation.

(a) Searchlight Switch. The SRCH LT switch (Figure 2-15) ON position illuminates the light. The OFF position deactivates the light. The STOW position retracts the light into the fuselage well.

(b) Searchlight Control Switch. The searchlight control switch (Figure 2-15) EXT position extends the light from the fuselage well and moves it forward. RETR position moves the light aft. The L/R position moves the light left and right.

b. Skid Landing Light.

(1) General. A fixed landing light is installed on the left side of the aircraft attached to the forward landing gear crosstube (Figure 2-1). This light provides a white light capability for use during night operation without NVG. The landing light is powered by the dc essential bus and protected by the SKID LDG LT circuit breaker.

(2) Operation. The SKID LDG LT switch (Figure 2-4) ON position illuminates the light. The OFF position deactivates the light. The elevation of the landing light beam is adjustable on the ground only.

NOTE

The IR filter and 150 watt bulb may be installed on the skid landing light with the 450 watt bulb installed in the standard searchlight housing. This configuration provides a slewable white searchlight and a ground-adjustable IR light.

2-66. COCKPIT UTILITY LIGHTS.

a. General. The pilot (two) and the gunner (one) utility lights are powered by the dc essential bus and protected by the CKPT LT circuit breaker. The lights are supplied in various configurations. All configurations have on-off and bright/dim capabilities and provide NVG compatible light. Adjustable extensions have been provided for pilot (right) and gunner utility lights. An alternate light bracket is provided for the pilot (left) utility light.

NOTE

The cockpit utility light lens selector must be placed in the "white" position in order to provide adequate illumination with NVG filters installed.

b. Operation. The pilot/gunner determines the configuration of his light and operates it accordingly.

2-67. PILOT STATION LIGHTING.

a. General. The cockpit is illuminated by integral lights, post lights, flood lights, and bezel lights. The lights are powered by the dc essential bus and protected by the PLT INST LT circuit breaker.

b. Night Vision Feature. NVG compatibility is provided by using blue-green lighting, in various configurations, to illuminate instruments, avionics and control panels. The NVG ENBL/OFF switches (Figure 2-21) and LTS switch (Figure 2-14) have been disabled.

c. Operation. The pilot rheostat knobs (Figure 2-21) OFF position deactivates the lights. The between OFF and BRT position controls the brightness of the instruments, avionics, and control panel lights as follows:

(1) Console. ROCKETS (RMS), ARMT Control panel, COMM CONT panel, miscellaneous control panel, FM radio, VHF AM radio, horizontal situation indicator (HSI) control panel left and right console, light rheostat control panel APR 39 radar warning, HUD control panel and reflex sight controls. The MASTER CAUTION, RPM and OVERTORQUE lights will dim to a preset intensity, when the CAUTION panel (BRIGHT/DIM) switch is in DIM and the CONSOLE rheostat is on. NVG compatible flip filters have been provided for the MASTER CAUTION, RPM, OVERTORQUE, FIRE, and CAUTION panel lights (Figure 2-6). NVG compatible filters are also provided for the ROCKETS control panel (Figure 4-11), APR 39 radar warning (Figure 3-20), and the switches on the armament (ARMT) panels (Figure 2-6, Figure 2-7, and Figure 4-17).

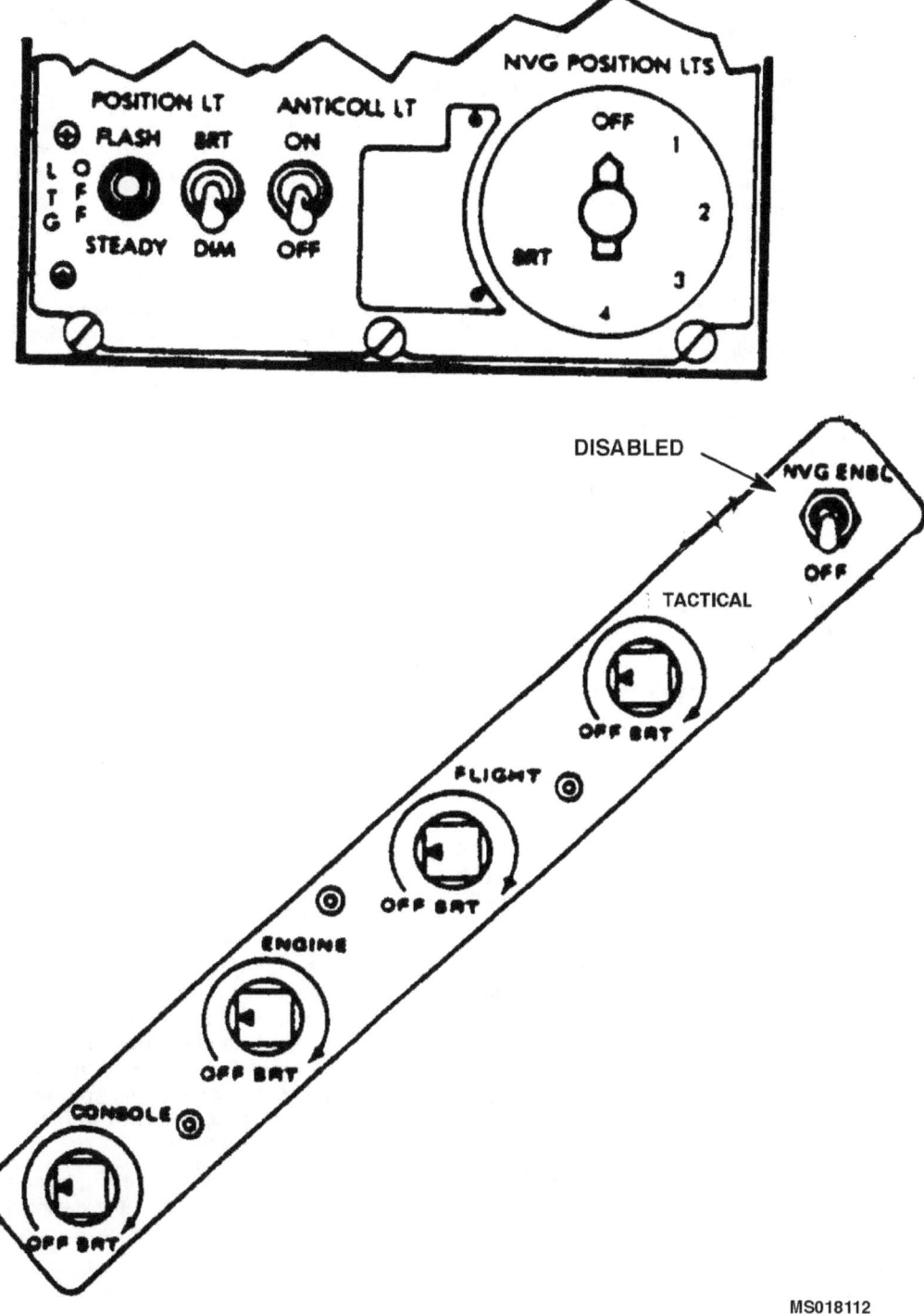

Figure 2-21. Pilot Light Control Panel

WARNING

Caution/Warning flip filters are to remain in the open (unfiltered) position during day flight to insure that caution/warning lights are readily visible.

(2) **Engine.** Fuel quantity, engine temperature/pressure, transmission temperature/pressure, dual tachometer, TGT, volt/ammeter, N1, and torque.

(3) **Flight.** Airspeed indicator, attitude indicator, HSI, vertical speed indicator (VSI), pressure altimeter, radar altimeter, and clock.

(4) **Tactical.** Torque, low airpeed attitude indicator, HSI, radar altimeter, and clock.

NOTE

With tactical rheostat in the ON position, only the listed instruments will be illuminated.

2-68. GUNNER STATION LIGHTING.

a. **General.** The gunner instrument panel is illuminated by NVG compatible flood lights. The armament control panel, (Figure 4-17) is illuminated by an NVG compatible edgelit panel. The magnetic compass (Figure 2-5) is illuminated by one post light. The lights are powered by the dc essential bus and protected by the GNR INST LT circuit breaker.

b. **Night Vision Feature.** NVG compatibility is provided by blue-green lighting, in various configurations to illuminate instruments, avionics and control panels. The LT NORMAL/NVG switch (Figure 2-12) and LTS switch (Figure 2-14) have been disabled. The LT NORMAL/NVG switch (Figure 2-12) has been reconnected and is used in conjunction with the ARMT LT RHEOSTAT to provide the FLIR display with three intensity levels (Figure 2-11)

c. **Operation.** The gunner rheostat knobs (Figure 2-7 and Figure 2-12) OFF position deactivates the lights. The between OFF and BRT position control the brightness of the instrument, avionics, and control panels lights as follows:

(1) **Console.** CSL LT, WING STORES JETTISON and EMER HYDR pump/boresight control panel, COMM CONT Panel, FM radio, ARM STBY, and doppler NAV CONTROL PANEL. The MASTER CAUTION light will dim when the caution panel (BRT/DIM) switch is in DIM and the CSL LT rheostat is on. Doppler MEM/MAL, ARMED/STBY, and PILOT IN CONT lights will dim to a preset intensity when CSL LT rheostat is on. A NVG compatible flip filter has been provided for the MASTER CAUTION panel lights (Figure 2-7), and the doppler NAV control panel displays (Figure 3-17) have permanent filters installed.

WARNING

Flip filters are to remain in the open (unfiltered) position during day flight to insure that the caution lights are readily visible.

(2) **Instrument.** INST LT Airspeed indicator, attitude indicator, pressure altimeter, vertical speed indicator (VSI), radio magnetic indicator (RMI), dual tachometer TGT. N1. torque and standby compass.

(3) **Armament Consoles.** ARMT LT: TOW control Panel (TCP), FLIR control panel (FCP), FLIR intensity settings. The ARMT LT RHEOSTAT is used in conjunction with the LT NORMAL/NVG switch to provide the FLIR display with three levels (day mode, night mode and NVG mode) of intensity for varying missions/atmospheric conditions.

(a) **Day Mode** - Brightest level generally used in day operations. This mode provides the greatest observation ranges.

CAUTION

Day mode operation used for extended periods at night/low light conditions may cause the CPG to experience one eye to be bright adapted by FLIR brightness, while the other eye night adapted. A flight safety problem could occur if the CPG, while operating the M65/C-NITE system, is required to take control of the aircraft to maintain safe flight operations.

(b) **Night Mode** - Reduced FLIR display intensity level generally used in low light conditions. This mode slightly reduces observation ranges.

(c) **NVG Mode** - This mode should be utilized when CPG is in a heads-up position at night and the pilot is using NVGs which prevents stray light from exiting the TSU, causing AN/PVS-NVGs to bloom. This mode should not be used for target detection.

SECTION XIII. FLIGHT INSTRUMENTS

2-69. AIRSPEED INDICATORS.

The pilot and gunner airspeed indicators (Figure 2-6 and Figure 2-7) display the helicopter indicated airspeed (IAS) in knots. The IAS is obtained by measuring the difference between impact air pressure from the pitot tube (Figure 2-1) and the static air pressure from the static ports (Figure 2-1). IAS is inaccurate due to instrument and installation errors.

NOTE

IAS below approximately 25 KIAS is inaccurate due to rotor downwash.

2-70. LOW AIRSPEED INDICATOR (LAI)

The low airspeed indicator, located in the pilot instrument panel, measures and displays low airspeed up to 50 knots by horizontal (fore-aft) and vertical (lateral) direction indicators. Airspeed is sensed by the airspeed and direction sensor. The intersection of the two direction indicators is related to the circular scale to obtain resultant airspeed. A three position flag is used to indicate system operational system failure or an overrange condition. The primary purpose is to provide windspeed to the FCC. Disregard forward airspeed indication when O/R flag is displayed. Refer to Figure 2-22 for airspeed examples and flag indications.

2-71. PRESSURE ALTIMETERS.

The pilot and gunner altimeters (Figure 2-6 and Figure 2-7) display the helicopter height above sea level in feet. The altimeters are supplied power by the dc essential bus and protected by the ALTM circuit breaker. The altimeter does not provide altitude reporting.

2-72. VERTICAL SPEED INDICATOR.

The pilot and gunner vertical speed indicator (Figure 2-6 and Figure 2-7) displays the helicopter ascent and descent speed in feet per minute. The indicator is actuated by the rate of atmospheric pressure change.

2-73. FREE AIR TEMPERATURE (FAT) INDICATOR.

The pilot FAT indicator (Figure 2-6) displays the outside air temperature in degrees Celsius.

2-74. MAGNETIC (STANDBY) COMPASS.

The magnetic compass (Figure 2-7) displays the magnetic heading of the helicopter. A compass correction card is attached to the compass.

2-75. RADIO AIDS TO NAVIGATION.

The FM radio, automatic direction finder, course indicator, and radio magnetic indicator are radio aids to navigation and are covered in Chapter 3.

2-76. MASTER CAUTION SYSTEM.

   a. Master Caution Lights. The pilot and gunner MASTER CAUTION lights (Figure 2-23) illuminate when a caution panel light illuminates. This illumination alerts the pilot and gunner to check caution panels for the specific fault condition.

   b. Caution Panels (Figure 2-23).

      (1) Caution Panel Lights. The pilot and gunner caution panel lights illuminate to identify specific fault conditions. The caution light lettering is readable only when the light illuminates. The light will remain illuminated until the fault condition is corrected.

      (2) Test/Reset and Test Switches. The pilot caution panel has a TEST/RESET toggle switch. The gunner caution panel has a TEST switch. Momentarily placing the pilot switch to the test position will cause pilot caution panel and MASTER CAUTION lights in both pilot's and gunner's station to illuminate. Pressing the gunner's test switch will cause gunner's caution panel to illuminate. Testing of the system will not change the existing fault condition indications. Momentarily placing the pilot switch in the RESET position will extinguish and reset the pilot and gunner MASTER CAUTION lights so they will illuminate again should another fault condition occur.

      (3) Bright-Dim Switches. The caution panels have a BRIGHT-DIM (pilot), BRT-DIM (gunner) switch to control the brightness of the panel caution lights and the MASTER CAUTION lights. This switch will not function if the pilot CONSOLE rheostat (Figure 2-21) of the gunner INST LT rheostat (Figure 2-12) is in the OFF position. The caution lights and the MASTER CAUTION lights will be at full brightness when the pilot/gunner rheostats are in the OFF position.

   c. Electrical Circuit. The master caution system is powered by the dc essential bus and protected by the CAUT LT circuit breaker.

TM 1-1520-236-10

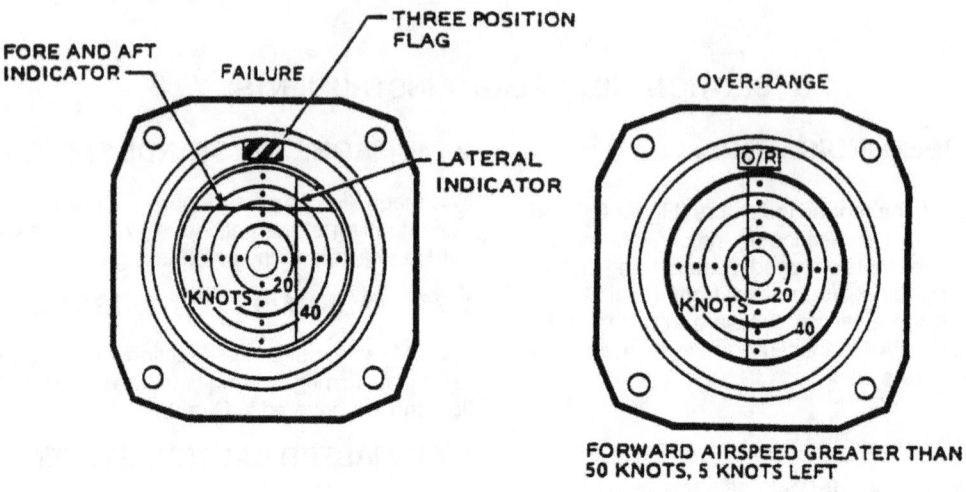

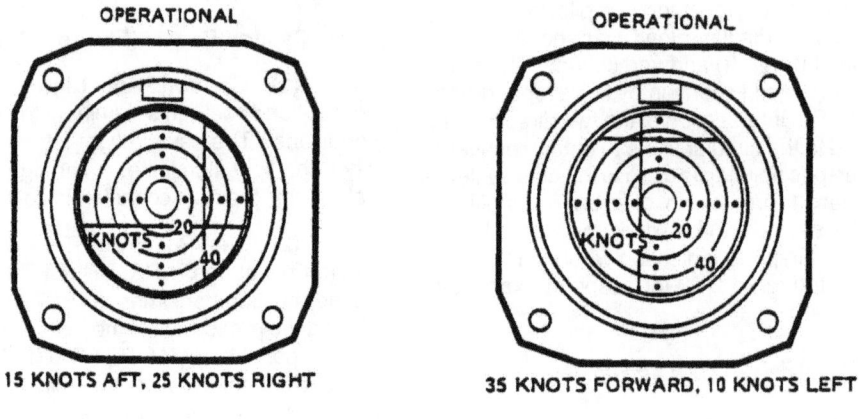

Figure 2-22. Low Airspeed Indicator (LAI)

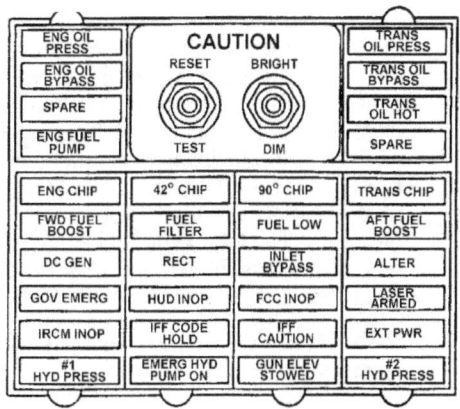
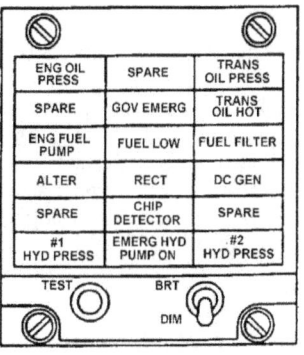

Gunner Panel

CAUTION PANEL WORDING	FAULT CONDITION	CAUTION PANEL WORDING	FAULT CONDITION
ENG OIL PRESS	Engine oil pressure below operating minimum (25 psi).	DC GEN	DC generator has failed or GEN switch is OFF.
TRANS OIL PRESS	Transmission oil pressure is below minimum (below 30 psi).	RECT	Transformer rectifier unit has failed or alternator is not supplying power.
ENG OIL BYPASS	Engine oil bypass switch OFF - Oil system level down 3.8 quarts from full.	RDRCM INOP	Radar countermeasures set has failed.
		GOV EMERG	Governor switch in emergency position.
	Engine oil bypass switch AUTOMATIC - Oil system level down 3.8 quarts from full and bypassing cooler.	ALTER	Alternator has failed. ALTNER switch is OFF, or ROTOR RPM is below 91%.
		GOV EMERG	Governor switch in emergency position.
TRANS OIL BYPASS	Transmission oil bypassing oil cooler.	*HUD INOP	Head up display has failed.
		*FCC INOP	Fire control computer has failed.
TRANS OIL HOT	Transmission oil temperature is at or above red line.	*LASER ARMED	LASER ARM switch is in 1st or LAST position.
ENG FUEL PUMP	One side and/or both sides of engine fuel pump producing low pressure.	IRCM INOP	Indicates system failure or 60 second cooldown period, then light should go out.
		*IFF CODE HOLD	Cold hold switch in the hold position.
ENG CHIP	Metal particles in engine.		
42° CHIP	Metal particles in 42 degree gearbox.	IFF CAUTION	IFF system inoperative.
90° CHIP	Metal particles in 90 degree gearbox.	EXT PWR	External power receptacle door open.
TRANS CHIP	Metal particles in transmission.	#1 HYD PRESS	System 1 hydraulic pressure is low.
FWD FUEL BOOST	Forward fuel boost pump pressure low (below 5 psi).	*EMERG HYD PUMP ON	Emergency hydraulic pump is operating.
FUEL FILTER	Fuel filter is partially obstructed.	*GUN ELEV STOWED	Turret weapon is in stowed position.
FUEL LOW	Low fuel quantity.	#2 HYD PRESS	System 2 hydraulic pressure is low.
AFT FUEL BOOST	Aft fuel boost pump pressure low (below 5 psi).	CHIP DETECTOR	Metal particles in transmission, engine, 42 degree gearbox, or 90 degree gearbox.
		*Illuminate aviation green.	

Figure 2-23. Pilot and Gunner Caution Panels

2-77. RPM HIGH-LOW LIMIT WARNING SYSTEM.

The system provides an immediate warning to check instruments for high or low rotor rpm or low engine rpm. The audio warning will be heard in the pilot and gunner headsets. The audio is a varying oscillating frequency starting low and building up to a high pitch, on for 0.85 second interval, then off for 1.25 seconds, then repeating cycle. The light warning and audio warning functions when the following rpm conditions exist:

a. Warning Light Only:

(1) For rotor rpm of 102-104 percent (High Warning).

(2) For rotor rpm of 93-95 percent (Low Warning).

(3) For engine rpm of 93-95 percent (Low Warning).

(4) Loss of signal (circuit failure) from either rotor tachometer generator or power turbine tachometer generator.

b. Warning Light and Audio Warning Signal Combination:

(1) For rotor rpm of 93-95 percent and engine rpm of 93-95 percent (Low Warning).

(2) Loss of signal (circuit failure) from both rotor tachometer generator and power turbine tachometer generator.

NOTE

It is possible to have an unmodified warning system in the aircraft. On unmodified warning systems, an audio signal will be heard if either rotor or engine RPM drops below low limits.

c. RPM Warning Light. The RPM light (Figure 2-6) illuminates (red) to provide a visual warning of high or low rotor rpm or low engine rpm. For low rpm warning, the audio warning functions in conjunction with the light.

d. RPM Switch - Low Audio. The pilot RPM switch (Figure 2-10) OFF position prevents audio warning from functioning for engine starting when the audio might be objectionable. The switch automatically resets to WARNING position when the engine and rotor reach normal rpm.

e. Electrical Circuit. The RPM high-low limit warning system is powered by 28V dc essential bus and protected by the RPM WARN SYS circuit breaker.

2-78. LOW G WARNING SYSTEM.

The system, provides and audio/visual warning to enable the pilot to recover and avoid entering a low G flight condition. The light and audio are activated when the helicopter enters a 0.559 flight condition. A counter, located under the pilot left console, will record a low G encounter each time the helicopter experiences a 0.45g or less flight condition. The warning light (Figure 2-6) is located on the right side of the pilot instrument panel. Pressing the light will test the lamp and audio. The circuit is powered by the essential bus and is protected by the LGW circuit breaker located in the aft electrical compartment.

2-79. OIL DEBRIS DETECTION SYSTEM (ODDS)

ODDS improves oil filtration and reduces nuisance chip indications caused by normal wear particles on detector gaps. When a chip gap is bridged by conductive particles, a power module provides an electrical pulse which burns away wear particles.

a. *Powerplant ODDS* Components Include:

(1) Oil separator (Lubriclone) in engine compartment.

(2) Oil filter, with 3-micron element, in engine compartment.

(3) Chip detector at bottom of oil separator. Detector is wired to ENG CHIP caution light.

b. *Drive System ODDS* Components Include:

(1) Full-flow debris monitor in transmission sump. Monitor replaces pre-ODDS conventional filter.

(2) External filter with 3-micron element bracket-mounted on transmission case. Filter replaces pre-ODDS 25-micron filter.

(3) Three chip detectors, one in debris monitor and one each in 42- and 90-degree gearboxes. Detectors are wired to TRANS, 42°, and 90° CHIP caution lights.

c. *Electrical System Component*: Power module in cabin provides electrical power to pulse (burn) away ferrous (iron or steel) debris less than 0.005 inch in cross section. Larger debris will not pulse away, but bridges gap and closes circuit to caution light.

2-80. OVER TORQUE CAUTION LIGHT.

The OVER TORQUE caution light (Figure 2-6) provides an immediate indication to check the torque meter for an over torque condition. The light illuminates at 100 ± 0.5% torque and will extinguish at 96 ± 0.5% torque. The system is powered by dc essential bus and protected by CAUT LT circuit breaker.

2-81. ENGINE FIRE DETECTION SYSTEM.

a. General. The system provides the pilot with a visual indication of a fire/overheat condition in the engine compartment. The system is powered by the dc essential bus and protected by the FIRE DETR circuit breaker.

b. Fire Detector Light. The pilot red FIRE light (Figure 2-6) illuminates when sensing elements detect excessive heat in the engine compartment. The sensing elements are attached to the tail rotor driveshaft tunnel.

c. Fire Detector Test Switch. Holding the pilot press-to-test FIRE DET TEST switch (Figure 2-6) in the test position will cause the FIRE light to illuminate. This illumination indicates that the system is operational.

2-82. PILOT CHECKLIST HOLDER.

The pilot checklist holder provides storage for the checklist. The holder is located on the pilot right console.

2-83. GUNNER MAP CASE.

The gunner map case provides storage for mission required maps and charts. The case is located in the gunner right console.

2-84. NIGHT VISION GOGGLE (NVG) BAGS.

Two NVG bags are provided for storing night vision goggles. The gunner bag is located on the right bulkhead forward of the seat. The pilot bag is located to the left of the seat.

SECTION XIV. SERVICING, PARKING, AND MOORING

2-85. SERVICING.

a. Servicing Diagram. Refer to Figure 2-24.

b. Approved Military Fuels, Oils, Fluids and Unit Capabilities. Refer to Figure 2-25.

c. Fuel Settling. Settling time for AVGAS is 15 minutes per foot of tank depth and one hour per foot depth for jet (JP) fuels. Allow (JP) fuel to settle for a minimum of 3.3 hours before any fuel samples are taken.

2-86. APPROVED COMMERCIAL FUELS, OILS, AND FLUIDS.

a. Fuels. Refer to Figure 2-26.

b. Oils. Refer to Figure 2-27.

c. Fluids. Refer to Figure 2-28.

2-87. TYPES AND USES OF FUELS.

a. Fuel types.

(1) Standard Fuel. JP-4 is designated as the Army standard fuel to be used in this helicopter. JP-4 contains icing inhibitor blended at the refinery. Commercial Jet B is a JP-4 type fuel; its mixture might or might not contain icing inhibitor.

(2) Alternate Fuel. JP-5 and JP-8 are designated as the alternate fuel to be used in this helicopter. JP-5 and JP-8 contain icing inhibitor blended at the refinery. Jet A and Jet A1 are JP-5 type fuels without icing inhibitor.

(3) Emergency Fuel. Aviation gasolines (MIL-G-5572) without Tricersyl Phosphate (TCP) are designated as the emergency fuels to be used in this helicopter.

b. Use of Fuels.

(1) No restrictions are imposed on the engine or aircraft when JP-4 is used.

(2) JP-5 and JP-8 type fuels may be added to JP-4 type fuels in any quantity in helicopter fuel tank.

(3) Aviation gasoline may also be added to turbine engine fuels in any quantity in the aircraft fuel tank. A fuel mixture which contains over 10 percent leaded gasoline shall be recorded as all leaded gasoline on DA Form 2408-13-1. Maximum allowable engine operating time when using aviation gasoline without TCP is 50 hours/with TCP it is 25 hours.

2-88. FUEL SYSTEM SERVICING.

Servicing personnel shall comply with all safety precautions and procedures specified in FM 10-68 Aircraft Refueling field manual.

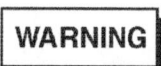

Infrared countermeasure set must be shut down at least one minute prior to any refueling operation and may not be restarted or originally started until the aircraft is in motion.

CAUTION

Ensure that servicing unit pressure is not above 125 psi while refueling.

a. Refer to Figure 2-25 for tank capacities.

b. Refer to Figure 2-26 for approved fuel.

c. The helicopter may be serviced by any of the methods described as follows:

   (1) **Closed Circuit Refueling (Power Off).**

   (a) Refer to Figure 2-24 for fuel filler location.

   (b) Assure fire guard is in position with fire extinguisher.

   (c) Ground servicing unit to ground stake.

   (d) Ground servicing unit to helicopter.

   (e) Ground fuel nozzle to ground receptacle located adjacent to fuel receptacle on helicopter.

   (f) Remove fuel filler cap, and assure that refueling module is in locked position.

   (g) Remove nozzle cap and insert nozzle into fuel receptacle and lock into position.

   (h) Activate flow control handle to ON or FLOW position. Fuel flow will automatically shut off when fuel cell is full. Just prior to normal shutoff, fuel flow may cycle several times, as maximum fuel level is reached. Pin at base of nozzle will indicate when fuel flow stops.

   (i) Assure that flow control handle is in OFF or NO FLOW position and remove nozzle.

   (j) Replace fuel nozzle cap.

   (k) Replace fuel filler cap.

   (l) Disconnect fuel nozzle ground.

   (m) Disconnect ground from helicopter to servicing unit.

   (n) Disconnect servicing unit ground from ground stake.

   (o) Return fire extinguisher to designated location.

   (2) **Gravity or Open-Port Refueling (Power Off).**

   (a) Refer to Figure 2-24 for fuel filler location.

   (b) Assure that fire guard is in position with fire extinguisher.

   (c) Ground servicing unit to ground stake.

   (d) Ground servicing unit to helicopter.

   (e) Ground fuel nozzle to ground receptacle located adjacent to fuel receptacle on helicopter.

   (f) Remove fuel filler cap.

   (g) Using latch tool, attached to filler cap cable, open refueling module if equipped with closed circuit receptacle.

   (h) Remove nozzle cap and insert nozzle into fuel receptacle.

   (i) Activate flow control handle to ON or FLOW position. Fuel flow will automatically shut off when fuel cell is full.

   (j) Assure that flow control handle is in OFF or NO FLOW position and remove nozzle.

   (k) Replace fuel nozzle cap.

   (l) Close refueling module by pulling cable until latch is in locked position, if equipped with closed circuit receptacle.

   (m) Replace fuel filler cap.

   (n) Disconnect fuel nozzle ground.

   (o) Disconnect ground from helicopter to servicing unit.

   (p) Disconnect servicing unit ground from ground stake.

   (q) Return fire extinguisher to designated location.

   (3) **RAPID (HOT) Refueling (Closed Circuit).**

   (a) Before RAPID Refueling.

   <u>1</u> Throttle – Idle.

   <u>2</u> FORCE TRIM switch – FORCE TRIM.

WARNING

In case of helicopter fire, observe fire emergency procedures in Chapter 9.

   (b) During RAPID Refueling. A crewmember shall observe the refueling operation (performed by authorized refueling personnel) and stand fireguard as required. One crewmember shall remain in the helicopter to monitor controls. Only emergency radio transmission should be made during RAPID refueling. Radar and infrared countermeasures equipment shall be placed in standby or turned off unless it is needed for defense of the aircraft.

    (c) Use same procedures as for POWER OFF refueling.

    (d) After Refueling. The pilot shall be advised by the refueling crew or other crewmember after refueling of the following.

        1 Fuel cap – secured.

        2 Grounding cables – Removed.

(4) RAPID (HOT) GRAVITY Refueling.

    (a) Before RAPID Refueling.

        1 Throttle – Idle.

        2 FORCE TRIM switch – FORCE TRIM.

WARNING

In case of helicopter fire, observe fire emergency procedures in Chapter 9.

    (b) During RAPID Refueling. A crewmember shall observe the refueling operation (performed by authorized refueling personnel) and stand fireguard as required. One crewmember shall remain in the helicopter to monitor controls. Only emergency radio transmission should be made during RAPID refueling.

Radar and infrared countermeasures equipment shall be placed in standby or turned off unless it is needed for defense of the aircraft.

    (c) Use same procedures as for POWER OFF refueling.

WARNING

During RAPID GRAVITY Refueling, exercise extreme caution to prevent fuel splashing from fuel cell or fuel nozzle. Any fuel leakage could be extremely hazardous if ingested into engine air intake.

    (d) After Refueling. The pilot shall be advised by the refueling crew or other crewmember after refueling of the following:

        1 Fuel cap – secured.

        2 Grounding cables – removed.

TM 1-1520-236-10

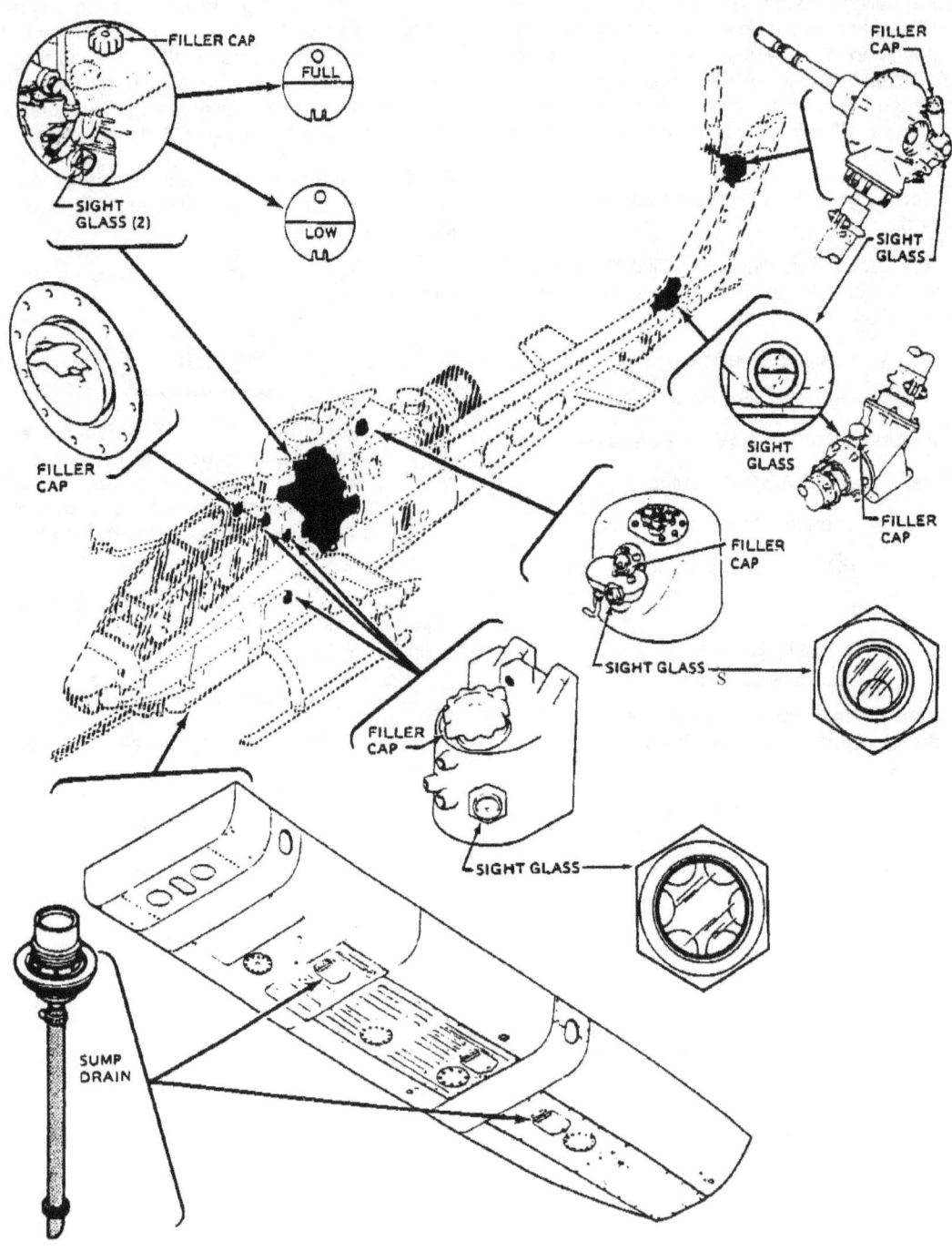

Figure 2-24. Servicing Diagram (Typical)

TM 1-1520-236-10

SYSTEM	SPECIFICATION	NOTE	CAPACITY
FUEL	MIL-T-5624 (JP-4)	1	260 U.S. Gals. Usable 262 U.S. Gals Total
OIL			
Engine	MIL-L-7808 MIL-L-23699	2,4 3,4	
Transmission	MIL-L-7808 MIL-L-23699 DOD-L85734	2,4 3,4	
42° Gearbox	MIL-L-7808 MIL-L-23699 DOD-L85734	2,4 3,4	
90° Gearbox	MIL-L-7808 MIL-L-23699 DOD-L-85734	2,4	
HYDRAULIC			
System No. 1	MIL-H-5606 MIL-H-83282	5 6	
System No. 2	MIL-H-5606 MIL-H-83282	5 6	
Reservoir No. 1 & 2	MIL-H-5606 MIL-H-83282	5	
Emergency System	MIL-H-5606 MIL-H-83282	5 6	

Figure 2-25. Approved Military Fuels, Oils, Fluids and Unit Capacities (Sheet 1 of 2)

2-43

TM 1-1520-236-10

NOTE:

1. MIL-T-5624 JP-4 (NATO F-40).
   Alternate fuel is MIL-T-5624 JP-5 (NATO F-44) or MIL-T-83133 JP-8 (NATO F-34).
   Emergency fuel is MIL-G-5572 AV GAS (NATO F-12, F-18, F-22).
   The helicopter shall not be flown when the cumulative engine operating time exceed 50 hours when AV GAS without TCP is used as emergency fuel or 25 hours when AV GAS with TCP is used as emergency fuel. Any mixture using AV GAS is considered emergency fuel.

2. MIL-L-7808 (NATO 0-148).
   For use in abient temperatures below minus 32°C/25°F.
   May be used when MIL-L-23669 oil is not available.

3. MIL-L-23699 (NATO 0-156).
   For use in abient temperatures below mius 32°C/25°F.
   DOD-L-85734 for use in ambient temperatures above minus 40°C (minus 40°F).

Under no circumstances shall MIL-L-23699 or DOD-L-85734 oil be used in ambient temperatures below minus 32°C/25°F.

4. It is not advisable to mix MIL-L-7808 and MIL-L-23699 or DOD-L-85734 oils, except during an emergency. An entry on DA Form 2408-13-1 is required when the oils are mixed.

5. MIL-H-5606 (NATO H-515).
   For use in ambient temperatures below minus 40°C/40°F.

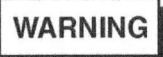

When handling hydraulic fluid (MIL-H-83282), observe the following:

- **Prolonged contact with liquid or mist can irritate eyes and skin.**

- **After any prolonged contact with skin, immediately wash contacted area with soap and water. If liquid contacts eyes, flush them immediately with clear water.**

- **If liquid is swallowed, do not induce vomiting; get immediate medical attention.**

- **Wear rubber gloves when handling liquid. If prolonged contact with mist is likely, wear an appropriate respirator.**

- **When fluid is decomposed by heating, toxic gases are released.**

6. MIL-H-83282.
   For use in ambient temperatures above minus 40°C/40°F.

Figure 2-25. Approved Military Fuels, Oils, Fluids and Unit Capacities (Sheet 2 of 2)

SOURCE	PRIMARY OR STANDARD FUEL	ALTERNATE FUEL	
US MILITARY FUEL	JP-4 (MIL-T-5624)	JP-5 (MIL-T-5624) or JP-8 (MIL-T-83133)	
NATO CODE NO.	F-40 (WIDE CUT TYPE)	F-44 OR F-34 (HIGH Flash Type)	
COMMERCIAL FUEL (ASTM-D-1655)	JET B	JET A	JET A-1 NATO F-34
American Oil Co.	American JP-4	American Type A	
Atlantic Richfield	Aerojet B	Aerojet A	Aerojet A-1
Richfield Div.		Richfield A	Richfield A-1
B.P. Trading	B.P.A.T.G.		B.P.A.T.K.
Caltex Petroleum Corp.	Caltex Jet B		Caltex Jet A-1
Cities Service Co.		CITGO A	
Continental Oil Co.	Conoco JP-4	Conoco Jet-50	Conoco Jet-60
Gulf Oil	Gulf Jet B	Gulf Jet A	Gulf Jet A-1
EXXON Co., USA	EXXON Turbo Fuel B	EXXON A	EXXON A-1
Mobil Oil	Mobil Jet B	Mobil Jet A	Mobil Jet A-1
Phillips Petroleum	Philjet JP-4	Philjet A-50	
Shell Oil	Aerosol JP-4	Aeroshell 640	Aerosol 650
Sinclair		Superjet A	Superjet A-1
Standard Oil Co.		Jet A Kerosene	Jet A-1 Kerosene
Chevron	Chevron B	Chevron A-50	Chevron A-1
Texaco	Texaco Avjet B	Avjet A	Avjet A-1
Union Oil	Union JP-4	76 Turbine Fuel	
FOREIGN FUEL	NATO F-40	NATO F-44	
Belgium	BA-PF-2B		
Canada	3GP-22F	3-6P-24e	
Denmark	JP-4 MIL-T-5624		
France	Air 3407A		
Germany	VTL-9130-006	UTL-9130-007/UTL 9130-010	
Greece	JP-4 MIL-T-5624		
Italy	AA-M-C-1421	AMC-143	
Netherlands	JP-4 MIL-T-5624	D. Eng RD 2493	
Norway	JP-4 MIL-T-5624		
Portugal	JP-4 MIL-T-5624		
Turkey	JP-4 MIL-T-5624		
United Kingdom (Britain)	D. Eng RD 2454	D. Eng RD 2498	

NOTE

Anti-icing and Biocidal Additive for Commercial Turbine Engine Fuel - The fuel system icing inhibitor shall conform to MIL-I-27686. The additive provides anti-icing protection and also functions as a biocide to kill microbial growths in helicopter fuel systems. Icing inhibitor conforming to MIL-I-27686 shall be added to commercial fuel not containing an icing inhibitor during refueling operations, regardless of ambient temperatures. Refueling operations shall be accomplished in accordance with accepted commercial procedures. This additive (prist or eq.) is not available in the Army Supply System, but will be locally procured when needed.

Figure 2-26. Approved Commercial Fuels - Equivalents for JP-4, JP-5 and JP-8

APPROVED COMMERCIAL MIL-L-7808 TYPE OILS

MANUFACTURER'S NAME	MANUFACTURER'S DESIGNATION
American Oil and Supply Co.	PQ Turbine Oil 8365
Humbie Oil and Refining Co.	ESSO/ENCO Turbo Oil 2389
Mobile Oil Corp.	RM-201A

CAUTION

Do not use Shell Oil Co., Part No. 307, Qualification No. 7D-1 oil (MIL-L-7808). It can be harmful to seals made of silicone.

APPROVED COMMERCIAL MIL-L-23699 TYPE OILS

MANUFACTURER'S NAME	MANUFACTURER'S DESIGNATION
American Oil and Supply Co.	PQ Turbine Lubricant 6423/8878/9595
Bray Oil Co.	Brayco 899/899-S
Castrol Oil Inc.	Castrol 205
Chevron International Oil Co., Inc.	Jet Engine Oil 5
W.R. Grace and Co. (Hatco Chemical Div.)	HATCOL 3211/3611
Exxon	Turbo Oil 2380 (WS-6000)/2395 (WS-6459)
Mobil Oil Corp.	RM-139A/RM-147A/Avrex S Turbo 260/Avrex S Turbo 265
Royal Lubricants Co.	Royco 899 (C-915)/899SC
Shell Oil Co., Inc.	Aeroshell Turbine Oil 500
Standard Oil Co., of California	Chevron Jet Engine Oil 5
Stauffer Chemical Co.	Stauffer 6924/Jet II
Texaco, Inc.	SATO 7730. TL-8090

Figure 2-27. Approved Commercial Oils - Equivalents for MIL-L7808 and MIL-L-23699 Oils

APPROVED COMMERCIAL MIL-H-5606 TYPE FLUID

MANUFACTURER'S NAME	MANUFACTURER'S DESIGNATION
American Oil and Supply Co.	"PO" 4226
Bray Oil Co.	Brayco 757B Brayco 756C Brayco 756D
Castrol Oils, Inc.	Hyspin A
Humble Oil and Refining Co.	Univis J41
Mobile Oil Corp.	Aero HFB
Pennsylvania Refining Co.	Petrofluid 5606B Petrofluid 4607
Royal Lubricants Co.	Royco 756C/D DS-437
Shell Oil Co.	XSL 7828
Standard Oil Co. of California	PED 3565 PED 3337
Texaco, Inc.	TL-5874
Stauffer Chemical Co.	Aero Hydroil 500
Union Carbide Chemical Co.	YT-283
Union Carbide Corp.	FP-221

Figure 2-28. Approved Commercial Fluids - Equivalents for MIL-H-5606

CHAPTER 3
AVIONICS

SECTION I. GENERAL

3-1. GENERAL.

This chapter covers the electronic equipment configuration installed in Army AH-1F helicopter. It includes a brief description of the electronic equipment, its technical characteristics, and capabilities. This chapter contains complete operating instructions for all signal equipment installed in the helicopter. For mission avionics equipment, refer to Chapter 4, Mission Equipment. During equipment operation, it is assumed that the power is applied and applicable circuit breakers are energized. The terms megahertz (MHz) and kilohertz (KHz) are used in this chapter, regardless of equipment markings.

3-2. ELECTRONIC EQUIPMENT CONFIGURATION.

Avionics equipment installed in the helicopter with their common names, use, and operational range is presented in Figure 3-1. Antenna locations are shown in Figure 3-2.

SECTION II. COMMUNICATIONS

3-3. INTERPHONE CONTROL.

3-4. DESCRIPTION – INTERPHONE CONTROL.

This communications systems control C-6533( )/ARC provides an intercommunication capability between the pilot and gunner. Two of the panels are installed in the helicopter. The system is used for intercommunication and radio control. It may be used in any one of three different modes as determined by the setting of the switches and controls on the panel. The three modes of operation are: two-way radio communication; radio receiver monitoring; and intercommunication between the pilot, gunner, and ground crews.

3-5. CONTROLS AND FUNCTIONS – INTERPHONE CONTROL.

Refer to Figure 3-3.

3-6. OPERATION – INTERPHONE CONTROL.

a. Transit interphone selector switch – As required.

b. Receivers switches – As required.

c. HOT MIKE switch – As required.

d. VOL control – Adjust.

3-7. VHF/FM RADIO SET AN/ARC-114A.

3-8. DESCRIPTION – VHF/FM RADIO SET AN/ARC-114A.

The AN/ARC-114A provides two-way frequency modulated (FM) narrow band voice communications, with homing capability, in the frequency range of 30.00 to 75.95 MHz. However, homing is primarily in the 30.00 to 60.00 MHz range. The set operates on 920 channels for a distance of approximately 50 miles as limited by line of sight. A guard receiver is incorporated within the unit, with a guard frequency of 40.50 MHz. Course homing information is presented to the course deviation pointer on the Altitude Director Indicator (ADI) and course deviation bar on the Horizontal Situation Indicator (HSI). FM signal strength is presented by the guideslope deviation pointers on both the HSI and ADI, and moves up with increasing signal strength. The FM homing display is selected by means of a course select switch on the HSI control panel. The VHF/FM radio set must also be set to HOMING. The set utilizes position number 1 of the C-6533 ( )/ARC intercommunications control panel.

NOMENCLATURE	COMMON NAME	USE	RANGE
Control, Intercommunications Set C-65330/AIC	Interphone Control	Interphone for pilot and gunner, integrates all communication equipment.	Stations within helicopter.
Radio Set AN/ARC-114A or ARC-201	VHF/FM Radio	Two-way voice communication and homing.	Line-of-sight
Communications Security Equipment TSEC/KY-28	Voice Security Equipment	Together with the FM radio set provides secure two-way voice communications.	
Radio Set AN/ARC-115 or ARC-186	VHF/AM Radio	Two-way voice communication.	Line-of-sight
Radio Set AN/ARC-116 or ARC-164	UHF Radio	Two-way voice communication.	Line-of-sight
Horizontal Situation Indicator ID-2103/A or 209-075-660-3	HSI	Determines heading, position and direction of flight.	
Direction Finder Set AN/ARN-89B	ADF Set	Radio range navigation.	150 to 200 miles average
Gyromagnetic Compass Set AN/ASN-43	Compass Set	Navigation aid.	
Radio Set AN/ARN-123(V)1	VOR SET	With appropriate instrumentation provided: VHF omnirange (VOR), localizer (LOC), glideslope (GS), and marker beacon (MB) position information.	Line-of-sight
Transponder Set AN/APX-72 AN/APX-100	IFF Transponder Radio	Transmit a special coded reply for radar interrogator systems.	Line-of-sight
Radar Signal Detector Set AN/APR-39(V)1 or AN/APR-39A(V)1	Radar Warning Set	Provides high radar threat warning and aids evasion and mission completion.	Line-of-sight
Indicator, Attitude Director ID-2104/A or 209-075-661-1	ADI	Provides altitude reference and command information for the direction of flight; to include localizer, glideslope and rate-of-turn deviation indications.	Line-of-sight
Indicator, Radio Magnetic Compass ID-2105/A or ID-250/A	RMI	Provides bearing information to selected radio station relative to magnetic heading.	Line-of-sight
Radar Altimeter APN-209	Radar Altimeter	Provides attitude indication above terrain.	0 to 1500 ft. AGL
Navigation set Airborne AN/ASN-128	Doppler Navigation	Provides navigation information position, bearing, time, and distance to selected destination.	
Laser Detection Set AN/AVR-2	Laser Detecting Set (LDS)	Detects and displays to the aircraft pilot information concerning the laser environment around the aircraft.	Line-of-sight
Trimpack	GPS	Provides navigation information position, velocity, waypoint, time and steering.	
AIM-1/EXL IR Laser	AIM-1	Night sight for aiming 20 mm gun.	Line-of-sight

Figure 3-1. Communication and Associated Electronics Equipment

TM 1-1520-236-10

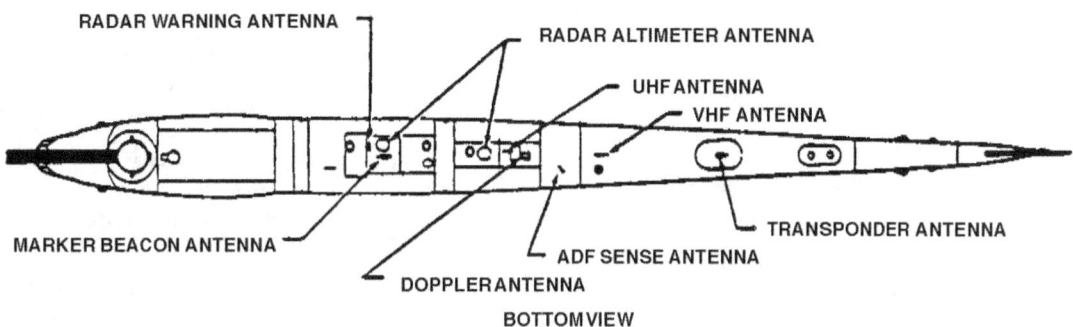

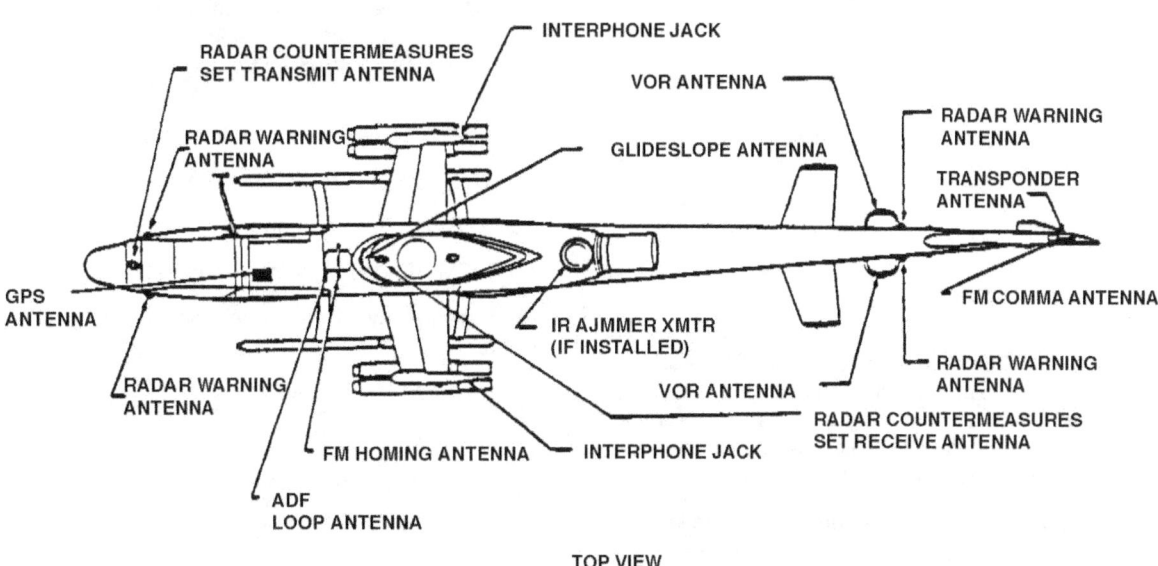

Figure 3-2. Antenna Locations (Typical)

3-3

3-9. CONTROLS AND FUNCTIONS – VHF/FM RADIO AN/ARC-114A.

Refer to Figure 3-4.

3-10. OPERATION – VHF/FM RADIO SET AN/ARC-114A.

    a. Function selector – As required.

    b. Frequency – Select.

    c. RCVR TEST switch – Press.

    d. AUDIO – Adjust.

    e. Interphone transmit - receiver switches – Number 1 position.

    f. Transmit keying switch – Press.

    g. Function selector – OFF.

3-11. VHF/FM RADIO SET AN/ARC-201.

3-12. DESCRIPTION – VHF/FM RADIO SET AN/ARC-201.

The AN/ARC-201 provides two-way frequency modulated (FM) narrowband voice communications.

    a. The following items form the airborne radio system:

Item	Description
1	Receiver-Transmitter Radio Panel Mounted (RT-1476)
2	Adapter, Data Rate (CV-3885)

    b. **Essential Operational Technical Characteristics.** Except where specifically indicated otherwise, the following operation/technical parameters are the minimum essential characteristics. Unless otherwise specified, they apply to each radio configuration.

    c. **Frequency range.** The frequency range is 30 to 87.975 MHz channelized in tuning increments of 25 KHz. In addition a frequency offset tuning capability of -10 KHz, -5 KHz, +5 KHz and +10 KHz is provided on both receive and transmit mode. This frequency is not used in the ECCM mode.

3-13. CONTROLS AND FUNCTIONS – VHF/FM RADIO SET AN/ARC-201.

Refer to Figure 3-5.

3-14. OPERATION – VHF/FM RADIO SET AN/ARC-201.

NOTE

The FM receiver-transmitter may cause interference in the VOR/ILS receiver and UHF receiver-transmitter when the 2nd harmonic (FREQ x 2) or 3rd harmonic (FREQ X 3) of the FM transmitter frequency approaches the operating frequency of the VOR/ILS receiver and UHF receiver.

This interference may cause the VOR pointer of the pilots HSI and gunners RMI to rotate to the park position with the NAV flag appearing. The FM harmonic can also interfere with UHF reception by blocking the received signal or degrading communication by producing a squeal in the UHF audio.

All FM receiver transmitters used in AH-1 aircraft (AN/ARC-201, AN/ARC-114, AN/ARC-114A) may produce this condition.

    a. FUNCTION selector switch – Set as required.

    b. MODE selector switch – Set as required.

    c. PRESET selector switch – Set as required.

    d. IFM RF PWR selector switch – Set as required.

    e. Frequency – Select frequency using key pad as follows:

       – press FREQ key

       – press CLR key

       – key in desired frequency

       – press STO/ENT key

    f. VOL – Adjust.

    g. Transmit – Press SEND key.

    h. FUNCTION selector switch – Off.

NOTE

To operate radio set in frequency hopping mode, perform the following steps before PRESET selection:

i. FUNCTION selector switch – LD-V.

j. MODE selector switch – FH.

k. PRESET channel select switch – MAN.

Display reads FILL T.

l. Connect an ECCM fill device to radio set FILL connector. Set ECCM device power switch to ON and selector switch to T1.

m. On radio set, H-LD/O key – Press.

Display reads STO T, then COLD.

n. On ECCM device, T1 switch – 1.

o. On radio set, FUNCTION selector switch – LD.

p. H-LD/O – Press

Display reads hopset number.

q. STO/ENT – Press.

Key pad 1 – Press.

This stores HOPSET data in PRESET 1 selection.

r. Repeat steps i through q for remaining PRESET numbers 2 through 6. FUNCTION selector switch – Set as required.

NOTE

To operate Time of Day (TOD), both radios must be within 1 minute of each other in order to establish communications in steps s through x.

s. TIME key – Press one time.

t. Then press: – LR key

– enter day

– ENT key

– TIME key

– CLR key

– enter hour

– enter minute

– ENT key

u. FUNCTION selector switch – SQ OFF.

v. MODE selector switch – FH.

w. PRESET selector switch – 1.

x. Establish communications.

y. FUNCTION selector switch – OFF.

NOTE

To operate in VHF FM homing mode, perform steps z through ab.

z. MODE selector switch – HOM

aa. Frequency – Select EM homing station frequency using key pad as follows:

– press FREQ key

– press CLR key

– key in desired frequent

– press STO/ENT key

ab. Homing information – Observe on HSI and ADI.

3-15. VOICE SECURITY EQUIPMENT TSEC/KY-58.

3-16. DESCRIPTION – VOICE SECURITY EQUIPMENT TSEC/KY-58.

The voice security equipment is used with the FM Command Radio to provide secure two way communication. The equipment is controlled by the control-indicator (Z-AHP). The POWER switch must be in the ON position, regardless of the mode of operation, whenever the equipment is installed.

3-17. CONTROLS AND FUNCTIONS – VOICE SECURITY EQUIPMENT TSEC/KY-58.

Refer to Figure 3-6.

3-18. OPERATING PROCEDURES – SECURE VOICE.

To talk in secure voice, the KY-58 must be "Loading" with any number of desired variables.

a. Set the MODE switch to OP.

b. Set the FILL switch to the storage register which contains the crypto-net variable (CNV) you desire.

c. Set the POWER switch to ON.

d. Set the PLAIN C/RAD switch to C/RAD.

e. If the signal is to be retransmitted, set the DELAY switch to ON.

TM 1-1520-236-10

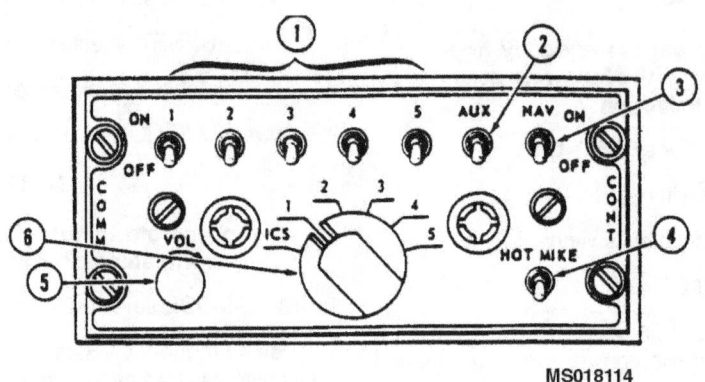

CONTROL/INDICATOR	FUNCTION

1. Receiver Switches
 	
   1 - VHF/FM ARC-114A or ARC-201
   2 - UHF ARC-116 or ARC-164
   3 - VHF/AM ARC-115 or ARC-186
   4 - Not used
   5 - Not used
	Connect (ON) or disconnect (OFF) communications receivers from the headsets.

2. AUX Receiver switch	Connect (ON), or disconnect (OFF), VOR set receiver ARN-123(V)1 from the headset.
3. NAV Receiver switch	Connects (ON), or disconnects (OFF), ADF navigation receiver ARN-89B from headset.
4. HOT MIKE switch	Permits hand-free intercommunications with transmit-interphone selector in the ICS position.
5. VOL control	Adjusts volume from receivers. Adjusts intercommunications volume.

6. Transmit-Interphone selector
 	
   1 - VHF/FM ARC-114A or ARC-201
   2 - UHF ARC-116 or ARC-164
   3 - VHF/AM ARC-115 or ARC-186
   4 - Not used
   5 - Not used
   ICS
	Selects transmitter to be keyed and connects microphone to transmitters.
	
	Connects the microphone to the intercommunications system only, disconnecting microphone from transmitters.

Figure 3-3. Interphone Control Panel C-6533/( )/ARC

TM 1-1520-236-10

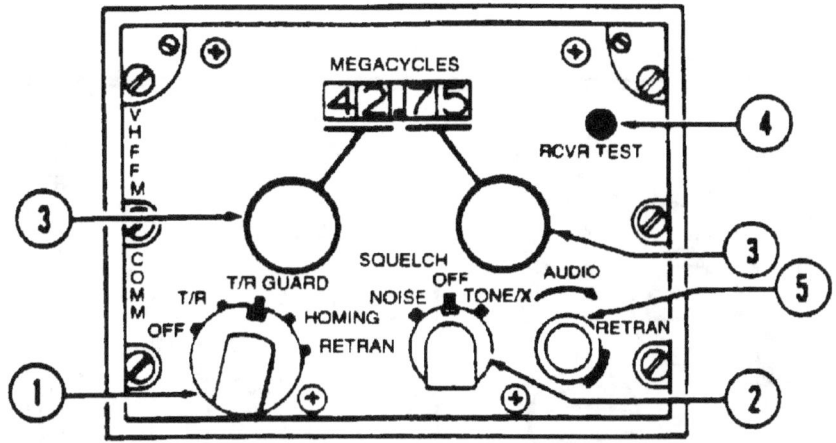

CONTROL/INDICATOR	INDICATOR
1. Function Selector	
OFF	Power off.
T/R	Receiver – ON. Transmitter – Standby.
T/R GUARD	Guard receiver – ON. Transmitter – Standby. Receiver – ON. **NOTE** **Reception on the guard receiver is unaffected by frequencies selected for normal communications.** **NOTE** **The guard frequency can be selected on the main receiver.**
HOMING	Activates the homing mode and displays on attitude indicator. May also be used for normal voice communications. The communications antenna is automatically selected when the transmitter is keyed.
RETRAN	Retransmission may be accomplished when the second FM radio set is installed.
2. Squelch Selector	
NOISE	Eliminates background noise in headsets.
OFF	Deactivates squelch.
TONE/X	Squelches background noise in headsets. Use TONE/X for secure voice operation.
3. Frequency Selectors - Indicator	
Left	Selects first two digits of desired frequency.
Right	Selects third and fourth digits of desired frequency.
4. RCVR TEST Switch	When pressed, audible tone indicates proper receiver performance.
5. AUDIO Control	Adjust receiver volume.

Figure 3-4. VHF/FM Radio Set AN/ARC-114A

TM 1-1520-236-10

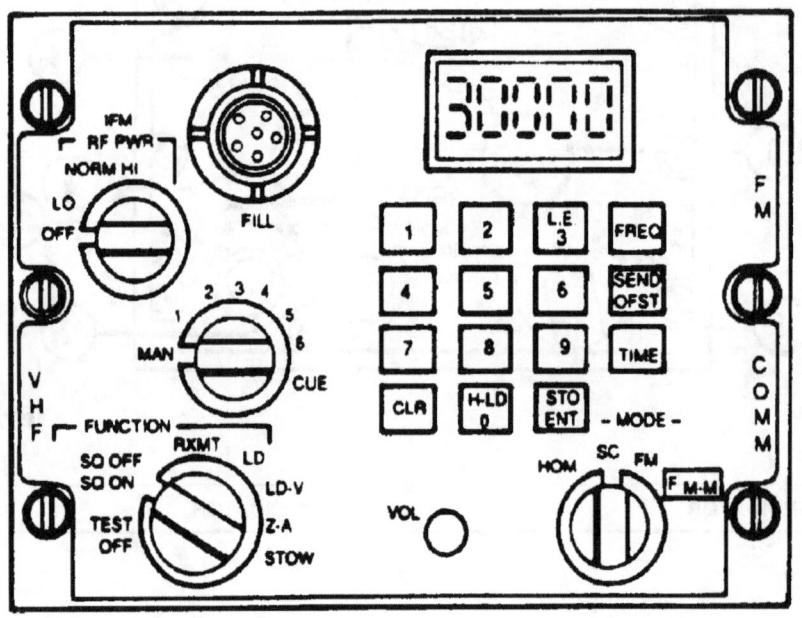

CONTROL/INDICATOR	FUNCTION
1. Function Selector	
1 - OFF	Primary power OFF. Memory battery power ON.
2 - TEST	RT and ECCM modules are tested. Results; GOOD or FAIL.
3 - SQ ON	RT on with squelch.
4 - SQ OFF	RT on with no squelch.
5 - RXMT	RT in RECEIVE mode. Used as a radio relay link.
6 - LD	Keyboard loading of preset frequencies.
7 - LD-V	TRANSEC variable loading is enabled.

Figure 3-5. VHF/FM Radio Set AN/ARC-201 (Sheet 1 of 3)

3-8

CONTROL/INDICATOR	FUNCTION
8 - Z-A	Not on operational position. Used to clear the TRANSEC variable.
9 - Stow	All power removed. Used during extended storage.
2. MODE Switch	Homing antennas are active; communication antenna is disconnected. Provides pilot with steering, station approach, and signal strength indicators.
1 - SC	Single channel mode of operation. Operating frequency selected by PRESET switch or keyboard entry.
2 - FH	Frequency hopping mode selected. PRESET switch positions 1-6 select frequency hopping met parameters.
3 - FM-M	Frequency hopping-master position selects control station as the time standard for communicating equipment.
3. Preset Switch	
1 - MAN	Used in single mode to select any operating frequency in 25 KHz increments.
2 - POS. 1-6	In single channel mode, preset frequencies are selected or loaded. In FH or FM-M mode, frequency hopping nets are selected.
3 - CUE	Used by a non-ECCM radio to signal to CUE or ECCM radio.
4. IFM RF	
1 - OFF	(Bypass) - 10 watts.
2 - LO	(Low Power) - 2.5 watts.
3 - NORM	(Normal) - 10 watts.
4 - HI	(High power) - 40 watts.
5. Display	The display generally operates in conjunction with the keyboard. Other displays may be selected by the FUNCTION and MODE switches.

Figure 3-5. VHF/FM Radio Set AN/ARC-201 (Sheet 2 of 3)

CONTROL/INDICATOR	FUNCTION
6. Keyboard	A 15-button array of switches in a 4x4 matrix, used to insert data or select data for display. The keyboard is comprised of 10 numerical buttons, three special functions, and two command buttons.
1 - Switches 1-9	Used to key in frequencies, load time information, or offsets.
2 - CLR	Used to zeroize the display, or to clear erroneous entries.
3 - 0 (H • LD)	Used to enter zeroes. Second function (hold) initiates transfer of ECCM parameters.

Figure 3-5. VHF/FM Radio Set AN/ARC-201 (Sheet 3 of 3)

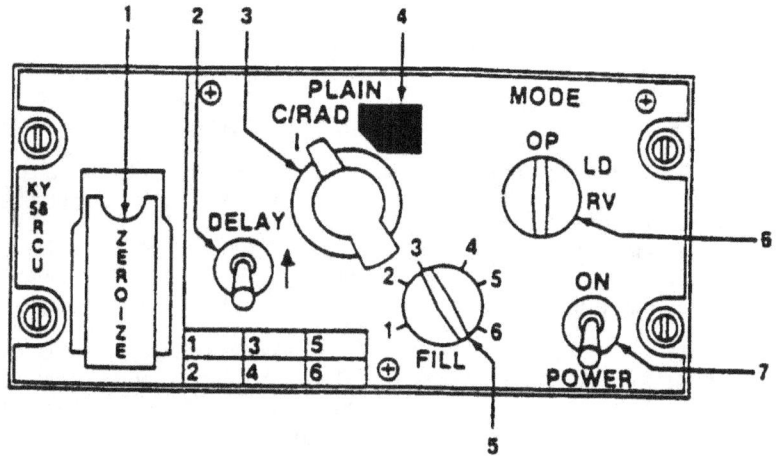

CONTROL/INDICATOR	FUNCTION
1. ZEROIZE switch (two-position) momentary toggle, under spring loaded cover	Zeroize the KY-58. Clears any encoding in the system.
2. DELAY switch 2-position toggle	Used when signal is to be retransmitted.
3. PLAIN-C/RAD1 Switch rotary 2-position selector switch	In the PLAIN position, permits normal (unciphered) communications on the associated FM radio set. In the C/RAD1 position, permits ciphered communications on the associated radio set.
4. N/A	
5. FILL switch 6-position rotary switch	Permits pilot to select one of 6 storage registers for filling.
6. MODE Switch 3-position rotary	In the OP position KT-58 normal operating. In the LD position for filling.
	In the RV position KY-58 in Receive-Variable. Filled from another external source.
7. POWER ON switch 2-position toggle.	Connects power to the associated TSEC/KY-58 cipher equipment in the ON (forward) position, and disconnects power from the equipment in the OFF (aft) position. Turns on power to TSCE/KY-58.

Figure 3-6. Voice Security Equipment T/SEC KY-58

f. At this time a cryptoalarm and background noise in the aircraft audio intercom system should be heard. To clear this alarm, press and release PTT in the aircraft audio/intercom system. Secure voice communication is now possible.

NOTE

When operating in either secure or clear (plain) voice operations the aircraft audio intercom system should be heard. To clear this alarm, press and release PTT in the aircraft audio/intercom system. Secure voice communication is now possible.

3-19. OPERATING PROCEDURES – CLEAR VOICE.

a. Set the RCU PLAIN-C/RAD 1 switch to PLAIN.

b. Operate the equipment.

3-20. OPERATING PROCEDURES – ZEROING.

Instructions should originate from the Net Controller or Commander as to when to zeroize the equipment and power must be on.

a. Lift the red ZEROIZE switch cover on the RCU.

b. Lift the spring-loaded ZEROIZE switch. This will zeroize positions 1-6.

c. Close the red cover.

3-21. OPERATING PROCEDURES – AUTOMATIC REMOTE KEYING.

Automatic Remote Keying (AK) causes an "old" cryptonet variable (CNV) to be replaced by a "new" CNV. Net Controller simply transmits the "new" CNV to your KY-58.

a. The Net Controller will use a secure voice channel with directions to stand by for an AK transmission. Calls must not be made during this standby action.

b. Several beeps should now be heard in headset. This means that the "old" CNV is being replaced by a "new" CNV.

c. Using this "new" CNV, the Net Controller will ask for a "radio check."

d. After the "radio check" is completed, the Net Controller instructions will be to resume normal communications. No action should be taken until the net controller requests a "radio check."

3-22. OPERATING PROCEDURES – MANUAL REMOTE KEYING.

The Net Controller will make contact on a secure voice channel with instructions to stand by for a new cryptonet variable (CNV) by a Manual Remote Keying (MK) action. Upon instructions from the controller:

a. Set the RCU FILL switch to position 6. Notify the Net Controller by radio, and stand by.

b. When notified by the Net Controller, set the Z-AHP MODE switch to RV (receive variable). Notify the Net Controller, and stand by.

c. When notified by the Net Controller, set the Z-AHP FILL switch to any storage position selected to receive the new CNV (may be unused or may contain the variable being replaced). Notify the Net Controller, and stand by.

NOTE

When performing Step c., the storage position (1 through 6) selected to receive the new CNV may be unused, or it may contain the variable which is being replaced.

d. When notified by Net Controller, listen for a beep in headset, wait two seconds and set the RCU MODE switch to OP. Confirm if:

(1) The MK operation was successful, the Net Controller will now contact you via the new CNV.

(2) The MK operation was not successful, the Net Controller will contact you via clear voice (plain) transmission; with instructions to set your Z-AHP FILL selector switch to position 6, and stand by while the MK operation is repeated.

3-23. KY-58 AUDIO TONES – NORMAL AND EQUIPMENT MALFUNCTION.

a. Continuous beeping, with background noise, is cryptoalarm. This occurs when power is first applied to the KY-58, or when the KY-58 is zeroized. This beeping is part of normal KY-58 operation. To clear this tone, press and release the PTT button on the Z-AHQ after the Z-AHQ LOCAL switch has been pressed. Also the PTT can be pressed in the cockpit.

b. Background noise indicates that the KY-58 is working properly. This noise should occur at TURN ON of the KY-58, and also when the KY-58 is generating a cryptovariable. If the background noise is not heard at TURN ON, the equipment must be checked out by maintenance personnel.

c. Continuous tone could indicate a "parity alarm." This will occur whenever an empty storage register is selected while holding the PTT button in. This tone can mean any of three conditions:

    (1) Selection of any empty storage register.

    (2) A "bad" cryptovariable is present.

    (3) Equipment failure has occurred. To clear this tone, follow the "Loading Procedures" in TM 11-5810-262-OP. If this tone continues, have the equipment checked out by maintenance personnel.

d. Continuous tone could also indicate a cryptoalarm. If this tone occurs at any time other than in Step c. above, equipment failure may have occurred. To clear this tone, repeat the "Loading Procedures" in TM 11-5810-262-OP. If this tone continues, have the equipment checked out by the maintenance personnel.

e. Single beep, when RCU is not in TD (Time Delay), can indicate any of three normal conditions:

    (1) Each time the PTT button is pressed when the KY-58 is in C (cipher) and a filled storage register is selected, this tone will be heard. Normal use (speaking) of the KY-58 is possible.

    (2) When the KY-58 has successfully received a cryptovariable, this tone indicates that a "good" cryptovariable is present in the selected register.

    (3) When you begin to receive a ciphered message, this tone indicates that the cryptovariable has passed the "parity" check, and that it is a good variable.

f. A single beep, when the RCU is in TD (Time Delay) occuring after the "preamble" is sent, indicates that you may begin speaking.

g. A single beep, followed by a burst of noise after which exists a seemingly "dead" condition indicates that your receiver is on a different variable than the distant transmitter. If this tone occurs when in cipher text mode: Turn RCU FILL switch to the CNV and contact the transmitter in PLAIN text and agree to meet on a particular variable.

3-24. VHF/AM RADIO SET AN/ARC-115.

3-25. DESCRIPTION – VHF/AM RADIO SET AN/ARC-115.

The AN/ARC-115 Radio Set provides amplitude - modulated (AM) narrow band voice communications with the frequency range of 116.000 to 149.95 MHz on 1360 channels. The set is effective at a distance of approximately 50 miles, line of sight. A guard receiver is incorporated with the unit, which is fixed tuned to121.500 MHz.

The radio set control panel is labeled VHF/AM COMM and utilizes position 3 of the C-6533( )/ARC interphone control panel.

3-26. CONTROLS AND FUNCTIONS – VHF/AM RADIO SET AN/ARC-115.

Refer to Figure 3-7.

3-27. OPERATION – VHF/AM RADIO SET AN/ARC-115.

    a. Function selector – As required.

    b. Frequency – Select.

    c. RCVR TEST – Press.

    d. AUDIO – Adjust.

    e. Interphone transmit-receive switches – Number 3 position.

    f. Transmit keying switch – Press.

    g. Function selector – OFF.

3-28. UHF/AM RADIO SET AN/ARC-116 or AN/ARC-164.

3-29. DESCRIPTION – UHF/AM RADIO SET AN/ARC-116 or AN/ARC-164.

The AN/ARC-116 or AN/ARC-164 provides two-way UHF amplitude modulated (AM) narrow band voice communications within the frequency range of 225.00 to 399.95 MHz on 3500 channels for a distance of approximately 50 miles as limited by conditions. A guard receiver is incorporated in the set and is fixed tuned to 243.00 MHz. Both receivers are disabled during transmitter operation. The radio set control panel is marked UHF. The UHF radio transmitter and main receiver operate on the same frequency and are simultaneously tuned by frequency selector knobs on the panel. When the function selector switch is placed in the T/R GUARD (AN/ARC-116) or BOTH (AN/ARC-164) position, constant monitoring of the UHF guard frequency (243.00 MHz) is possible regardless of main receiver-transmitter frequency selected. The set utilizes selector switch (6, Figure 3-3) position number 2 of the interphone control panel.

The UHF set is used for transmission and reception. The audio signal level is adjusted by the volume control and the signal is then applied to the interphone control panels for selection. When the No. 2 receiver switch is on, the audio signal lever is further adjusted by the interphone control panel volume (VOL) control and is fed to the headset. When the No. 2 transmit position is selected and the microphone output is amplified in the audio control panel and applied to the UHF command transmitter. Sidetone audio is routed back to the headset in the same way as receiver audio.

TM 1-1520-236-10

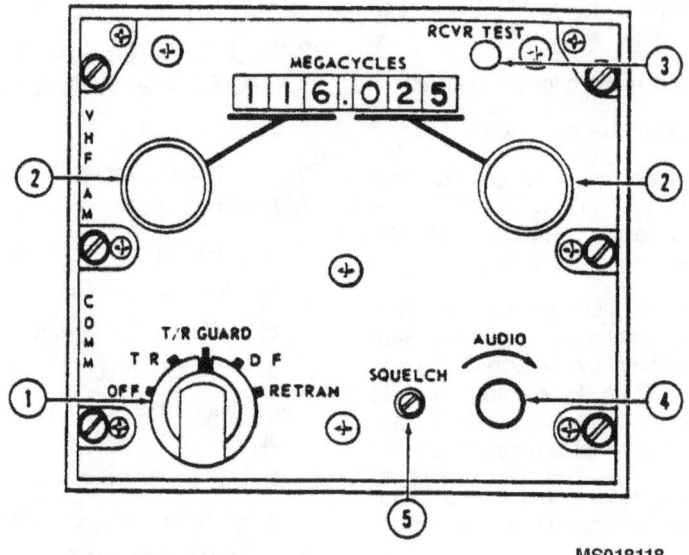

CONTROL/INDICATOR	FUNCTION
1. Function Selector	
OFF	Power off.
T/R	Receiver – On; Transmitter – Standby.
T/R GUARD	Receiver – On; Transmitter – Standby; Guard receiver – On.
	NOTE
	Reception on the guard receiver is unaffected by frequencies selected for normal communications.
D/F	Not used.
RETRAN	Not used.
2. Frequency Selectors	
Left	Selects first three digits of desired frequency.
Right	Selects fourth, fifth and sixth digits of desired frequency.
3. RCVR TEST Switch	When pressed, audible signal indicates proper receiver performance.
4. AUDIO Control	Adjusts receiver volume.
5. SQUELCH control	Squelch control adjusted by maintenance personnel only.

Figure 3-7. VHF/AM Radio Set AN/ARC-115

3-30. CONTROLS AND FUNCTIONS – UHF/AM RADIO SET AN/ARC-116 or AN/ARC-164.

Refer to Figure 3-8.

3-31. OPERATION – UHF/AM RADIO SET AN/ARC-116 or AN/ARC-164.

    a. **UHF/AM Radio Set (ARC-116).**

        (1) Function selector – As required.

        (2) Frequency – Select.

        (3) RCVR TEST – Press-to-test.

        (4) AUDIO – Adjust.

        (5) Interphone transmit-receive switches – Number 2 position.

        (6) Transmit keying switch – Press.

        (7) Function selector – OFF.

    b. **UHF/AM Radio Set (ARC-164).**

        (1) Function selector – As required.

        (2) Frequency – Select.

        (3) TONE switch – Press.

        (4) VOL control – Adjust.

        (5) Interphone transmit-receive switches – Number 2 position.

        (6) Transmit keying switch – Press.

        (7) Function selector – OFF.

    c. **Channel Preset Procedure (ARC-164).**

        (1) UHF switch – MAIN.

        (2) Mode switch – PRESET.

        (3) Frequency selector switch – Set frequency.

        (4) Channel selector switch – Set channel.

        (5) Cover – Open.

        (6) PRESET switch – Press.

        (7) Cover – Close.

3-32. EMERGENCY OPERATION – UHF/AM RADIO SET AN/ARC-116 or AN/ARC-164.

    a. **UHF/AM Radio Set (ARC-116).** Place function selector in T/R GUARD. Select 243.00 MHz and transmit.

    b. **UHF/AM Radio Set (ARC-164).** Place mode switch to GUARD position. Radio is ready to transmit and receive on 243.00 MHz.

3-33. RADIO SET AN/ARC-186(V).

NOTE

The normal electrical configuration of the AH-1F does not allow the AN/ARC-186 VHF radio to be used in the FM mode. The band lockout selector should be set to the FM position so that the FM portion of the radio is locked out and will not function.

3-34. DESCRIPTION – RADIO SET AN/ARC-186(V). Refer to Figure 3-9.

The radio set is a VHF FM-AM transceiver that provides in the clear and secure voice communication capability of frequencies in both VHF, AM and FM bands. Over a frequency range of 108.00 MHz to 115.975 MHz, Radio Set AN/ARC 186(V) functions as a receiver for the reception of amplitude-modulated (AM) transmissions. At frequencies in the range of 116.000 MHz to 151.975 MHz, the set operates both as an AM receiver and AM transmitter. From 108.000 MHz, to 151.975 MHz, a total of 1790 AM voice communication channels spaced at 25 KHz, are provided by the set. In a range of frequencies extended from 30.000 MHz to 87.975 MHz, Radio Set AN/ARC-186(V) functions both as an FM receiver and FM transmitter. Operating in this frequency range, Radio Set AN/ARC-186(V) provides 2320 FM voice communication channels. The channels are spaced at 25 KHz. Radio Set AN/ARC-186(V) also provides 20-channel presets which can be any combination of AM or FM frequencies. Automatic tuning to both AM and FM emergency frequencies (121.5 MHz and 40.5 MHz, respectively) is provided by setting only one control. Power output of the transmitter section of the transceiver is 10 watts.

3-35. CONTROLS AND FUNCTIONS – RADIO SET AN/ARC-186(V).

Refer to Figure 3-9.

3-36. OPERATION – CONTROL (MODE) SETTINGS.

    a. TR mode: two-way in the clear and secure voice communication. Refer to paragraphs 3-15 through 3-20 for voice security system.

    b. Not functional this installation.

    c. EMER AM-FM mode: emergency two-way voice communication on selected guard channel.

3-37. OPERATION – TRANSMIT/RECEIVE (TR) MODE.

a. Set OFF-TR-D/F mode select switch to TR.

b. Set EMER AM/FM-MAN-PRE frequency selector switch to MAN for manual frequency selection or to PRE for present channel selection.

c. To manually select a frequency, rotate the four MHz selector switches until desired frequency is displayed at indicator windows.

d. To select a preset channel, rotate preset channel selector switch until the number (1 to 20) of the desired channel is displayed in preset CHAN indicator window. The radio set will automatically tune to the preset channel in both TR and DF modes.

3-38. OPERATION – AM EMERGENCY (EMER AM) MODE.

a. Set OFF-TR-DF mode select switch to either TR or D/F.

b. Set Emer AM/FM-MAN-PRE frequency control/emergency select switch to EMER AM. This mode will automatically disable the secure speech function and enable in the clear voice communication.

3-39. OPERATION – FM EMERGENCY (EMER FM) MODE.

The FM Emergency mode enables voice reception/transmission on a prestored guard frequency of 40.500 MHz.

a. Set OFF-TR-D/F mode select switch to either TR or D/F.

b. Set EMER AM/FM-MAN-PRE frequency control/emergency select switch to EMER FM. This mode will automatically disable the secure speech function and enable in the clear voice communication.

3-40. OPERATING PROCEDURES – RADIO SET AN/ARC-186.

a. Squelch Disable – SQ DIS/TONE switch to SQ DIS. Squelch will remain disabled (open) until switch is returned to center position.

b. Tone Transmission – SQ DIS/TONE switch to the momentary TONE position to transmit (FM or AM) tone frequency of approximately 1000 Hz. Releasing the switch disables the tone frequency.

c. Loading Preset Channels.

(1) Set OFF-TR-D/F mode select switch to TR.

(2) Set EMER AM/FM-MAN-PRE frequency control emergency select switch to MAN.

(3) Rotate the four MHz selector switches until desired frequency is displayed in indicator windows.

(4) Rotate CHAN preset channel selector switch until desired channel is displayed in the indicator window.

(5) Remove SNAP-ON-COVER.

(6) Momentarily hold WB-NB-MEM LOAD switch to MEM LOAD. Preset frequency is now loaded into memory.

d. Wideband/Narrowband Selection.

(1) Remove SNAP-ON-COVER.

(2) For wideband operation, set WB-NB MEM LOAD switch to WB.

(3) For narrowband operation, set WB-NB-MEM switch to NB.

NOTE

This switch shall he placed in the WB position at any time the MEM LOAD function is not being accomplished. The NB position is not used in this installation.

e. Band Lockout Selection.

(1) Remove SNAP-ON-COVER.

(2) Ensure LOCKOUT-FM-AM switch is in LOCKOUT position (indicated by a white dot on the switch).

NOTE

With the LOCKOUT-FM-AM switch set to AM or FM, the frequency of the band selected will be locked out. This will cause an audible warning to occur whenever a frequency in a locked out band is selected. For this installation, operational AM and FM bands are required and the LOCKOUT-AM-FM switch must be set to the LOCKOUT position.

TM 1-1520-236-10

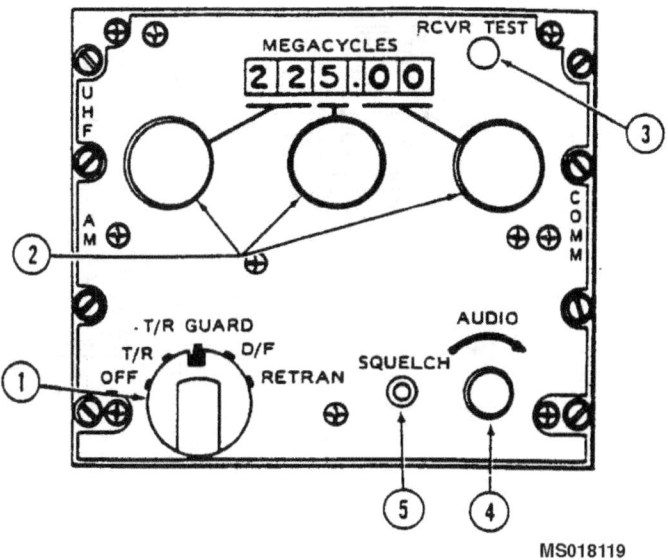

AN/ARC-116

CONTROL/INDICATOR	FUNCTION
1. Function Selector	
OFF	Power off.
T/R	Receiver – ON. Transmitter – Standby.
T/R GUARD	Receiver – ON. Transmitter – Standby. Guard Receiver – ON.
D/R	Not used.
RETRAN	Not used.
2. Frequency Selectors - Indicator	
Left	Selects first two digits of desired frequency.
Middle	Selects third digit (1 MHz) of desired frequency.
Right	Selects last two digits of desired frequency.
3. RCVR TEST Switch	When pressed, audible tone indicates proper receiver performance.
4. AUDIO Control	Adjusts receiver audio volume.
5. SQUELCH Control	Squelch control adjusted by maintenance personnel only.

Figure 3-8. UHF/AM Radio Set (Sheet 1 of 2)

3-17

TM 1-1520-236-10

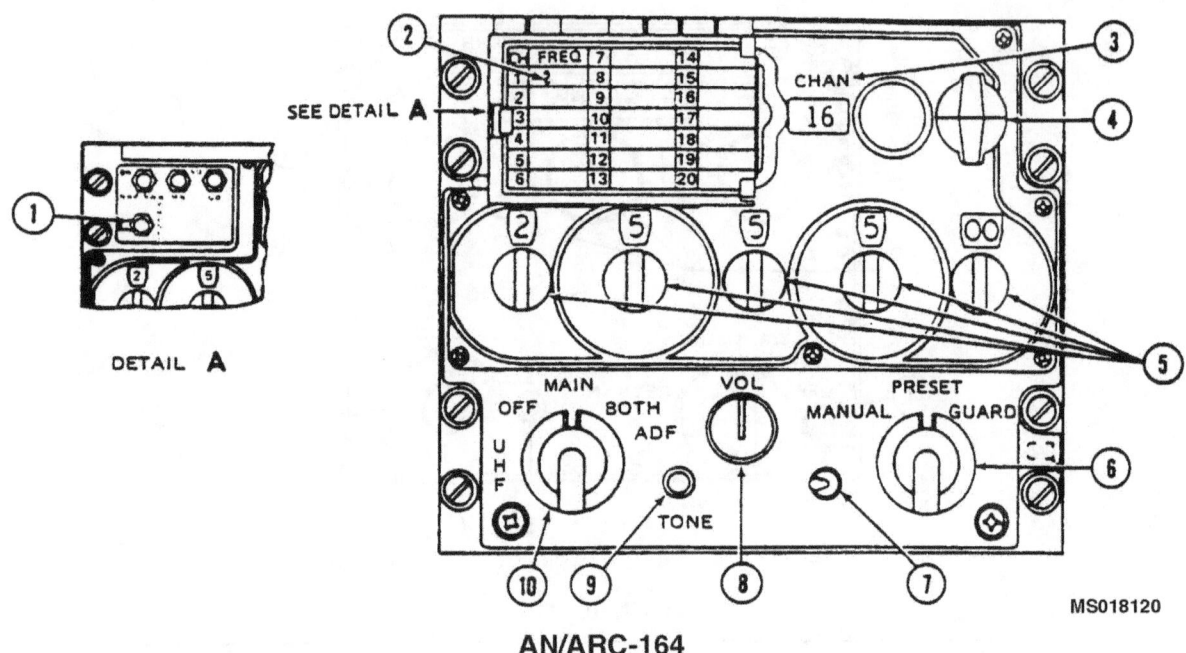

AN/ARC-164

CONTROL/INDICATOR	FUNCTION
1. PRESET	Press - Sets selected frequency in desired preset channel.
2. Channel frequency card	Provides space to record selected frequency.
3. CHAN window	Indicator selected channel.
4. Channel selector knob	Selects preset channel.
5. Frequency selector	Selects desired frequency.

6. Mode selector
    MANUAL
    PRESET
    GUARD
	Frequency selected with frequency selector knobs.
	Selects preset channel as desired by CHAN selector.
	Frequency is automatically positioned to guard channel (243.000 MHz).

7. SQUELCH
    OFF
    ON
	Received unsquelched.
	Received squelch operating.

8. VOL knob	Adjusts autio volume.
9. TONE pushbutton	When pressed, audible tone indicated proper receiver performance.

10. UHF knob
 	
    OFF
    MAIN
    BOTH
    ADF
	
	Power off.
	Main receiver on, transmitter in standby.
	Main and guard receiver on, main transmitter in standby.
	Not used.

Figure 3-8. UHF/AM Radio Set (Sheet 2 of 2)

TM 1-1520-236-10

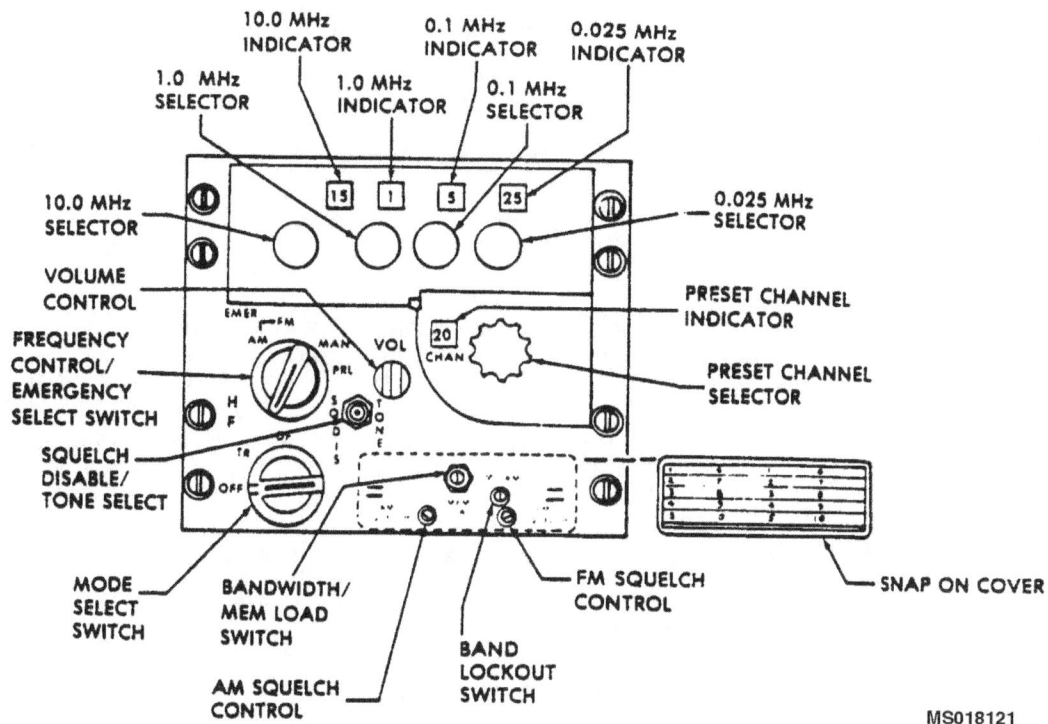

CONTROL/INDICATOR	FUNCTION
0.025 MHz selector	Rotary switch. Selects r/t frequency in 0.025 MHz increments. Clockwise rotation increases frequency.
0.025 MHz indicator	Indicates manually selected r/t frequency in 0.025 MHz increments.
0.1 MHz selector	Rotary switch. Selects r/t frequency in 0.1 MHz increments. Clockwise rotation increases frequency.
0.1 MHz indicator	Indicates manually selected r/t frequency in 0.1 MHz increments.
1.0 MHz selector	Rotary switch. Selects r/t frequency in 1.0 MHz increments. Clockwise rotation increases frequency.
1.0 indicator	Indicates manually selected r/t frequency in 1.0 increments.
10 MHz selector	Rotary switch. Selects r/t frequency in 10 MHz increments from 30 to 150 MHz. Clockwise rotation increases frequency.
10 MHz indicator	Indicates manually selected r/t frequency in 10 MHz increments from 30 to 150 MHz.

Figure 3-9. Radio Set AN/ARC-186(V) (Sheet 1 of 2)

3-19

CONTROL/INDICATOR	FUNCTION
Preset channel selector	Rotary switch. Selects preset channel from 1 to 20. Clockwise rotation increases channel number selected.
Preset channel indicator	Indicates selected preset channel.
Volume control	Potentiometer. Clockwise rotation increases volume.
Squelch disable/tone select	Three-position switch. Center position enables squelch. SQ DIS position disables squelch. Momentary TONE position transmits tone of approximately 1000 Hz.
Frequency control/emergency select switch	Four-position rotary switch. EMER AM-FM selects a prestored guard channel. MAN position enables manual frequency selection. PRE position enables preset channel selection.
Mode select switch	Three-position rotary switch. OFF position disables r/t TR position enables transmit receive modes. D/F position enables FM homing.
Bandwidth/memory load switch	Three-position switch. NB position enables narrow-band selectivity. WB enables wideband selectivity in the FM band. Momentary MEM LOAD allows manually selected frequency to go into selected preset channel memory.
AM squelch control	Screwdriver adjustable potentiometer. Squelch overridden at maximum counterclockwise position. Clockwise rotation increases input signal. Required to open the squelch.
FM squelch control	Screwdriver adjustable potentiometer. Squelch overridden at maximum counterclockwise position. Clockwise rotation increases input signal required to open the squelch.
Band lockout switch	Will lock out the AM or FM frequency of the band selected. Presently set to the center (LOCKOUT) position to receive both AM and FM bands.

Figure 3-9. Radio Set AN/ARC-186(V) (Sheet 2 of 2)

SECTION III. NAVIGATION

3-41. HORIZONTAL SITUATION INDICATOR (HSI).

3-42. DESCRIPTION – HORIZONTAL SITUATION INDICATOR (HSI).

The HSI (Figure 3-10) is located in the pilot instrument panel. This indicator is used in conjunction with the Direction Finder Set; the VHF/FM Radio operating in the homing mode; the Gyromagnetic Compass Set; the VOR-LOC-GS-MB System, which supplies landing approach information; and Doppler NAV for range, bearing, course information. Part of the information to the HSI is controlled by the HSI Display Control Panel (Figure 3-11) located in the pilot instrument panel.

3-43. CONTROLS AND FUNCTIONS – HORIZONTAL SITUATION INDICATOR (HSI).

Refer to Figure 3-10 and Figure 3-11.

3-44. OPERATION – HORIZONTAL SITUATION INDICATOR (HSI).

   a. **ADF Operation.**

   (1) ADF frequency – As required.

   (2) BRG PTR 1 or BRG PTR 2 selector knob – ADF position.

   (3) HDG SEL knob – Set to desired heading.

   b. **VOR/ILS/LOC Operation.**

   (1) VOR frequency – As required.

   (2) BRG PTR 1 or BRG PTR 2 selector knob – VOR position.

   (3) COURSE switch – VOR.

   (4) HDG SEL knob – Set to desired heading.

   (5) CRS SEL knob – Set to desired VOR course.

   c. **FM Homing Operation.**

   (1) FM frequency – As required.

   (2) FM function selector knob – HOMING.

   (3) COURSE switch – FM HOME.

   (4) HDG SEL knob – Set to desired heading.

   d. **Doppler Operation.**

   (1) BRG PTR 1 selector knob – DPLR.

   (2) COURSE switch – DPLR position.

   (3) Follow Doppler Operation, paragraph 3-44.

3-45. DIRECTION FINDER SET.

3-46. DESCRIPTION – DIRECTION FINDER SET.

The Direction Finder Set (ADF) RCVR AN/ARN-89B, located in the pilot right console, is used in conjunction with the VOR/LOC, gyromagnetic compass, and intercommunications systems. Also, the set is interfaced with both the RMI and HSI bearing indicators. The ADF set operates in the 100 to 3,000 kHz frequency range and is used to receive continuous wave (cw) or amplitude modulated (am) radio frequency signals. Two modes of operation for the ADF set include automatic homing in the COMP mode, and as a communications receiver in the ANT mode.

3-47. CONTROLS AND FUNCTIONS – DIRECTION FINDER SET.

Refer to Figure 3-12.

3-48. OPERATION – DIRECTION FINDER SET.

   a. **ADF operation.**

   (1) Interphone control panel receiving NAV switch – ON.

   (2) Function selector – COMP.

   (3) Frequency – Select.

TM 1-1520-236-10

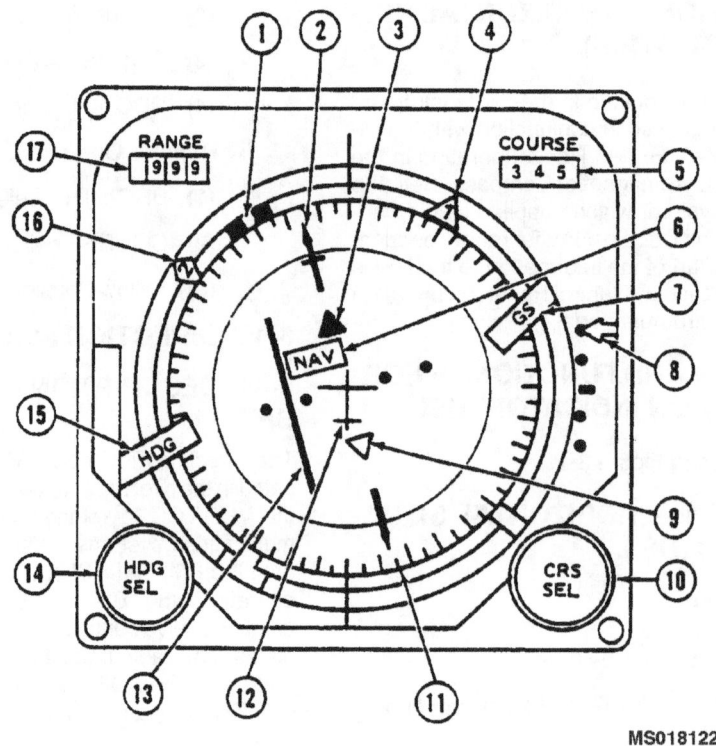

1. Heading marker
2. Course pointer
3. To indicator
4. Bearing pointer number 1
5. Course readout indicator
6. Navigation warning flag
7. Glideslope flag
8. Glideslope deviation pointer
9. From indicator
10. Course select knob
11. Azimuth indicator
12. Aircraft symbol
13. Course deviation bar
14. Heading select knob
15. Heading flag
16. Bearing pointer number 2
17. Range readout

Figure 3-10. Horizontal Situation Indicator (HSI) (Sheet 1 of 2)

CONTROL/INDICATOR	FUNCTION
1. Heading marker	Enables pilot, by adjusting HDG SEL knob, to set the marker to a desired heading reference.
2. Course pointer	Indicates selected course.
3. To indicator	Indicates selected course is in the direction, within plus or minus 90 degrees, of the course to the station.
4. Bearing pointer number 1	Indicates bearing relative to a ground station (ADF-VOR), as determined by the HSI Display Control Panel (figure 3-9).
5. COURSE indicator	Provides selected course readout (in degrees) to indicate course pointer.
6. NAV warning flag	Indicates loss of radio navigational signal.
7. GS flag	Indicates loss or unreliable glideslope radio signal.
8. Glideslope deviation pointer	Indicates aircraft position relative to glideslope centerline.
9. FROM pointer	Indicates selected course is within plus or minus 90 degrees to the course from the station.
10. CRS SEL knob	Manually adjusts, course pointer and COURSE readout, to set desired course to track fro VOR and LOC.
11. Azimuth indicator	Indicates aircraft heading.
12. Aircraft symbol	Provides immediate indication of azimuth relative to desired course and course deviation.
13. Course deviation bar	Indicates aircraft deviation from desired VOR, LOC or FM course or track.
14. HDG SEL knob	Manually adjusts to select desired aircraft heading.
15. HDG flag (warning)	Indicates loss of instrument power or directional gyro information is invalid.
16. Bearing pointer number 2	Indicates bearing relative to a ground radio station (ADF-VOR) as determined by HSI Display Control Panel.
17. RANGE readout	Indicates range to destination.

Figure 3-10. Horizontal Situation Indicator (HSI) (Sheet 2 of 2)

TM 1-1520-236-10

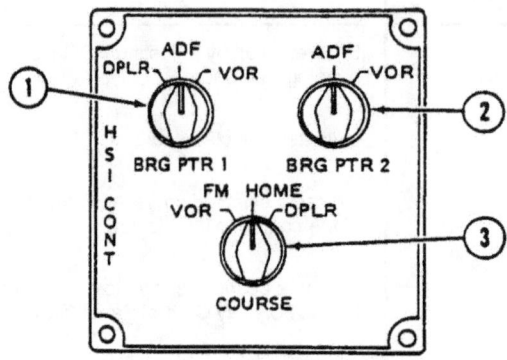

CONTROL/INDICATOR	FUNCTION
1. BRG PTR 1 switch DPLR	Doppler bearing information is presented on HSI bearing pointer number 1.
ADF	ADF bearing information is presented on HSI bearing pointer number 1.
VOR	VOR bearing information is presented on HSI bearing pointer number 1 and VOR bearing is presented on gunner RMI bearing pointer number 2.
2. BRG PTR 2 switch ADF	ADF bearing information is presented on HSI bearing pointer number 2 and ADF bearing is presented on gunner RMI ADF bearing pointer number 1.
VOR	VOR bearing information is presented on HSI bearing pointer number 2 and VOR bearing information is presented on gunner RMI bearing pointer number 2.
3. COURSE switch VOR	Presents selected VOR/LOC station displacement signal information to the HSI course deviation bar and glideslope deviation pointer and VOR/LOC signal information is also presented to the ADI course bar.
FM HOME	Presents FM homing course and glideslope deviation displacement information to both the ADI and HSI pointers.
DPR	Presents selected doppler coordinates course deviation to the HSI course deviation bar, doppler signal validity information to the navigation flag of HSI, and displays range to selected destination in range window of HSI.

Figure 3-11. HSI Display Control Panel

3-24

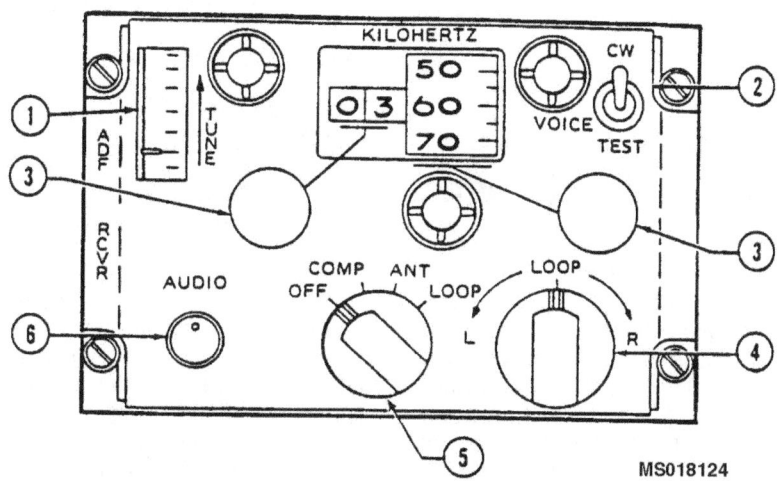

CONTROL/INDICATOR	FUNCTION
1. TUNE indicator	Up deflection of the needle indicates most accurate tuning of the receiver.
2. CW VOICE TEST switch	
CW	Provides tone that may be used for identification, turning, or CW station.
VOICE	Permits normal aural reception.
TEST	Rotates ADF bearing pointer to provide a check of pointer accuracy with function selector in the COMP position, inoperative in LOOP and ANT positions. The switch is spring loaded away from TEST position.
3. Frequency Selectors	
Left (course tune)	Selects first two digits of desired frequency.
Right (fine tune)	Selects third and fourth digits of desired frequency.
4. LOOP control	Manual positioning of loop antenna when ADF is operating in manual direction finding mode.
5. Function selector	
OFF	Power off.
COMP	ADF operation as an automatic direction finder.
ANT	Receiver provides aural information only.
LOOP	ADF operation as a manual direction finder using the loop antenna only.
6. AUDIO control	Adjusts receiver volume.

Figure 3-12. Direction Finder Set AN/ARN-89

(4) AUDIO – Adjust.

(5) TUNE meter – tune for maximum up needle deflection.

b. **Function selection** – OFF.

3-49. GYROMAGNETIC COMPASS SET.

3-50. DESCRIPTION – GYROMAGNETIC COMPASS.

The gyromagnetic compass AN/ASN-43 set is a directional sensing system which provides an accurate visual reference indication of magnetic heading (MAG) of the helicopter. The information provided by the system is used for navigation and to control the flight path of the helicopter. The system may also be used as a free directional gyro (DG) in areas where magnetic reference is unreliable. The compass set supplies information to the Horizontal Situation Indicator (HSI) located on the pilot instrument panel (Figure 3-10) and a course indicator (RMI) (Figure 3-15) located on the gunner instrument panel. The compass system functions is determined by the compass controller C-6347( )/ASN-43 located in the pilot right console.

3-51. CONTROLS AND FUNCTIONS – GYROMAGNETIC COMPASS.

Refer to Figure 3-13.

3-52. OPERATION – GYROMAGNETIC COMPASS.

a. DG/MAG switch – As desired; DG operation is recommended when flying in latitudes greater than 70 degrees.

b. In MAG mode, the gyromagnetic compass system will remain synchronized during normal flight maneuvers. In normal operation, the annunciator will oscillate slightly about center position; however, during certain aircraft maneuvers, compass system may become unsynchronized, as evidenced by the annunciator moving off center. The slaving circuits in the compass system will slave slowly to remove errors and synchronize the system. If fast slaving is desired, turn the synchronizing knob in the direction indicated by the annunciator until the annunciator is centered.

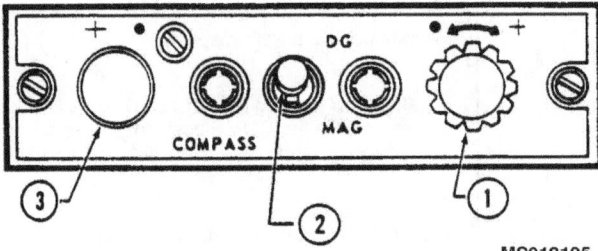

CONTROL/INDICATOR	FUNCTION
1. Synchronizing Control	Corrects heading indication when operating in the MAG mode or used as a heading set knob in the DG mode as shown by annunciator null.
2. MAG-DG Switch	
MAG	Provides magnetically slaved information.
DG	Provides for free directional gyro operation.
3. Annunciator	Moves left (+) or right (•) to indicate nonsynchronization or oscillates between (+) and (•) to indicate synchronization.

Figure 3-13. Compass Control Panel C-6347( )ASN-43

c. In the DG mode, the annunciator is inoperative and the gyro is unslaved. Approximately each 15 minutes, update the heading to the standby compass by rotating the synchronizing knob.

3-53. VOR/LOC/GS/MB SYSTEM.

3-54. DESCRIPTION – VOR/LOC/GS/MB SYSTEM.

The VOR/LOC/GS/MB Radio Receiving Set AN/ARN-123(V)1 receives the combined VOR (VHF omnirange) and LOC (localizer) signals over a frequency range of 108.00 to 117.95 MHz, GS (glideslope) signals over a frequency range of 329.15 to 335.00 MHz, and MB (marker beacon) signals on 75.00 MHz from ground transmitters. The signals drive the pilot HSI (Figure 3-10) and ADI (Figure 3-14) as applicable, the gunner RMI (Figure 3-15) radio bearing pointers, and the marker beacon lights as required. Audio signals may also be received, from the ground transmitters, through the helicopter's intercommunications system by placing the interphone control AUX switch in ON. The set enables the operator to determine his present position, direction to a given point, and fly a predetermined flightpath to a desired destination relative to a VOR facility. The localizer circuitry provides a visual display of the helicopter position relative to a localizer course. The marker beacon circuitry provides a visual display and aural tone to indicate helicopter position relative to a marker beacon transmitter.

3-55. CONTROLS AND FUNCTIONS – VOR/LOC/GS/MB SYSTEM.

Refer to Figure 3-16.

3-56. OPERATION – VOR/LOC/GS/MB SYSTEM.

    a. NAV VOL control – On and adjust.

    b. MB VOL control – On and adjust.

    c. CRS SEL Knob – Rotate to 315 degrees. Note course display and VOR/MB switch – Test. Note deviation indicator centers ± 5 degrees.

    d. Frequency selectors – As required.

    e. MB SENS switch – As required.

    f. HSI control panel COURSE switch – VOR.

    g. HSI control panel BRG PTR 1 or BRG PTR 2 – VOR.

    h. Interphone control panel AUX switch – ON.

    i. Interphone control panel VOL control – Adjust.

3-57. DOPPLER NAVIGATION SET.

3-58. DESCRIPTION – DOPPLER NAVIGATION SET.

The Doppler Navigation Set, AN/ASN-128, in conjunction with the helicopter heading and vertical reference systems, provides helicopter velocity, position, and steering information from ground level to 10,000 feet. To achieve best results with the set, pitch and roll angles should be limited to 30 degree pitch and 45 degree roll, and moderate maneuver rates should be employed. The Doppler Navigation System is a completely self-contained navigation system and does not require any ground-based aids. The system provides world-wide navigation, with position readout available in both Universal Transverse Mercator (UTM) and Latitude and Longitude (LAT/LONG). Navigation and steering is done using LAT/LONG coordinates, and a bilateral UTM-LAT/LONG conversion routine is provided for UTM operation. Up to ten destinations may be entered in either format and not necessarily the same format. Present position data entry format is also optional and independent of destination format. The set is powered by dc essential bus and protected by the DPLR NAV circuit breaker.

3-59. RESTRICTION – DOPPLER NAVIGATION SET.

The Doppler Navigation Set may be unreliable above 10,000 feet AGL, over land in bank angles above 45 degrees or pitch angles above 30 degrees, over water (Beaufort 1 or less) in bank angles above 30 degrees or pitch angles above 20 degrees. Beaufort 1 is, defined as direction of wind shown by smoke but not by wind vanes. This set shall not be used for IFR flight.

3-60. CONTROLS AND FUNCTIONS – DOPPLER NAVIGATION SET.

Refer to Figure 3-17.

3-61. OPERATION – DOPPLER NAVIGATION SET.

    a. MODE switch – LAMP TEST. All lights illuminate.

    b. MODE switch – TEST. After 15 seconds, GO illuminates.

    c. Refer to TM 11-5841-281-12 for operation.

    d. MODE switch – OFF.

TM 1-1520-236-10

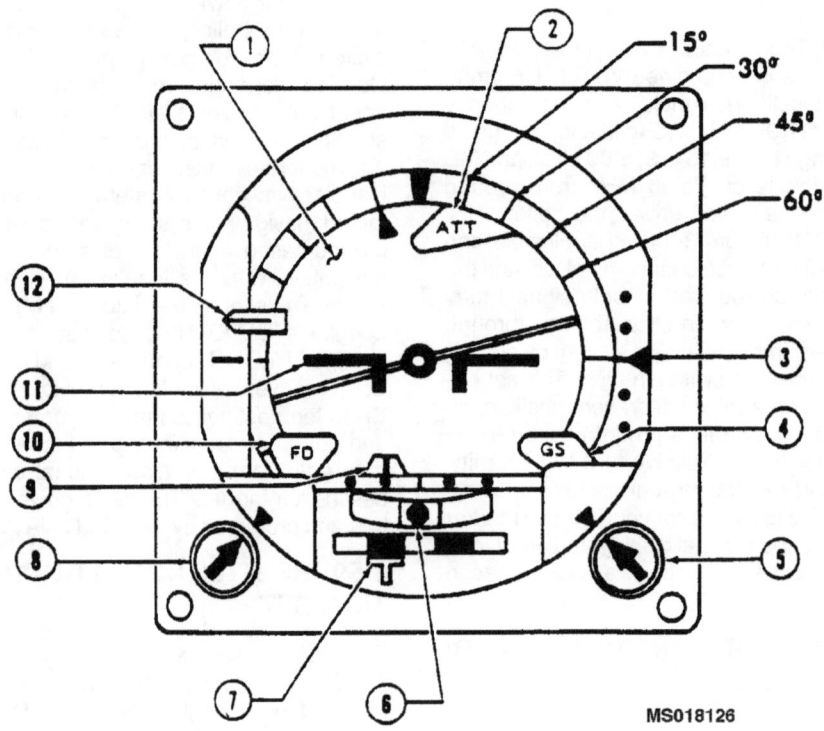

1. Sphere
2. Attitude gyro flag
3. Vertical deviation (GS)
4. Glideslope flag
5. Pitch trim
6. Inclinometer
7. Rate-of-turn
8. Roll trim
9. Horizontal deviation
10. Flight director flag
11. Horizontal reference
12. Not used

Figure 3-14. Attitude Direction Indicator (Sheet 1 of 2)

CONTROL/INDICATOR	FUNCTION
1. Sphere	Indicates position of horizon relative to the helicopter. Figure 3-12 shows level pitch, 15 degrees right bank.
2. Attitude Gyro Flag	Indicates loss of vertical gyro power or ADI malfunction.
3. Vertical Deviation (GS)	Indicates helicopter position relative to glideslope centerline (ILS) or signal strength (FM homing).
4. Glideslope Flag	Indicates loss of or unreliable radio signal (ILS, FM homing).
5. Pitch Trim	Adjusts artificial horizon up (climb) or down (dive).
6. Inclinometer	Indicates helicopter trim.
7. Rate of Turn	One needle width (4 minute turn); two needle widths (2 minute turn).
8. Roll Trim	Adjusts artificial horizon right or left.
9. Horizontal Deviation	Indicates helicopter deviation from desired VOR, LOC, or FM course or track, and deviation from desired doppler course.
10. Flight Director Flag	Not used.
11. Horizontal Reference	Indicates helicopter position relative to artificial horizon.
12. Not Used	

Figure 3-14. Attitude Direction Indicator (Sheet 2 of 2)

TM 1-1520-236-10

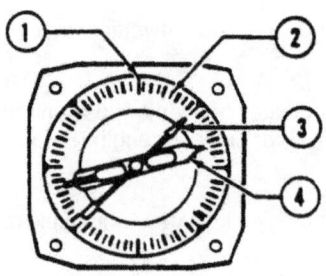

MS018127

CONTROL/INDICATOR	FUNCTION
1. Fixed reference	Provides reference point for rotating scale dial.
2. Scale dial	Rotates to indicate helicopter heading relative to the fixed reference point.
3. Pointer No. 1	Indicates course to selected ADF station.
4. Pointer No. 2	Indicates course to selected VOR station.

Figure 3-15. Course Indicator (RMI) Gunner

3-30

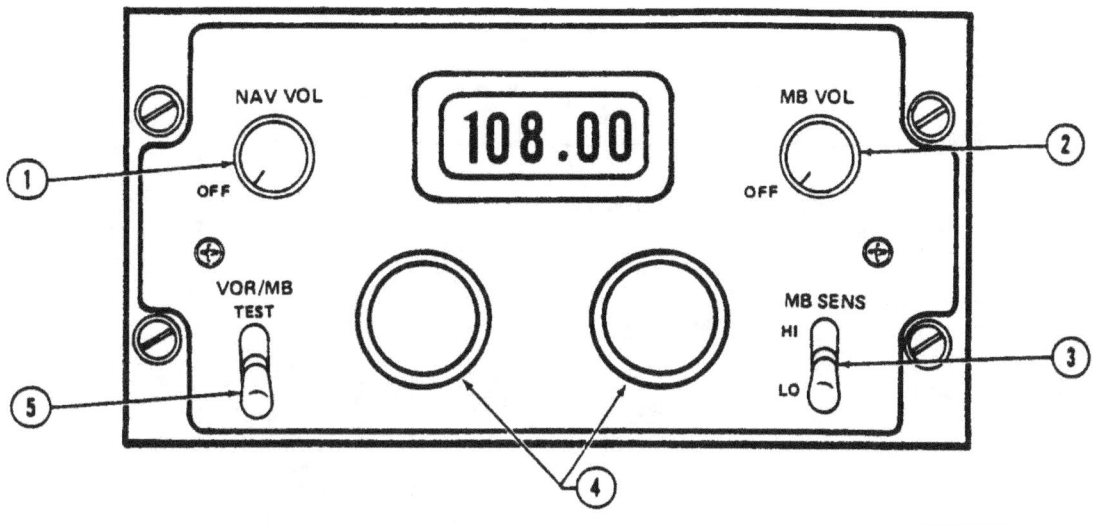

CONTROL/INDICATOR	FUNCTION
1. NAV VOL power switch and volume control	
NAV VOL	Turns set on and controls receiver volume.
OFF	Turns set OFF.
2. MB VOL power switch and volume control	
MB VOL	Turns set on and controls volume.
OFF	Turns set OFF.
3. MB SENS switch	
HI	Increases MB lamp brilliance and audible output as required.
LO	Decreases MB lamp brilliance and audible output as required.
4. Frequency selectors	
Right	Selects the fractional megahertz portion of the desired frequency.
Left	Selects the whole megahertz portion of the desired frequency.
5. VOR/MB-TEST switch	Adjusts receiver volume.
	Provides on and off capability for the VOR/MB self-test circuits within the receiver.

Figure 3-16. VOR/LOC/GS/MB Control Panel C-10048/ARN-123

TM 1-1520-236-10

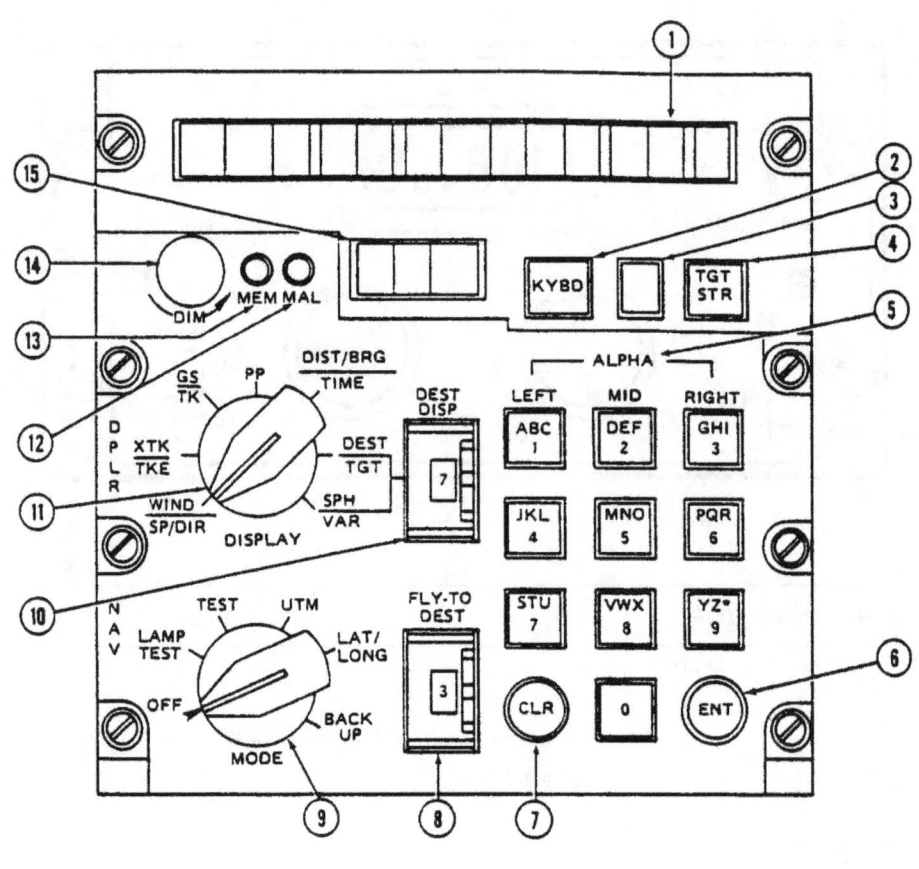

MS018129

NOTE
NVG compatible filters installed in items 1, 3, 12, 13, and 15.

CONTROL/INDICATOR	FUNCTION
1. Left Center and Right Display Lamps	Displays alpha numeric characters as determined by alpha keyboard entry.
2. KYBD Pushbutton	Enables keyboard for data entry.
3. TGT STR Indicator	Displays destination number (memory location) in which present position will be stored when the TGT STR push button is pressed.
4. TGT STR	Stores present position data.
5. ALPHA: Left, Mid, Right	Keyboard for entering information into Doppler Navigation System. Alphanumeric characters are by left, center and right display lamps.
6. ENT	Data entry to memory bank.

Figure 3-17. Doppler Navigation System (Sheet 1 of 2)

3-32

CONTROL/INDICATOR	FUNCTION
7. CLR	Pressed once clears last character entered by ALPHA key. Pressed twice clears entire entry.
8. Fly-to-Dest	Selects destination to which steering information is desired.
9. MODE Switch	Selects Doppler Navigation System (DNS) mode.
OFF	Turns set off.
LAMP TEST	Checks operation of lamps.
TEST	Initiates built-in-test (BIT) exercise.
UTM	Selects UTM (Universal Transverse Mercator) display/entry.
LAT/LONG	Selects latitude/longitude display/entry.
BACKUP	Places navigation set in true air speed plus remembered wind mode of operation, or estimated velocity.
10. DEST DISP	Used in conjunction with DEST/TGT and SPH/VAR positions of the DISPLAY switch to select the destination whose coordinates or magnetic variation are desired.
11. Display Switch	
WIND SP/DIR	Left display - wind speed (km/h). Right display - direction (degrees).
XTK/TKE	Left display - distance crosstrack error (XTK).
	Right display - degrees of track angle error (TKE).
GS/TK	Left display - ground speed (GS) is Km/h.
	Right display - track angle (TK).
PP	Present position, used in conjunction with MODE switch.
DIST/BRG/TIME	Distance to fly to destination. Bearing to fly to destination Time to fly to destination.
DEST/TGT	Destination or target number.
SPH/VAR	SPH spheroid (figure) of destination. VAR magnetic variation in degrees.
12. MAL Indicator Lamp	Illumination indicates malfunction detected by BIT.
13. MEM Indicator Lamp	Indicates radar portion of navigation set is in nontrack condition.
14. DIM Control	Controls light intensity of navigation set.
15. Zone Display	UTM zone.

Figure 3-17. Doppler Navigation System (Sheet 2 of 2)

3-62. GPS TRIMPACK.

3-63. DESCRIPTION – GPS TRIMPACK.

The Trimpack is a GPS navigation receiver which provides world-wide, day/night, all weather position and velocity data. The Trimpack is a self-contained GPS receiver and has an integrated antenna/preamplifier. The GPS Trimpack utilizes three sequencing signal processing channels to compute three-dimensional position and velocity and to manage and maintain the satellite tracking process. The Trimpack receives GPS satellite signals using a fixed pattern antenna. The GPS Trimpack displays time-tagged position and velocity at intervals of approximately one second. Output information is communicated digitally via an RS-422 data channel at a data rate of 9600 baud. The GPS Trimpack allows for position readout in Universal Transverse Mercator (UTM), Latitude and Longitude (LAT/LONG), and Military Grid Reference System (MGRS).

3-64. CONTROLS AND FUNCTIONS – GPS TRIMPACK.

Refer to Figure 3-18.

3-65. OPERATION – GPS TRIMPACK.

    a. Rotary knob – STS. Built-in test (BITE).

        FIX – As required.

        P05 – As required.

        R + A – As required.

        NAV – As required.

        WPT – As required.

        OPS – As required.

    b. L-R switch – As required.

    c. INC-DEC switch – As required.

    d. Rotary knob – OFF.

SECTION IV. TRANSPONDER AND RADAR

3-66. TRANSPONDER SET.

3-67. DESCRIPTION – TRANSPONDER SET.

The transponder set AN/APX-100 enables the helicopter to identify itself automatically when properly challenged by friendly surface and airborne radar equipment. The control panel, located on right hand console, enables the set to operate in modes 1, 2, 3A, 4, and test. When computer KIT-1A/C/TSEC (classified) is installed, mode 4 is operational. The range of the receiver-transmitter is limited to line of sight transmission since its frequency of operation is in the UHF band making range dependent on altitude.

3-68. CONTROLS AND FUNCTIONS – TRANSPONDER SET.

Refer to Figure 3-19.

3-69. OPERATION – TRANSPONDER SET.

    a. MASTER control – STBY, Allow approximately 2 minutes for warm-up.

    b. MODE and CODE – As required.

    c. MASTER control – NORM.

    d. TEST – As required.

    e. ANT – As desired.

    f. IDENT – As required.

    g. Stopping procedure. MASTER control – OFF.

3-70. EMERGENCY OPERATION – TRANSPONDER SET.

MASTER control – EMER.

3-71. MODE 4 OPERATION (APX-100).

    a. Before Exterior Check.

        (1) MASTER switch – OFF.

        (2) CODE switch – HOLD.

        (3) CODE HOLD switch (on the pilots misc. control panel) – HOLD. If the CODE HOLD switch is OFF and the MASTER switch is in any position other than OFF, MODE 4 codes will zeroize when the battery switch is turned off during the BEFORE EXTERIOR check.

TM 1-1520-236-10

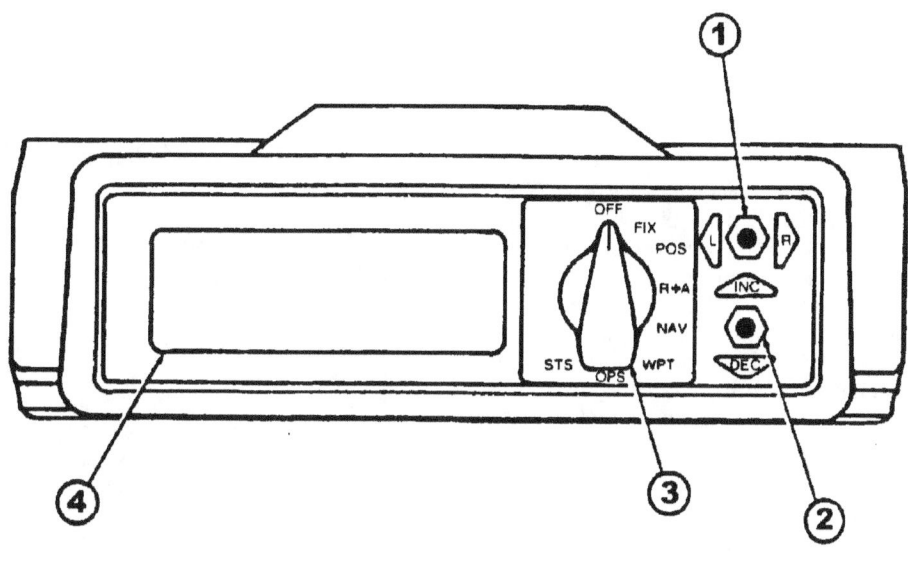

MS018130

CONTROL/INDICATOR	FUNCTION
1. L-R Switch	Moves the cursor within the display to select the field when user option selection or data entry is required.
2. INC-DEC Switch	Selects options, alter values, or change screens depending on the field that has been selected.
3. Rotary Knob	Selects mode of operation.
OFF	Turns GPS Trimpack off.
FIX	Computes a position fix (within 3 minutes) and displays it for 30 seconds, after which it automatically powers down.
POS	Computes a position fix, except that the position fix remains displayed until another mode is selected.
R + A	Displays the range, azimuth, and vertical difference from your present position to any 3 waypoints on a single screen.
NAV	Provides steering and other navigation data relative to user-selected waypoints.
WPT	Enables the user to enter waypoint designators and coordinate data for up to 26 waypoints.
OPS	Provides selectable functions that support other operating modes: COPY, CALCulate, DISTance, and AVERAGING.
STS	Provides current status information concerning reception and maintenance conditions; to select operating parameters for the required application and communicate over the digital data port with other GPS Trimpaks.
4. Display	Provides information and cursor position to assist in data entry and selection.

Figure 3-18. GPS Trimpack

3-35

b. Aircraft Runup – Test.

    (1) MASTER switch – STDY for 2 minutes.

    (2) CODE switch – A.

    (3) MODE 4 TEST/ON/OUT switch – ON.

    (4) MODE 4 AUDIO/LIGHT/OUT switch – AUDIO.

    (5) MODE 4 TEST/ON/OUT switch – TEST momentarily. The REPLY light should be on. If the REPLY light is not on or the IFF caution light goes on when the switch is at TEST; a malfunction is indicated and MODE 4 shall not be used. Release the switch to the ON position. Further testing to check for correct coding responses is done with ground test equipment by moving the MASTER switch to NORMAL. When the ground test equipment is moved within 50 feet of the aircraft antenna following indications should be observed if coding is correct.

    (6) APX-100.

        (a) REPLY light should go on.

        (b) If the REPLY light does not illuminate and/or the audio tone is heard select the opposite code (A or B) and repeat check.

    (7) If the aircraft transponder does not respond correctly to ground test interrogation, the IFF caution light should illuminate. If there is any indication of an unsatisfactory test, MODE 4 shall not be used.

c. Zeroizing. Mode 4 codes may be zeroized by either of the following methods:

    (1) CODE switch – ZERO.

    (2) MASTER switch – OFF.

    (3) Aircraft electrical power. – OFF.

d. Before Takeoff. CODE HOLD switch (on the pilot's misc. control panel) – OFF.

e. Engine Shutdown. If MODE 4 codes are to be held (not zeroized):

NOTE

If master switch or aircraft power is turned OFF prior to holding codes and master switch is returned to NORMAL or power is turned back on within 10 seconds, zeroizing may not occur.

    (1) CODE HOLD switch (on the pilot's misc. control panel) – HOLD.

    (2) CODE switch (on transponder) – HOLD position momentarily and release to positton A or B (as required) and turn MASTER switch to OFF.

3-72. RADAR WARNING SET AN/APR-39(V)1.

3-73. DESCRIPTION – RADAR WARNING SET AN/APR-39(V)1.

The Radar Signal Detecting Set AN/APR-39(V)1 provides the pilot with visual and audible warning when a hostile fire-control threat is encountered. The equipment responds to hostile fire-control radars but non-threat radars are generally excluded. The equipment also receives missile guidance radar signals and when signals are time-concident with a radar tracking signal, the equipment identifies the combination as an activated hostile surface-to-air missile (SAM) radar system. The visual and aural displays warn the pilot of potential threat so that evasive maneuvers can be initiated. The AN/AVR-2 Laser Warning Receiver interfaces with the AN/APR-39(V)1 providing early warning against laser threats.

3-74. CONTROLS AND FUNCTIONS – RADAR WARNING SET AN/APR-39(V)1.

Refer to Figure 3-20.

3-75. OPERATION – RADAR WARNING SET AN/APR-39(V)1.

> **CAUTION**
>
> To prevent damage to the receiver detector crystals, ensure that the AN/APR-39(V)1 antennas are at least 60 meters from active ground radar antennas or 6 meters from active airborne radar antennas. Allow an extra margin for new, unusual, or high power emitters.

a. PWR switch – ON. Allow one minute warmup.

b. DSCRM switch – OFF.

c. SELF TEST switch – press and hold. The forward and aft strobes appear and a 2.5 KHz audio is present in the headset. In approximately six seconds, the MA light will start flashing and the audio becomes intermittent.

d. BRIL control – Rotate, check indicator illumination.

e. AUDIO control – Set.

f. SELF TEST switch – Release.

g. DSCM switch – ON.

h. SELF TEST – Press and hold. One of the strobes appear and a 1.2 KHz audio is present after approximately four seconds. Within approximately six seconds, the other strobe will appear and the audio tone will double. Several seconds later an alarm audio is heard and missile activity light illuminates.

i. SELF TEST – Release. With AN/AVR-2 installed, after approximately five seconds, flashing strobe at 45, 135, 225, and 315 degrees is displayed along with a flashing MA lamp (Figure 3-21).

TM 1-1520-236-10

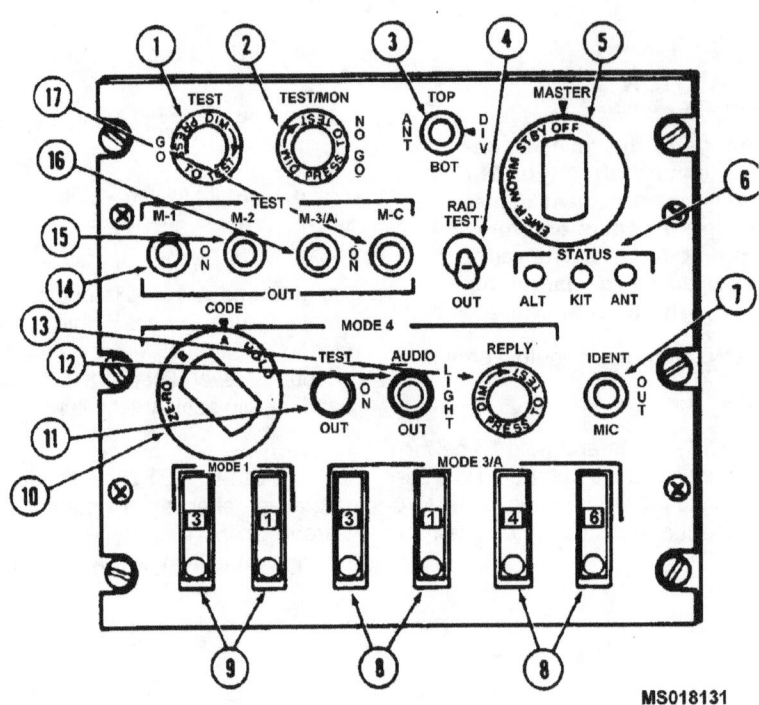

CONTROL/INDICATOR	FUNCTION
1. TEST GO	Indicates successful built in test (BIT).
2. TEST/MON NO GO	Illuminates to indicate unit malfunction.

3. ANT
   TOP
   BOT
   DIV
	
	Selects antenna located on top of helicopter.
	Selects antenna located on bottom of helicopter.
	Monitor received signals from both antennas and allows transmission via antenna receiving the strongest signal.

4. RAD TEST switch
   RAD TEST
   OUT
	
	Enables set to reply to TEST mode interrogations.
	Disables to RAD TEST features.

5. MASTER control
   OFF
   STBY
   NORM
   EMER
	
	Turns set off.
	Places in warmup (standby) condition.
	Set operates at normal receiver sensitivity.
	Transmits emergency replay signal to MODE 1, 2, or 3/A interrogations regardless of mode control settings.

6. STATUS indicators
   ANT
 	
   KIT
 	
   ALT
	
	Indicates that built in test (BIT) or monitor (MON) failure is due to high voltage standing wave ratio (VSMR) in antenna.
	Indicates that built in test (BIT) or monitor (MON) failure is due to external computer.
	Indicates that built in test (BIT) or monitor (MON) failure is due to altitude digitizer.

Figure 3-19. Transponder Set (AN/APX-100) Control Panel (Sheet 1 of 2)

CONTROL/INDICATOR	FUNCTION
7. IDENT-MIC switch 　　DENT 　　OUT 　　MIC	Initiates identification reply for approximately 25 seconds. Prevents triggering of identification reply. Spring loaded to OUT. Not used.
8. MODE 3/A code 　　select switches	Selects and indicates the MODE 3/A four-digit reply code number.
9. MODE 1 code 　　select switches	Selects and indicates the MODE 1 two-digit reply code number.
10. MODE 4/CODE control 　　HOLD/A/B/ZERO	Selects condition of code changer in remote computer.
11. MODE 4 TEST switch 　　TEST 　　ON 　　OUT	Selects MODE 4 BIT operation. Selects MODE 4 ON operation. Disables MODE 4 operation.
12. MODE 4 AUDIO/LIGHT 　　control 　　AUDIO 　　LIGHT 　　OUT	 MODE 4 is monitored by audio. MODE 4 is monitored by a light. MODE 4 not monitored.
13. MODE 4 REPLY	Indicates that a MODE 4 reply is generated.
14. TEST/M-1 　　TEST/ON/OUT	Selects ON, OFF or BIT of MODE 1 operation.
15. TEST/M-2 　　TEST/ON/OUT	Selects ON, OFF or BIT of MODE 2 operation.
16. TEST/M-3/A 　　TEST/ON/OUT	Selects ON, OFF or BIT of MODE 3/A operation.
17. TEST/M-C 　　TEST/ON/OUT	Selects ON, OFF or BIT of MODE C operation.

Figure 3-19. Transponder Set (AN/APX-100) Control Panel (Sheet 2 of 2)

TM 1-1520-236-10

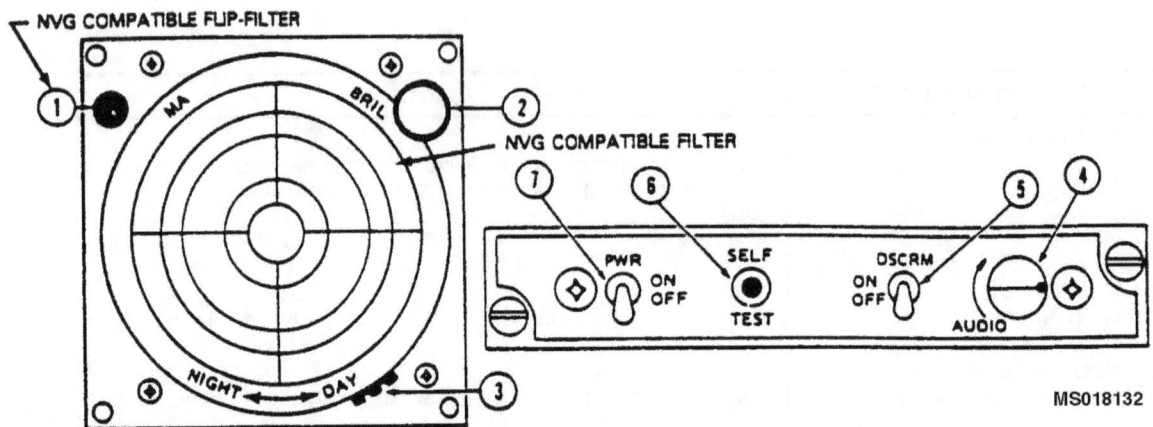

CONTROL/INDICATOR	FUNCTION
1. MA indicator	Flashing indicates high radar missile threat.
2. BRIL control	Adjusts indicator illumination.
3. NIGHT - DAY control	Adjust indicator intensity.
4. AUDIO control	Adjusts radar warning audio volume.
5. DSCRM switch:	
OFF	Without missile activity - Provides strobe lines for ground radar and normal audio indications.
	With missile activity - Provides strobe lines for ground radar, flashing strobe line(s) for missile activity, and flashing MA (missile alert) light.
ON	Without missile activity - Threat acquisition and track radar strobes only.
	With missile activity - Flashing strobe lines for missile activity (no strobe lines for ground radar), flashing MA light, and audio warning.
6. SELF TEST switch: with DSCRM switch OFF PWR switch ON (NOTE: One minute warmup) Monitor CRT and audio & press and hold SELF TEST	Forward and aft strobes appear, extending to approximately the third circle on the indicator graticule and 2.5 khz PRF audio present immediately.
Rotate indicator BRIL control CW & CCW	Within approximately 6 seconds, alarm audio present and MA lamp starts flashing.
Rotate control unit AUDIO control between maximum CCW and maximum CW	Indicator strobes brighten (CW) and dim as control is rotated.
Release SELF TEST	AUDIOS not audible at maximum CCW and clearly audible at maximum CW.
Set DSCRM to ON Press & hold SELF TEST	All indications cease.
	Within approximately 4 seconds a FWD or AFT strobe and 1.2 khz PRF audio present. Within approximately 6 seconds the other strobe will appear and APRF audio will double.
Release SELF TEST	With AN/AVR-2 installed, after approximately five seconds, a flashing strobe at 45, 135, 225, and 315 degrees is displayed along with a flashing MA lamp (figure 3-18.1).
7. PWR switch:	
ON	Applies power to radar set.
OFF	De-energizes radar set.

Figure 3-20. Radar Warning Indicator and Control AN/APR-39

TM 1-1520-236-10

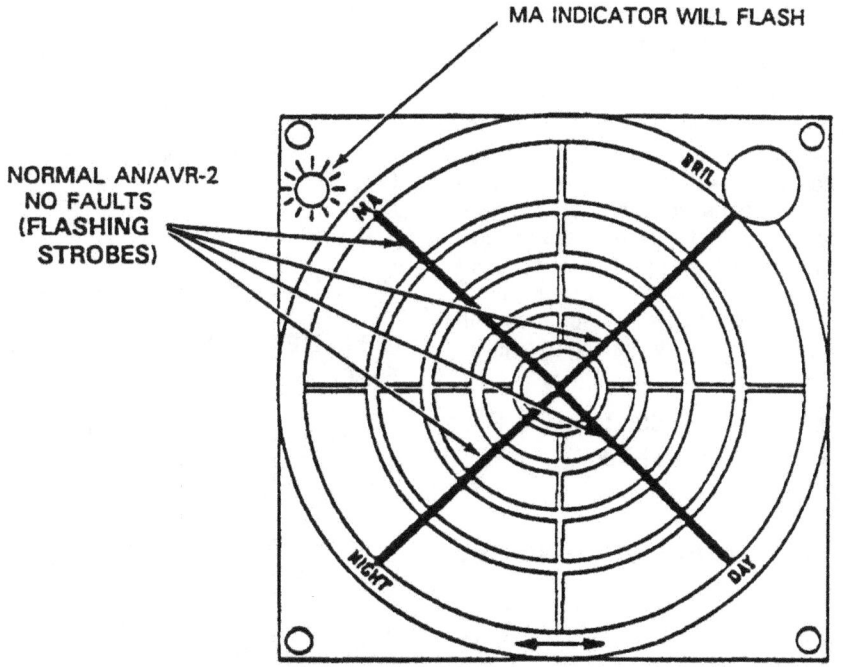

Figure 3-21. Radar Warning Indicator Self-Test Displays AN/APR-39(V)1

3-76. RADAR WARNING SET AN/APR-39(V)1.

3-77. DESCRIPTION – RADAR WARNING SET AN/APR-39(V)1.

The Radar Signal Detecting Set AN/APR-39A(V)1 provides the pilot with visual and audible warning when a hostile fire-control threat is encountered. Antenna-detectors provide frequency coverage into the millimeter-wave region of the RF spectrum, identifying radar sources using an Emitter Identification Data (EID) module located in the processor. The Processor is software controlled, and updates to the EID can be installed with minimum effort. Search radars and fire control radars operating in search mode are shown as strobes at edge of Indicator Display. Search is defined here as a signal that has not yet been identified. Once identified, search radar strobes are replaced by a generic symbol denoting threat type. The symbol is modified to show changing threat status (new threat, acquiring, tracking, launch). Intercepted signals that do not match specific threat parameters in the EID are displayed as unknowns (Symbol U). Threats are displayed on the Indicator at their relative bearing from the aircraft. Synthetic voice messages give threat location to the nearest clock position over the aircraft ICS so that evasive maneuvers can be initiated. The AN/AVR-2 Laser Warning Receiver interfaces with the AN/APR-39A(V)1 providing early warning against laser threats.

3-78. CONTROLS AND FUNCTIONS – RADAR WARNING SET AN/APR-39(V)1.

Refer to Figure 3-22.

3-79. OPERATION – RADAR WARNING SET AN/APR-39(V)1.

   a. PWR switch – ON. Listen for synthetic voice message "APR-39 POWER UP".

   b. BRIL control – Rotate, check indicator display of (+) symbol.

   c. MODE switch – MODE 1, MODE 2 as required.

   d. Self-test operation.

      (1) MODE switch – MODE 1.

      (2) TEST switch – Press.

         (a) Listen for "SELF-TEST ADJUST VOLUME 1,2,3,4,5,6,7,8,9,10,11,12" in the headset.

         (b) Check for correct software version numbers on indicator (Figure 3-23).

            1 OFP = Operational Flight Program

            2 EID = Emitter Identification Data

         (c) Forward and aft triangles appear at 6 and 12 o'clock (Figure 3-23).

         (d) With AN/AVR-2 installed, an asterisk appears in each quadrant (Figure 3-23).

         (e) No AN/AVR-2 installed, an asterisk will flash in each quadrant (Figure 3-23).

         (f) Listen for synthetic voice status message.

            1 "APR-39 OPERATIONAL"

            2 "APR-39 FAILURE"

      (3) MODE switch – MODE 2.

      (4) TEST switch – Press.

         Listen for "SELF-TEST ADJUST VOLUME 5,4,3,2,1."

   e. PWR switch – OFF.

3-80. LASER DETECTING SET.

3-81. DESCRIPTION – LASER DETECTING SET.

The Laser Detecting Set (LDS) AN/AVR-2 consists of five components: four Sensor Units mounted on the forward pylon fairing assembly (one facing forward and one facing aft on the left and right side of the aircraft) and one Interface Unit Comparator mounted inside the battery compartment. The AN/APR-39(V)1 and AN/APR-39A(V)1 Family Radar Signal Detecting Sets (RSDS) control panel, display indicator, and processing are used with the AVR-2 LDS to provide testing capability, and visual and audio interface to the operator. This interface between the AN/AVR-2 LDS and AN/APR-39(V) series RSDS allows them to function as an integrated radar and laser warning system. The AN/AVR-2 LDS detects, identifies, and characterizes laser signals 360 degrees in four 100 degree fields-of-view and ±45 degrees in elevation around the aircraft. The AN/AVR-2 LDS detects laser radiation illuminating the aircraft, processes laser threat data into laser threat messages, and transmits the messages to the AN/APR-39(V) series RSDS for visual display indicating the direction of the threat. Audio signals will also be available through the helicopter's intercommunications system. The AVR-2 LDS provides threat data so that countermeasures can be taken, improving the aircraft's survivability. For additional information on visual displays and audio signals, refer to TM 11-5841-301-30-2.

3-82. CONTROLS AND FUNCTIONS – LASER DETECTING SET.

Refer to Figure 3-20 (AN/APR-39(V)1).

Refer to Figure 3-22 (AN/APR-39A(V)1).

NOTE

AN/AVR-2 LDS is controlled by AN/APR-39(V) series RSDS control, and threat information is displayed on AN/APR-39(V) series RSDS indicator.

3-83. OPERATION – LASER DETECTING SET (AN/APR-39(V)1 AND AN/APR-39A(V) FAMILY).

  a. System Operation.

    (1) AN/APR-39(V)1.

      (a) PWR switch – ON.

      (b) AUDIO control – Adjust.

      (c) BRIL control – Adjust.

      (d) NIGHT-DAY control – Adjust.

      (e) DSCRM switch – OFF.

    (2) AN/APR-39A(V) FAMILY.

      (a) PWR switch – ON.

      (b) BRIL control – Adjust.

      (c) MODE switch – MODE 1, MODE 2 as required.

  b. Self-Test Operation.

    (1) AN/APR-39(V)1.

      (a) SELF TEST switch – Press and hold SELF TEST switch. Verify RADAR SIGNAL DETECTING SET self-tests properly. Refer to paragraph 3-58.

      (b) SELF TEST switch – Release. After approximately five seconds, a flashing strobe at 45, 135, 225, and 315 degrees is displayed along with a flashing MA lamp (Figure 3-18.1).

    (2) AN/APR-39A(V) Family

      (a) TEST switch – Press. Verify RADAR SIGNAL DETECTING SET self-tests (go/no go) properly. Refer to paragraph 3-80.

      (b) An asterisk appears in each quadrant (Figure 3-18.3).

  c. Stopping Procedure.

    PWR switch – OFF.

TM 1-1520-236-10

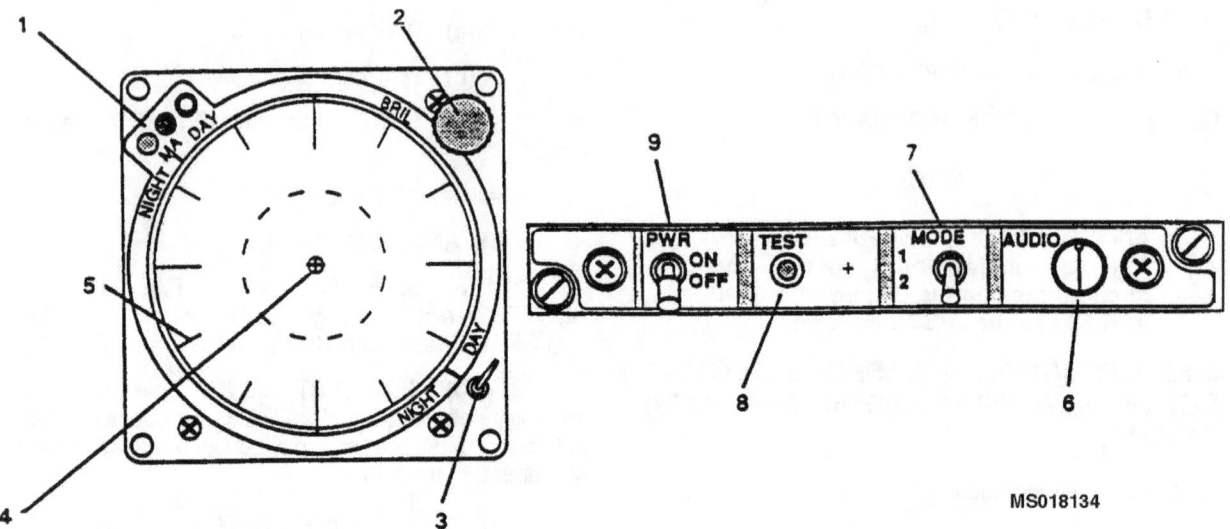

CONTROL/INDICATOR	FUNCTION
1. MA indicator	Missile Alert (MA) lamps are not used in AN/APR-39A(V)1 System. Night MA lamp is ANVIS yellow. Day MA lamp is red.
2. BRIL control	Adjusts indicator display brightness.
3. NIGHT - DAY control	Not Used.
4. Plus (+) symbol	Indicates system is ON.
5. Bearing marks	Provide relative bearing reference at 15 degree increments.
6. AUDIO control	Adjusts radar warning synthetic voice audio volume.
7. MODE switch MODE 1 (up)	Selects normal synthetic voice message format. Indicated by solid (+) symbol.
MODE 2 (down)	Selects abbreviated message format. Indicated by flashing (+) symbol and by the synthetic voice message "THREAT DETECTION DEGRADED"
	NOTE Will automatically return to normal when signal density in the environment decreases. The synthetic voice message "THREAT DETECTION RESTORED" will occur.
8. TEST switch	Provides a go/no-go test of system.
9. PWR switch: ON	Applies power to radar set.
OFF	De-energizes radar set.

Figure 3-22. Radar Warning Indicator and Control AN/APR-39A(V)1

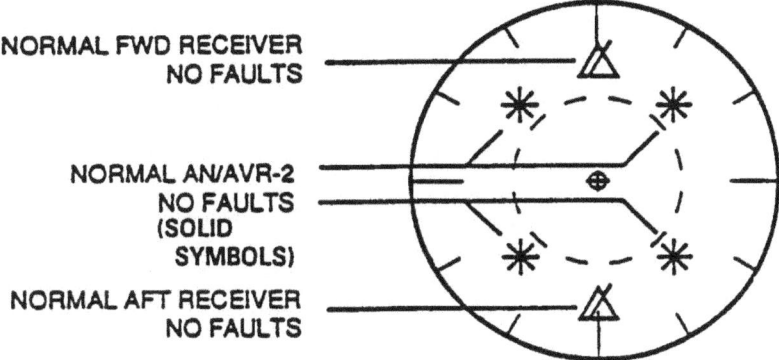

Normal Self-test Display - No Faults Displayed

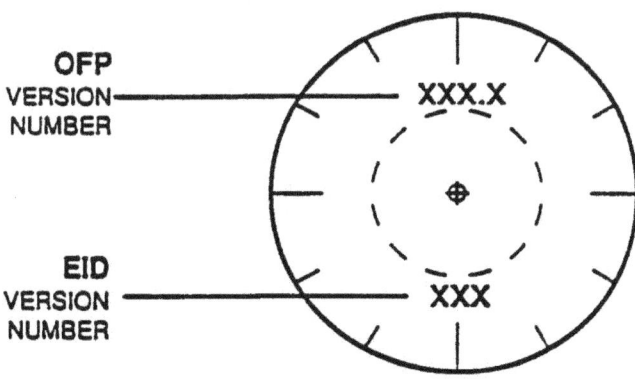

OFP and EID Version Number Display

Figure 3-23. Radar Warning Indicator Self-Test Displays AN/APR-39A(V)1

TM 1-1520-236-10

CHAPTER 4

MISSION EQUIPMENT

SECTION I. MISSION AVIONICS

4-1. DESCRIPTION – INFRARED COUNTERMEASURE SET AN/ALQ-144.

WARNING

The countermeasure set must be shut down at least one minute prior to any refueling operation and not restarted or, originally started, until the aircraft is in motion.

Do not operate the countermeasure set when the aircraft is in a refueling area.

CAUTION

When energized, the countermeasures set should remain on for a minimum of 15 minutes. Otherwise the life of the source may be drastically shortened.

Complete provisions are provided for the installation of an infrared countermeasure system. Provisions are provided to mount an IR jammer transmitter on top of the engine exhaust suppressor and a control panel in the pilot instrument panel. A failure light is incorporated in the pilot caution panel.

4-2. CONTROLS AND FUNCTIONS – INFRARED COUNTERMEASURES SET.

   a. Preflight, countermeasure set – Checks.

   (1) Loosen the strap and remove the protective cover from the transmitter.

   (2) Energize the aircraft 28VDC circuit breakers for the operator control unit (OCU) and the transmitter.

   (3) Locate the OCU and pull ON/OFF switch out and up to the ON position.

   (4) Wait 60 seconds. If at the end of 60 seconds, the IRCM INOP legend caution light does not display an INOP, the countermeasures set is operating and ready for use.

   (5) Set the OCU ON/OFF switch to OFF.

   (6) Observe that the IRCOM INOP legend light goes on when the OCU ON/OFF switch is set to off.

   (7) After 60 seconds, observe that the IRCM INOP lamp goes out.

   (8) Install the protective cover on the transmitter and tighten the strap.

4-3. DESCRIPTION – RADAR JAMMER SET AN/ALQ-136.

Control of the radar set is provided on the radar/infrared countermeasures control panel located in the pilot center instrument panel (Figure 2-6). The radar jammer control switch, RDCM, is placed in the STBY position for a 3 minute warm-up. If the radar jammer is indifferently placed in the ON position directly from the OFF position, the system will not respond to threat signals until the 3 minute warm-up period has expired. The system also requires a 3 minute warm-up if the control switch is inadvertently switched from the ON or STBY position to the OFF position. The radar jammer control switch is placed in the ON position to activate the system. When in the ON position, the radar jammer immediately and automatically responds to threat radar energy at the receive antenna by providing appropriate jamming energy at the transit antenna. Placing the control switch to the OFF position removes all power to the radar jammer set. The radar jammer set receives power from the DC non-essential bus (Figure 2-18) and protected by radar jammer circuit breaker (Figure 2-20, sheet 2 of 2).

4-4. OPERATION – RADAR COUNTERMEASURES SET. Refer to Figure 4-1.

   a. Warmup – Control switch to STBY. Allow three minutes warmup. An internal timer will prevent the equipment from operating until warmup is complete.

   b. Check that RDRCM-INOP failure light on pilot caution panel is not illuminated.

4-1

c. Listen to verify that blower in receiver-transmitter is operating. Turn equipment off if the blower fails unless it is needed for defense of the aircraft. Operating the CM set when the blower is not functioning may cause premature failure of the equipment.

d. Standby – After warmup, with control switch in STBY position, the CM set is in standby, ready for immediate operation. Leave CM set in standby when anticipating a need for its use.

e. Operate – Control switch to OPR when within range of hostile radar.

f. OFF – Control switch to OFF. Leave CM set off when not needed. this will extend the service life of the equipment.

4-5. MILES/AGES.

Operations of Miles/Ages: Refer to TM 9-1270-223-10.

SECTION II. ARMAMENT

4-6. AUTHORIZED ARMAMENT CONFIGURATIONS.

Figure 4-2 shows the authorized armament loading configurations.

4-7. INTERRELATION OF ARMAMENT.

The armament subsystems are interfaced with one another. Completely operational armament systems are dependant upon the following fully-functional equipment.

   a. Telescopic sight unit (TSU).
   b. Helmet sight subsystem (HSS).
   c. Universal turret subsystem.
   d. Rocket management subsystem (RMS).
   e. TOW missile subsystem.
   f. Air data subsystem.
   g. Laser range finder.
   h. Head-up display system (HUD).
   i. Airborne laser tracker (ALT).
   j. Attitude reference gyro.
   k. Gyro magnetic compass set.
   l. Radar altimeter.
   m. Torquemeter.
   n. Doppler navigation system.
   o. Fire control computer (FCC).
   p. AIM-1/EXL infrared laser gun sight system.

Figure 4-3 shows the pilot and gunner control components in relationship to each armament subsystem.

4-8. ARMAMENT FIRING MODES.

NO TAG shows the switch positions for principal firing modes.

4-9. INTEGRATED ARMAMENT FUNCTIONAL DESCRIPTION.

The following is a functional description of the integrated armament system.

TOW Modes. The HUD is used in conjunction with the TMS by displaying the TOW prelaunch window in order to assist the pilot in maneuvering the helicopter to achieve the required missile prelaunch constraints. The HUD display will also indicate when those constraints have been satisfied, and notifies the pilot when to commence evasive maneuvers after the TOW missile launch. A post-launch HUD display window indicates the maneuver limits for TOW missile steering.

   a. TOW Prelaunch. Attack Mode (Flashing gunner LOS). The prelaunch constraint window will appear in the pilot HUD and the missile image will appear on the side of the window to correspond to the missile the gunner has selected when the ACTION switch is pressed. Ready Mode (Steady gunner LOS). The gunner LOS will appear steady when the pilot has satisfied all prelaunch constraints.

   b. TOW Fired Mode. An "X" will appear over the missile image to show pilot that the firing sequence has started. Once the trigger is pulled, the "X" will appear for about 1.5 seconds prior to the postlaunch mode appearing on the display.

   c. TOW Postlaunch Mode. This mode will appear until wire cut on the missile and the pilot is free to maneuver the helicopter within the postlaunch constraints.

d. PHS to TSU Acquisition. The gunner enters this mode by placing the ATS switch to TRK, then placing the ACQ switch to the Pilot Helmet Sight (PHS) position when the pilot identifies to him that he has a target in the Helmet Sight Line of Sight (LOS). The ACQ switch is located in the lower right side of the gunner's instrument panel. Entering this mode causes the TSU to come into alignment with the PHS, thus shortening target acquisition time for the TSU.

e. GHS to TSU Acquisition. The gunner enters this mode by engaging the ATS switch to ACQ on the sight hand control when he desires to align the TSU LOS to his helmet LOS. Entering this mode causes the TSU to come into alignment with the gunner helmet sight.

f. ALT to TSU Acquisition. The gunner enters this mode by engaging the ACQ switch to ALT. This mode allows the TSU to be slaved to the ALT while the ALT is locked onto (tracking) a target.

g. Solutions Gun and Rocket Fire. The Fire Control Computer (FCC) provides for concurrent turret gun fire and rocket fire solutions.

In the case of concurrent helmet sight-turret and rocket fire, both modes operate concurrently without degrading either mode using manual range input.

In the case of concurrent TSU-Turret and rocket fire, both modes operate concurrently as far as the computer is concerned; however, while the TSU is being used to support turret gunfire, it cannot be supporting rocket fire. The rocket solution is valid only in the direct mode with RMS estimated range as explained below.

While the TSU is supporting gunfire, the rocket solution may be degraded for two reasons. First, the laser range will be correct for the gun target but not for the rocket target.

Second - Since the TSU is not pointing at the rocket target, LOS information will not be corrected for use in the rocket solution in indirect mode.

h. Manual Range Guns. No range countdown is available for the manual range gun mode. The range utilized by the gun solution is SHORT = 1000m, MED = 1500m, LONG = 2000m.

i. Gun Moding Discretes. Three discretes from the IFCU to the FCC tell the FCC which gun solution is currently allowed.

PHS-GUN -	Pilot ACTION switch applies.
GHS-GUN -	
TSU-GUN -	Gunner ACTION switch applies.

However, a gun solution will not actually start until the appropriate ACTION switch is pressed.

j. Helmet Sight - Gun With Rocket (estimated or laser range). All rocket modes can operate concurrently with either helmet sight-gun mode because the TSU is not needed in helmet sight modes.

k. TSU-Gun (laser range). If the "TSU-GUN" mode is selected, laser data will be applied to both the TSU gun and the rocket solutions if both are currently operating. The TSU gun solution will be computed if the TSU-GUN is selected and the gunner ACTION switch is pressed. Initially, if no laser range is available, range data is provided by the setting of the gunner RANGE switch. Laser range information will be used as soon as available and will be extrapolated for 6-seconds after the last laser input. After 6 seconds, manual range will again be used until the next laser input. The Fire Control Solution for the 20mm is limited to 2000m and will not exceed this value even if laser range is higher. Firings beyond 2000m should not be attempted.

l. Rocket solutions.

(1) Rocket Solution (laser range). In this mode, the RNG-km switch must be in the "A" position for the FCC to use laser range to calculate the rocket solution. Do not use the "A" mode on the RNG-km switch unless the Laser Range finder is operational.

The FCC will position the fire control reticle to 0°az, 0°ei on the HUD; Range display is F0. The rocket solution will not be calculated during this time. As soon as laser data is received, the rocket solution will start and the laser data will be used. This data will be extrapolated for 15 seconds after the last laser input. After 15 seconds, the rocket solution will stop and the fire control reticle will be positioned by the FCC to 0°az, 0°ei on the HUD; Range display is F0. While laser data is being extrapolated, the current value used in the extrapolation is displayed on the HUD. After the 15 second time elapses, range goes to F0. The rocket ballistic solution does not make any allowance for target motion.

If the TSU is being used to fire the gun and the gunner lases on the gun target, the rocket solution will be incorrect in both the direct and indirect modes, unless both the gun and rockets are firing on the same target.

(2) Rocket Solution (RMS estimated range). In this mode, the rocket solution will be calculated continuously. The range value displayed in the RMS RNG-km switches will be used for the initial range value and displayed on the HUD. This range will not be counted down except following a change in the setting.

A change in the setting will be the signal to start counting down range based on velocity inputs. Range will count down for 15 seconds or until the range is less than 700 meters, whichever occurs first. It will then reset to the initial value and will not count down again until the switches are changed again. If the aircraft moves such that the target is not straight ahead, the computer uses magnetic heading, vertical gyro, and doppler information to extrapolate the range correctly. In either manual range mode (Direct or Indirect), whenever the switches are first set or changed, the aircraft must be aligned such that the target is straight ahead. During the countdown sequence, the HUD will display the current counted down range. As the range counts down, the range value used in the rocket solution will be limited to a minimum of 700 meters.

If firing FUSE SET rockets, the RNG-km switches sets the fuse at the range selected on the switches regardless of what range is displayed in the HUD. If the laser is operational and the RNG-km switch is in "A", the time of functions for the fuse set comes from the computer.

(3) **Related Items.**

(a) **Rocket Mode Lasing.** In both direct and indirect rocket modes, the computer allows the gunner to begin lasing before the ship is aligned with the target and this laser data be applied correctly to the solution. In the indirect mode, the TSU must be on the target when the rockets are fired. This is not true for the direct mode. In both direct and indirect modes after lasing stops for 1/4 second, the computer uses magnetic heading, vertical gyro, and doppler to extrapolate range in the off-axis situation.

(b) **Laser Ranging.** If the gunner holds the laser trigger down, the laser sends data to the FCC at a rate of 4 times per second. The FCC will continue to use the data, integrated with doppler data, for the fire control solution and will send time of function to the RMS for fuse setting. Along with range data displayed on the HUD, will be one of two letters - F or L. They define the source of the range data being displayed.

L - Raw Laser Range (in case of FCC failure).

F - Range from FCC.

4-10. PILOT SWITCHES AND INDICATORS.

Pilot panels and switches are interfaced with other pilot/gunner panels and switches for weapon operations and wing stores jettison. Figure 4-3 and Figure 4-4 shows switch interface.

a. **Pilot Armament Control Panel.** Refer to Figure 4-12.

b. **Recoil Compensation Switch Panel.** The rotary switch provides variable recoil compensation feel as desired. Refer to Figure 4-12.

c. **Rocket Management Subsystem (RMS) Display Unit.** Refer to Figure 4-16.

d. **Wing Stores Jettison Switch.** The guarded jettison switch is on the gunner collective stick switchbox. Activation of the switch will jettison the weapons from the inboard, outboard, or all four of the wing ejector racks. Refer to Figure 4-21 for various jettison combinations.

e. **Pilot Jettison Select Switches.** Refer to Figure 4-21.

f. **Pilot Armament Circuit Breakers.** Refer to Figure 4-24.

g. **Heads Up Display.** Refer to Figure 4-5.

h. **Pilot Helmet Sight.** Refer to Figure 4-6.

i. **Cyclic Armament Switches.** Refer to Figure 2-14.

j. **ALT Control Panel.** Refer to Figure 4-22.

4-11. GUNNER SWITCHES AND INDICATORS.

Gunner panels and switches are interfaced with other gunner/pilot panels and switches for weapon operations and wing stores jettison. Figure 4-3 and Figure 4-4 shows switch interface.

a. **Cyclic Armament Switches.** Refer to Figure 2-14.

b. **Helmet Sight Subsystem (HSS).** Refer to Figure 4-6.

c. **Telescopic Sight Unit (TSU).** Refer to Figure 4-8.

d. **CN Telescopic Sight Unit (TSU) with C-NITE.** Refer to Figure 4-9.

e. **Armament Control Panel.** Refer to Figure 4-13.

f. **CN FLIR Control Panel (FCP).** Refer to Figure 4-10.

g. **Wing Stores Jettison Switch.** The guarded switch is on the gunner instrument panel. The switch is powered and protected by a toggle CB located with AC circuit breakers beneath pilot collective control stick. Refer to Figure 4-21 for various jettison combinations.

h. **Gunner Sight Hand Control (SHC).** Refer to Figure 4-14.

TM 1-1520-236-10

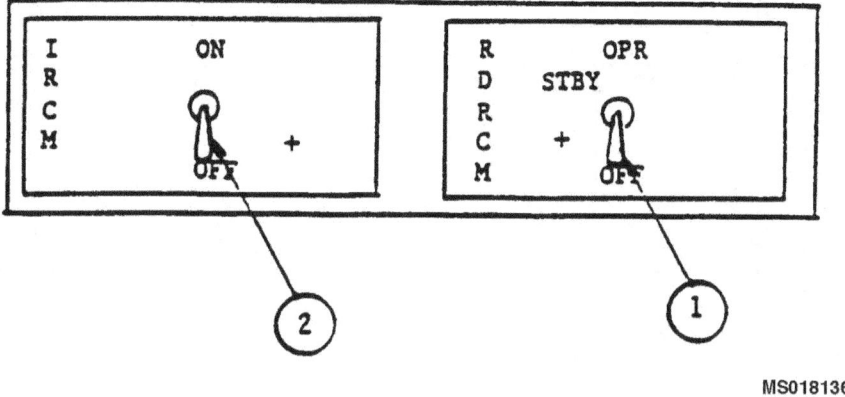

CONTROL/INDICATOR	FUNCTION
1. Switch/ALQ136	
OFF	Turns CM set off.
STBY	Places CM set in standby (warmup) condition.
OPR	Places CM set in operating condition after 3 minute warmup.
2. Switch/ALQ144	Operates ALQ144.

Figure 4-1. Radar Countermeasures Set Control Indicator

4-5

TM 1-1520-236-10

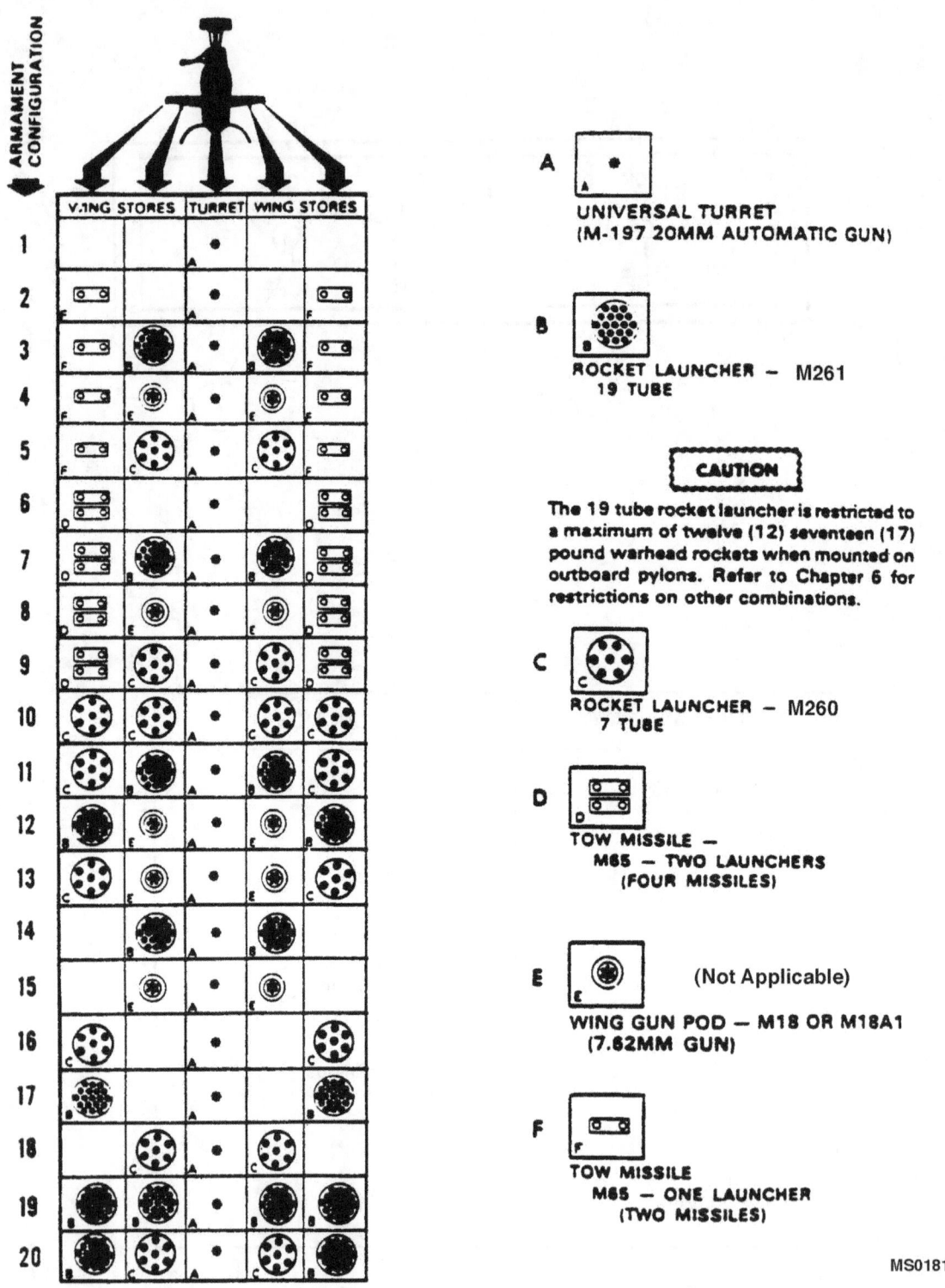

Figure 4-2. Authorized Armament Configuration

i. Gunner TOW Control Panel (TCP). Refer to Figure 4-7.

j. Laser Range Finder Control Panel. Refer to Figure 4-15. The laser range finder is used to find distance from helicopter to target. This range information is displayed on the TSU range readout and heads up display (HUD). Range information is also sent to the fire control computer (FCC) to be used for weapons trajectory calculations.

4-12. ARMAMENT DESCRIPTION.

a. Electronic Processor Unit (EPU). The electronic processor unit computes and converts AADS outputs into airspeed components and temperature and pressure outputs.

b. Low Airspeed Indicator (LAI). Refer to Chapter 2. Weapon firing in the 26 to 32 knot airspeed range will result in degraded accuracy in helicopters equipped with K747 blades.

c. ADS versus Radar Altimeter Relationship. The Air Data System (ADS) uses the input from the radar altimeter AN/APN-209 to determine IGE or OGE effect on airspeed. If the radar altimeter is turned OFF or failed the ADS will be based on data based on 33 feet regardless of helicopter altitude. This function can be checked while hovering IGE by pushing the test switch on the radar altimeter and observing the jump in the low airspeed indicator bar. In the test condition, the AN/APN-209 tells the ADS that the helicopter is at 1000 ft. +/– 100 ft.

d. Fire Control Computer (FCC). The fire control computer data received from the telescopic sight unit, helmet sight subsystem, universal turret subsystem, rocket management subsystem, TOW missile subsystem air data subsystem, laser rangefinder, head-up display system, airborne laser tracker, attitude reference gyro, gyro magnetic compass set, radar altimeter, torquemeter, and doppler navigation system. The solution data derived from the integration of the inputs from the above listed components is used to develop electrical signals to head-up display system for the rocket fire control reticle, to provide fuse settings to the rocket management system and to provide ballistics corrections for the 20mm universal turret system through the interface control unit. Flight information, torque, magnetic heading, and radar altimeter altitude is displayed in the HUD.

e. Air Data Subsystem (ADS). The air data subsystem (ADS) (TM 96-1270-219-13) consists of an airspeed and direction sensor (AADS) (Figure 2-1), a low airspeed indicator (LAI) (Figure 2-22) and an electronic processor unit (EPU) which is mounted on the bulkhead aft of the pilot seat. The ADS interfaces with the fire control computer (FCC), doppler navigation system, radar altimeter to enhance weapon accuracy. The ADS electrical circuit is powered by 28vdc and protected by the ADS PWR circuit breaker (Figure 2-20).

f. Airspeed and Direction Sensor (AADS). The airspeed and direction sensor is a swiveling pilot-static probe which measures pitot and static pressures, the angles of the airflow relative to the helicopter and the free stream air temperature.

CONTROL COMPONENTS	TURRET	TOW MISSILE	WING STORES		TARGET ACQUIRE FOR TSU	WING STORES JETTISON
			ROCKETS	GUNPOD		
Pilot Station						
Armament Control Panel	X	X	X	X	X	
Rocket Management System (RMS) Display Unit			X			
Jettison Select Switches						X
Head Up Display	X	X	X	X		
Helmet Sight	X				X	
Cyclic Switches	X		X	X		
AIM Switch	X					
Gunner Station						
Cyclic Switches	X		X	X		
Helmet Sight	X				X	
Telescopic Sight Unit	X	X				
Left-Hand Grip	X	X				
Armament Control Panel	X		X	X		
Wing Store Jettison Switches						X
Sight Hand Control	X	X			X	
TOW Control Panel	X	X			X	
Acquisition Panel					X	
FLIR Control Panel	X	X			X	

Figure 4-3. Control Components in Relationship to Armament Subsystems

TM 1-1520-236-10

COLUMN	FIRING MODES	Armament Panel					Cyclic Grip					HUD		RMS				
			WPN CONTR	MAN RANGE	WING STORE	RECOIL	ACTION	GUN	WING ARM FIRE	RKT	PWR	MODE	ZONE ARM	PEN-M	RATE	MODE	QTY	RNG-KM
1	TSU Firing Gun	ARM	GUNNER			COMPEN												
2	GHS Firing Gun	ARM	GUNNER			COMPEN												
3	PHS Firing Gun	ARM	GUNNER / PILOT	Select		COMPEN	Press	Press										
4	Fixed Firing Gun	ARM	FIXED				Press	Press			ON	NORM						
5	Rocket Direct Mode	ARM			RKT				Press	DIR	ON	NORM	Select	Select	Select	Select	Select	A Select
6	Rocket Indirect Mode	ARM			RKT				Press	INC	ON	NORM	Select	Select	Select	Select	Select	A Select
7	Rockets Without FCC	ARM			RKT				Press	DIR	ON	NORM	Select	Select	Select	Select	Select	Select
8	Rockets Without FCC OR LRF	ARM			RKT				Press		ON	STAD	Select	Select	Select	Select	Select	Select
9	PLT ORIDE Rockets/Gun																	
10	TOW Prelaunch Mode	ARM	GUNNER								ON	NORM						
11	TOW Post-launch Mode	ARM	GUNNER								ON	NORM						
12	PHS to TSU Acquisition	ARM	GUNNER															
13	GHS to TSU Acquisition	ARM	GUNNER															
14	ALT to TSU Acquisition	ARM	GUNNER															
15	HUD TEST Mode										ON	TEST						
16	LRF FIRE	ARM																

Figure 4-4. Armament Firing Modes (Sheet 1 of 2)

TM 1-1520-236-10

COLUMN	Gunner Switches																
	TCP		LASER RANGE		Right Console						Left Hand Grip			Sight Hand Control	Panel	Cyclic Grp		
	TSU Filter	MODE Select	LASER ARM	MIN RANGE	RANGE	PLT ORIDE	WING STORE	TURRET DEPR LIMIT	TUR SLEW	AC-TION	TRIG-GER	LASER	ACO TRK STOW	ACO	WIG ARM FIRE	ACTION	GUN
1	LASER	TSU GUN	SELECT	SELECT	SELECT	OFF		OFF	NORM	PRESS	PRESS	PRESS	TRK				
2					SELECT	OFF		OFF	NORM	PRESS	PRESS		STOW				
3						OFF		OFF	NORM								
3						OFF											
4						OFF											
5	LASER	TSU GUN	SELECT	SELECT		OFF		OFF				PRESS	TRK				
6	LASER	TSU GUN	SELECT	SELECT		OFF		OFF				PRESS	TRK				
7	LASER	TSU GUN	SELECT	SELECT		OFF		OFF				PRESS	TRK				
8						OFF											
9					SELECT	PLT ORIDE	RKT / GUN								PRESS	PRESS	PRESS
10		ARMED				OFF				PRESS	AS Desired		TRK				
11		ARMED				OFF				PRESS	PRESS						
12		TSU GUN OR TOW				OFF							TRK	PHS ACO			
13		TSU GUN OR TOW				OFF								ACO			
14		TSU GUN OR TOW				OFF								ALT ACO			
15																	
16	LASER		SELECT	SELECT				OFF			PRESS						

Figure 4-4. Armament Firing Modes (Sheet 2 of 2)

4-13. Heads Up Display (HUD). The HUD visually presents required symbology for flight and weapons firing on a partially reflective beam splitter superimposed on real world image. The primary use of the HUD is for aiming the helicopter to fire rockets and to provide the pilot steering indications for meeting the helicopter constraints in operation of the TOW missile system. The secondary use of the HUD is for display of the engine torque, radar altitude, magnetic heading, and range for flight safety purposes when the pilot is flying head-up with eyes focused outside the cockpit. The components of the HUD are the head-up display, signal processor, and HUD boresightable mount.

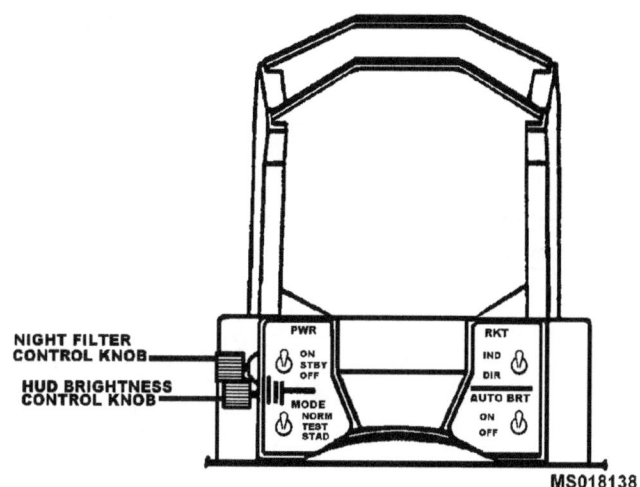

ITEM	FUNCTION
PWR Switch	
ON	Electrical power applied, symbols displayed depend on MODE switch position.
STBY	Electrical power applied, STAD reticle can be displayed.
OFF	All electrical power removed from HUD circuits.
MODE Switch	
NORM	Displays basic symbols according to firing mode selected.
TEST	Displays all heads up display symbols except the stadiametric reticle.
STAD	Displays stadiametric reticle which is a backup reticle.
RKT Switch	
IND	Displays a continually computed rocket release point.
DIR	Displays a continuously computed rocket impact point.
AUTO BRT Switch	
ON	Allows brightness of displayed symbols to be automatically adjusted.
OFF	Disables automatic brightness control feature.
	CAUTION Do not leave in night filter position in sunlight. Sunlight will damage the night filter beyond repair.
NIGHT FILTER Control Knob	Selects usage of night filter by rotating knob.
HUB BRIGHTNESS Control Knob	Controls brightness of heads up display element when rotated as shown by BRIGHT arrow.

Figure 4-5. Heads Up Display (Sheet 1 of 4)

TM 1-1520-236-10

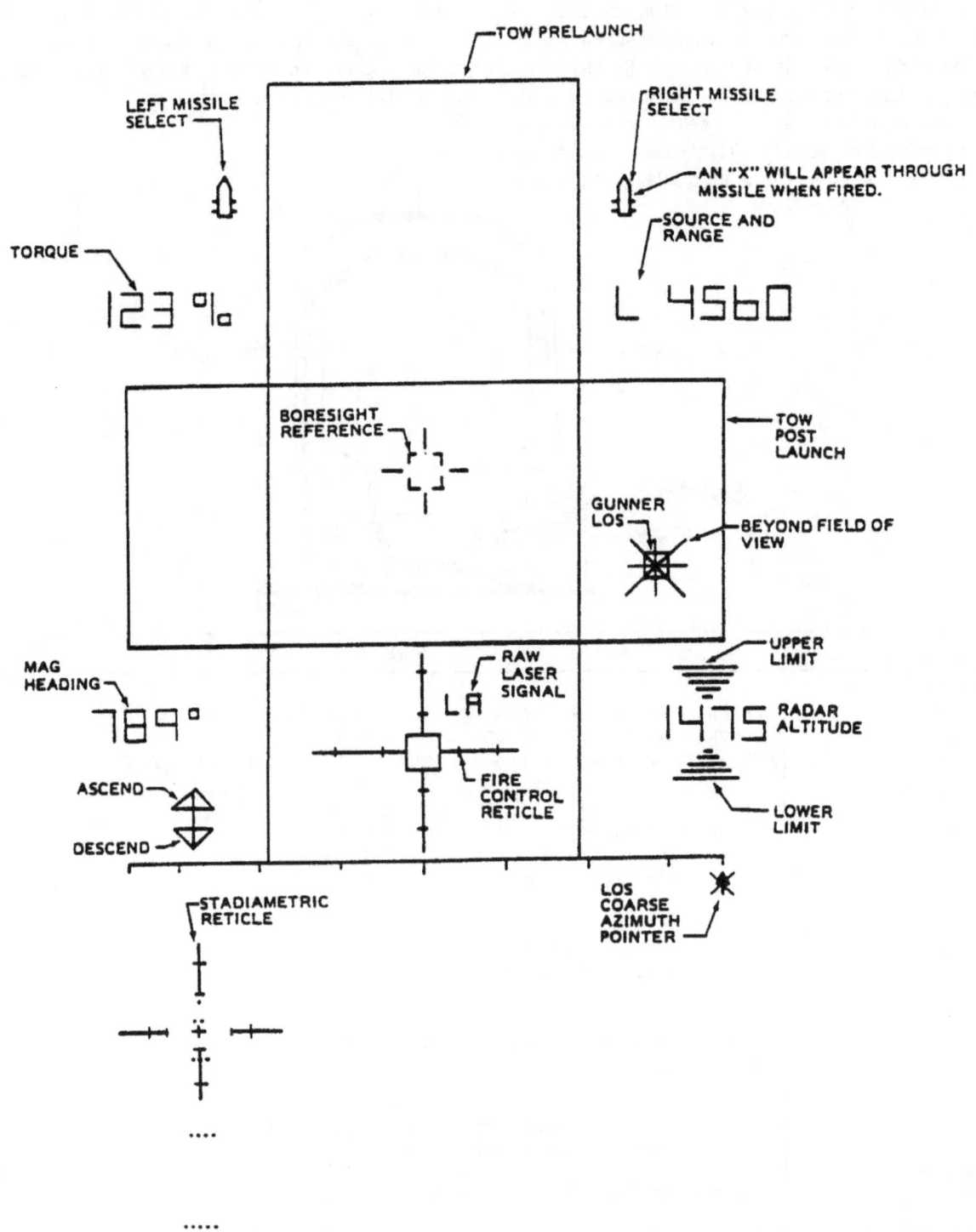

Figure 4-5. Heads Up Display (HUD) Symbols (Sheet 2 of 4)

SYMBOL	FUNCTION
Missile Select	Indicates TOW missile selected for firing from left or right launcher.
TOW Prelaunch Constraint	Represents boundary within which the pilot must keep the gunner LOS and target prior to and during TOW missile launch.
TOW Prelaunch Constraint	Represents boundary within which the pilot must keep the gunner LOS after TOW missile launch and until wire cut or missile impact.
Ascent - Descend	ON - Indicates nose of helicopter must be raised or lowered to meet prelaunch constraints. OFF - Indicates helicopter attitude and line-of-sight rate are compatible.
Torque	Indicates engine torque in percent.
Source and Range	Displays range in meters and source of range: F - Range from fire control computer (FCC). L - Range from laser (displayed when FCC fails).
Heading	Displays magnetic heading of helicopter.
Radar Altitude	Displays altitude above ground level in five feet increments. When absolute altitude exceeds 1495 feet, the numbers will blank and will not unblank until the altitude drops below 1475 feet.
Upper Limit - Lower Limit	Illuminates when within 25 feet of present upper or lower altitude limits selected on AN/APN-209 radar altimeter.
Boresight Reference	Used for boresighting weapons and serves as aircraft datum line (ADL) reference symbol during flight. It is used during indirect firing of rockets.
Gunner LOS	Displays line of sight as commanded by telescopic sight unit (TSU).
Beyond Field of View Caution	An X superimposed on gunner LOS to indicate LOS has exceeded field of view limits.
Fire Control Reticle	Indicates target area for rocketing firing.
LA	Superimposes on fire control recticle and indicates FCC has failed and raw laser range is being used.
LOS Coarse Azimuth Pointer	Indicates azimuth reading of gunner TSU LOS.
Stadiametric Reticle	Displays when HUD MODE switch is in STAD position and is used as a back up reticle.

Figure 4-5. Heads Up Display (HUD) Symbols (Sheet 3 of 4)

TM 1-1520-236-10

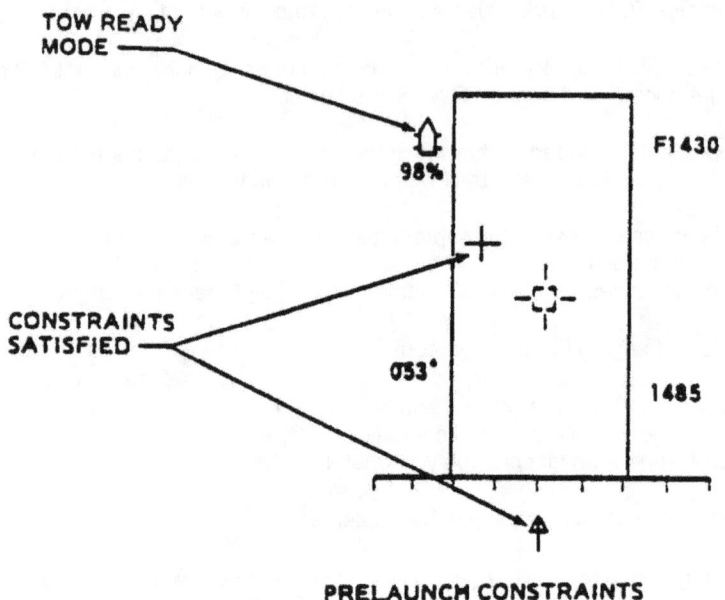

PRELAUNCH CONSTRAINTS

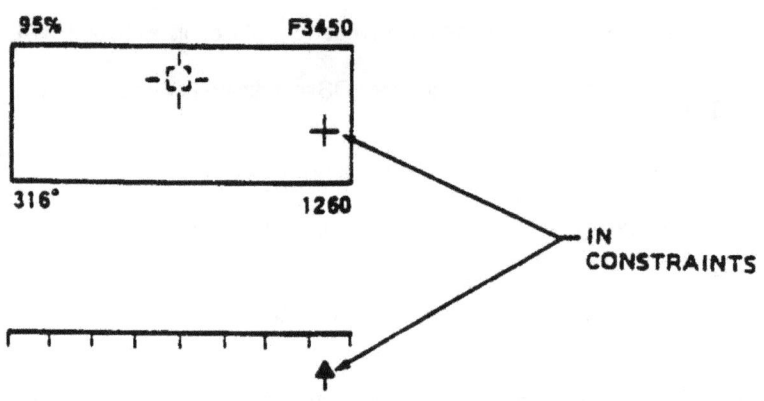

POSTLAUNCH CONSTRAINTS

Figure 4-5. Heads Up Display (HUD) Symbols (Sheet 4 of 4)

4-14. Helmet Sight Subsystem (HSS). The HSS (TM 9-1270-212-14) permits the pilot or gunner to rapidly acquire visible targets and to direct the turret and/or the telescopic sight unit (TSU) to those targets.

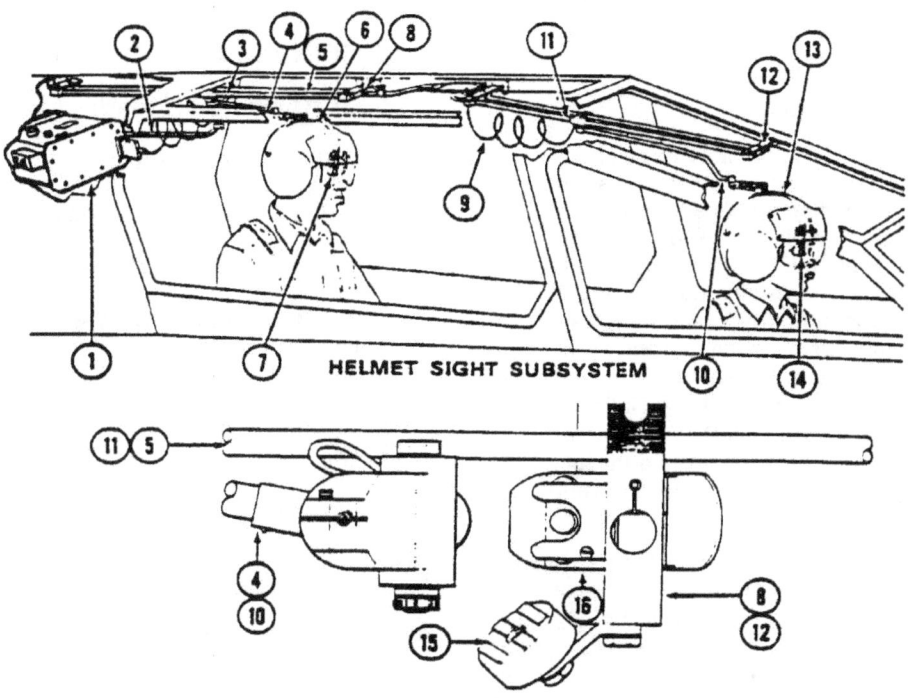

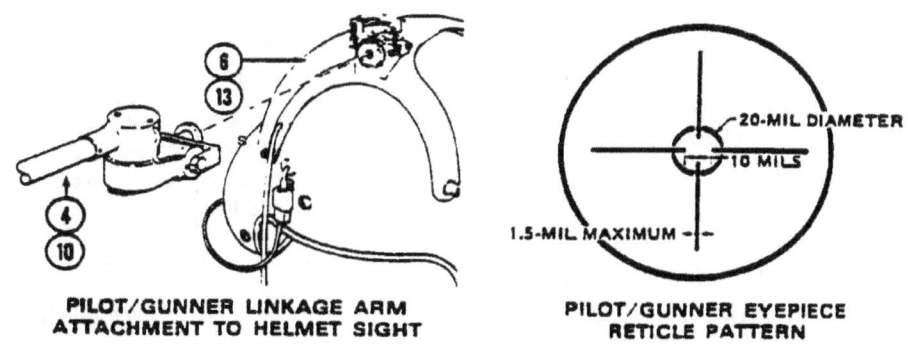

1. Electronic interface assembly
2. Gunner extension casble
3. Pilot linkage cable
4. Pilot linkage arm
5. Pilot linkage rails
6. Pilot helmet sight
7. Pilot eyepiece
8. Pilot linkage front support
9. Gunner linkage cable
10. Gunner linkage arm
11. Gunner linkage rails
12. Gunner linkage front support
13. Gunner helmet sight
14. Gunner eyepiece
15. BIT magnet
16. Stow bracket

Figure 4-6. Helmet Sight Subsystem (HSS)

4-15. TOW Missile. The TOW (tube-launched, optically-tracked, wire command link) missile subsystem (TM 9-1425-473-20) is a heavy antitank/assault weapon. The subsystem utilizes optical and IR (infrared) means to track a target and guide the missile. Isolation from helicopter motions and vibrations is provided. One or two TML (TOW Missile Launcher) (Figure 4-11) supports two missiles each on the outboard ejector racks.

NOTE

The subsystem is designed to be effective during daylight conditions. Use at night may be effective if flares are used to augment visibility. Problems with glare on sight reticles, inability to adjust reticle in intensity during target tracking, and difficulty in acquiring targets at unknown locations during darkness, will degrade system performance during night operations. **CN** Helicopters equipped with M65/C-NITE system have enhanced target acquisition during night or obscured battlefield conditions.

CN M65/C-NITE System. The M65/C-NITE system is a modification of the M65 and M65/laser augmented airborne TOW (LAAT) system. In addition to the existing direct view optics (DVO) of the M65, a forward looking infrared (FLIR) sensor is added. The FLIR provides thermal imaging, thus providing the ability to detect and recognize targets at night and under obscured battlefield conditions. The M-65/C-NITE system incorporates a video thermal tracker which allows tracking of the thermal tracker which allows tracking of the thermal beacon on the TOW 2 family of missiles. This compatibility allows the missile to be tracked through obscured battlefield conditions and provides a tracking capability against electro-optic countermeasures. In addition to tracking the TOW 2 missile, the FLIR is used to accurately direct turret and rocket fire, FLIR power supply (FPS) is powered by 28 vdc and is protected by FPS PWR circuit breaker located in the aft electrical compartment.

NOTE

The FLIR sensor requires several minutes to stabilize thermal imaging. DET HOT is displayed in FLIR mode indicator until sensor is stabilized. Sensor must be stabilized if FLIR use is anticipated.

4-16. LASER RANGE FINDER FIRING IS ACCOMPLISHED AS FOLLOWS:

    a. MASTER ARM switch – ARM.

    b. LASER SAFE/TURRET DEPR LIMIT switch – OFF.

    c. TCP MODE SELECT – As desired, except OFF.

    d. TCP LASER ARM switch – As desired.

    e. TSU filter lever – Set to L.

    f. SHC AQC/TRK/STOW switch – TRK.

NOTE

A Green information/system status light will illuminate on the pilots Caution Panel indicating LASER ARMED.

    g. LASER RANGE MIN RANGE DISPLAY switch – DISPLAY.

    h. LRD Knob – Adjust brightness.

    i. LASER RANGE MIN RANGE SET switch – Select desired minimum range (setting displayed in TSU).

    j. LASER RANGE MIN RANGE DISPLAY switch – OFF.

NOTE

Setting MIN RANGE DISPLAY in the TSU will not allow the LASER Range Finder to identify any target range between 200 meters and the range set into the TSU. If the LASER is fired at a range less than the MIN RANGE DISPLAYED in the TSU a no-valid return will be displayed in the TSU (red light).

    k. TSU reticle – On target.

    l. LHG HI LO MAG switch – As desired.

    m. LHG LASER switch – Press. Switch must be positively held in position to obtain range data.

    n. LHG LASER switch – Release.

    o. MASTER ARM switch – STBY.

TM 1-1520-236-10

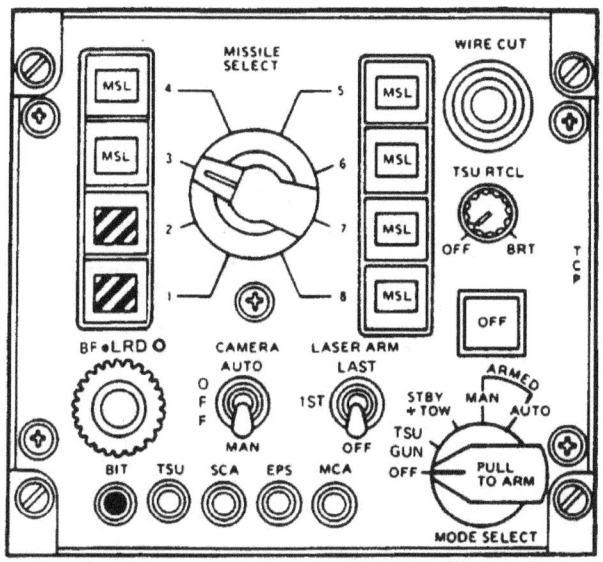

LOCATION: GUNNER INSTRUMENT PANEL
MS018142

ITEM	FUNCTION
MODE SELECT Switch	Off - Deactivates TSU and TMS circuits. TSU/GUN - Selects turret operation for gunner. STBY TOW - Permits gunner to control TMS. MAN - Permits gunner to select missile to be fired manually. AUTO - Missile to be fired is automatically selected.

ITEM	FUNCTION	
TSU/SCA/ EPS/MCA Unit Fail Indicators	Black Flag - Indicates unit operational during performance or built-in-test. White Flag - Indicates unit failure during performance or built-in-test. EPS indicates failure during performance, built-in-test, or non-performance.	
BIT Switch	Performs manual built-in-test when pressed.	
BF Knob LRD Knob	Inner Knob - Adjusts brightness of TSU battle flags. Outer Knob - Adjusts brightness of TSU range readout.	
CAMERA Switch	Not normally used:	
LASER ARM Switch	FIRST - ALLOWS laser range finder to compute target distance by using first laser pulse reflected from target (<u>WHEN TARGET IS UNOBSTRUCTED FROM VIEW</u>). LAST - Allows laser range finder to compute target distance by using last laser pulse reflected from target (<u>WHEN VIEW OF TARGET IS OBSTRUCTED BY CLUTTER</u>). OFF - Deactivates laser range finder.	
OFF/PWR/ON/ ARMED/TEST System Status Annunciator	OFF	- Indicates MODE SELECT switch is in the OFF position.
	PWR ON	- Indicates MODE SELECT switch is in the TSU GUN or STBY TOW position.
	ARMED	- Indicates MODE SELECT switch is in the ARMED position.
	TEST	- Indicates built-in test is being performed.
TSU RTCL Switch	OFF	- Deactivates the TSU reticle circuit. Varies intensity of TSU reticle lights when turned.
WIRE CUT Switch	Permits gunner to manual cut missile command wire when pressed.	
MSL/Barberpole Missile Status Indicators	MSL	- Indicates missile is present in a specific location of launcher.
	Barberpole	- Indicates missile is not present in a specific location of launcher.
MISSILE SELECT Switch	1/2/3/4 5/6/7/8	- Indicates missile selected (Manual or automatic) for firing.

Figure 4-7. Gunner TOW Control Panel (TCP)

4-17

TM 1-1520-236-10

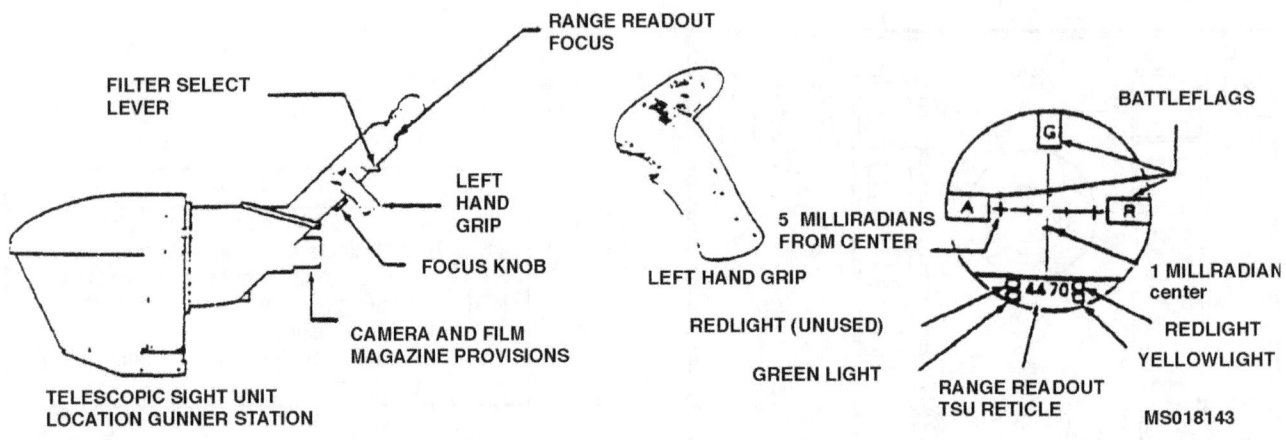

ITEM	FUNCTION
Left-hand grip switches	
MAG switch	LO - Magnifies target two times.
	HI - Magnifies target 13 times.
TRIGGER switch	- Fires TOW if selected in first or second detent.
	- Fires turret if selected in first or second detent.
	- First Detent Limited to 16 round burst.
	- Second detent - Continuous burst.
ACTION switch	- Activates TOW launchers
	- Slaves turret to TSU or gunner helmet sight.
LASER switch	- Fires laser pulses at target for range finding.
TSU Reticle	
G battle flag	- When flashing, indicates TCP MODE SELECT switch is TSU/GUN position and turret not aligned with TSU or turret has activated a limit switch: upper, lower, left, right or turret depression limit.
	- When steady, indicates TCP MODE SELECT switch is in TSU/GUN position and turret is aligned with TSU.
A battle flag	- Indicates TCP MODE SELECT switch is in the ARMED position. All requirements have been met except prelaunch constraints.
R battle flag	- Indicates pilot has achieved prelaunch constraints for TOW firing.
Red light	- Indicates no-valid laser return pulse.
Green light	- Indicates multiple targets detected by laser range finder.
Yellow light	Steady - Indicates laser range finder malfunction.
	Flashing - Indicates laser range finder overtemperature.
Range readout	- Indicates range from helicopter to target.
Filter select leve	- Selects filter of different light intensities.
	Red: Use when firing a TOW missile to reduce glare from the IR source on the missile and thus allow proper tracking of the target.
	Clear: To be used during low light level conditions, such as hazy (smoke, fog, dust) days or under twilight conditions.
	Neutral Density: To be used on bright clear days or to reduce the glare reflected from bodies of water.
	Laser Filter: To be used during any laser ranging operations to protect the eyes from laser radiation energy.
Range readout	
Focus knob	- Focus battle and range readout display.
Focus knob	- Focus target image.

Figure 4-8. Telescopic Sight Unit (TSU)

4-18

TM 1-1520-236-10

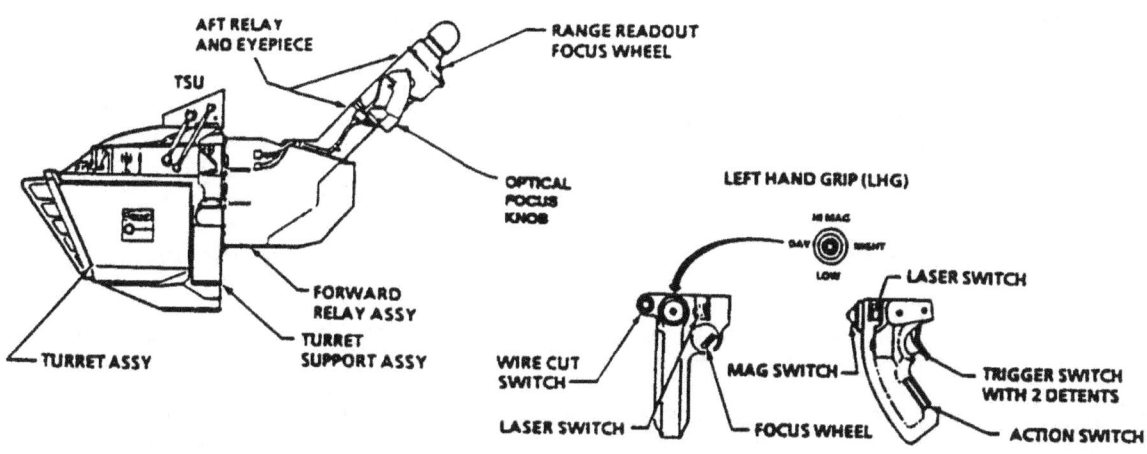

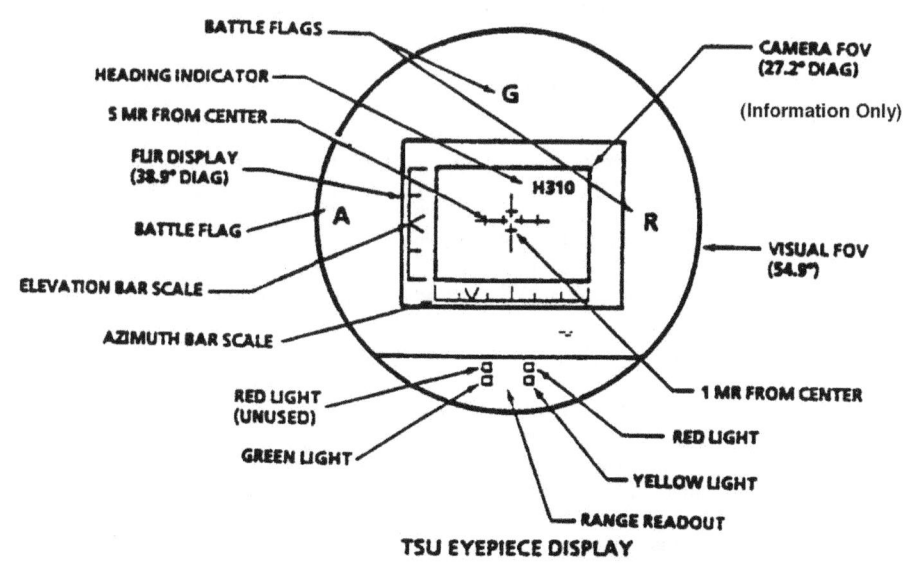

TSU EYEPIECE DISPLAY

MS018144

ITEM	FUNCTION
Left-hand grip switches MAG switch	LO - Magnifies target two times in DAY mode, five times NIGHT mode. HI - Magnifies target 13 times in DAY mode, 15.5 times NIGHT mode. DAY - Selects direct view optics. NIGHT - Selects FLIR display.

TRIGGER switch	- Fires TOW when pressed to first or second detent.
	- Fires turrent when pressed to:
	    First detent - Limited to 16 round burst.
	    Second detent - Continuous burst.

CN Figure 4-9. Gunner Telescopic Sight Unit (TSU) With FLIR (Sheet 1 of 2)

ITEM	FUNCTION
ACTION Switch	- Acticates TWO launchers. - Slaves turret to TSU or gunner helmet sight.
LASER switch	- Fires laser pulses at target for range finding.
TSU Reticle	
G battle flag	Steady - Indicates TCP MODE SELECT switch is in TSU/GUN position and turret is aligned with TSU. Flashing - Indicates TCP MODE SELECT switch is in TSU/GUN position and turret is not aligned with TSU.
A battle flag	- Indicates TCP MODE SELECT switch is in ARMED position, missile has been selected, action switch pressed, and ready for prelaunch constraints to be met.
R battle flag	- Indicates pilot has achieved prelaunch constraints for TOW firing.
Heading Indicator	- Indicates magnetic heading of TSU line-of-sight.
Elevation Bar Scale	- Indicates elevation of TSU line-of-sight relative to helicopter in 25 degree increments.
Azimuth	- Indicates azimuth of TSU line-of-sight relative to helicopter in Bar Scale 30 degree increments.
Red light	- Indicates no valid laser return pulse.
Green light	- Indicates multiple targets detected by laser range finder.
Yellow light	Steady - Indicates laser range finder malfunction. Flashing - Indicates laser range finder overtemperataure.
WIRE CUT Switch	- Permits gunner to manually cut missile command wire when pressed (Pilots MASTER ARM switch must be set to ARMED).
Range readout	- Indicates range from helicopter to target.
Range readout focus wheel	- Focuses battle flags and range readout display.
Focus wheel	- Focuses FLIR target image.
Optical Focus Knob	- Focuses daysight optics (Day Mode) and FLIR reticle (Night Mode).

CN Figure 4-9. Gunner Telescopic Sight Unit (TSU) With FLIR (Sheet 2 of 2)

TM 1-1520-236-10

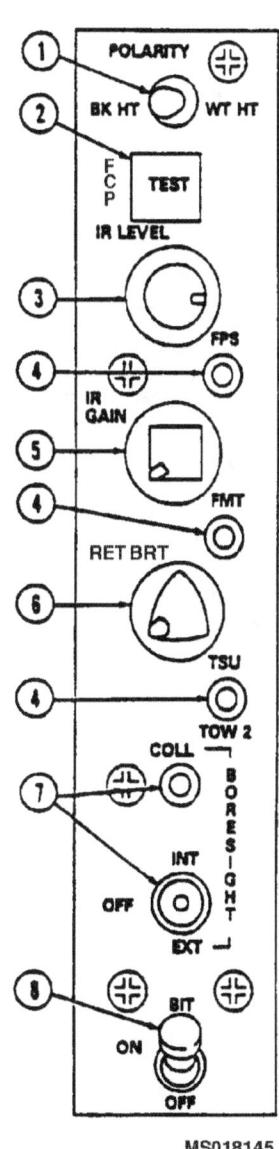

ITEM	FUNCTION		
1. POLARITY switch	BK HT	-	Displays FLIR video with targets in black hot and differentially cold white environments.
	WT HT	-	Displays FLIR video with targets in white hot and differentially cold black environments.
2. Mode indicator	OFF	-	Indicates FLIR subsystem is off.
	TEST	-	Indicates FLIR subsystem is performing BIT.
	DET HOT	-	Indicates FLIR subsystem has not yet stabilized for thermal imaging.
	PWR ON	-	Indicates FLIR subsystem is on and FLIR sub system sensor is stabilized for thermal imaging.
3. IR LEVEL Control			Adjusts brightness of FLIR video in TSU.
4. BIT indicators	FPS	-	Indicates white when FLIR power supply fails BIT.
	FMT	-	Indicates white when FLIR missile tracker fails BIT (TOW 2 EOCCM capability is inoperable).
	TSU TOW 2	-	Indicates white when TOW 2 signal to TSU has failed (TOW 2 EOCCM capability may be degraded).
5. IR GAIN Control		-	Adjusts contrast of FLIR video in TSU.
6. RET BRT Control		-	Adjusts reticle brightness in TSU from black to white.
7. BORESIGHT switch and indicator	COLL	-	For maintenance use only.
	EXT	-	For maintenance use only.
	INT	-	For maintenance use only.
8. FLIR control panel OFF/ON/BIT switch	OFF	-	Turns FLIR subsystem off. The switch is overridden when: TCP MODE SELECT switch - ARMED, MASTER ARM switch - ARM and WPN CONTR switch - GUNNER.
	ON	-	Turns FLIR subsystem on. PWR ON displays in mode indicator after FLIR subsystem stabilizes for thermal imaging.
	BIT	-	Holding switch in BIT position displays a self test bar across FLIR video in TSU. When switch is released from BIT position to ON, the system initiates FLIR subsystem BIT. TEST is displayed in mode indicator until BIT is completed. DET HOT displays after BIT completes and remains a few minutes until FLIR subsystem is stabilized for thermal imaging. PWR ON then displays in mode indicator. BIT cannot be run with TCP indicating ARMED.

CN Figure 4-10. FLIR Control Panel (FCP)

4-21

TM 1-1520-236-10

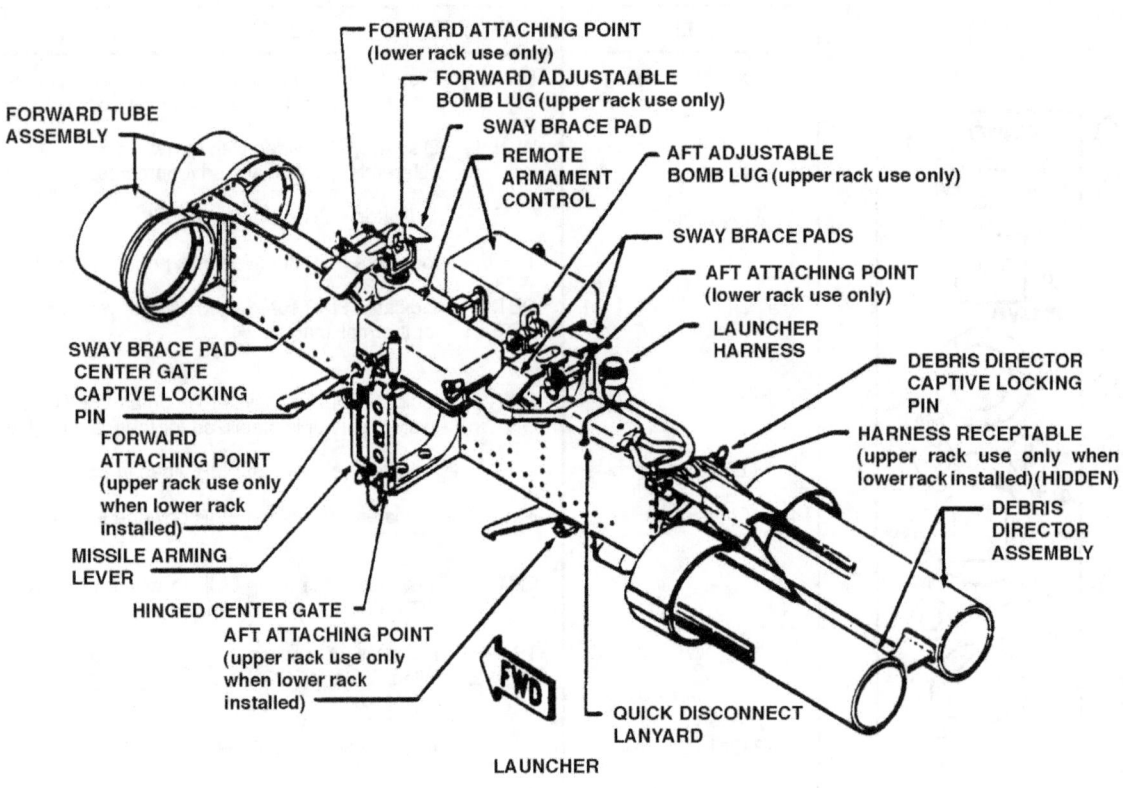

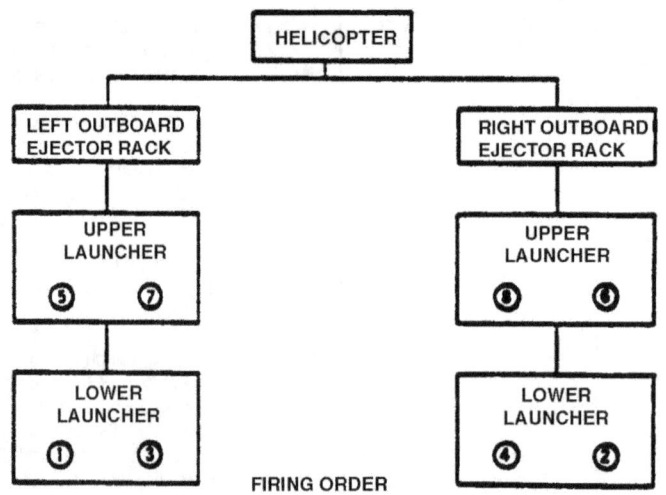

Figure 4-11. TOW Missile Launcher

4-22

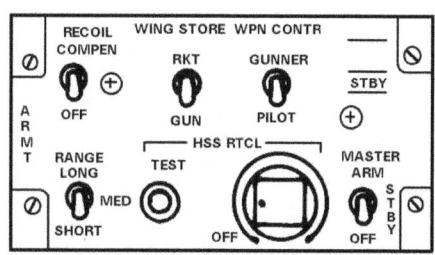
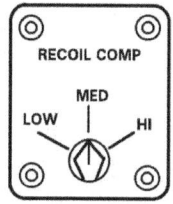

LOCATION PILOT INSTRUMENT PANEL   MS018147

ITEM		FUNCTION
MASTER ARM Switches		**WARNING** MASTER ARM switch bypassed when gunner pit oride switch in ORIDE.
	OFF STBY	Deactivates all sights (but HUD) and weapon control/firing circuits. Activates all sights (but HUD) turret and TOW missile current circuits. Charges wing gun pod battery.
		NOTE MASTER ARM OFF and STBY position disable CPG wire cut switches.
	ARM-	Activates all sights (but HUD) weapon control/firing circuits. Charges wing gun pod battery.
WPN CONTR Switch	PILOT-	Permits pilot to fire turret using HS. Illuminates gunner PILOT IN CONT light.
	FIXED-	Permits pilot to fire turret using HUD. Illuminates gunner PILOT IN CONT light.
	GUNNER	Permits gunner to fire turret using helmet sight or TSU and TOW using TSU.
HSS RTCL OFF/BRT Switch	OFF- Rotate-	Deactivates pilot HS reticle lamps. Varies intensity of pilot HS reticle lamps.
HSS RTCL TEST Switch	TEST-	Tests pilot HS reticle.
ARMED/STBY Indicator	ARMED-	Indicates MASTER ARM switch in ARM or gunner PLT ORIDE switch in PLT ORIDE (amber light).
	STBY- OFF- Press-	Indicates MASTER ARM switch in STBY (green light). Indicates MASTER ARM switch is off. Tests indicator lights.
WING STORE Switch	RKT- GUN-	Permits pilot or gunner to fire rockets. Permits pilot or gunner to fire wing mounted gun.
RECOL Switch	OFF- COMPEN-	Deactivates turret recoil compensation circuits. Activates turret recoil compensation circuits in SCAS.
RANGE Switch	LONG/- MED/- SHORT-	Provides range to target data to turret elevation compensation circuits. LONG - 2000 m. MID - 1500 m. SHORT - 1000 m.
RECOIL CCMP Switch	LOW- MED- HI-	Provides low SCAS input to fight controls during turret fire. Provides medium SCAS input to fight controls during turret fire. Provides high SCAS input to fight controls during turret fire.

Figure 4-12. Pilot Armament Control Panel

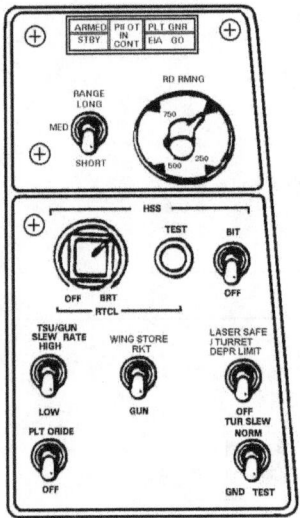

LOCATION: GUNNER RIGHT CONSOLE MS018148

ITEM		FUNCTION
ARMED/ STBY Indicator	ARMED	- Indicates pilot MASTER ARM switch in ARM (red light).
	STBY	- Indicates pilot MASTER ARM switch is STBY (green light).
	Off	- Indicates pilot MASTER ARM switch if OFF.
	Press	- Tests indicator lights.
PILOT IN CONT Indicator	ON	- Pilot has control of turret.
	OFF	- Gunner has control of turret or pilot MASTER ARM Switch is OFF.
	Press	- Tests indicator light.
PLT/ GNR/ EIA/ GO Indicators	PLT	- Indicates failure in pilot helmet linkage.
	GNR	- Indicates failure in gunner helmet linkage.
	EIA	- Indicates failure in electronic interface assembly.
	GO	- Indicated HSS operating properly.
	Press	- Tests indicator lights.
	Off	- Indicates HSS built-in-test not being conducted.
RANGE Switch	SHORT/	- Provides target range data to compensation circuit. Short - 1000 m.
	MED/	- Med - 1500 m.
	LONG	- Long - 2000 m.
RD RMNG Counter	Gradations	- Indicates quantity of ammunition remaining for turret weapon.

ITEM		FUNCTION	ITEM		FUNCTION
HSS/ RETICLE OFF/BRT Switch	OFF	- Deactivates gunner HSS reticle lights. Varies intensity of gunner HSS reticle lights when turned.	LASER SAFE/ TURRET DEPR LIMIT switch	OFF	- Permits turret travel between minimum to maximum elevation.
				LASER SAFE/ TURRET DEPR LIMIT	- Limits downward travel to prevent turret weapon from striking ground and prevents laser from firing.
HSS RTCL TEST Switch	TEST	- Tests gunner HSS reticle.	PLT ORIDE Switch	OFF	- Permits pilot armament control panel to control the weapons.
HSS BIT Switch	OFF	- Deactivates pilot and gunner HSS built-in-test circuit.		PLT ORIDE	- Overrides pilot armament control panel. Permits gunner to fire turret using HSS, and wing stores (not TOW) without sight. Deactivates TSU left hand grip trigger.
	BIT	- Tests pilot and gunner HSS when linkage arms attached to BIT magnets.			
TSU/GUN SLEW RATE Switch	HIGH	- Selects high slew rate for TSU when the TOW control panel made select switch is in the TSU/GUN position.	TUR SLEW Switch	NORM	- Drives turret azimuth and elevation at 60 degrees per second.
	LOW	- Used for more accurate firing by engaging circuit so TSU will move at TOW mode - Hi MAG slew rate.		GND TEST	- Used for ground operations servicing only (drives turret azimuth and elevation at 4 to 8 degrees per second).
WING STORE Switch	RKT	- Permits gunner to fire rockets.			
	GUN	- Permits gunner to fire wing mounted gun.			

Figure 4-13. Gunner Armament Control Panel

TM 1-1520-236-10

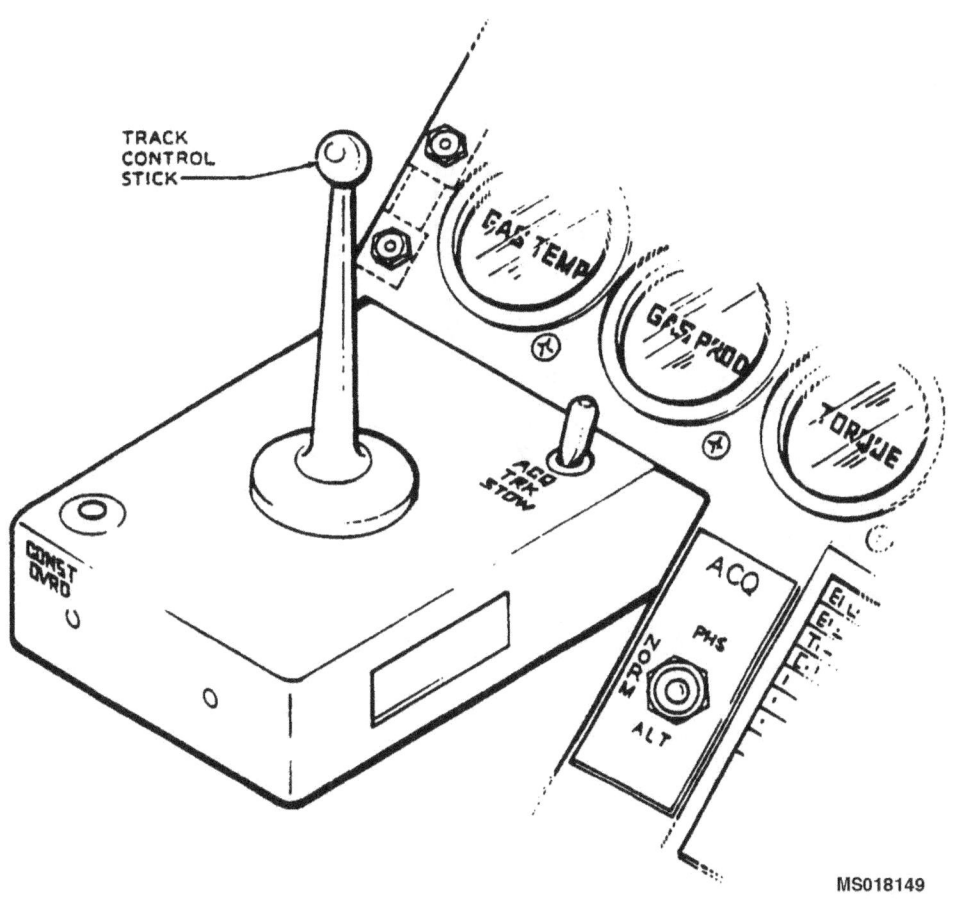

LOCATION: GUNNER INSTRUMENT PANEL

ITEM	FUNCTION	
Track control Stick		Positions TSU in azimuth and elevation.
ACQ/TRK/STOW Switch	ACQ	- Slaves TSU to gunner HS for target acquisition.
	TRK	- Permits track control handle to position TSU.
	STOW	Stows TSU 0°AZ and 0°EL.
ACQ Switch Located on Instrument Panel	NORM	- Track control stick controls TSU.
	PHS	- Slaves TSU to PHS when mode switch is in track.
	ALT	- Slaves TSU to ALT.
CONST OVRD Switch		Permits TOW firing when helicopter is not within the prelaunch constraints when pressed.

Figure 4-14. Gunner Sight Hand Control (SHC)

TM 1-1520-236-10

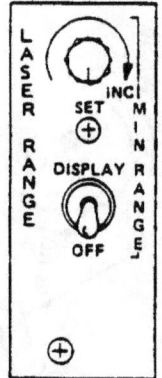

MS018150

ITEM	FUNCTION
MIN RANGE SET knob	Sets minimum range which laser range finder will recognize.
DISPLAY switch DISPLAY	Displays minimum range in eye piece display in TSU and resets displayed range to zero.
OFF	Deactivates minimum range display circuit and permits normal range display.

Figure 4-15. Laser Range Finder Control Panel

NOTE

If the Gunner is in TSU GUN position on the TCP MODE select and the ACTION switch depressed the range data will be supplied to the 20MM through the FCC for 6 seconds. If the ACTION switch is not depressed range data will be supplied to the rockets, through the FCC for 15 seconds. When firing rockets the Pilot must be in the A position on the RMS RNG - km selector to use LASER range data.

4-17. TOW OPERATION – INFLIGHT PROCEDURES.

TOW firing is accomplished as follows:

a. MASTER ARM switch – ARM.

b. WPN CONTR switch – GUNNER.

c. TCP MODE SELECT switch – ARMED MAN for manual missile selection, ARMED AUTO for automatic missile selection. TCP system status annunciator displays ARMED.

d. TCP MISSILE SELECT switch – Set to first loaded missile if TCP MISSILE SELECT switch is ARMED MAN.

e. TSU LHG MAG switch – LO. Switch must be positively held in position before releasing.

WARNING

On aircraft modified to fire the TOW 2B, note launcher location of each TOW 2B missile. In addition, ensure flight path of the TOW 2B missile is not over friendly forces.

f. Gunner HS reticle – On target.

g. SHC ACQ/TRK/STOW switch – Release to ACQ.

h. SHC ACQ/TRK/STOW switch – Release to TRK.

i. TSU reticle – On target.

j. TSU LHG MAG switch – HI. Switch must be positively held in position before releasing.

k. SHC track control stick – Move as required to keep TSU crosshairs on target.

l. Helicopter position – Maneuver to keep flashing gunner LOS symbol in HUD field of view.

m. TSU LHG ACTION switch – Press and hold. Gunner TSU reticle A battle flag comes on, HUD displays prelaunch constraint and missile symbol. LOS symbol flashing if outside of constraint and ascend/descend pointer appears when maneuver required. Keeping the TSU LHG ACTION switch pressed provides motion compensation by the TSU for a target during tracking.

n. Helicopter position – Maneuvered to align gunner LOS symbol within prelaunch window of HUD and maintain a roll attitude of less than ±5° Gunners LOS symbol ceases flashing and TSU gunner reticle R battle flag comes on.

o. TSU LHG TRIGGER switch – Pressed when helicopter is within range of target. Pilot HUD X symbol appears over missile symbol. After 1.5 seconds missile symbol and prelaunch constraint disappear and gunner TSU A and R battle flags go out. Gunner cannot fire if the helicopter is not within the prelaunch constraint boundary. Gunner can override the prelaunch constraint boundary limitation by pressing the CONST OVRD switch on the SHC; however degraded capture probability should be expected. Smoke may emerge from launcher after TRIGGER is pressed and before missile exits launcher. The smoke is caused by the missile gyro and battery squibs firing and should not be regarded as a misfire. A misfire has occurred if missile fails to exit launcher within 1.5 seconds. Do not press the LH TRIGGER during wire cutting because another missile will be launched if the TCP MODE SELECT switch is in the ARMED AUTO position and the helicopter is within prelaunch constraints.

WARNING

Do not turn helicopter to the side from which a missile is fired. The helicopter may strike the command wire.

NOTE

If missile fails to fire in ARMED MAN mode reselect missile on TCP.

WARNING

On aircraft modified to fire the TOW 2B, note launcher location of each TOW 2B missile, in addition, ensure flight path of the TOW 2B missile is not over friendly forces.

p. LHG TRIGGER switch – Release.

q. LHG ACTION switch – Release.

r. Helicopter position – Maneuvered to keep gunner LOS symbol within postlaunch constraint of HUD until wire cut or missile impact, Postlaunch constraint disappears on wire cut or missile impact.

CAUTION

Loss of missile guidance could result if a maneuver exceeding postlaunch constraint boundary is made.

Loss of missile guidance may occur when firing TOW missiles over high voltage lines or in the vicinity of strong RFI emitters. Contact of TOW wires with high voltage lines may result in damage to TOW system.

s. TSU reticle crosshairs – On target until wire cut or missile impact. Gunner SHC track control stick used to keep crosshairs on target.

t. LHG CN or TCP WIRE CUT switch – Press.

NOTE

When smoke or TOW jammers are present, system automatic wirecut will not operate until approximately 27 seconds after trigger pull. LHG or TCP wirecut switches may be used to minimize time to wirecut.

Manual wirecut should be performed immediately following missile impact for all night shots (whenever command wires cannot be visually verified to be cut).

During night operations (when command wires cannot be visually verified to be cut) the pilots should press the collective wire cut switch in case of system malfunction or prior to repositioning the helicopter.

Pilot Master Arm switch must be in Armed position for wire cut to occur automatically.

u. Additional missile firing – The next missile is selected automatically if the gunner TCP MODE SELECT switch is on ARMED AUTO, manually selected by the MISSILE SELECT switch if switch is on ARMED MAN.

(1) HUD – Displays which side missile has been selected when LHG ACTION switch is pressed.

(2) TSU LHG MAG switch – LO. Switch must be positively held in position before releasing.

(3) Fire missile – Repeat steps f. through u.

v. SHC ARQ/TRK/STOW switch – Stow.

w. MASTER ARM switch – STBY.

x. Emergency procedures – Refer to paragraph 9-52.

4-18. Rockets. The Rocket Management Subsystem (RMS) (TM 9-1090-207-13) is a light anti-personnel assault weapon. The RMS consists of a Display Unit (Rockets) panel located in the pilot station and two Operations Units located in the leading edge of the wings, one for each of the inboard wing stores racks. The RMS permits the pilot to select the desired type of 2.75 inch folding fin aerial rocket (FFAR) warhead, fuze, quantity, range, and rate. Seven or 19 tube launchers can be mounted on each of the inboard and outboard wing stores racks. The rocket launchers are divided into zones as shown in Figure 4-18. Prior to loading or unloading 2.75 inch rockets, the wing stores power circuit breaker will be pulled.

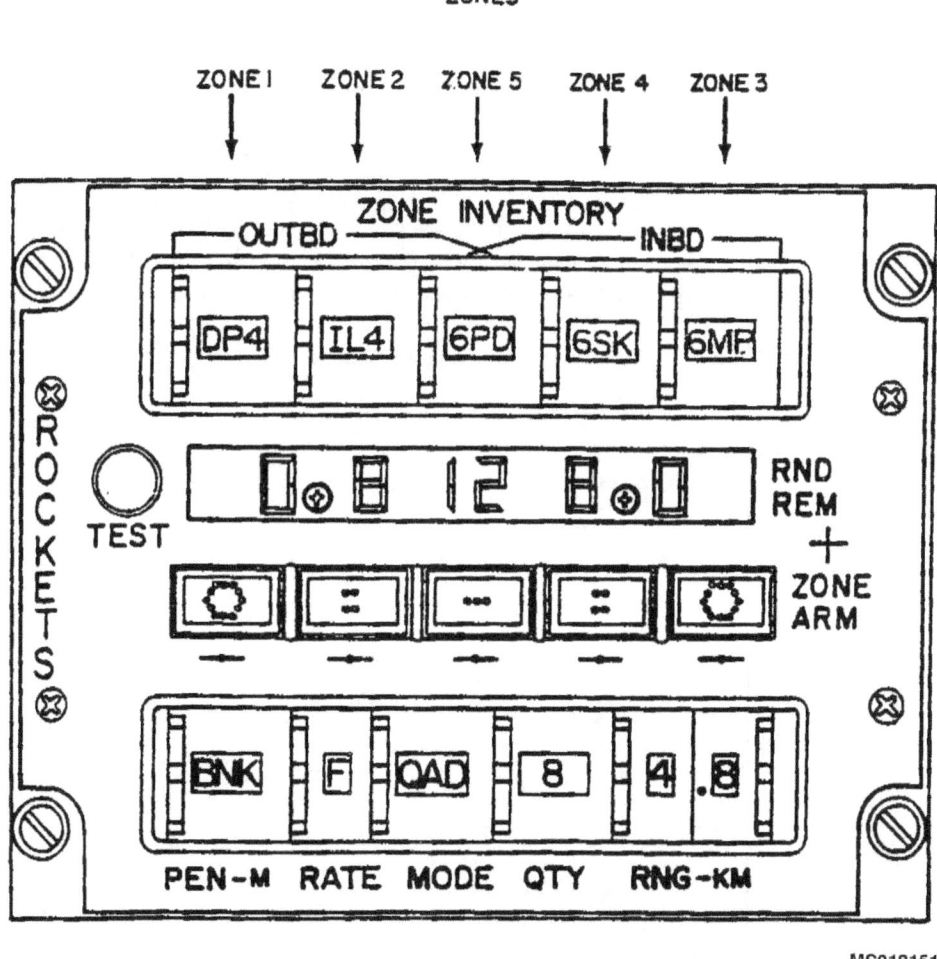

Figure 4-16. M147 Rocket Management Subsystem (RMS) Display Unit

M147 Rocket Management System allows firing of both the MK40 and MK66 2.75" rockets

SELECTOR	FUNCTION
Zone Inventory: Indicators/Selectors	a. Selector must match type of rocket in that zone. b. Selector must be set before power is applied to the RMS. To change setting, the Master Arm must be turned off. c. MK40 rocket motor settings. DP4 - HE dual purpose warhead (M247, WDU-4A/A, -13/A). d. MK66 rocket motor settings. e. The BLANK setting is used for any warhead/fuze combination not listed.
PEN-M (Penetration in meters, used with M433 Fuze only) Indicator/Selector	a. Number settings, in 5 meter increments, cause fuze to delay detonation after initial contact with forest canopy or light roof. Number signifies the distance the rocket will travel at terminal velocity before detonation. b. BNK (bunker) delays detonation of fuze until calculated penetration depth of 3 meters into log and dirt bunker. c. SQ (Superquick) causes immediate detonation on contact.

Figure 4-17. M147 Rocket Management System (Sheet 1 of 4)

SELECTOR	FUNCTION
RATE Indicator/Selector	Sets the time interval between pairs of rockets fired when more than one pair is selected in MODE or QTY. a. F – Fast fires pairs at 60 millisecond intervals. b. S – Slow fires pairs at 180 millisecond intervals. c. A – Uninventoried tubes (RMS thinks they are empty) will be displayed in the Rounds Remaining (RND-REM) window. Pilot may attempt to fire these tubes: firing voltage is applied to "empty" tubes (dependent upon selected mode and quantity) one at a time each time the arm fire button is pressed. Rockets will be fired at fast rate.
MODE Indicator/Selector	Sets the number of rocket pods to fire each time. a. QAD – Used when rocket pods are installed inboard and outboard. The outboard pods will delay firing for 30 milliseconds. The SECU circuit breaker must be pulled to deactivate the outboard pylon actuators. b. PRS – Fires one rocket from each side of the A/C in the armed zone (inboard or outboard pods). c. SNG – Single rockets alternating sides of A/C.
QTY (quantity) Indicator/Selector	A multiple of whatever is set in MODE. a. ALL – Ripple fires all rockets in armed zones. b. 8, 4, 2, or 1 multiplies the MODE selection.

Figure 4-17. M147 Rocket Management System (Sheet 2 of 4)

TM 1-1520-236-10

SELECTOR	FUNCTION
RNG-KM (Range In Kilometers) Indicators/Selectors	Sends range data to the FCC for rocket ballistic solutions. This selector must be set to the desired range when using the M439 Fuze and the new submunitions warhead (M261). When laser range data is not available, estimated range set in the window is sent to the FCC. In hover fire the Fire Control Reticle (FCR) is relatively stationary and becomes the aiming point on target. In running fire it becomes a Continuously Computed Impact Point for 15 seconds after range is set or changed. After the 15 sec countdown, the ballistic solution returns to the range set in the window and doesn't compensate for A/C forward motion. a. Left Thumbwheel – Numbers for 1 to 6 indicate 1000M increments (there's also a blank for ranges less than 1K) b. Left Thumb wheel – A – Used only with laser range finder. FCC will use laser range compute ballistic solution for 15 seconds. Before the gunner lases the target, and after the 15 second countdown is complete, the FCR will be fixed at 0/0 in the HUD and can't be used to aim rockets. c. Right Thumbwheel – Numbers from 0 to 9 indicate 100M increments. d. The M147 RMS is programmed for ranges from 700-6900M. Settings below 700M will still compute at 700 M.
TEST Switch	Tests digital display segment and indicator lamps (RND REM) and subsystem (including helicopter wiring) from end to end. Does not check firing circuits.
ZONE ARM (Zone Arming) Indicator/Selectors	Pressing appropriate ZONE ARM switch arms selected zone. When any one zone is selected (ARMED) all other zones with identical rounds are automatically armed and visually indicated by appropriate ZONE ARM switch(es). Any round selected by pressing a ZONE ARM switch, which is different (different zone) will automatically de-arm previously selected zone(s).

Figure 4-17. M147 Rocket Management System (Sheet 3 of 4)

SELECTOR	FUNCTION	
Warhead/Fuze Matching	1. <u>Warheads</u>:	<u>Fuzes</u>:
	a. M151 – 10 lb HE	M423, M429, M433
	b. M229 – 17 lb HE	M423, M429, M433
	c. M247 – HEAT/frag (shaped charge)	M438
	d. WDU-4A/A – Flechettes (2200 20gr)	M113A
	e. WDU-13/A – Flechettes (700 60gr)	M113A
	f. M262 – Illum	M439
	g. M261 – Smokescreen	M439
	h. M261 – Submunition (9 shaped charges)	M439
	2. <u>Fuzes</u>:	<u>Warheads</u>:
	a. M423 – PD, armed 43-92 M downrange	M151, M229
	b. M429 – Prox, arms 150-300 M downrange detonates at 5-12 ft	M151, M229
	c. M113A – Flechette burst, arms 140-300 ft det. at 12-15 G's	WDU-13/A WDU-4A/A
	d. M438 – PD, armed 500-1000 ft downrange	M247
	e. M433 – Time Delay, remote set by PEN-m	M151, M229
	f. M439 – Time Delay, remote set by RNG-km "A" setting using laser ranging or manual input.	M262, M264, M261

Figure 4-17. **M147 Rocket Management System (Sheet 4 of 4)**

LAUNCHER ZONING

ZONE 1 - Outer ring of 19 tube launcher when installed on outboard wing stores rack for a total of 24 rockets.

ZONE 2 - Two top and two bottom tubes of the inner ring of 19 tube launcher or two top and two bottom tubes of the outer ring of 7 tube launcher, when installed on outboard wing stores rack for a total of 8 rockets.

ZONE 3 - Outer ring of 19 tube launcher when installed on inboard wing stores rack for a total of 24 rockets.

ZONE 4 - Two top and two bottom tubes of the inner ring of 19 tube launcher or two top and two bottom tubes of the outer ring of 7 tube launcher, when installed on inboard wing stores rack for a total of 8 rockets.

ZONE 5 - Center three tubes of 19 tube and 7 tube launchers for a total of 12 rockets.

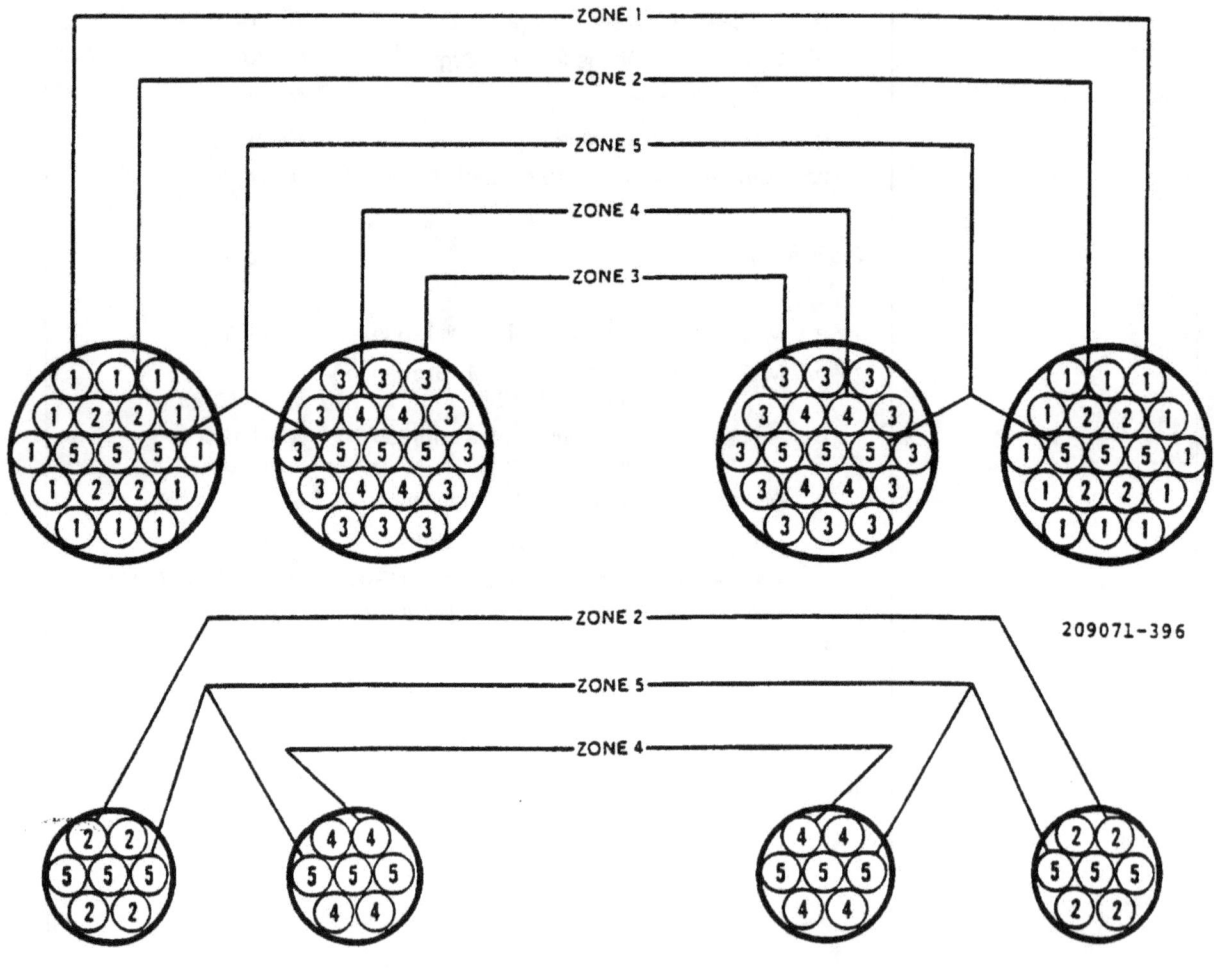

Figure 4-18. Folding Fin Aerial Rocket (2.75 inch) Launcher

4-19. ROCKET OPERATION – INFLIGHT PROCEDURES.

CAUTION

Firing multiple Mark 66 rockets in excess of 8 pair, less than 20 feet skid height with the engine inlet shield installed may result in surge damage to the drive system and engine. The probability of an engine surge decreases as the number of rockets fired in a salvo decreases and/or the helicopter altitude above the ground increases.

NOTE

A rocket induced engine surge is characterized by engine torque fluctuations, rising TGT, and an audible change in the engine noise. A lateral airframe oscillation may be present after the rockets have fired. When firing multiple Mark 66 rockets, it is normal to see the TGT rise more than 50 degrees even though no engine surge occurred.

NOTE

Do not use an MK-66 Rocket motor that has been continuously stored above 140 degrees Fahrenheit for more than 24 hours. Discard any rocket that has been dropped. MK-66 Mod 2 motors are prohibited.

   a. Rocket direct with laser ranging is accomplished as follows:

    (1)   MASTER ARM switch – ARM.

    (2)   WING STORE switch – RKT.

    (3)   RMS QTY selector – As desired.

    (4)   RMS ZONE ARM switches – ARM.

    (5)   RMS MODE selector – As desired.

    (6)   RMS RNG - km selector – A.

    (7)   RMS PEN-M selector – As desired.

    (8)   HUD RKT switch – DIR.

    (9)   Helicopter position – Maneuver to put HUD fire control reticle on target. The HUD fire control reticle will continue to get accurate rocket solution, based on movement of the helicopter, for fifteen seconds after gunner has stopped firing the laser range finder.

    (10) Cyclic WING ARM FIRE switch – Press.

    (11) Cyclic WING ARM FIRE switch – Release.

   b. Rocket direct with estimated range is accomplished as follows:

    (1)   MASTER ARM switch – ARM.

    (2)   WING STORE switch – RKT.

    (3)   RMS QTY selector – As desired.

    (4)   RMS ZONE ARM switches – ARM.

    (5)   RMS MODE selector – As desired.

    (6)   RMS RATE selector – As desired.

    (7)   RMS RNG-km selector – Select estimated range.

    (8)   RMS PEN-M selector – As desired.

    (9)   HUD RKT switch – DIR.

    (10) Helicopter position – Maneuver to put HUD fire control reticle on target. The Fire Control System will provide a fire control ballistic solution for rockets in the HUD based on the F range displayed in the HUD. This range will change based on the movement of the aircraft for 15 seconds after the RMS RNG-km switch is moved to a new range. After 15 seconds the steady solution presented in the HUD and the F range in the HUD will be the same as the RMS range selected. If FCC power is lost for a period beyond one second, turn the MASTER ARM switch OFF and back ON to restore the data communication between the two systems. This communication can be checked by determining if the range selected on the RMS is displayed in the HUD with the FCC on.

    (11) Cyclic WING ARM FIRE switch – Press.

    (12) Cyclic WING ARM FIRE switch – Release.

    (13) MASTER ARM switch – STBY.

   c. Rocket indirect with laser ranging is accomplished as follows:

    (1)   MASTER ARM switch – ARM.

    (2)   WING STORE switch – RKT.

    (3)   HUD RKT switch – IND.

    (4)   RMS QTY selector – As desired.

    (5)   RMS ZONE ARM switches – ARM.

    (6)   RMS MODE selector – As desired.

    (7)   RMS RATE selector – As desired.

    (8)   RMS RNG-km selector – A.

TM 1-1520-236-10

(9) RMS PEN-M selector – As desired.

(10) Gunner TSU reticle – On target.

(11) Helicopter position – Maneuver to superimpose fire control reticle over boresight reference symbol. The HUD fire control reticle will continue to get an accurate rocket solution based on movement of the aircraft for 15 seconds after the gunner ceases to FIRE the LASER RANGE FINDER.

(12) Cyclic WING ARM FIRE switch – Press.

(13) Cyclic WING ARM FIRE switch – Release.

(14) MASTER ARM switch – STBY.

d. Rocket indirect with estimated ranging is accomplished as follows:

(1) MASTER ARM switch – ARM.

(2) WING STORE switch – RKT.

(3) RMS QTY selector – As desired.

(4) RMS ZONE ARM switches – ARM.

(5) RMS MODE selector – As desired.

(6) AMS RATE selector – As desired.

(7) RMS RNG-km Selector – Select estimated range.

(8) RMS PEN-M selector – As desired.

(9) HUD RKT switch – IND.

(10) TSU reticle – On target.

(11) Helicopter position – Maneuver to superimpose HUD fire control reticle over boresight reference symbol. The Fire Control System will provide a fire control ballistic solution for rockets in the HUD based on the range displayed in the HUD. This range will change based on the movement of the aircraft for 15 seconds after the RMS RNG-km switch is moved to a new range. After 15 seconds the steady solution presented in the HUD and the F range in the HUD will be the same as the RMS Range selected. If FCC power is lost for a period beyond one second, turn the MASTER ARM switch OFF and back ON to restore the data communication between the two systems. This communication can be checked by determining if the range selected on the RMS is displayed in the HUD with the FCC on.

(12) Cyclic WING ARM FIRE switch – Press.

(13) Cyclic WING ARM FIRE switch – Release.

(14) MASTER ARM switch – STBY.

e. Rocket firing without FCC is accomplished as follows:

NOTE

Stadiametric reticle must be used when firing in this method.

(1) MASTER ARM switch – ARM.

(2) WING STORE switch – RKT.

(3) RMS QTY selector – As desired.

(4) RMS ZONE ARM switches – Arm.

(5) RMS MODE selector – As desired.

(6) RMS RATE selector – As desired.

(7) RMS RNG-KM selector – Set in estimated range.

NOTE

Range must be set into the RMS RNG-KM selector for remote fuses. Rockets will not fire in the A position.

(8) RMS PEN-M selector – As desired.

(9) HUD MODE select switch – STAD.

(10) Helicopter position – Maneuver to put stadiametric reticle an target.

(11) WING ARM FIRE switch – Press.

(12) WING ARM FIRE switch – Release.

(13) MASTER ARM switch – STBY.

f. Indirect rocket firing using ADI/HSI is used when the target is not visible and or the HUD is inoperative. It should be accomplished as follows:

NOTE

Attitude Directional Indicotor (ADI) and Horizontal Situation Indicator (HSI) must be used when firing in this method.

(1) Determine range to the target and required pitch attitude from Figure 4-19.

(2) WING STORE switch – RKT.

(3) RMS PEN-M selector – As desired.

(4) RMS RATE selector – As desired.

(5) RMS MODE selector – As desired.

(6) RMS QTY selector – As desired.

(7) MASTER ARM switch – ARM.

(8) RMS ZONE ARM switches – ARM.

WARNING

The pilot must anticipate the effect of tuck and the possible rearward movement of the helicopter when the rocket is fired. The pilot should select reference points and avoid areas of limited contrast to prevent spatial disorientation.

(9) Helicopter position – Maneuver to the required heading and pitch attitude.

NOTE

The pitch-up maneuver is initiated with forward airspeed and applying aft cyclic, while collective pitch is added to keep the tail rotor clear of obstacles. The forward airspeed will be determined by the range to the target. The greater the range the more forward airspeed will be required.

(10) WING ARM FIRE switch – Press and release.

(11) MASTER ARM switch – STBY.

4-20. UNIVERSAL TURRET. The universal turret system (TM 9-1090-206-12) provides for positioning, sighting, ammunition feeding, and firing of the M-197 20 mm gun. The system consists of a turret assembly, turret control unit, logic control unit, pressure transducer, ammunition feed system with boost assembly, gun control unit, recoil assembly, slider assembly and gun drive assembly. The turret is operated by 28 vdc and 115 vac 400 hertz power provided by the helicopter electrical system. The turret weapon can be fired in the fixed or flexible mode by the pilot, flexible mode by the gunner. The turret can travel 110 degrees left or right in azimuth and 13 to 21 degrees up (varying with the turret azimuth position) and 50 degrees down in elevation. The turret fires a burst of 16 ± 4 rounds per minute when the cyclic trigger switch is pressed to the first detent and fires a continuous burst at 730 ± 50 rounds per minute when the cyclic trigger switch is pressed to the second detent. When the turret is slewed more than five degrees in azimuth, the wing stores lockout circuitry is activated and the turret will stow to zero degrees azimuth and elevation to preclude the possibility of a turret round detonating the rockets or missile in close proximity to the helicopter. If the turret is slewed less than 5 degrees in azimuth, and an action switch is pressed to enable firing rockets or TOW missiles, the wing stores lockout circuitry becomes activated which stops the gun from firing, and the turret will not stow to zero degrees azimuth or elevation. The capacity of the ammunition and feed system is 750 rounds of continuously belted ammunition.

AIM-1/EXL. The AIM-1/EXL aiming light is mounted on the gun saddle of the universal turret (Figure 4-20, detail B). It enables low-light/night target acquisition for the turret gun by using a boresighted infrared laser beam that can only be viewed with night vision goggles (NVG). The AIM-1/EXL subsystem can be used in conjunction with the Helmet Sight Subsystem (HSS) when NVG are worn. The AIM-1/EXL aiming light can operate in continuous mode or activated when ACTION switch on pilot cyclic control is pressed. Subsystem operations are controlled by the switch/relay assembly located on the outboard side of pilot's ash receiver (Figure 2-4). When switch is in NORM position the ACTION switch governs the laser emission. When switch is in CONT position the laser emissions are continuous. To disable the subsystem place switch in OFF position. Power (28 Vdc) is supplied to the AIM-1/EXL subsystem through the TURRET DRIVE MOTOR circuit breaker 19CB7 located on the pilot armament circuit breaker panel.

TM 1-1520-236-10

INDIRECT FIRE (ADI & HSI) FOR MK66 WITH M151 AND M274 WARHEADS

RANGE (M)	PITCH ATTITUDE QE 71 mils	TIME OF FLIGHT (SECONDS)	MAXIMUM TRAJECTORY HEIGHT (FEET)	*MAXIMUM TRAJECTORY RANGE (METERS)
800	-2	1.7	7	371
2,000	-1	4.0	49	1,136
2,800	0	6.2	127	1,665
3,400	+1	8.1	231	2,037
3,900	+2	9.8	355	2,359
4,600	+4	12.9	650	2,827
5,200	+6	15.7	992	3,231
5,600	+8	18.3	1,374	3,504
6,400	+12	23.2	2,233	3,988
6,900	+16	27.6	3,196	4,371
7,500	+21	32.9	4,559	4,693

* At this range, the rocket will reach maximum trajectory height.

INDIRECT FIRE (ADI & HSI) FOR MK66 WITH M261 AND M267 WARHEADS (SUBMUNITIONS)

RANGE (M)	PITCH ATTITUDE QE 71 mils
1,000	+10
1,500	+7
2,000	+6
2,500	+6
3,000	+6
3,500	+7
4,000	+7
4,500	+8
5,000	+10
5,500	+11
6,000	+13
6,500	+15
7,000	+18

NOTE: Submunition expulsion is the result of fuse function, and is based on range/fuse time; launch attitude provides optimum downrange rocket/warhead altitude for the RAD deployment/fuse arming and dispersion pattern of the submunitions.

Figure 4-19. Indirect Fire (ADI & HSI) for MK66 Rockets

TM 1-1520-236-10

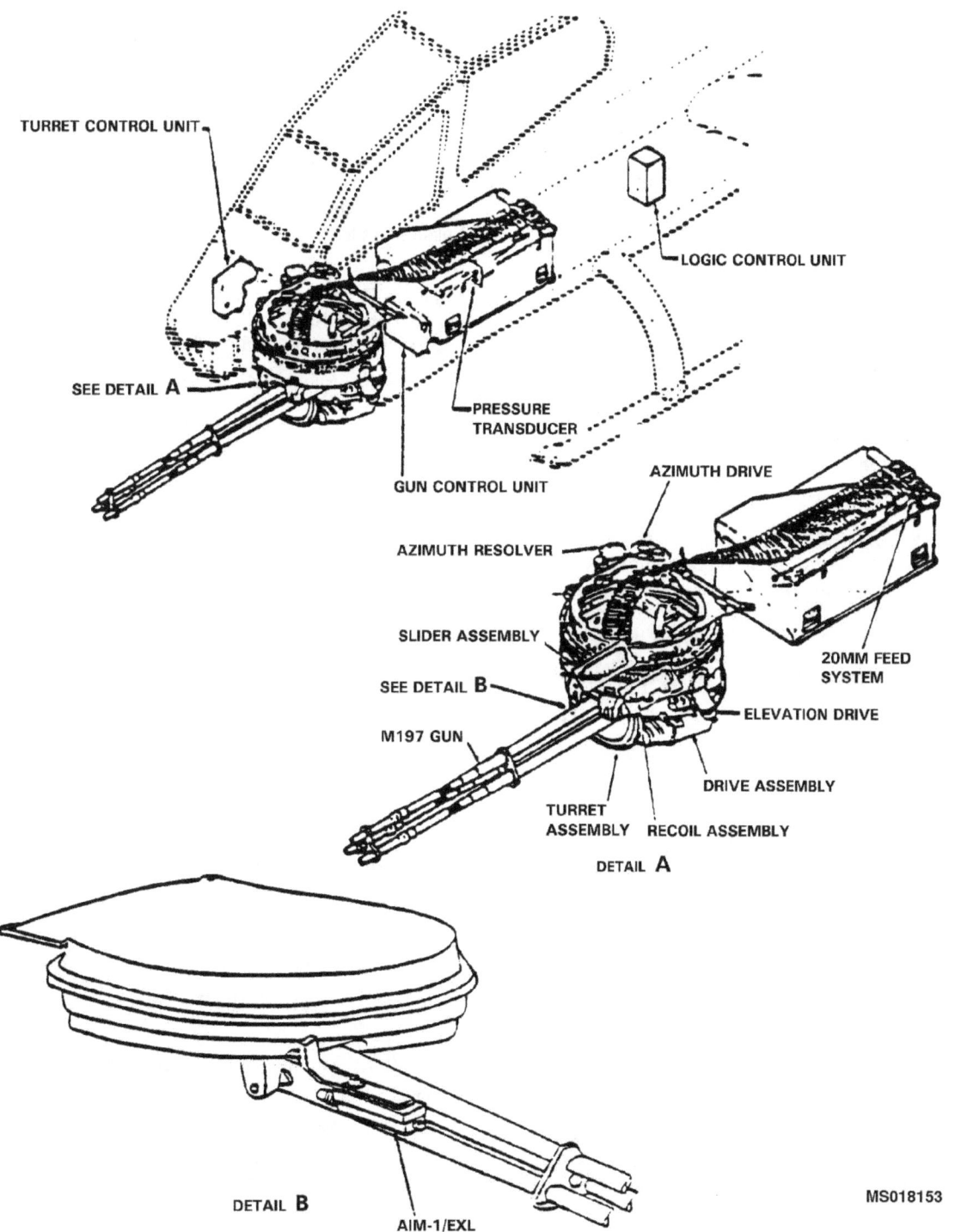

Figure 4-20. Universal Turret Components

4-39

4-21. TURRET OPERATION – INFLIGHT PROCEDURES.

> **CAUTION**
>
> The M-197 gun is restricted to a firing schedule not to exceed a 450-round burst with a minimum of 6 minutes cooling time prior to firing the remaining 300 rounds.

> **CAUTION**
>
> Prior to reducing N2 below 91 percent, insure the TCP MODE SELECT switch is in the STBY TOW position to prevent any gun movement and possible damage to the SCA as the TCP cycles through BIT.

NOTE

The possibility of interruptive fire exists at any time the gun is fired at a near 0 degree azimuth with the helicopter in an extreme nose low altitude. This is due to the gun reaching the upper limit.

a. Turret Firing (TSU) is accomplished as follows:

(1) MASTER ARM switch – ARM.

(2) WPN CONTR switch – GUNNER.

(3) RECOIL switch – COMPEN.

(4) RECOIL COMP switch – As desired.

(5) Gunner-RANGE switch – As desired.

(6) TSU/GUN SLEW RATE – As desired.

(7) LASER SAFE/TURRET DEPR LIMIT switch – OFF.

(8) TCP MODE SELECT switch – TSU/GUN.

(9) SHC/ACQ/TRK/STOW switch – TRK.

NOTE

TSU FLIR display dims when GNR misc control panel A RMT LTG switch is set to other than OFF. Display dims further when NVG switch is set to NVG.

(10) Gunner LHG HI LO MAG switch – As desired.

(11) **CN** LHG MAG switch – As desired.

(12) LHG ACTION switch – Press.

(13) TSU reticle – On target.

(14) LHG TRIGGER – Press.

(15) LHG TRIGGER – Release.

(16) LHG ACTION switch – Release.

(17) MASTER ARM switch – STBY.

b. Turret firing (Gunner Helmet Sight) is accomplished as follows:

TCP MODE SELECT switch must be in OFF position or with MODE SELECT switch in TSU/GUN position the SHC/ACQ/TRK/STOW switch must be in STOW position to fire the turret with GHS.

(1) Pilot MASTER ARM switch – ARM.

(2) WPN CONTR switch – GUNNER.

(3) RECOIL switch – COMPEN.

(4) RECOIL COMP switch – As desired.

(5) Gunner RANGE switch – As desired.

(6) LASER SAFE/TURRET DEPR LIMIT switch – OFF.

(7) LHG ACTION switch – Press.

(8) GHS reticle – On target.

(9) LHG TRIGGER switch – Press.

(10) LHG TRIGGER switch – Release.

(11) LHG ACTION switch – Release.

(12) MASTER ARM switch – STBY.

c. Turret firing (Gunner Helmet Sight Pilot Override) is accomplished as follows:

(1) PLT ORIDE switch – PLT ORIDE.

(2) Gunner RANGE switch – As desired.

(3) LASER SAFE/TURRET DEP LIMIT switch – OFF.

(4) Gunner cyclic TRIGGER ACTION switch – Press.

(5) GHS reticle – On target.

(6) Gunner cyclic TRIGGER TURRET FIRE switch – Press.

(7) Gunner cyclic TRIGGER TURRET FIRE switch – Release.

(8) Gunner cyclic TRIGGER ACTION switch – release.

(9) TCP – STBY TOW.

(10) PLT ORIDE switch – OFF.

d. Turret firing (Pilot Helmet Sight) is accomplished as follows (WPN CONTR switch – PILOT):

(1) MASTER ARM switch – ARM.

(2) PILOT RANGE switch – As desired.

(3) WPN CONTR switch – PILOT.

(4) RECOIL switch – COMPEN.

(5) RECOIL COMP switch – As desired.

(6) LASER SAFE/TURRET DEPR LIMIT switch – OFF.

(7) Pilot cyclic TRIGGER ACTION switch – Press.

(8) PHS reticle – On target.

(9) Pilot cyclic TRIGGER TURRET FIRE switch – Press.

(10) Pilot cyclic TRIGGER TURRET FIRE switch – Release.

(11) Pilot cyclic TRIGGER ACTION switch – Release.

(12) MASTER ARM switch – STBY.

e. Turret firing (Pilot Helmet Sight) is accomplished as follows (WPN CONTR switch – GUNNER).

NOTE

This method allows the pilot to fire the turret using his helmet sight while the gunner is targeting with the TSU. Switch positions are the same except the following:

(1) Pilot WPN CONTR switch – GUNNER.

(2) TCP MODE SELECT – STBY TOW, ARMED MAN or AUTO.

f. Turret firing (Pilot Fixed Gun) accomplished as follows:

(1) MASTER ARM switch – ARM.

(2) WPN CONTR switch – FIXED.

(3) Pilot cyclic TRIGGER ACTION switch – Press.

(4) HUD fire control reticle – On target.

(5) Pilot cyclic TRIGGER TURRET FIRE switch – Press. The FCC provides no ballistic compensation for the FIXED MODE. The GUN is aligned to the boresight reference symbol in the HUD approximately 1350 meters.

(6) Pilot cyclic TRIGGER TURRET FIRE switch – Release.

(7) Pilot cyclic TRIGGER ACTION switch – Release.

4-22. Wing Stores Jettison. Each of the four ejector racks are equipped with an electrically operated ballistic device to jettison the attached weapon during an emergency. Each device has two cartridges.

When four TOW missile launchers are installed on outboard wing stations the TOW missile launchers will jettison prior to the inboard stores regardless of the jettison select switches position.

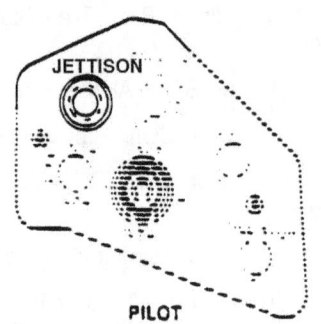
PILOT

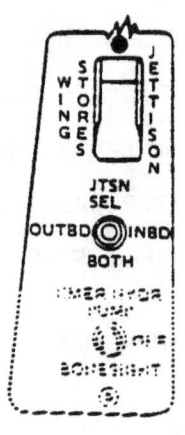
GUNNER

PILOT JETTISON

MS018154

PLT JETT Circuit Breaker Position	Pilot JETTISON SELECT Switch Position	Pilot Jettison Switch Position	Wing Stores Jettisoned	
			2 TOW	4 TOW
Off	•	•	None	None
PLT JETT (On)	Inbd	Pressed	Inbd	Both
PLT JETT (On)	Outbd	Pressed	Outbd	Outbd
PLT JETT (On)	Inbd/Outbd	Pressed	Both	Both

GUNNER JETTISON

GNR JETT Circuit Breaker Position	Gunner JTSN SEL Switch Position	Gunner Wing Stores Jettison Switch Position	Wing Stores Jettisoned	
			2 TOW	4 TOW
Off	•	•	None	None
GNR JETT (On)	Inbd	Up (On)	Inbd	Both
GNR JETT (On)	Outbd	Up (On)	Outbd	Outbd
GNR JETT (On)	Both	Up (On)	Both	Both

*Switch position makes no difference.

In the BOTH jettison sequence the outboard stores leave first followed by the inboard.

The electrical circuit interface will allow jettison of the inboard stores if only two missile launch tubes are installed on the outboard racks.

Figure 4-21. Wing Stores Jettison

4-23. Airborne Laser Tracker (ALT). The airborne laser tracker (Figure 4-23) is used to automatically scan the terrain, detect and lock onto a laser designated target. The ALT automatically tracks the target and when commanded, aims the telescopic sight unit to the ALT line of sight. The ALT consists of a receiver, electronics assembly, and control panel. The receiver is a barrel-shaped housing with a glass dome that contains the laser seeker, and is located in forward pylon fairing assembly. The electronics assembly contains the ALT plug-in modules and power supply, and is located in the aircraft behind the receiver. The control panel (Figure 4-22) contains the ALT controls and indicators, and is located in the pilot's cockpit.

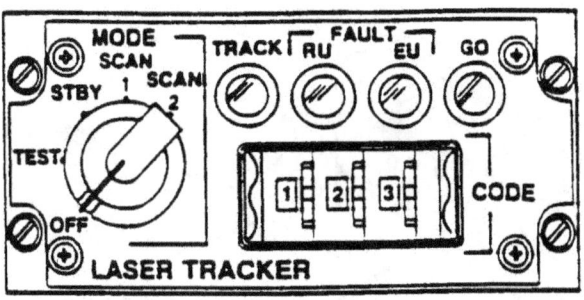

MS018155

ITEM	FUNCTION
MODE SWITCH	OFF - TURNS ALT POWER OFF (TRACKER GIMBALS ARE FREE TO MOVE). TEST STARTS ALT SELF-TEST. STBY - CENTERS ALT OPTICS (ALT READY TO SCAN). SCAN 1 - SCANS 0 TO -8.3 DEGREES ELEVATION AND ±15 DEGREES AZIMUTH. SCAN 2 - SCANS 0 TO -25 DEGREES ELEVATION AND ±60 DEGREES AZIMUTH.
TRACK LAMP	LIGHTS WHEN SYSTEM ACQUIRES A REFLECTED LASER SIGNAL FROM TARGET. SYSTEM MUST BE IN SCAN 1 OR SCAN 2 MODE. REFLECTED LASER SIGNAL CODE MUST MATCH CODE SELECTED AT CODE THUMBWHEEL SWITCHES. TRACK LAMP ALSO LIGHTS IN TEST MODE.
FAULT LAMPS	RU - LIGHTS IN TEST MODE IN RECEIVER IS DEFECTIVE. EU - LIGHTS IN TEST MODE IF ELECTRONICS ASSEMBLY IS DEFECTIVE.
GO LAMP	LIGHTS IN TEST MODE IF SELF-TEST IS GOOD. LIGHTS WITH TRACK LAMP AFTER 25 SECONDS. THE GO LAMP WILL TURN OFF AGAIN AFTER 30 SECONDS.
CODE THUMB-WHEEL SWITCH	SELECTS A CODED 3 DIGIT NUMBER THAT MATCHES CODE OF TARGET'S LASER SIGNAL.

NOTE

If RU FAULT or EU FAULT lamps light in TEST mode, rotate MODE switch to STBY and back to TEST. If either lamp lights again, refer to higher category of maintenance. The TRACK lamp may light a few times in the TEST mode.

NOTE

It will take about 25 seconds until GO lamp and TRACK lamp light. The GO lamp goes off after about 30 seconds.

Figure 4-22. ALT Control Panel

TM 1-1520-236-10

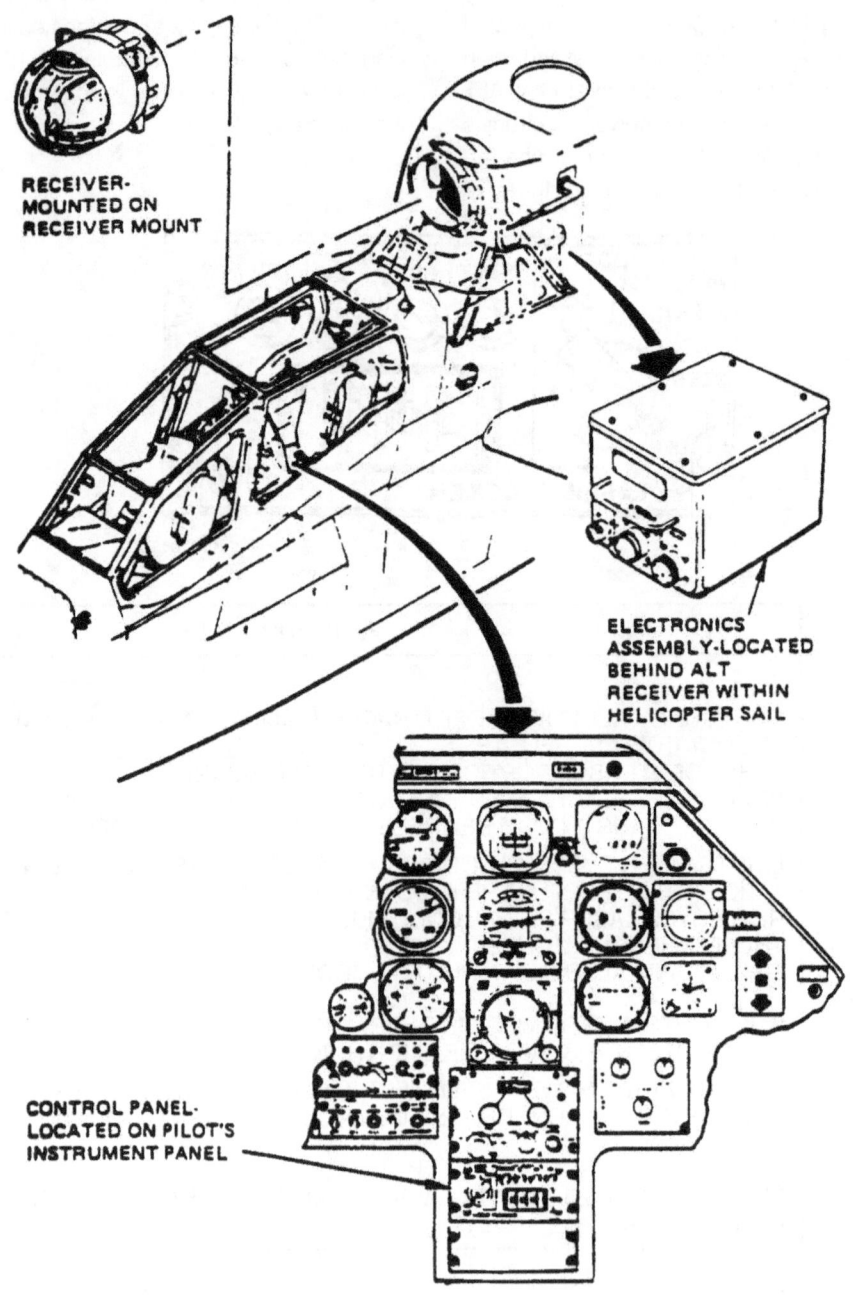

Figure 4-23. ALT Major Components - Helicopter Locations

★ 4-24. ARMAMENT – SYSTEMS CHECK.

WARNING

The following checks shall not be performed with TOW missiles installed. If missiles are installed TOW arming handle(s) will be in the full up (safed) position.

CAUTION

Do not drive the turret to the stops while performing the armament system checks.

a. TOW built-in-test – Ensure TOW completes BIT (Only performed in STBY TOW). Check as follows:

(1) TCP – TSU/SCA/EPS/MCA indicators display black on black. White on black indicates failed BIT.

(2) TCP BIT switch – Press and hold. Check for battle flags A\G\R displayed in the TSU. Pilot checks for ascend/descend arrows and pre-launch constraints box displayed in HUD.

NOTE

TOW BIT override may be accomplished by placing ATS switch to track or by placing TCP to an armed TOW mode.

(3) TCP BIT switch – Release. BIT completed within approximately 120 seconds. Indicator moves from TEST to PWR ON at completion.

(4) Barber pole indicators – Display black on black.

(5) TCP missile status indicator displays Barber poles.

b. TSU tracking – Ensure TSU moves at fast rate in LOW MAG and at slow rate in HI MAG, check as follows:

(1) TSU LHG HI/LOW MAG switch – LOW MAG.

(2) SHC ATS switch – Track and check TSU focus as required.

(3) SHC – Press. Check TSU full travel left, right, up, and down. SHC is released after each check to ensure TSU reticle is stationary and does not rotate.

Pilot confirms Gunner LOS on HUD indicates left, right, up, and down.

(4) SHC ATS switch – STOW.

(5) TSU LHG HI/LOW MAG switch – HI MAG.

(6) SHC ATS switch – TRK.

(7) SHC – Press to the right or left.

(8) TSU LHG action switch – Press and hold. TSU continues moving (Motion compensation check).

(9) SHC – Release. TSU continues to move.

(10) TSU LHG action switch – Release. TSU stops.

(11) TSU LHG HI/LOW MAG switch – LOW MAG.

(12) SHC ATS switch – STOW.

c. HSS built-in-test – Check as follows:

(1) HS arm assemblies – Attach to BIT magnets.

(2) Test segment lights. All panels illuminate.

(3) HSS BIT switch – BIT. Test passed if Go light illuminates, failed if PLT/GNR/EIA lights illuminate. If failed, ensure HSS arm assemblies are secure on BIT magnets, check all cable connections, and press BIT again.

NOTE

If continued failure occurs, recycle MASTER ARM switch to clear BIT fail indication. HSS will not function properly with BIT fail indication preset.

d. HSS to TURRET – Check. Ensure turret follows HSS reticle line of sight.

(1) HS arm assemblies – Attach to helmet. Extend eyepiece over eye, adjust reticle brightness and test.

(2) TCP Mode select switch – TSU GUN.

(3) Gunner looks left or right at least 45 degrees. TSU LHG action switch press. Reticle flashes until gun line is coincident with HS line of sight. LHG action switch release.

(4) TCP Mode select switch – STBY TOW.

(5) PLT ORIDE switch – ORIDE. Press cyclic action switch and repeat steps in c. above.

(6) TCP Mode select switch – TSU GUN once the TOW BIT is completed.

(7) WPN CONTR switch – Pilot.

(8) Pilot looks left or right at least 45 degrees. Cyclic action switch press. Reticle flashes until gun line is coincident with HS line of sight. Cyclic action switch release.

(9) WPN CONTR switch – Gunner.

e. **HSS to TSU and TSU to TURRET** – Ensure TSU follows HSS line of sight and turret follows TSU line of sight, check as follows:

(1) Gunner's HS reticle on a target at least 45 degrees to the left or right.

(2) SHC ATS switch – ACQ and release. Gunner HS reticle retracts. TSU displays target.

(3) LHG action switch – Press. GUN flag flashes until gun line is coincident with TSU, LHG action switch release, turret stows.

(4) Gunner's HS eyepiece – Extend over eye.

WARNING

The next step arms the system. Do not press the gunner cyclic trigger.

(5) Pilot HS reticle – On a target and announces Gunner target.

(6) ACQ switch – PHS and release. Gunner's eyepiece retracts, and target is dislayed in TSU.

(7) SHC ATS switch – STOW.

f. **RMS built-in-test** – Ensure RMS passes a BIT, check as follows:

(1) Test switch – Press. Eight 8s and zone arm lights illuminate and then 7s appear for each LRU. Release test switch.

g. **HUD** – Check as follows:

(1) Mode switch – Test. All symbols displayed except Stadiametric reticle.

(2) Mode switch – NORM.

(3) RKT switch – DIR then IND check FCRs.

(4) Night Filter contr – Day position (Green for day/Red for night).

h. **ALT** – Check as follows:

(1) Mode switch – STBY.

(2) Press to test lamps – Test.

(3) Mode switch – Test Approximately 25 sec. GO and TRACK lights illuminate. GO light off after approximately 30 sec.

(4) Mode switch – As desired.

i. **(O) FLIR** – Check as follows:

(1) FCP Mode Indicator – Check POWER ON.

(2) FCP BIT Indicator – Check for black on black.

(3) POLARITY switch – As desired (White/Black Hot)

(4) IR LEVEL control knob – Adjust approximately to the 2 o'clock position.

(5) IR GAIN control – Adjust approximately to the 2 o'clock position.

(6) LHG MAG switch – NIGHT.

(7) Gunner – Check for FLIR picture, adjust LHG focus as desired, adjust IR Level and IR Gain as desired.

(8) LHG MAG switch – As desired.

NOTE

FLIR subsystem can be turned ON or OFF at any time without damage to the system.

NOTE

FLIR BIT is performed once automatically upon power up. Thereafter it is performed only when FCP OFF/ON/BIT switch is moved to BIT position and released.

NOTE

If FLIR BIT indicator FPS/FMT/TSU show white, reinitiate FLIR BIT. If second BIT fails, turn system OFF, and make appropriate write-up on DA Form 2403-13-1.

★ 4-25. GUNNERY CHECKLIST – ENGINE RUN-UP PROCEDURE.

NOTE

Units may modify the following checks because of possible range constraints or safety reasons.

NOTE

The following procedure is only used when the helicopter has been shutdown IAW Chapter 8 and paragraph 4-27 Engine Shutdown Cold Arming procedure.

a. Wing store pins – Remove.

b. Grounding cable – Remove.

c. Ground crews – Clear.

d. ANTI-COLLISION – ON (indicates helicopter is not safe to approach).

e. TURRET STOW circuit breaker – IN.

f. WING STORE PWR circuit breaker – IN.

g. JETTISON SELECT switches – OUTBD/INBD.

h. Continue with paragraph 8-23. ENGINE RUNUP.

★ 4-26. GUNNERY CHECKLIST – ENGINE SHUTDOWN HOT/COLD ARMING PROCEDURES.

NOTE

Units may modify the following checks because of possible range constraints or safety reasons.

NOTE

Steps a. through k. below apply to both HOT and COLD rearming procedures.

a. JETTISON SELECT switches – OFF.

b. ANTI-COLLISION – OFF (indicates aircraft is safe to approach).

c. Ground crews – Approach aircraft.

d. Wing stores pins – Installed.

e. Grounding cable – Install.

f. TOW launcher – Missile arming lever up (if TOW missiles are installed).

g. W2P1 – Disconnected.

WARNING

Stray voltage check is required prior to loading rockets. First stray voltage check of the day does not satisfied this requirement.

h. Stray voltage – Check (if loading rockets).

(1) RMS ZONE INVENTORY selector – 6PD.

(2) MASTER ARM switch – ARMED.

(3) FCC circuit breaker – ON.

(4) RMS RATE selector – "A" position.

(5) RMS ZONE ARMING switches – ARMED.

(6) Stray voltage check – Completed.

(7) FCC circuit breaker – OFF.

(8) MASTER ARM switch – OFF.

i. RMS ZONE INVENTORY selector – As required.

j. RMS RATE selector – As desired.

k. WING STORE PWR circuit breaker – OFF.

NOTE

If performing COLD ARMING PROCEDURES continue with paragraph 8-28 ENGINE SHUTDOWN item number 13. SCAS POWER switch - OFF.

If performing HOT ARMING PROCEDURES continue with step 1. below once arming/rearming is completed.

l. W2P1 – Connect.

m. TOW launcher – Missile arming lever down.

n. Grounding cable – Remove.

o. Wing stores pins – Remove.

p. Ground crew – Clear.

q. ANTI-COLLISION – ON (indicates aircraft is not safe to approach).

r. HUD PWR – STBY.

s. HSS LINKAGE – As desired.

t. LASER SAFE/TURRET DEPR LIMIT switch – As desired.

u. TUR SLEW switch – NORM.

v. MASTER ARM – STBY.

TM 1-1520-236-10

w. TCP switch – STBY TOW.

x. Throttle – 100%.

y. TURRET STOW circuit breaker – IN.

z. ADS PWR circuit breaker – IN.

aa. FCC switch – ON.

ab. WING STORE PWR circuit breaker – ON.

ac. JETTISON SELECT switches – OUTBD/INBD.

ad. HUD PWR switch – ON.

ae. FORCE TRIM switch – OFF.

af. BEFORE TAKE OFF – CHECK.

4-27. ALT – INFLIGHT PROCEDURES.

a. Pilot ALT control panel – Set as follows:

(1) CODE Thumbwheel switches – Set to assigned code.

NOTE

Prior to moving MODE switch to SCAN 1 or SCAN 2, allow 20 seconds for ALT gyros to warm up.

(2) MODE switch – SCAN 1 for scanning 0 to -8.3 degrees elevation and ±15 degrees azimuth or SCAN 2 for scanning 0 to -25 degrees elevation and ±60 degrees azimuth.

NOTE

When the ALT locks onto your target, the TRACK lamp will light. To maintain lock on, keep the target forward (azimuth: 180°, elevation: 30° up and 60° down) of your aircraft. If TRACK lamp goes off, the ALT has lost lock on. In this case, the ALT will automatically resume the scanning mode selected on the MODE switch.

b. Maneuver switch – Direction of target.

c. TRACK lamp – Verify on.

NOTE

If the ALT lock on is lost in Step (1), the TSU will move full right and down, and it may be necessary to recycle to the STOW position with the ACQ TRACK STOW switch before another acquisition can be initiated.

d. Gunner ACQ switch – ALT position to aim TS to ALT line of sight.

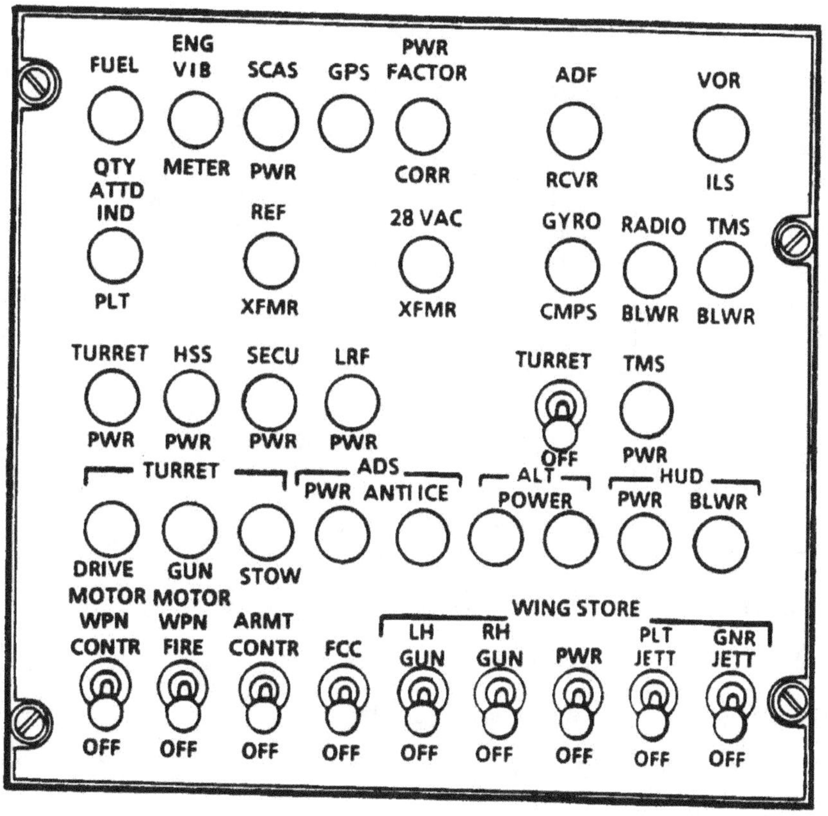

Figure 4-24. Pilot Armament Circuit Breakers (Sheet 1 of 2)

CIRCUIT BREAKER	FUNCTION - Applies Power to and Protects Circuit for:
REF XFMR	Reference transformer.
TMS BLWR	TOW missile system blower.
TURRET PWR	Turret power.
HSS PWR	Helmet sight subsystem power.
SECU PWR	Servo electronic control unit power.
LRF PWR	Laser rangefinder power.
TMS PWR	TOW missile system power.

TURRET
  DRIVE MOTOR
 	
  GUN MOTOR
  STOW
	
	Turret drive motor.
	AIM-1/EXL IR laser gunsight subsystem.
	Turret gun motor.
	Turret stow control.

ADS
  PWR
  ANTI-ICE
	
	Air data subsystem power.
	Air data subsystem anti-ice.

ALT POWER	 Airborne laser tracker power.

HUD
  PWR
  BLWR
	
	Heads up display power.
	Heads up display blower.

WPN CONTR	Master arm switch standby power.
WPN FIRE	Master arm switch fire power.
ARMT CONTR	Gun control assembly.
FCC	Fire control computer.

WING STORE
  LH GUN
  RH GUN
  PWR
  PLT JETT
  GNR JETT
	
	Left inboard wing gun pod firing.
	Right inboard wing gun pod firing.
	Left/right inboard/outboard rocket firing.
	Wing store jettison - pilot.
	Wing store jettison - gunner.

Figure 4-24. Pilot Armament Circuit Breakers (Sheet 2 of 2)

SECTION III. ACTIVE AND PASSIVE DEFENSE EQUIPMENT

4-28. WIRE STRIKE PROTECTION SYSTEM.

The wire strike protection system (Figure 4-25) consists of three cutter assemblies, a windshield channel and a nose deflector. An upper cutter assembly is mounted on top of the pilot station, forward of the ADF loop antenna. A chin cutter assembly is mounted under the nose just forward of the gunner station. A lower cutter assembly is mounted on the forward fuselage, under the ammunition compartment. The wire strike protection system is designed to protect the helicopter from wire obstructions at low levels of flight.

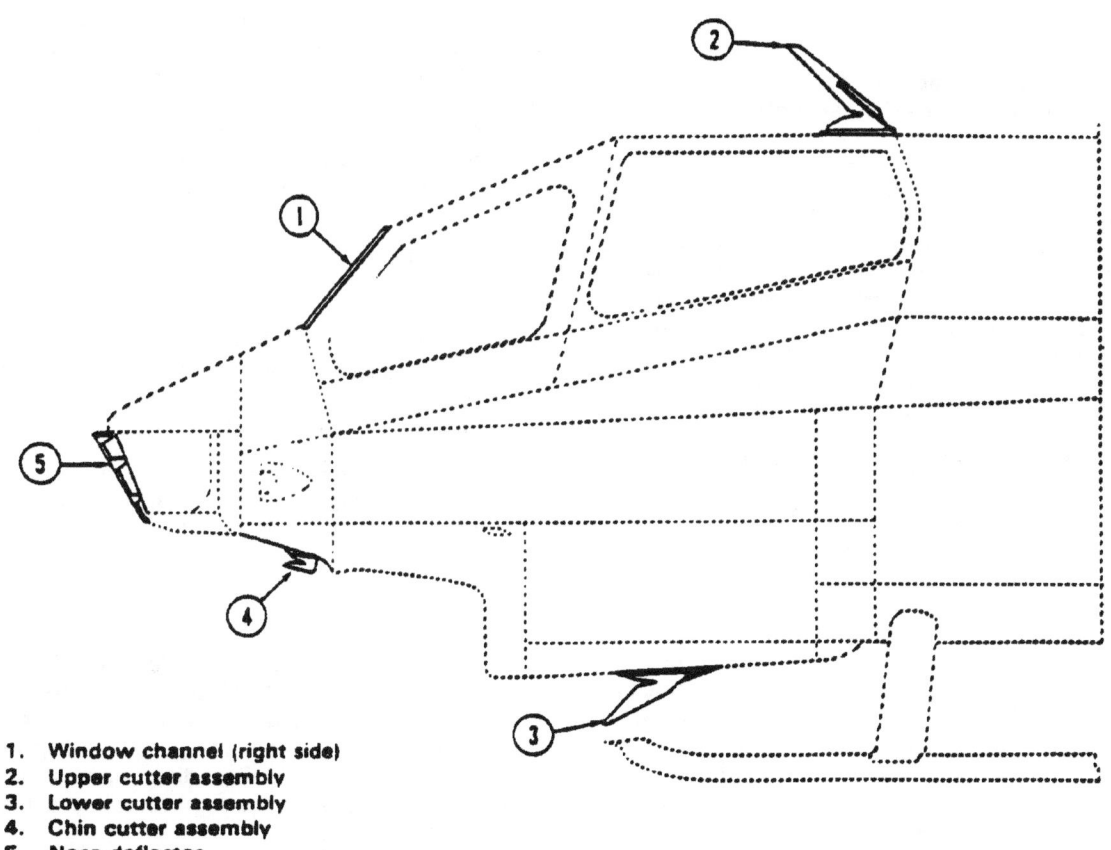

1. Window channel (right side)
2. Upper cutter assembly
3. Lower cutter assembly
4. Chin cutter assembly
5. Nose deflector

Figure 4-25. Wire Strike Protection System

4-29. DESCRIPTION OF DISPENSER, GENERAL PURPOSE, M-130.

The dispenser, general purpose, aircraft, M130 (NSN 1095-01-036-6886) consists of a single system (dispenser assembly, payload module assembly, electronics module, and dispenser control panel) designed to dispense chaff M-1 from U.S. Army helicopters and fixed wing aircraft. The system, common to Army aircraft, provides effective survival countermeasures against radar guided weapon systems threats. The dispenser system M130 has the capability of dispensing up to 30 chaff cartridges.

NOTE

The flare dispenser function is not employed in the AH-1 helicopter.

The dispenser system functions in the following manner: When a crew member sights a missile launch or receives a radar warning, he will press a firing switch. The aircraft's power supply (28V dc) will immediately pulse (via the dispenser control panel) the programmer section of the electronics module, and signal the dispenser assembly. This activates the sequencer assembly, completing the circuit to the contact pin in the breech assembly. The current in this completed circuit initiates the impulse cartridge forcing the chaff out of the payload.

4-30. DISPENSER SUB-SYSTEMS.

a. Dispenser Control Panel. The dispenser control panel (DCP) contains a manual ARM-SAFE switch which is provided to arm the dispenser system. When the ARM-SAFE switch is moved to the ARM position and the safety flag pin(s) has been removed from the system safety switch(s), the ARM lamp will light. The control panel counters indicate the number of chaff (cartridges) remaining in the payload module. The counters are manually set prior to each mission to agree with the number of chaffs loaded. The two-way MANUAL, PROGRAMMED switch controls the firing of chaff. When the switch is in PROGRAMMED position, the number of bursts (series of shots) per salvo (any number of bursts) fired is automatically controlled by the preset programmer. The MANUAL position of the switch by-passes the programmer and fires one chaff cartridge each time the firing switch is activated.

b. Dispenser Assembly. The dispenser assembly contains the breech assembly, flare sensor, selector switch for flare or chaff (marked C or F), reset switch, and a housing containing the sequencer assembly. The sequencer assembly receives power through the firing switches circuit and furnishes pulses to each of the 30 contacts of the breech assembly, in sequential order 1 through 30, thus firing each of the impulse cartridges.

c. Payload Module Assembly. The payload module assembly consists of the payload module and retaining plate assembly. The payload module has 30 chambers which will accept either chaff or flares. Flares or chaff are loaded through the studded end of the payload module, one per chamber, and secured in place by the retaining plate assembly. The payload module assembly is assembled to the dispenser assembly.

d. Electronics Module Assembly. The EM contains a programmer and a cable assembly which includes a 28-volt supply receptacle and a safety switch activated by insertion of the safety pin with flag assembly. On some aircraft installations the 28-volt supply receptacles and the safety switch have been included in the aircraft cable and are therefore remote from the EM. The programmer consists of a programming circuit which allows for the setting of chaff burst number, chaff salvo number, chaff burst interval and chaff salvo interval.

4-31. CHAFF DISPENSER, M-130.

a. The function of the M130 chaff countermeasure system is to provide an effective airborne countermeasure against enemy infrared missiles and radar controlled weapons, thereby reducing an enemy's capability to damage or destroy U.S. Army aircraft.

b. Aircrew members are required to maintain visual coverage around the aircraft when in a hostile area for IR missiles that have been launched against the aircraft. The crew member who observes a missile launch will initiate the dispensing of the counter-measure flares in accordance with prescribed tactics for the aircraft.

c. The aircraft's radar warning receiver (RWR) will provide the alert to the pilot and co-pilot when the aircraft is being tracked by a radar-guided anti-aircraft weapon system. To be effective as a radar decoy the dispensing of chaff must be accompanied with an appropriate aircraft maneuver in accordance with prescribed tactics for the aircraft.

d. Upon receiving an alert from the aircraft radar warning system, the pilot or gunner will dispense chaff by depressing his chaff dispensing switch and initiate an evasive maneuver. The number of burst/salvo and number of salvo/program and their intervals will be set into the programmer, as indicated above, prior to take-off. If desired, the operator may override the programmed operational mode and fire chaff countermeasures manually. Manual operation is achieved by changing the position of the two-way MANUAL PROGRAMMED switch from PROGRAMMED to MANUAL and then depressing firing switch.

e. The M130 dispenser system should not be fired unless a missile launch is observed or radar-guided weapon system is detected with lock on. If a system malfunction is suspected, the aircraft commander may authorize attempt(s) to dispense chaff to test the system.

f. The crew member who observes the missile launch or a radar warning indication and dispenses the first flares or chaff will advise the other crew members that a missile launch has been observed or a radar warning signal has been received and that a flare or chaff has been dispensed. Other crew members will continue watching for additional missile launches.

g. The chaff dispenser will eject chaff one at a time in the manual mode or according to the setting of the programmer when set in the PROGRAM mode. The following program settings are provided.

```
Number of burst/salvo            1 2 3 4 6 8
Burst interval (sec)         0.1   0.2   0.3   0.4
Number salvo/program 1 2 4 8 C (Continuous)
Salvo interval (sec)           1 2 3 4 5 8 R
R = Random (sec) = 3 5 2 4 3 5 2 4 3 5
```

NOTE

The small round dot on each control knob shall be aligned with each setting number as desired.

h. Crew Responsibilities.

(1) Perform daily PRE-FLIGHT/RE-ARM tests.

(2) Confirm that the number of chaff cartridges in the payload module are the same as shown on the dispenser control panel counter(s).

(3) Confirm chaff flare (CF) selector switch on dispenser assembly is set to proper dispense mode.

(4) Confirm pre-planned chaff program is properly set on electronics module if system is to dispense chaff.

(5) Remove safety pins(s) and flag assembly(s) prior to boarding aircraft.

(6) After the aircraft is airborne the aircraft commander assumes responsibility for arming the M130 system.

TM 1-1520-236-10

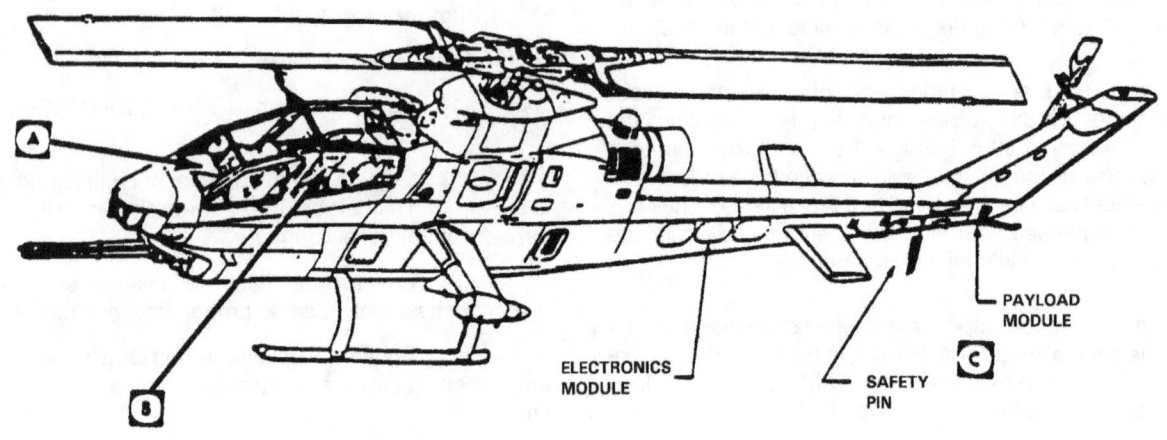

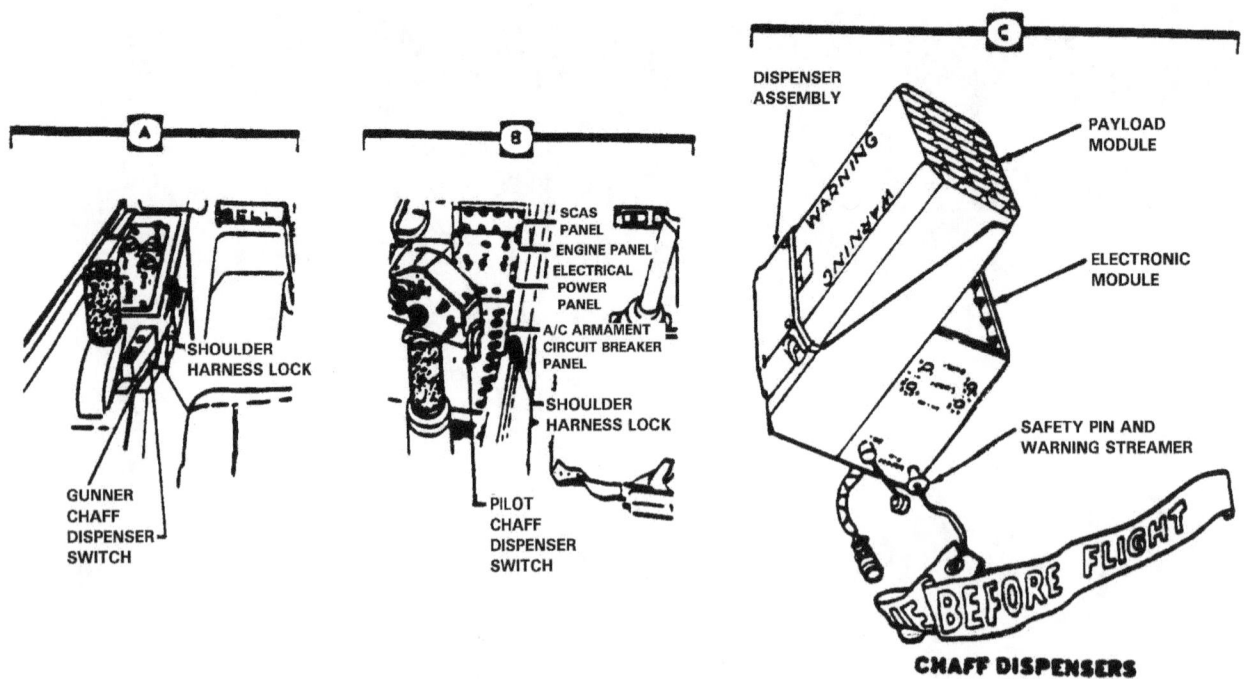

Figure 4-26. Chaff Dispenser, Gunner/Pilot

4-54

TM 1-1520-236-10

CHAPTER 5

OPERATING LIMITS AND RESTRICTIONS

SECTION I. GENERAL

5-1. PURPOSE.

This chapter identifies or refers to all important operating limits and restrictions that shall be observed during ground and flight operations.

5-2. GENERAL.

The operating limitations set forth in this chapter are the direct results of design analysis, tests, and operating experiences. Compliance with these limits will allow the pilot to safely perform the assigned missions and to derive maximum utility from the helicopter. Limits concerning maneuvers, weight, and center of gravity limitations are also covered in this chapter.

5-3. EXCEEDING OPERATIONAL LIMITS.

  a. Anytime an operational limit is exceeded, an appropriate entry shall be made on DA Form 2408-13-1. Entry shall state what limit or limits were exceeded, range, time above limits, and any additional data that would aid maintenance personnel in the maintenance action that may be required.

  b. The instruments in the pilot's station are the primary reference for determining aircraft operating limits.

5-4. MINIMUM CREW REQUIREMENTS.

The minimum crew requirement consists of a pilot whose station is in the aft cockpit.

SECTION II. SYSTEM LIMITS

5-5. INSTRUMENT MARKINGS (Figure 5-1).

  a. **Instrument Marking Color Codes.** Operating limitations and ranges are illustrated by the colored markings which appear on the dial faces of engine, flight, and utility system instruments. RED markings on the dial faces of these instruments indicate the limit above or below which continued operation is likely to cause damage or shorten life. The GREEN markings on instruments indicate the safe or normal range of operation. The YELLOW markings on instruments indicate the range when special attention should be given to the operation covered by the instrument. Operation is permissible in the yellow range, provided no other operating limit is exceeded.

  b. **Chevron.** A chevron (<) indicates above operating limits and to go in direction of point. The saw tooth red line is placed on the dial face with respect to the operating limit as follows:

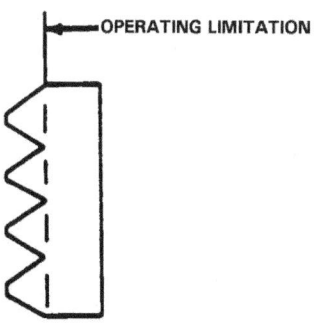

MS018160

5-6. ROTOR LIMITATIONS.

  a. **Normal Operating Range.** Refer to Figure 5-1.

5-1

TM 1-1520-236-10

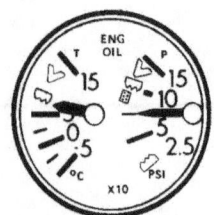

ENGINE OIL PRESSURE

▦ 80 to 100 PSI Continuous Operation
⌒ 25 PSI Minimum
⌣ 100 PSI Maximum

ENGINE OIL TEMPERATURE

⌣ 93°C maximum below 30°C FAT
100°C maximum at or above 30°C FAT
(Write-up is required any time 93°C is exceeded.)

TURBINE GAS TEMPERATURE

▦ 400°C to 820°C Continuous Operation
(Normal Power)
▩ 820°C to 880°C 30 Minute Limit
(Military Power)
⌣ 880°C thru 950°C Transient for
Starting and Acceleration (5 sec)
○ 950°C Maximum for Starting

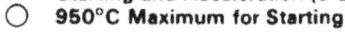

GAS PRODUCER TACHOMETER (N_1)

⌣ 106 Percent Maximum

TORQUE PERCENT

▦ 0 To 88 Percent Continuous Operation
▩ 88 To 100 Percent 30 Minute
⌣ 100 Percent Calibrated Torque Maximum.
Refer to Chapter 7 for indicated torque values.

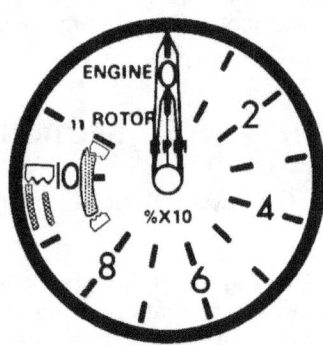

ROTOR TACHOMETER

⌒ 91 Percent RPM Minimum
▦ 91 to 100 Percent RPM Continuous Operation
⌣ 105 Percent RPM Maximum for Autorotation

ENGINE TACHOMETER (N_2)

▩ 91 to 97 Percent RPM Transient
▦ 97 to 100 Percent RPM Continuous Operation
⌣ 101.5 thru 104.5 percent RPM Maximum
Transient with TGT above 750°C (10 seconds).

104.5 Percent RPM Maximum

Legend	
▦	Green
▩	Yellow
☐	Red

MS018607

Figure 5-1. Instrument Markings (Sheet 1 of 2)

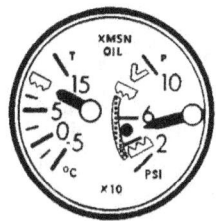

TRANSMISSION OIL PRESSURE

▽ 30 PSI Minimum
▓ 40 to 70 PSI Continuous Operation
▒ 30 to 40 PSI only below 91% (N_2)
△ 70 PSI Maximum

TRANSMISSION OIL TEMPERATURE

110°C Maximum

AIRSPEED

▒ 70 KIAS Not Applicable
▒ 100 KIAS Above 88% torque
▓ 0 TO 190 KIAS
△ 190 KIAS

See Figure 5-3 for Additional Limitations.

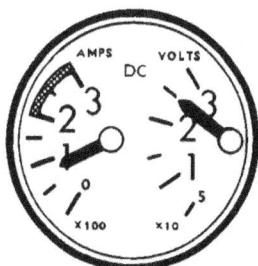

VOLT/AMP METER

▒ Transient. Operation in the yellow area may reduce generator life.

Legend	
▓	Green
▒	Yellow
☐	Red

Figure 5-1. Instrument Markings (Sheet 2 of 2)

b. Wind Limitations. The helicopter can be started in a maximum wind velocity of 30 knots or a maximum gust spread of 15 knots. Gust spreads are not normally reported. To obtain spread, compare minimum and maximum wind velocity.

SECTION III. POWER LIMITS

5-7. ENGINE LIMITATIONS (Figure 5-1).

a. Engine Overspeed: An engine overspeed exists under the following conditions:

(1) When N1 exceeds 106 percent.

(2) When N2 exceeds 104.5 percent.

(3) When N2 is between 101.5 percent and 104.5 percent for more than ten seconds with TGT above 750°C.

NOTE

The red line at 100 percent on the engine tachometer (Figure 5-1) represents the power-on rotor speed limit. Even though an engine write-up is not required unless the rpm limits of paragraph 5-7a (2) and (3) are exceeded, willful operation shall not be conducted with engine rpm above the redline limit of 100 percent. Maintenance test flights and operational checks IAW the appropriate test flight/maintenance manuals are not affected and will continue as required.

b. Maximum oil consumption is 0.3 gal. (2.4 pints) per hour.

c. Maximum starter energize time is 35 seconds with a one minute cooling time between start attempts with three attempts in any one hour.

d. Maximum TGT for environmental control system operation is 820°C.

e. 91 to 97 percent N2 transient.

SECTION IV. LOADING LIMITS

5-8. CENTER OF GRAVITY LIMITATIONS.

Center of gravity limits for the aircraft to which this manual applies and instructions for computation of the center of gravity are contained in Chapter 6.

NOTE

The lateral cg limits are 2.0 Inches (2 inches to the right and left of centerline of helicopter). These limits can not be exceeded due to normal weapon firing sequence and stores jettison procedure.

5-9. TURBULENCE RESTRICTIONS.

Intentional flight into severe or extreme turbulence is prohibited.

5-10. WEIGHT LIMITATIONS.

a. The maximum gross weight for this helicopter is 10,000 pounds.

b. Aircraft with single hydraulic system capability (collective authority check results) of less than 85 percent torque but more than 70 percent torque may be operated with restrictions. The aircraft configuration and gross weight shall be limited such that, in the event of a hydraulic system failure, a gross weight is achievable (jettisoning wing stores as appropriate) which does not exceed that corresponding to a 5 feet IGE hover capability at the recorded torque value.

SECTION V. AIRSPEED LIMITS

5-11. AIRSPEED LIMITATIONS.

a. Refer to Figure 5-2 for forward airspeed limits.

b. Sideward flight is 35 knots.

c. Rearward flight limit is 30 knots.

d. Maximum steady-state airspeed with SCAS OFF is 100 knots. With the SCAS inoperative and at an airspeed in excess of 100 KIAS, uncommanded roll, pitch and yaw oscillations will occur. The magnitude of the oscillation will increase as airspeed increases. Due to the nature of the oscillation, there is a tendency to introduce pilot induced oscillations which further aggravate the condition. Additionally, high power setting above 60 percent should be avoided when operating at airspeeds between 60 and 100 KIAS with inoperative roll and yaw SCAS channel because of instability.

e. Maximum steady-state autorotational airspeed is 120 knots.

f. All TOW series missiles shall be fired from a hover.

g. Airspeed limit for indicated torque greater than 88.0 percent is 100 KIAS. Airspeed limit for indicated torque greater than 62.5 percent is 150 KIAS.

5-12. CANOPY DOOR LIMITATIONS.

The canopy door can be opened only if engine RPM is at ground idle.

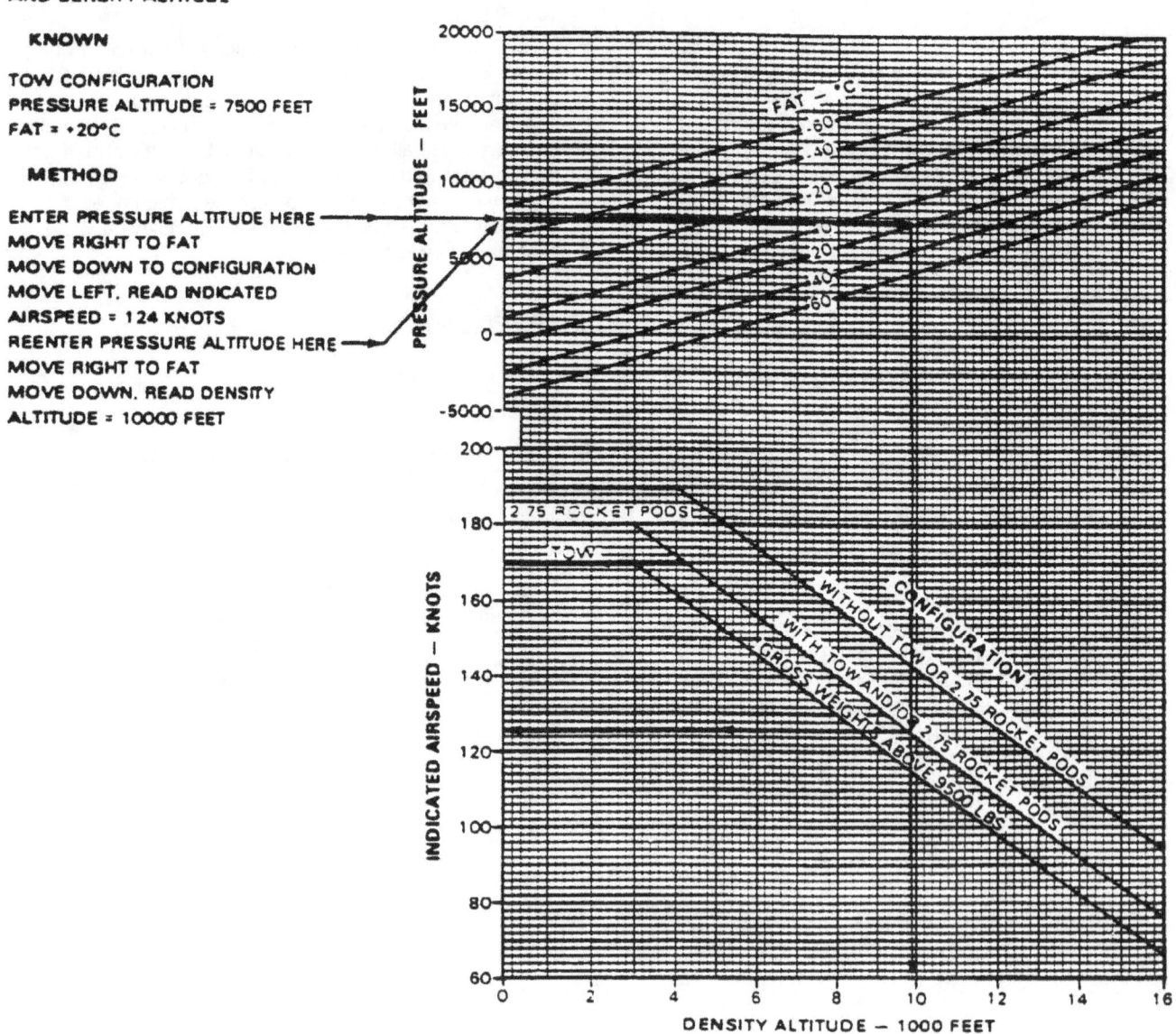

Figure 5-2. Airspeed Operating Limits Chart

TM 1-1520-236-10

SECTION VI. MANEUVERING LIMITS

5-13. PROHIBITED MANEUVERS.

a. Abrupt inputs of flight controls cause excessive main rotor flapping, which may result in mast bumping and must be avoided.

b. No aerobatic maneuvers permitted or intentional maneuvers beyond attitudes of ±30 degrees in pitch or ±60 degrees in roll are prohibited.

c. Intentional flight below + 0.5 "g's" is prohibited. Refer to "Low G Maneuvers", chapter 8, paragraph 8-41.

d. The speed for any and all maneuvers shall not exceed the airspeeds as stated on the Airspeed Operating Limit Chart, Figure 5-2.

e. Slope landing and take off limitation. Slope operations shall be limited to slopes of 8 degrees or less.

> **CAUTION**
>
> Caution is to be exercised for slopes greater than 5 degrees since rigging, loading, terrain and wind conditions may alter the slope landing capability.

f. Diving flight as defined in Chapter 8 is prohibited for aircraft equipped with B540 Main Rotor Blades. Maintenance test flight maneuvers IAW the appropriate test flight manuals are not affected and will continue as required.

SECTION VII. ENVIRONMENTAL RESTRICTIONS

5-14. ENVIRONMENTAL RESTRICTIONS.

a. This helicopter is not qualified for flight under instrument meteorlogical condition.

b. Environmental restrictions; refer to Section III and V of Chapter 8.

SECTION VIII. HEIGHT VELOCITY

5-15. AH-1 AIRCRAFT WITH MILES/AGES INSTALLED PER TM 9-1270-23-10 HAVE THE FOLLOWING RESTRICTIONS:

a. Airspeed Limitations. Maximum airspeed with the Ages/Advanced Development (AD) installed will not exceed 160 knots indicated airspeed. For density altitudes above 4400 ft., maximum airspeed limit will be determined by the "GROSS weights above 9500 lbs" line of Figure 5-2 of the operator's manual, reference 1c.

b. Maneuvering Limits.

(1) Simulated emergency procedures are not authorized.

(2) Practice touchdown autorotative landings with AGES/AD are prohibited.

(3) Aircraft shall be operated in balanced coordinated flight within one ball width on the turn and bank indicator.

(4) Emergency training maneuvers such as tail rotor loss simulation and hydraulic failures are not approved with the AGES/AD installed.

c. Actual firing of armament systems with the AGES/AD installed is prohibited.

d. Paragraph 8-50. Instrument flight with AGES/AD installed is prohibited.

e. Paragraph 8-58. First flight after installation shall be conducted during daylight. When night flying is planned, care should be taken to adjust or modify the age/ad cockpit indicators to be compatible with night vision devices.

f. Paragraph 9-51. Jettison of wing stores is permissible in coordinated level flights up to 130 knots (KIAS) and in autorotative descent at 85 KIAS.

g. Operational task 1, exterior check and interior check, reference 1b, will be completed as daily preflight inspection. In addition to these checks, inspection will ensure that detector belt, wiring and components do not interfere with aircraft equipment or antennas or cause damage to the aircraft.

CHAPTER 6
WEIGHT/BALANCE AND LOADING

SECTION I. GENERAL

6-1. GENERAL.

Chapter 6 contains sufficient instructions and data so that an aviator knowing the basic weight and moment of the helicopter can compute any combination of weight and balance.

6-2. CLASSIFICATION OF HELICOPTER.

For the purpose of clarity, Army AH-1F helicopters are in class 2. Additional directives governing weight and balance of class 2 helicopter forms and records are contained in AR 95-3, DA PAM 738-751, and TM 55-1500-342-23.

6-3. HELICOPTER STATION DIAGRAM.

Figure 6-1 shows the helicopter reference datum lines, fuselage stations, buttlines, and waterlines. The primary purpose of the figure is to aid personnel in the computation of the helicopter weight/balance and loading.

6-4. LOADING CHARTS.

a. Information. The loading data contained in this chapter are intended to provide information necessary to work a loading problem for the helicopters to which this manual is applicable.

b. Use. From the figures contained in this chapter, weight and moment are obtained for all variable load items and are added to the current basic weight and moment to obtain the gross weight and moment.

(1) The gross weight and moment are checked on Figure 6-9 to determine the approximate center of gravity (cg).

(2) The effect on cg by the expenditures in flight of such items as ammunition, etc., may be checked by subtracting the weights and moments of such items from the takeoff weight and moment and checking the new weight and moment on the Loading Limits Chart.

(3) If the weight and moment lines do not intersect, the cg is not within the fight limits.

NOTE

This check should be made to determine whether or not the cg will remain within limits during the entire flight.

TM 1-1520-236-10

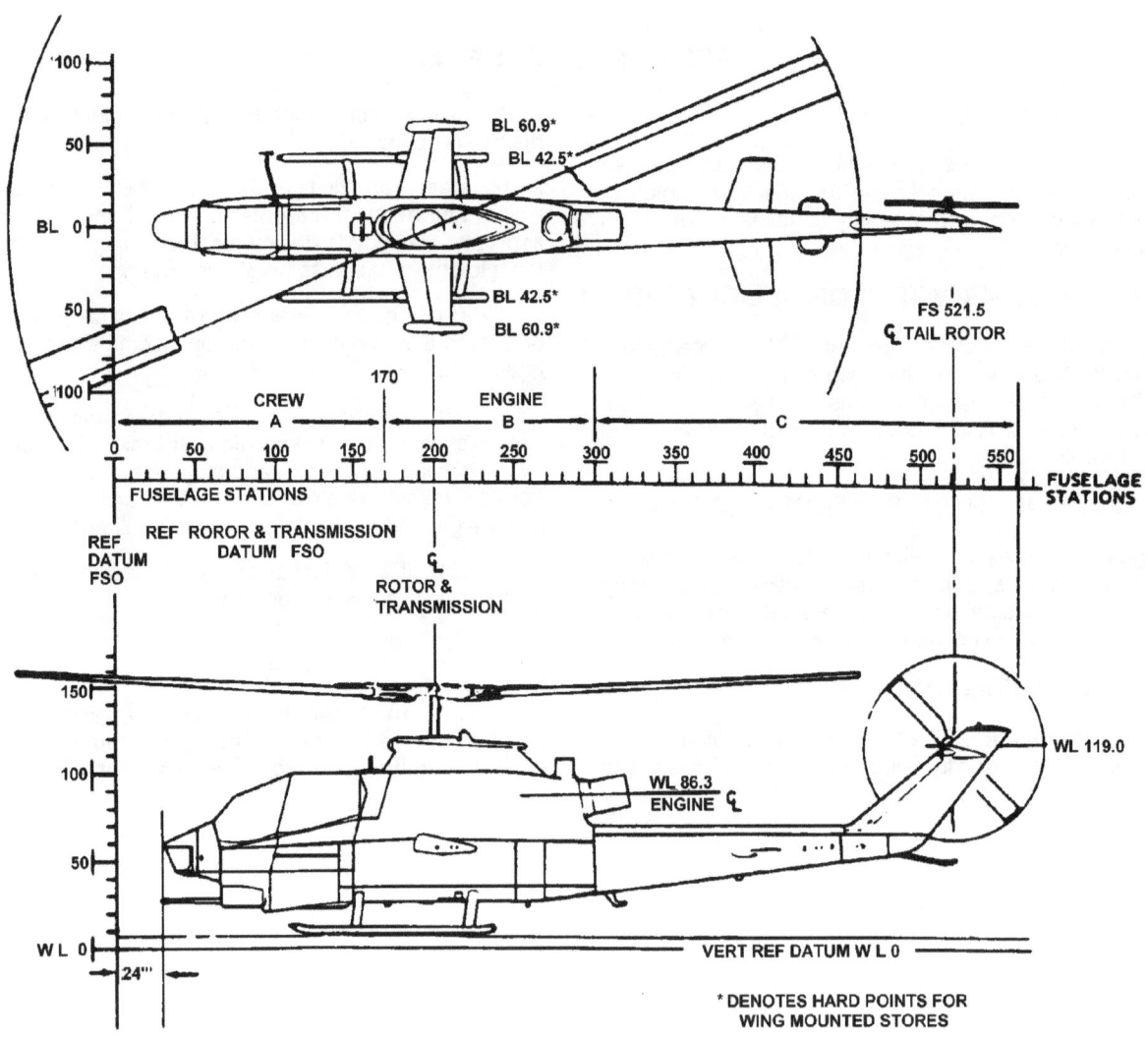

Figure 6-1. Helicopter Station Diagram (Typical)

6-2

SECTION II. WEIGHT AND BALANCE

6-5. WEIGHT AND BALANCE RECORDS.

Weight and Balance forms are maintained in the helicopter historical file. Refer to Section II, TM 55-1500-342-23 for additional information on DD Forms 365-1, -3 and -4.

SECTION III. PERSONNEL

6-6. PERSONNEL MOMENTS.

Refer to Figure 6-2 to compute pilot and gunner moments.

TM 1-1520-236-10

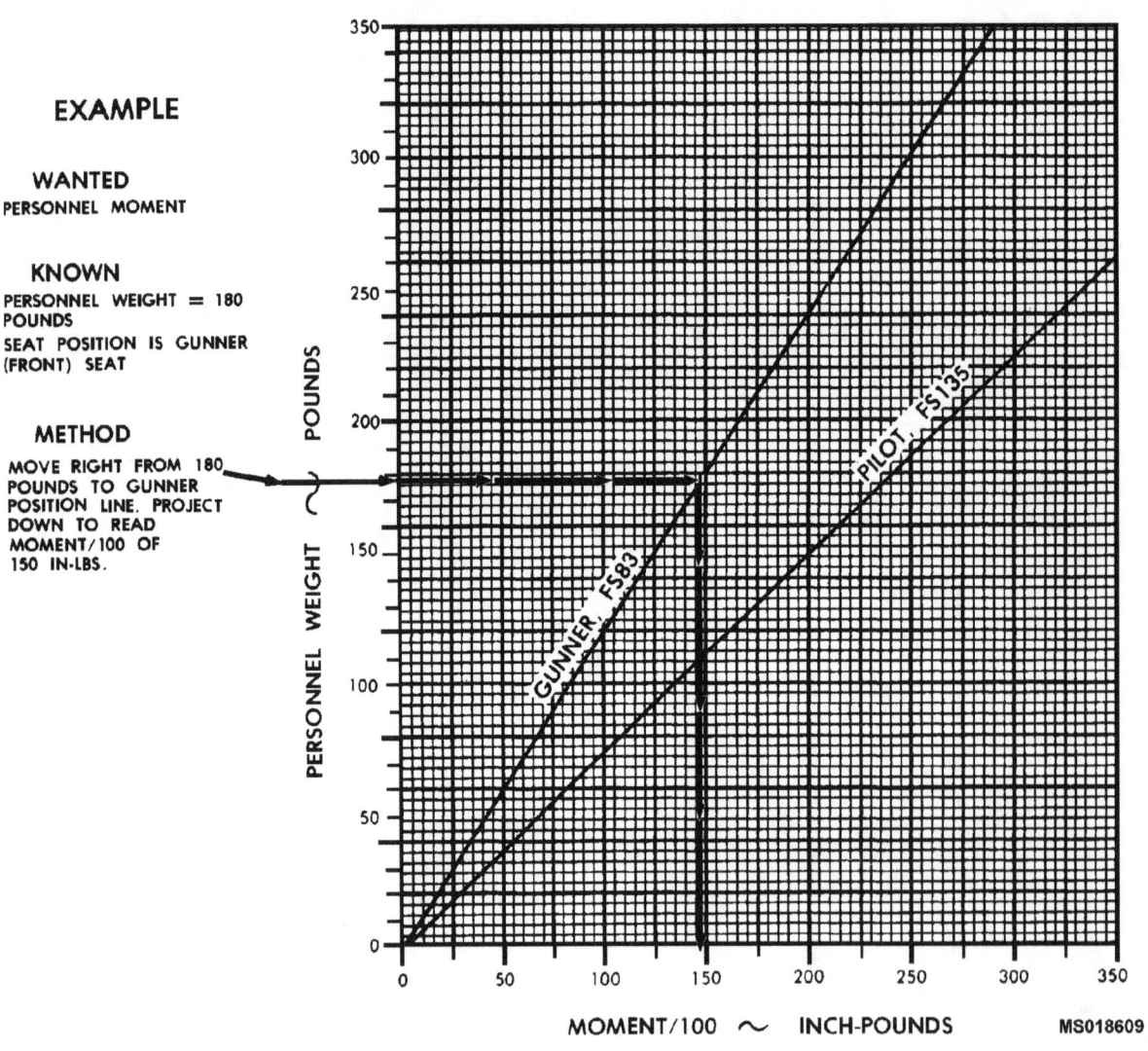

Figure 6-2. Personnel Moment Chart

SECTION IV. MISSION EQUIPMENT

6-7. WEIGHT AND BALANCE LOADING DATA.

Refer to Figure 6-3 through Figure 6-8 for the quantity, weight, and moment of each armament item up to maximum load.

6-8. 2.75 ROCKETS/19 ROUND PODS OUTBOARD WING STATIONS.

There are significant differences in the individual weights of available 2.75 rockets that can be installed. The weight differences pose no structural concern on the inboard wing stations. However, there is a limitation on the outboard wing stations of 12 heavy warhead rockets due to limited fatigue life predictions for the wing to fuselage attachment lugs. There are no outboard station limitations for the light warhead rockets.

There rocket weight differences are primarily due to the various types to warheads that range in weight from approximately 8.7 to 16.1 pounds. Also warhead weight variation of the forward end of the rockets drastically charges the pitch and yaw inertias of the overall rocket. Refer to Figure 6-4 for outboard wing station loading.

TM 1-1520-236-10

LAUNCHER	WEIGHT (POUNDS)	LOCATION ON WING	
		Inboard Moment/100	Outboard Moment/100
M260	35	70	72
M261	85	168.5	174.3

209900-826A

Figure 6-3. 2.75 Inch Rocket Launcher Moment Chart

Heavy Warhead Rockets	Light Warhead Rockets	Total No. Of Rockets For Each Combination
12	0	12
11	1	12
10	3	13
9	4	13
8	6	14
7	8	15
6	9	15
5	11	16
4	12	16
3	14	17
2	15	17
1	16	17

Figure 6-4. Combination of Light and Heavy 2.75 Rockets on Outboard Wing Stations
(19 Round Pod)

M151 WARHEAD/M429 FUSE
10 POUND WARHEAD WITH PROXIMITY FUSE
M40 ROCKET MOTOR

NO. OF ROCKETS	WEIGHT (POUNDS)	M261 LAUNCHER	
		(MOMENT/100) LOCATION ON WING	
		INBOARD	OUTBOARD
1	21	41	43
2	42	82	85
3	62	124	128
4	83	165	170
5	104	206	213
6	125	247	255
7	146	289	298
8	166	330	340
9	187	371	383
10	208	412	425
11	229	454	468
12	250	495	510
13	270	536	553
14	291	577	595
15	312	619	638
16	333	660	680
17	354	701	723
18	374	742	765
19	395	784	808

NO. OF ROCKETS	WEIGHT (POUNDS)	M260 LAUNCHER	
		(MOMENT/100) LOCATION ON WING	
		INBOARD	OUTBOARD
1	21	41	43
2	42	82	85
3	62	124	128
4	83	165	170
5	104	206	213
6	125	247	255
7	146	289	298

Figure 6-5. Folding Fin Aerial Rocket Moment Chart (Sheet 1 of 6)

M229 WARHEAD/M423 FUSE
17 POUND WARHEAD WITH POINT DETONATING FUSE
M40 ROCKET MOTOR

NO. OF ROCKETS	WEIGHT (POUNDS)	M261 LAUNCHER (MOMENT/100) LOCATION ON WING	
		INBOARD	OUTBOARD
1	28	54	55
2	56	107	111
3	84	161	166
4	112	215	222
5	140	269	277
6	167	322	332
7	195	376	388
8	223	430	443
9	251	483	499
10	279	537	554
11	307	591	609
12	335	644	665
13	363	698	
14	391	752	
15	419	806	
16	446	859	
17	474	913	
18	502	967	
19	530	1020	

NO. OF ROCKETS	WEIGHT (POUNDS)	M260 LAUNCHER (MOMENT/100) LOCATION ON WING	
		INBOARD	OUTBOARD
1	28	54	55
2	56	107	111
3	84	161	166
4	112	215	222
5	140	269	277
6	167	322	333
7	195	376	388

Figure 6-5. Folding Fin Aerial Rocket Moment Chart (Sheet 2 of 6)

M156 WARHEAD/M423 FUSE
10 POUND WARHEAD WITH POINT DETONATING FUSE
M40 ROCKET MOTOR

NO. OF ROCKETS	WEIGHT (POUNDS)	M261 LAUNCHER	
		(MOMENT/100) LOCATION ON WING	
		INBOARD	OUTBOARD
1	21	42	43
2	42	83	86
3	63	125	128
4	84	166	171
5	105	208	214
6	125	249	257
7	146	291	299
8	167	332	342
9	188	374	385
10	209	415	428
11	230	457	471
12	251	498	513
13	272	540	556
14	293	581	599
15	314	623	642
16	334	664	685
17	355	706	727
18	376	747	770
19	397	789	813

NO. OF ROCKETS	WEIGHT (POUNDS)	M260 LAUNCHER	
		(MOMENT/100) LOCATION ON WING	
		INBOARD	OUTBOARD
1	21	42	43
2	42	83	86
3	63	125	128
4	84	166	171
5	105	208	214
6	125	249	257
7	146	291	300

Figure 6-5. Folding Fin Aerial Rocket Moment Chart (Sheet 3 of 6)

M229 WARHEAD/M429 FUSE
17 POUND WARHEAD WITH PROXIMITY FUSE
M40 ROCKET MOTOR

NO. OF ROCKETS	WEIGHT (POUNDS)	M261 LAUNCHER (MOMENT/100) LOCATION ON WING	
		INBOARD	OUTBOARD
1	28	54	56
2	56	108	112
3	85	163	168
4	113	217	224
5	141	271	279
6	169	325	335
7	197	379	391
8	226	433	447
9	254	488	503
10	282	542	559
11	310	596	615
12	338	650	671
13	367	704	
14	395	758	
15	423	813	
16	451	867	
17	479	921	
18	508	975	
19	536	1029	

NO. OF ROCKETS	WEIGHT (POUNDS)	M260 LAUNCHER (MOMENT/100) LOCATION ON WING	
		INBOARD	OUTBOARD
1	28	54	56
2	56	108	112
3	85	163	168
4	113	217	224
5	141	271	280
6	169	325	336
7	197	379	392

Figure 6-5. Folding Fin Aerial Rocket Moment Chart (Sheet 4 of 6)

M247 WARHEAD/M438 FUSE
DUAL PURPOSE WARHEAD WITH POINT DETONATING FUSE (10 POUND)
<u>M40 ROCKET MOTOR</u>

NO. OF ROCKETS	WEIGHT (POUNDS)	M261 LAUNCHER (MOMENT/100) LOCATION ON WING	
		INBOARD	OUTBOARD
1	20	40	41
2	40	80	82
3	60	119	123
4	80	159	164
5	100	199	205
6	120	239	246
7	140	279	287
8	160	319	328
9	180	358	369
10	200	398	410
11	220	438	451
12	240	478	492
13	260	518	534
14	280	557	575
15	300	597	616
16	320	637	657
17	340	677	698
18	360	717	739
19	380	757	780

NO. OF ROCKETS	WEIGHT (POUNDS)	M260 LAUNCHER (MOMENT/100) LOCATION ON WING	
		INBOARD	OUTBOARD
1	20	40	41
2	40	80	82
3	60	119	123
4	80	159	164
5	100	199	205
6	120	239	246
7	140	279	287

Figure 6-5. Folding Fin Aerial Rocket Moment Chart (Sheet 5 of 6)

M151 WARHEAD/M423 FUSE
10 POUND WARHEAD WITH DETONATING FUSE
M40 ROCKET MOTOR

NO. OF ROCKETS	WEIGHT (POUNDS)	M261 LAUNCHER	
		(MOMENT/100) LOCATION ON WING	
		INBOARD	OUTBOARD
1	21	41	42
2	41	81	84
3	62	122	126
4	82	163	168
5	103	204	210
6	123	244	252
7	144	285	294
8	164	326	336
9	185	367	378
10	205	407	420
11	226	448	462
12	246	489	504
13	267	530	546
14	287	570	588
15	308	611	630
16	328	652	672
17	349	692	714
18	369	733	756
19	390	774	798

NO. OF ROCKETS	WEIGHT (POUNDS)	M260 LAUNCHER	
		(MOMENT/100) LOCATION ON WING	
		INBOARD	OUTBOARD
1	21	41	42
2	41	81	84
3	62	122	126
4	82	163	168
5	103	204	210
6	123	244	252
7	144	285	294

Figure 6-5. Folding Fin Aerial Rocket Moment Chart (Sheet 6 of 6)

M151 WARHEAD
M423 FUSE
MK66 ROCKET MOTOR
(10 POUND WARHEAD WITH POINT DETONATING FUSE)

ROCKETS (NUMBER)	WEIGHT (POUNDS) OF ROCKETS INDICATED	M261 LAUNCHER TYPE LOCATION ON WING	
		INBD: MOM/100	OUTBD: MOM/100
1	23	44	45
2	46	88	91
3	69	132	136
4	92	176	181
5	115	220	227
6	138	264	272
7	161	308	317
8	184	352	363
9	207	396	408
10	230	440	453
11	252	484	499
12	275	528	544
13	298	572	589
14	321	616	635
15	344	660	680
16	367	704	725
17	390	747	771
18	413	791	816
19	436	835	861

ROCKETS 22.95 LBS. EACH

Figure 6-6. Folding Fin Aerial Rocket Moment Chart (Sheet 1 of 14)

TM 1-1520-236-10

M151 WARHEAD
M423 FUSE
MK66 ROCKET MOTOR
(10 POUND WARHEAD WITH POINT DETONATING FUSE)

ROCKETS (NUMBER)	WEIGHT (POUNDS) OF ROCKETS INDICATED	M260 LAUNCHER TYPE LOCATION ON WING	
		INBD: MOM/100	OUTBD: MOM/100
1	23	45	47
2	46	90	93
3	69	136	140
4	92	181	186
5	115	226	233
6	138	271	280
7	161	316	326

ROCKETS 22.95 LBS. EACH

Figure 6-6. Folding Fin Aerial Rocket Moment Chart (Sheet 2 of 14)

M151 WARHEAD

M433 FUSE

MK66 ROCKET MOTOR

(10 POUND WARHEAD WITH MULTIPLE OPTION FUSE)

ROCKETS (NUMBER)	WEIGHT (POUNDS) OF ROCKETS INDICATED	M261 LAUNCHER TYPE LOCATION ON WING	
		INBD: MOM/100	OUTBD: MOM/100
1	24	46	47
2	48	91	94
3	72	137	141
4	95	182	188
5	119	228	235
6	143	273	282
7	167	319	329
8	191	364	376
9	215	410	422
10	239	455	469
11	262	501	516
12	286	546	563
13	310	592	610
14	334	637	657
15	353	683	704
16	382	728	751
17	405	774	798
18	429	819	845
19	453	865	892

ROCKETS 22.85 LBS. EACH

Figure 6-6. Folding Fin Aerial Rocket Moment Chart (Sheet 3 of 14)

M151 WARHEAD
M433 FUSE
MK66 ROCKET MOTOR
(10 POUND WARHEAD WITH MULTIPLE OPTION WARHEAD)

ROCKETS (NUMBER)	WEIGHT (POUNDS) OF ROCKETS INDICATED	M260 LAUNCHER TYPE LOCATION ON WING	
		INBD: MOM/100	OUTBD: MOM/100
1	24	47	48
2	48	94	96
3	72	140	145
4	95	187	193
5	119	234	241
6	143	281	289
7	167	328	338

ROCKETS 23.85 LBS. EACH

Figure 6-6. Folding Fin Aerial Rocket Moment Chart (Sheet 4 of 14)

M267 WARHEAD
M439 FUSE
MK66 ROCKET MOTOR
(13.5 POUND WARHEAD WITH RANGE SETABLE FUSE)

ROCKETS (NUMBER)	WEIGHT (POUNDS) OF ROCKETS INDICATED	M261 LAUNCHER TYPE LOCATION ON WING	
		INBD: MOM/100	OUTBD: MOM/100
1	27	51	52
2	54	101	104
3	81	152	157
4	109	202	209
5	138	253	261
6	163	303	313
7	190	334	365
8	217	405	418
9	244	455	470
10	272	506	522
11	299	556	574
12	326	607	626
13	353	658	679
14	380	708	731
15	407	769	783
16	434	809	835
17	462	860	887
18	489	910	940
19	516	961	992

ROCKETS 27.15 LBS. EACH

Figure 6-6. Folding Fin Aerial Rocket Moment Chart (Sheet 5 of 14)

M267 WARHEAD
M439 FUSE
MK66 ROCKET MOTOR
(13.5 POUND WARHEAD WITH RANGE SETABLE FUSE)

ROCKETS (NUMBER)	WEIGHT (POUNDS) OF ROCKETS INDICATED	M260 LAUNCHER TYPE LOCATION ON WING	
		INBD: MOM/100	OUTBD: MOM/100
1	27	52	54
2	54	104	107
3	81	156	161
4	109	208	215
5	136	260	268
6	163	312	322
7	190	364	376

ROCKETS 27.15 LBS. EACH

Figure 6-6. Folding Fin Aerial Rocket Moment Chart (Sheet 6 of 14)

M274 WARHEAD
MK66 ROCKET MOTOR
(10 POUND WARHEAD)

ROCKETS (NUMBER)	WEIGHT (POUNDS) OF ROCKETS INDICATED	M261 LAUNCHER TYPE LOCATION ON WING	
		INBD: MOM/100	OUTBD: MOM/100
1	23	44	45
2	46	88	91
3	69	132	136
4	92	176	181
5	115	220	227
6	138	264	292
7	161	308	317
8	184	352	363
9	207	396	408
10	230	440	453
11	252	484	499
12	275	528	544
13	298	572	589
14	321	616	635
15	344	660	680
16	367	704	725
17	390	747	771
18	413	791	816
19	436	835	861

ROCKETS 22.95 LBS. EACH

Figure 6-6. Folding Fin Aerial Rocket Moment Chart (Sheet 7 of 14)

M274 WARHEAD
MK66 ROCKET MOTOR
(10 POUND WARHEAD)

ROCKETS (NUMBER)	WEIGHT (POUNDS) OF ROCKETS INDICATED	M260 LAUNCHER TYPE LOCATION ON WING	
		INBD: MOM/100	OUTBD: MOM/100
1	23	45	47
2	46	90	93
3	69	136	140
4	92	181	186
5	115	226	233
6	138	271	280
7	161	316	326

ROCKETS 22.95 LBS. EACH

Figure 6-6. Folding Fin Aerial Rocket Moment Chart (Sheet 8 of 14)

M257 WARHEAD
M442 FUSE
MK66 ROCKET MOTOR
ILLUMINATION WARHEAD WITH DELAY FUSE

ROCKETS (NUMBER)	WEIGHT (POUNDS) OF ROCKETS INDICATED	M261 LAUNCHER TYPE LOCATION ON WING	
		INBD: MOM/100	OUTBD: MOM/100
1	24	48	49
2	48	96	99
3	72	144	148
4	96	192	197
5	120	240	246
6	144	289	295
7	168	337	344
8	192	385	393
9	216	433	442
10	240	481	492
11	264	529	541
12	288	577	590
13	312	626	639
14	336	674	688
15	360	722	737
16	384	770	786
17	408	818	835
18	432	866	885
19	456	914	934

ROCKETS 24.22 LBS. EACH

Figure 6-6. Folding Fin Aerial Rocket Moment Chart (Sheet 9 of 14)

TM 1-1520-236-10

M257 WARHEAD
M442 FUSE
MK66 ROCKET MOTOR
ILLUMINATION WARHEAD WITH DELAY FUSE

ROCKETS (NUMBER)	WEIGHT (POUNDS) OF ROCKETS INDICATED	M260 LAUNCHER TYPE LOCATION ON WING	
		INBD: MOM/100	OUTBD: MOM/100
1	24	48	49
2	48	96	98
3	72	144	148
4	96	192	197
5	120	240	246
6	144	289	295
7	168	337	344

ROCKETS 24.22 LBS. EACH

Figure 6-6. Folding Fin Aerial Rocket Moment Chart (Sheet 10 of 14)

M261 or M267 WARHEAD
M439 FUSE
MK66 ROCKET MOTOR
MULTIPURPOSE SUBMUNITION (MPSM) WARHEAD WITH REMOTE SET FUSE

ROCKETS (NUMBER)	WEIGHT (POUNDS) OF ROCKETS INDICATED	M261 LAUNCHER TYPE LOCATION ON WING	
		INBD: MOM/100	OUTBD: MOM/100
1	27	54	55
2	54	108	111
3	81	162	166
4	108	216	221
5	135	270	276
6	162	324	332
7	189	378	387
8	216	433	442
9	243	487	497
10	270	541	552
11	297	595	608
12	324	649	663
13	351	703	718
14	378	757	773
15	405	811	828
16	432	865	884
17	459	919	939
18	486	973	994
19	513	1028	1049

ROCKETS 27.1 LBS. EACH

Figure 6-6. Folding Fin Aerial Rocket Moment Chart (Sheet 11 of 14)

**M261 or M267 WARHEAD
M439 FUSE
MK66 ROCKET MOTOR
MULTIPURPOSE SUBMUNITION (MPSM) WARHEAD WITH REMOTE SET FUSE**

ROCKETS (NUMBER)	WEIGHT (POUNDS) OF ROCKETS INDICATED	M261 LAUNCHER TYPE LOCATION ON WING	
		INBD: MOM/100	OUTBD: MOM/100
1	27	54	55
2	54	108	111
3	81	162	166
4	108	216	221
5	135	270	276
6	162	324	331
7	189	378	387

ROCKETS 27.1 LBS. EACH

Figure 6-6. Folding Fin Aerial Rocket Moment Chart (Sheet 12 of 14)

WDU-4/A AND WDU-13/A WARHEADS
M113A FUSE
MK40 ROCKET MOTOR
FLECHETTE WARHEAD WITH DELAY FUSE

ROCKETS (NUMBER)	WEIGHT (POUNDS) OF ROCKETS INDICATED	M261 LAUNCHER TYPE LOCATION ON WING	
		INBD: MOM/100	OUTBD: MOM/100
1	27	38	39
2	54	76	78
3	81	114	117
4	108	152	156
5	135	190	195
6	162	228	234
7	189	266	272
8	216	304	311
9	243	342	350
10	270	380	389
11	297	418	428
12	324	456	467
13	351	494	506
14	378	532	545
15	405	570	583
16	432	609	622
17	459	647	661
18	486	685	700
19	513	723	739

ROCKETS 20.2 LBS. EACH

Figure 6-6. Folding Fin Aerial Rocket Moment Chart (Sheet 13 of 14)

WDU-4/A AND WDU-13/A WARHEADS
M113A FUSE
MK40 ROCKET MOTOR
FLECHETTE WARHEAD WITH DELAY FUSE

ROCKETS (NUMBER)	WEIGHT (POUNDS) OF ROCKETS INDICATED	M261 LAUNCHER TYPE LOCATION ON WING	
		INBD: MOM/100	OUTBD: MOM/100
1	27	38	39
2	54	76	78
3	81	114	117
4	108	152	156
5	135	190	195
6	162	228	233
7	189	266	272

ROCKETS 20.2 LBS. EACH

Figure 6-6. Folding Fin Aerial Rocket Moment Chart (Sheet 14 of 14)

20MM LINKED		
Rounds (Number)	Weight (lbs) For No. of Rounds Indicated	Moment/100
		F.S. 113.0
50	34	38
100	67	76
150	101	114
200	134	151
250	168	190
300	201	227
350	235	266
400	268	303
450	302	341
500	335	379
550	369	417
600	402	454
650	436	493
700	469	530
750	503	568

20MM AMM (LINKED) @
0.67 LBS. EACH

Figure 6-7. Ammunition Moment Table

BGM-71 OR BTM-71A TOW MISSILE

ITEM	WEIGHT (POUNDS)	OUTBOARD WING POSITION ONLY	
		UPPER LAUNCHER MOMENT/100	LOWER LAUNCHER MOMENT/100
(1) Launcher	60	123	122
(2) Launchers	120	246	244
(1) Tube	13	26	26
(2) Tubes	26	52	52
(3) Tubes	39	78	78
(4) Tubes	52	104	103
(1) BGM 71/71A (BASIC TOW)	41	82	82
(1) BGM 71C (ITOW)	43	86	86
(1) BGM 71D (TOW 2)	48	96	96
(1) BGM 71E (TOW 2A)	51	102	102
(1) BGM 71F (TOW 2B)	51	102	102

Figure 6-8. TOW Missile Moment Chart

M 130 CHAFF

CHAFF CARTRIDGES 30 RDS	
ARM = 490	
(SINGLE CHAFF WEIGHT = 0.33 LB)	
WEIGHT - LB	MOMENT/100
10	49

Figure 6-9. M 130 Chaff Moment Chart

SECTION V. CARGO LOADING

(Not Applicable)

SECTION VI. FUEL/OIL

6-9. FUEL DATA.

Refer to Figure 6-10 for fuel quantity, weight, and moment.

For a given weight of fuel there is only a very small variation in fuel moment with change in fuel specific weight. Fuel moments should be determined from the line on Figure 6-8 which represents the specific weight closest to that of the fuel being used.

The full tank usable fuel weight will vary depending upon fuel specific weight. The aircraft fuel gage system was designed for use with JP-4, but does tend to compensate for other fuels and provide acceptable readings. When possible the weight of fuel onboard should be determined by direct reference to the aircraft fuel gages.

The following information is provided to show the general range of fuel specific weights to be expected. Specific weight of fuel will vary depending on fuel temperature. Specific weight will decrease as fuel temperature rises and increase as fuel temperature decreases at the rate of approximately 0.1 lb/gal for each 15 degrees C change. Specific weight may also vary between lots of the same type fuel at the same temperature by as much as 0.5 lb/gal. The following approximate fuel specific weights at 15 degrees C may be used for most mission planning.

FUEL TYPE	SPECIFIC WEIGHT
JP-4	6.5 LB/GAL
JP-5	6.8 LB/GAL
JP-8	6.7 LB/GAL

6-10. OIL DATA.

For weight and balance purposes, oil is considered a part of aircraft basic weight.

TM 1-1520-236-10

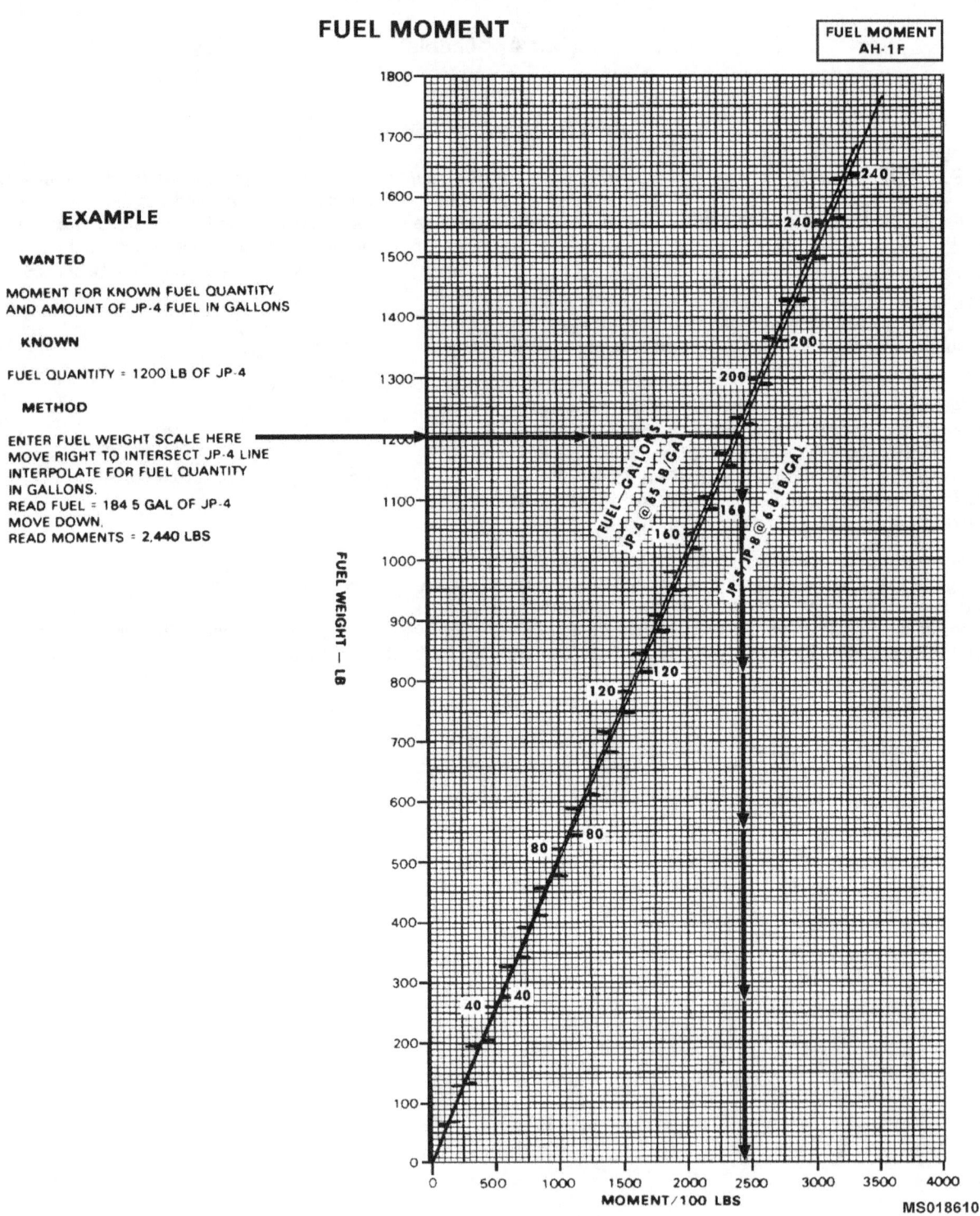

Figure 6-10. Fuel Moment Chart

SECTION VII. ALLOWABLE LOADING

Refer to TM 55-1500-342-23.

TM 1-1520-236-10

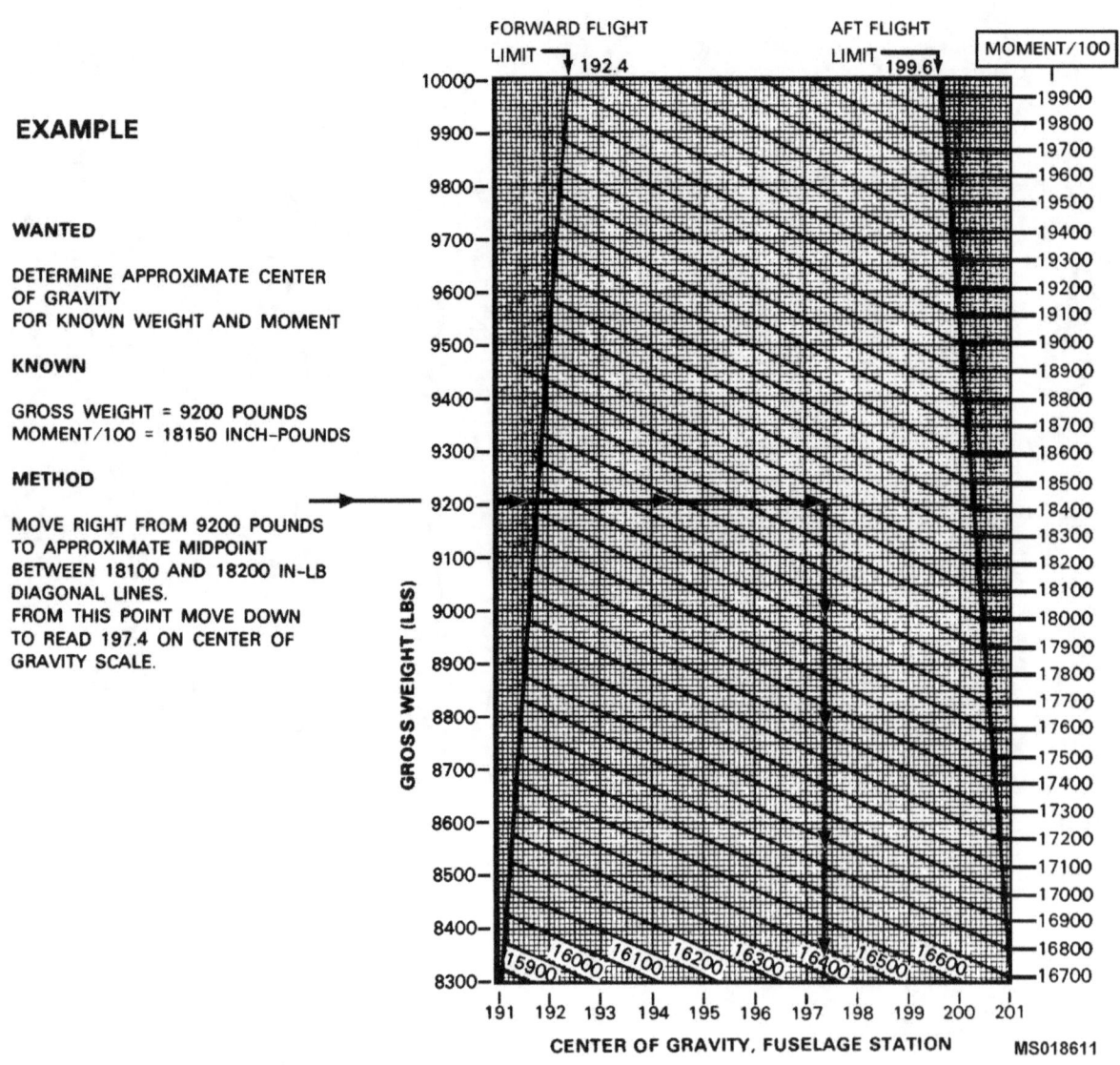

Figure 6-11. Center of Gravity Limits Chart (Sheet 1 of 2)

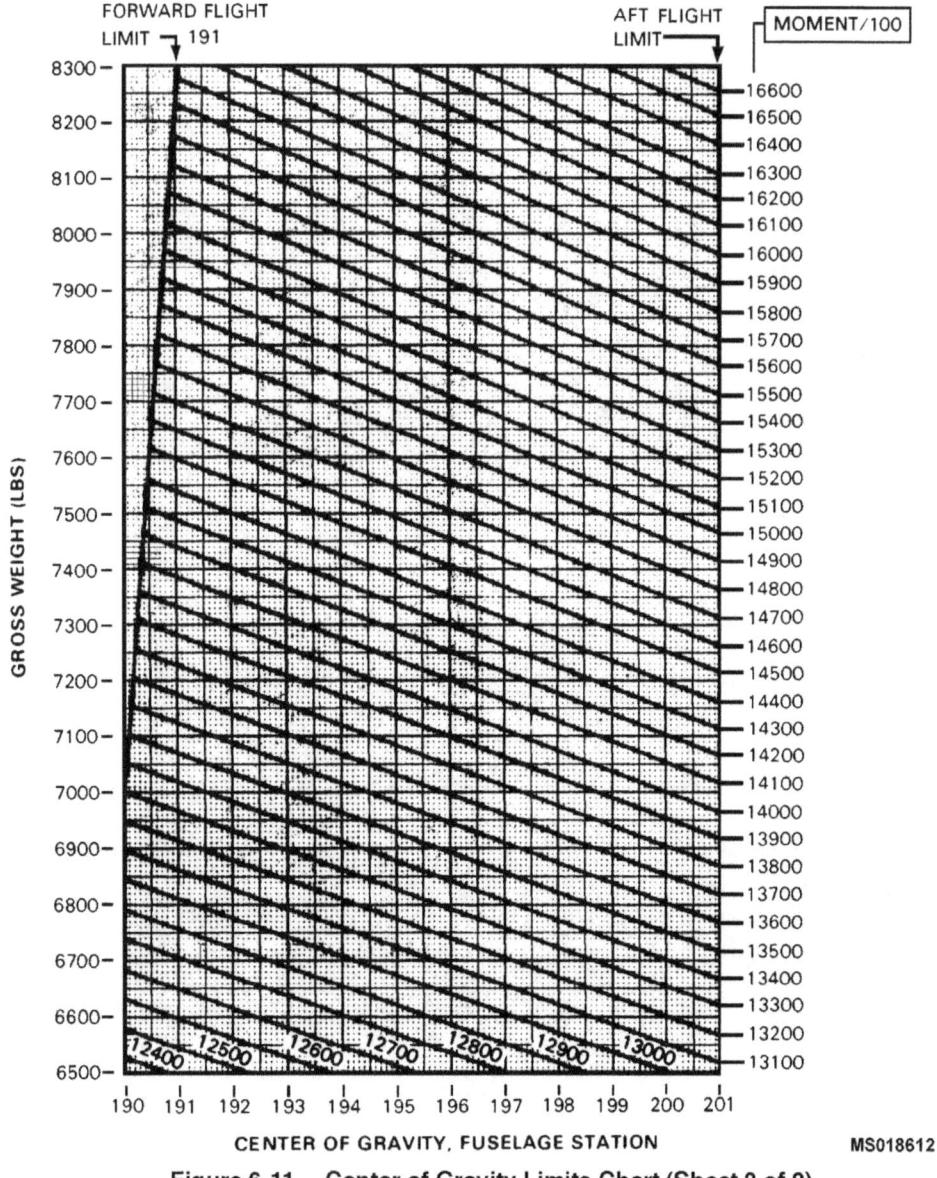

Figure 6-11. Center of Gravity Limits Chart (Sheet 2 of 2)

CHAPTER 7

PERFORMANCE DATA B540

SECTION I. INTRODUCTION

NOTE

Chapter 7 provides information for the AH-1F equipped with the B540 main rotor blade.

Chapter 7.1 provides information for the AH-1F equipped with the K747 main rotor blade.

7-1. PURPOSE.

The purpose of this chapter is to provide the best available performance data for the AH-1F helicopter equipped with the B540 main rotor blade. Regular use of this information will enable you to receive maximum safe utilization from the aircraft. Although maximum performance is not always required, regular use of this chapter is recommended for the following reasons.

a. Knowledge of your performance margin will allow you to make better decisions when unexpected conditions or alternate missions are encountered.

b. Situations requiring maximum performance will be more readily recognized.

c. Familiarity with the data will allow performance to be computed more easily and quickly.

d. Experience will be gained in accurately estimating the effects of variables for which data are not presented.

NOTE

The information provided in this chapter is primarily intended for mission planning and is most useful when planning operations in unfamiliar areas or at extreme conditions. The data may also be used inflight, to establish unit or area standing operating procedures, and to inform ground commanders of performance/risk tradeoffs.

7-2. CHAPTER 7 INDEX.

The following index contains a list of the sections and their titles, the figure numbers, subjects and page numbers of each performance data chart contained in this chapter.

INDEX

SECTION	SUBJECT		PAGE NO.
I	INTRODUCTION		7-1
II	PERFORMANCE PLANNING		7-5
	Figure 7-1	Temperature Conversion Chart	7-6
III	TORQUE AVAILABLE		7-7
	Figure 7-2	Maximum Torque Available (30 Minute Operation) Chart	
		Engine Deice Off, ECS Off	7-8
	Figure 7-3	Torque Available (Continuous Operation) Chart	
	Sheet 1 of 2	Engine Deice Off, ECS Off	7-9
	Sheet 2 of 2	Engine Deice Off, ECS On	7-10
	Figure 7-4	Calibration Factor Conversion Chart	7-11

INDEX (Cont)

SECTION	SUBJECT	PAGE NO.
IV	HOVER	7-12
	Figure 7-5　　　　　　Hover (Ceiling) Chart	
	Sheet 1 of 3　　　　　Maximum Torque Available (30 Minute Operation)	7-13
	Sheet 2 of 3　　　　　Example　B540	7-14
	Sheet 3 of 3　　　　　All Configurations 100% RPM	7-15
	Figure 7-6　　　　　　Directional Control Margin Chart	
	Sheet 1 of 2　　　　　Directional Control Margin Chart	7-16
	Sheet 2 of 2　　　　　Areas Derived From Sheet 1 of 2	7-17
V	CRUISE	7-18
	Figure 7-7　　　　　　Cruise Chart	
	Sheet 1 of 23 FAT = -30°C, Pressure Altitude = Sea Level	7-19
	Sheet 2 of 23 FAT = -30°C, Pressure Altitude = 2000 Ft	7-20
	Sheet 3 of 23 FAT = -30°C, Pressure Altitude = 4000 Ft to 6000 Ft	7-21
	Sheet 4 of 23 FAT = -30°C, Pressure Altitude = 8000 Ft to 10000 Ft	7-22
	Sheet 5 of 23 FAT = -30°C, Pressure Altitude = 12000 Ft to 14000 Ft	7-23
	Sheet 6 of 23 FAT = -15°C, Pressure Altitude = Sea Level to 2000 Ft	7-24
	Sheet 7 of 23 FAT = -15°C, Pressure Altitude = 4000 Ft to 6000 Ft	7-25
	Sheet 8 of 23 FAT = -15°C, Pressure Altitude = 8000 Ft to 10000 Ft	7-26
	Sheet 9 of 23 FAT = -15°C, Pressure Altitude = 12000 Ft to 14000 Ft	7-27
	Sheet 10 of 23 FAT = 0°C, Pressure Altitude = Sea Level to 2000 Ft	7-28
	Sheet 11 of 23 FAT = 0°C, Pressure Altitude = 4000 Ft to 6000 Ft	7-29
	Sheet 12 of 23 FAT = 0°C, Pressure Altitude = 8000 Ft to 10000 Ft	7-30
	Sheet 13 of 23 FAT = 0°C, Pressure Altitude = 12000 Ft to 14000 Ft	7-31
	Sheet 14 of 23 FAT = +15°C, Pressure Altitude = Sea Level to 2000 Ft	7-32
	Sheet 15 of 23 FAT = +15°C, Pressure Altitude = 4000 Ft to 6000 Ft	7-33
	Sheet 16 of 23 FAT = +15°C, Pressure Altitude = 8000 Ft to 10000 Ft	7-34
	Sheet 17 of 23 FAT = +15°C, Pressure Altitude = 12000 Ft to 14000 Ft	7-35
	Sheet 18 of 23 FAT = +30°C, Pressure Altitude = Sea Level to 2000 Ft	7-36
	Sheet 19 of 23 FAT = +30°C, Pressure Altitude = 4000 Ft to 6000 Ft	7-37
	Sheet 20 of 23 FAT = +30°C, Pressure Altitude = 8000 Ft to 10000 Ft	7-38
	Sheet 21 of 23 FAT = +45°C, Pressure Altitude = Sea Level to 2000 Ft	7-39
	Sheet 22 of 23 FAT = +45°C, Pressure Altitude = 4000 Ft to 6000 Ft	7-40
	Sheet 23 of 23 FAT = +45°C, Pressure Altitude = 8000 Ft to 10000 Ft	7-41
VI	DRAG	7-42
	Figure 7-8　　　　　　Drag Chart	7-43
VII	CLIMB-DESCENT	7-44
	Figure 7-9　　　　　　Climb – Descent Chart	7-45
VIII	IDLE FUEL FLOW	7-46
	Figure 7-10　　　　　100% RPM Fuel Flow Chart	7-47

7-3. GENERAL.

The data presented covers the maximum range of conditions and performance that can reasonably be expected. In each area of performance, the effects of altitude, temperature, gross weight and other parameters relating to that phase of flight are presented. In addition to the presented data, your judgment and experience will be necessary to accurately obtain performance under a given set of circumstances. The conditions for the data are listed under the title of each chart. The effects of different conditions are discussed in the text accompanying each phase of performance. Where practical, data are presented at conservative conditions. However, NO GENERAL CONSERVATISM HAS BEEN APPLIED. All performance data presented are within the applicable limits of the aircraft.

7-4. LIMITS.

Applicable limits are shown on the charts as red lines. Performance generally deteriorates rapidly beyond limits. If limits are exceeded, minimize the amount and time. Enter the maximum value and time above limits on DA Form 2408-13-1 so proper maintenance action can be taken.

7-5. USE OF CHARTS.

a. Chart Explanation. The first page of each section describes the chart(s) and explains its uses.

b. Coding and Shading. Chart codes are used as follows.

(1) Example guidlines have arrows.

(2) Bold is used for limit lines, which are also labeled.

(3) Shading or patterns are used for precautionary or time-limited operation.

c. Reading the Charts. The primary use of each chart is given in a example and a green guideline is provided to help up follow the route through the chart. The use of a straight edge (ruler or page edge) and a hard fine point pencil is recommended to avoid cumulative errors. The majority of the charts provide a standard pattern for use as follows: enter first variable on top left scale, move right to the second variable, reflect down at right angles to the third variable, reflect left at right angles to the fourth variable, reflect down, etc. until the final variable is read out at the final scale. In addition to the primary use, other uses of each chart are explained in the text accompanying each set of performance charts. Colored registration blocks located at the bottom and top of each chart are used to determine if slippage has occurred during printing. If slippage has occurred, refer to Chapter 5 for correct operating limits.

NOTE

An example of an auxiliary use of the charts referenced above is as follows: Although the hover chart is primarily arranged to find torque required to hover, by entering torque available as torque required, maximum skid height for hover can also be found. In general, any single variable can be found if all others are known. Also, the tradeoffs between two variables can be found. For example, at a given pressure altitude, you can find the maximum gross weight capability as free air temperature changes.

7-6. DATA BASIS.

The type of data used is indicated at the bottom of each performance chart under DATA BASIS. The data provided generally is based on one of four categories:

a. Flight Test Data. Data obtained by flight test of the aircraft by experienced flight test personnel at precise conditions using sensitive calibrated instruments.

b. Derived From Flight Test. Flight test data obtained on a similar rather than the same aircraft and series. Generally small corrections will have been made.

c. Calculated Data. Data bases on tests, but not on flight test of the complete aircraft.

d. Estimated Data. Data based on estimates having aerodynamic theory or other means but not verified by flight test.

7-7. SPECIFIC CONDITIONS.

The data presented are accurate only for specific conditions listed under the title of each chart. Variables for which data are not presented, but which may affect that phase of performance, are discussed in the text. Where data are available or reasonable estimates can be made, the amount that each variable affects performance will be given.

7-8. GENERAL CONDITIONS.

In addition to the specific conditions, the following general conditions are applicable to the performance data.

a. Rigging. All airframe and engine control are assumed to be rigged within allowable tolerances.

b. Pilot Technique. Normal pilot technique is assumed. Control movements should be smooth and continuous.

c. Aircraft Variation. Variations in performance between individual aircraft are known to exist; however, they are considered to be small and cannot be individually accounted for.

d. Instrument Variation. The data shown in the performance charts do not account for instrument inaccuracies or malfunctions.

e. Types Of Fuel. All flight performance data are based on JP-4 Fuel. The change in fuel flow and torque available, when using JP-5, JP-8, aviation gasoline or any other approved fuels, is insignificant.

7-9. PERFORMANCE DISCREPANCIES.

Regular use of this chapter will allow you to monitor instruments and other aircraft systems for malfunction, by comparing actual performance with planned performance. Knowledge will also be gained concerning the effects of variables for which data are not provided, thereby increasing the accuracy of performance predictions.

7-10. DEFINITIONS OF ABBREVIATIONS.

a. Unless otherwise indicated in Appendix B, abbreviations and symbols used in this manual conform to those established in Military Standard MIL-STD-12, which is periodically revised to reflect current changes in abbreviation usage. Accordingly, it may be noted that certain previously established definitions have been replaced by more current abbreviations and symbols.

b. Capitalization and punctuation of abbreviations varies, depending upon the context in which they are used. In general, lower case abbreviations are used in text material, whereas abbreviations used in charts and illustrations appear in full capital letters. Periods do not usually follow abbreviations; however, periods are used with abbreviations that could be mistaken for whole words if the period were omitted.

SECTION II. PERFORMANCE PLANNING

7-11. PERFORMANCE PLANNING.

Refer to the appropriate Aircrew Training Manual for preparing the performance planning card (PPC).

7-12. TEMPERATURE CONVERSION.

The temperature conversion chart (Figure 7-1) is arranged so that degrees Celsius can be converted quickly and easily by reading Celsius and looking directly across the chart for Fahrenheit equivalent and vice versa.

TEMPERATURE CONVERSION CHART

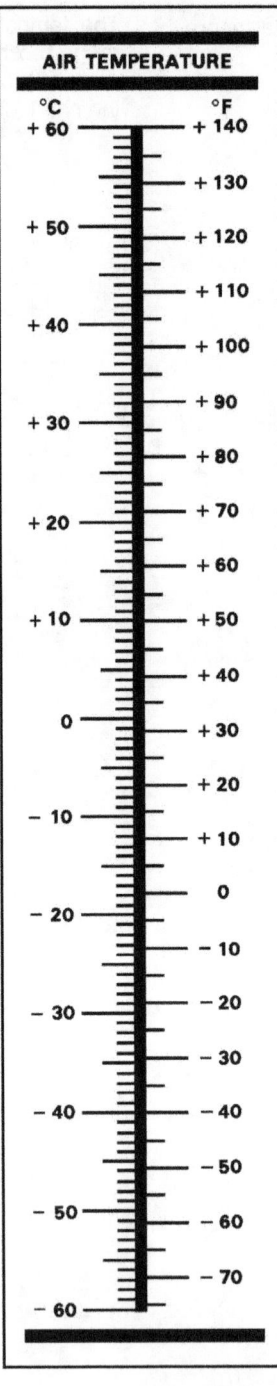

Figure 7-1. Temperature Conversion Chart

SECTION III. TORQUE AVAILABLE

7-13. DESCRIPTION.

The torque available charts show the effects of altitude and temperature on engine torque.

7-14. CHART DIFFERENCES.

Both pressure altitude and FAT affect engine power production. Figures 7-2 and 7-3 show power available data at 30 minute power and maximum continuous power ratings in terms of the allowable torque as recorded by the torquemeter (%Q).

> **CAUTION**
>
> **The power output capability of the T53-L-703 engine can exceed the transmission structural limit (100% Q) under certain conditions.**

a. Figure 7-2 (sheet 1) is applicable for maximum power, engine deice off and ECS off, 30 minute operation.

b. Figure 7-3 (sheet 1) is applicable for maximum continuous power, engine deice off, and ECS off.

c. Figure 7-3 (sheet 2) is applicable for maximum continuous power, engine deice off, and ECS on.

d. Prolonged IGE hover may increase engine inlet temperature as much as 10 degrees Celsius; therefore, a higher FAT must be used to correct for the increase under this condition.

7-15. USE OF CHARTS.

The primary use of the charts is illustrated by the examples. In general, to determine the maximum power available, it is necessary to know the pressure altitude and temperature. The calibration factor (Data Plate Torque), obtained from the engine data plate or from the engine acceptance records, is the indicated torque pressure at the actual output shaft torque, and is used to correct the error of individual engine torque indicating system.

7-16. CONDITIONS.

Charts (Figure 7-2 and Figure 7-3) are based upon speeds at 100 percent rpm with grade JP-4 fuel. The use of aviation gasoline will not influence engine power. Fuel grade of JP-5 will yield the same nautical miles per pound of fuel and being 6.8 pounds per gallon will only result in increased fuel weight per gallon. Because JP-4 and JP-5 have the same energy value per pound, then JP-5 fuel will increase range by almost 5 percent per gallon of fuel.

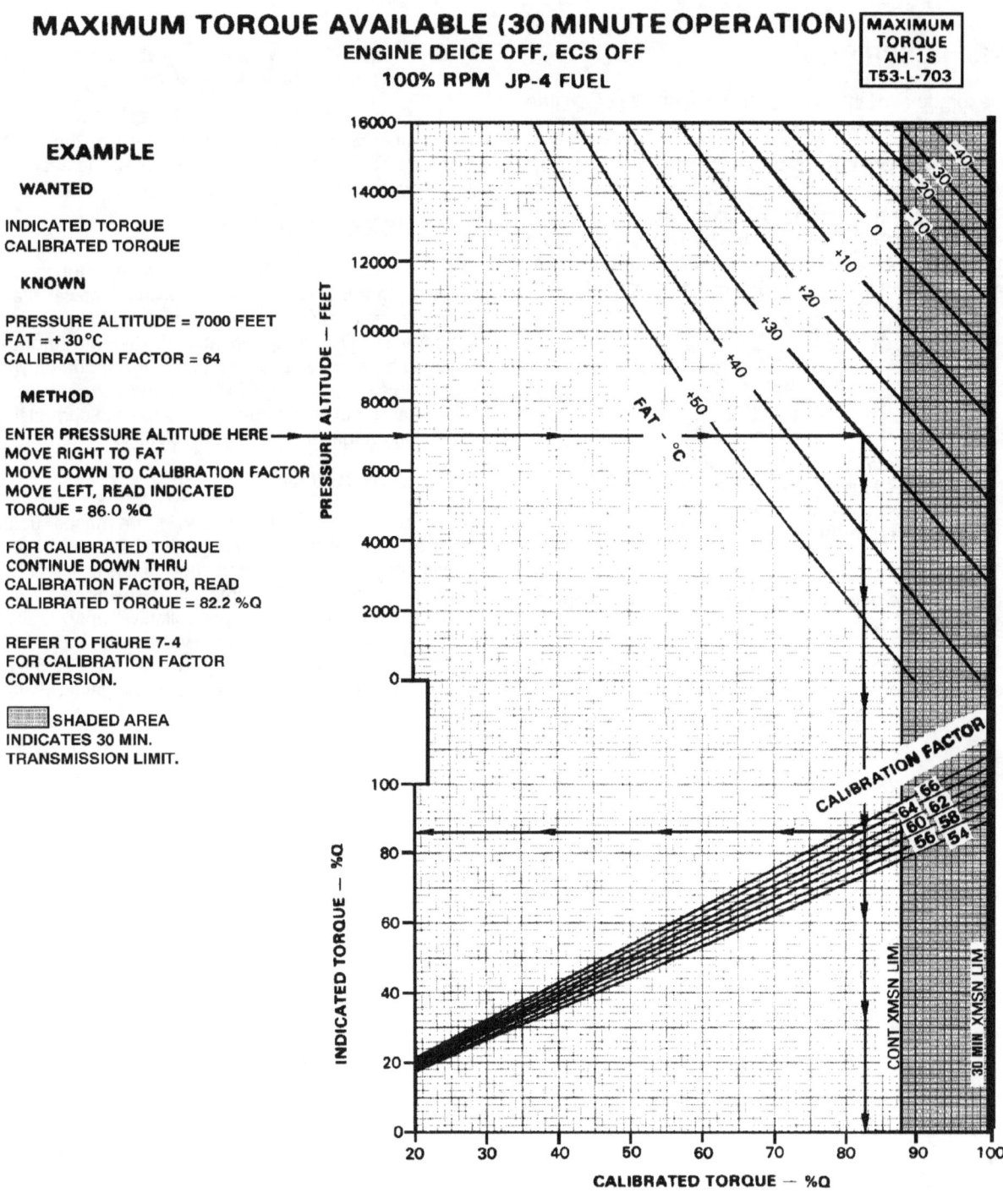

Figure 7-2. Maximum Torque Available (30-Minute Operation) Chart

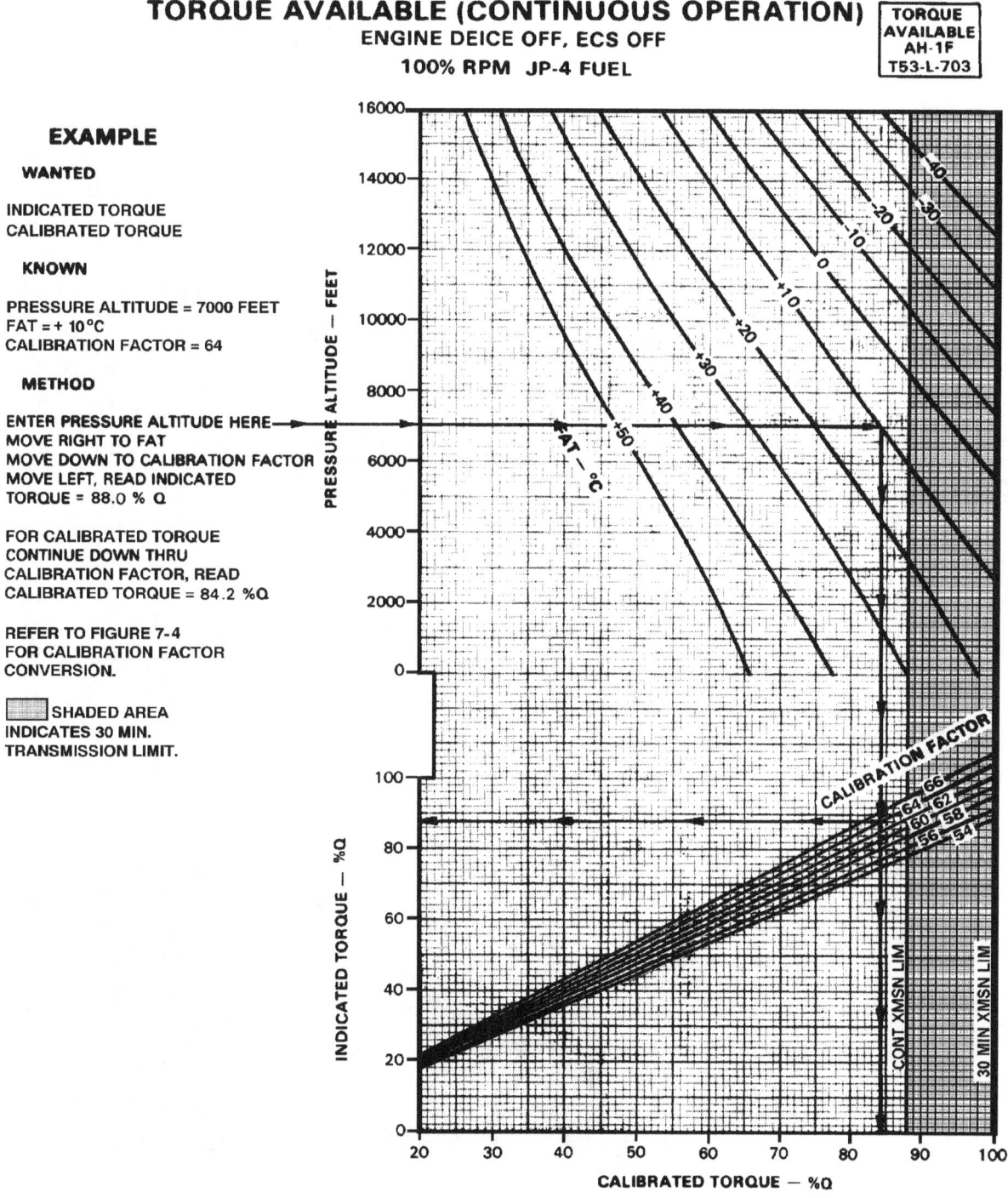

Figure 7-3. Torque Available (Continuous Operation) Chart (Sheet 1 of 2)

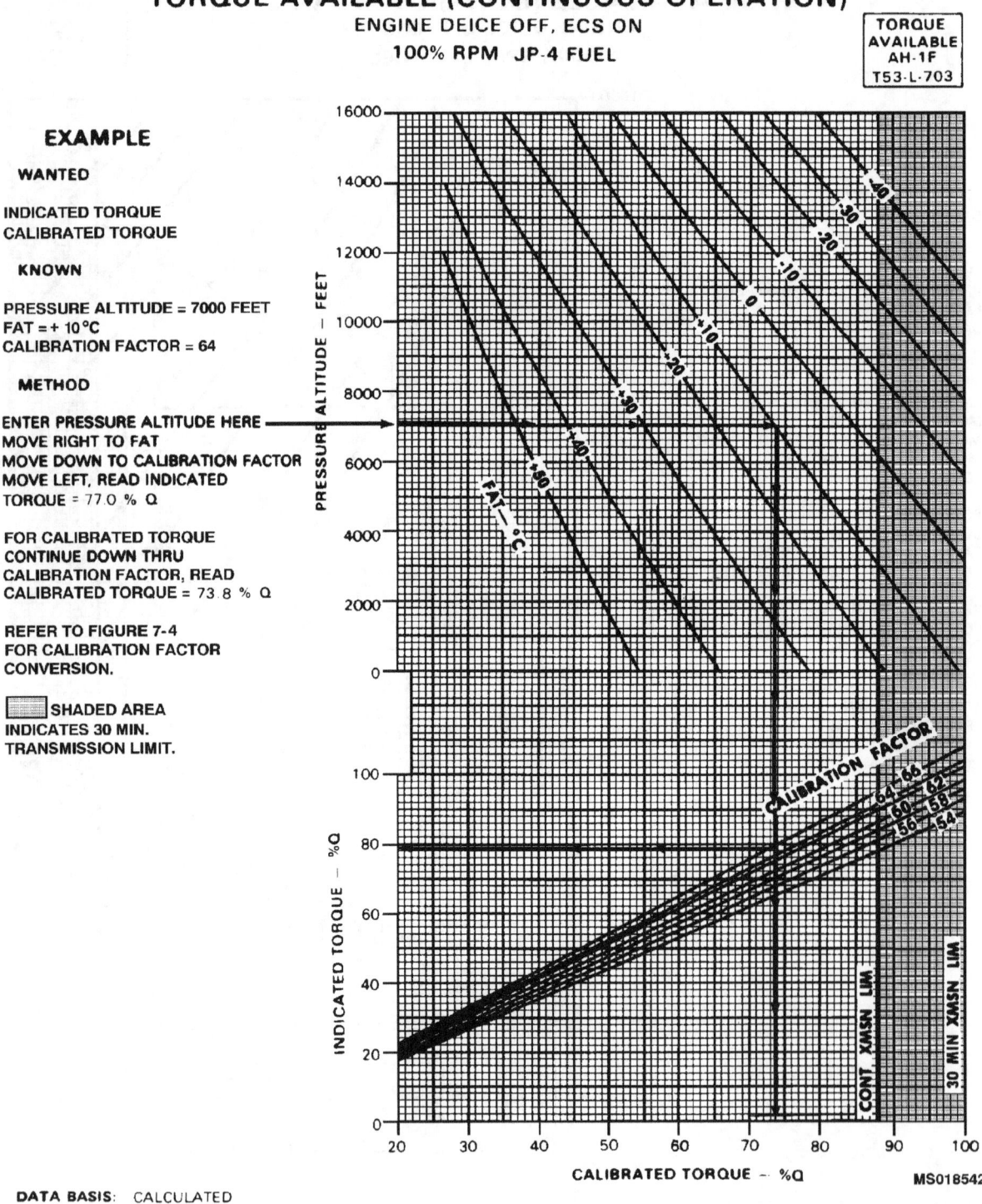

Figure 7-3. Torque Available (Continuous Operation) Chart (Sheet 2 of 2)

CALIBRATION FACTOR CONVERSION TABLE

CAL FACTOR CONVERSION TABLE									
64.0	63.9	63.8	63.7	63.6	63.5	63.4	63.3	63.2	63.1
4.2	4.1	4.0	3.8	3.7	3.6	3.5	3.4	3.3	3.2
63.0	62.9	62.8	62.7	62.6	62.5	62.4	62.3	62.2	62.1
3.1	2.9	2.7	2.5	2.2	2.0	1.8	1.6	1.4	1.2
62.0	61.9	61.8	61.7	61.6	61.5	61.4	61.3	61.2	61.1
1.0	0.9	0.8	0.7	0.6	0.5	0.4	0.3	0.2	0.1
61.0	60.9	60.8	60.7	60.6	60.5	60.4	60.3	60.2	60.1
0.0	-0.2	-0.4	-0.6	-0.8	-1.0	-1.2	-1.4	-1.6	-1.8
60.0	59.9	59.8	59.7	59.6	59.5	59.4	59.3	59.2	59.1
-2.0	-2.2	-2.3	-2.5	-2.7	-2.9	-3.1	-3.3	-3.5	-3.7
59.0	58.9	58.8	58.7	58.6	58.5	58.4	58.3	58.2	58.1
-3.8	-4.0	-4.2	-4.4	-4.6	-4.8	-4.9	-5.1	-5.3	-5.5

MS018543

EXAMPLE (UTILIZING TORQUE VALUE FROM FIGURES 7-2 OR 7-3)

WANTED

INDICATED TORQUE
CALIBRATED TORQUE

KNOWN

PRESSURE ALTITUDE = 7000 FEET
FAT = +30°C
CALIBRATION FACTOR = 64

METHOD

ENTER PRESSURE ALTITUDE
MOVE RIGHT TO FAT
FOR CALIBRATED TORQUE:
   CONTINUE DOWN THROUGH CALIBRATION FACTOR
   READ CALIBRATED TORQUE = 82.2%Q
FOR INDICATED TORQUE:
   ADD OR SUBTRACT CAL FACTOR CONVERSION TO CALIBRATED TORQUE
   FOR EXAMPLE: 4.2%Q + 82.2%Q = 86.4%Q INDICATED TORQUE

Figure 7-4. Calibration Factor Conversion Chart

SECTION IV. HOVER

7-17. DESCRIPTION.

The hover charts (Figure 7-5, sheets 1 through 3) show the hover ceiling and the torque required to hover respectively at various pressure altitudes, ambient temperatures, gross weights and skid heights. Maximum skid height for hover can also be obtained by using the torque available from Figure 7-2.

7-18. USE OF CHART.

a. The primary use of the charts is illustrated by the charts examples. In general, to determine the hover ceiling or the torque required to hover, it is necessary to know the pressure altitude, temperature, gross weight and the desired skid height.

b. The hover ceiling chart sheet 1 of 3 shows the maximum gross weight at which the helicopter may hover at maximum torque available. The chart shows OGE hover performance with trade-off curves for various skid heights (IGE) operation. To obtain maximum hover capability, proceed as follows:

(1) Enter chart at appropriate pressure altitude.

(2) Move right to FAT.

(3) Move down to gross weight (which represents OGE hover), if a specific skid height (IGE) desired proceed.

(4) Move down to desired skid height.

(5) Move left and read IGE gross weight capability at desired skid height.

c. In addition to its primary use, the hover chart (sheet 3) can also be used to determine the predicted maximum hover height. To determine maximum hover height, proceed as follows:

(1) Enter chart at appropriate pressure altitude.

(2) Move right to FAT.

(3) Move down to gross weight.

(4) Move left to intersection with maximum power available (obtained from Figure 7-2).

(5) Read predicted maximum skid height. This height is the maximum hover height.

7-19. CONTROL MARGIN.

Ten percent pedal margin is considered adequate for safe directional control. Figure 7-6 (sheet 1) shows the combinations of relative wind velocity and azimuth which may result in marginal directional control. Figure 7-6 (sheet 3) shows the maximum right crosswind, in knots true airspeed, which one can achieve and still maintain 10 percent directional control margin for given gross weights and density altitudes. This figure has zone letters which are to be used in conjunction with Figure 7-6 (sheet 3). If, for example, your operating gross weight and density altitude are such that the point lies in zone C on sheet 1 then go to sheet 3. The zone identified by the letter C shows the wind velocity in knots that one can achieve while still maintaining a 10 percent directional control margin (e.g., if the wind were from 45 degrees you could have 18.5 knots of wind whereas, if from 60 degrees, only 15.4 knots). The left vertical zone lines on sheet 3 represent 10 percent control margin. As you move toward the right for that gross weight and density altitude, the control margin approaches zero.

7-20. CONDITIONS.

The hover charts are based upon calm wind conditions, a level ground surface, and the use of 100 percent rpm. In ground effect hover data is based upon hovering over a level surface. If the surface over which hovering will be conducted is known to be steep, uneven, covered with high vegetation, or if the type of terrain is unknown, the flight should be planned for out of ground effect hover capability.

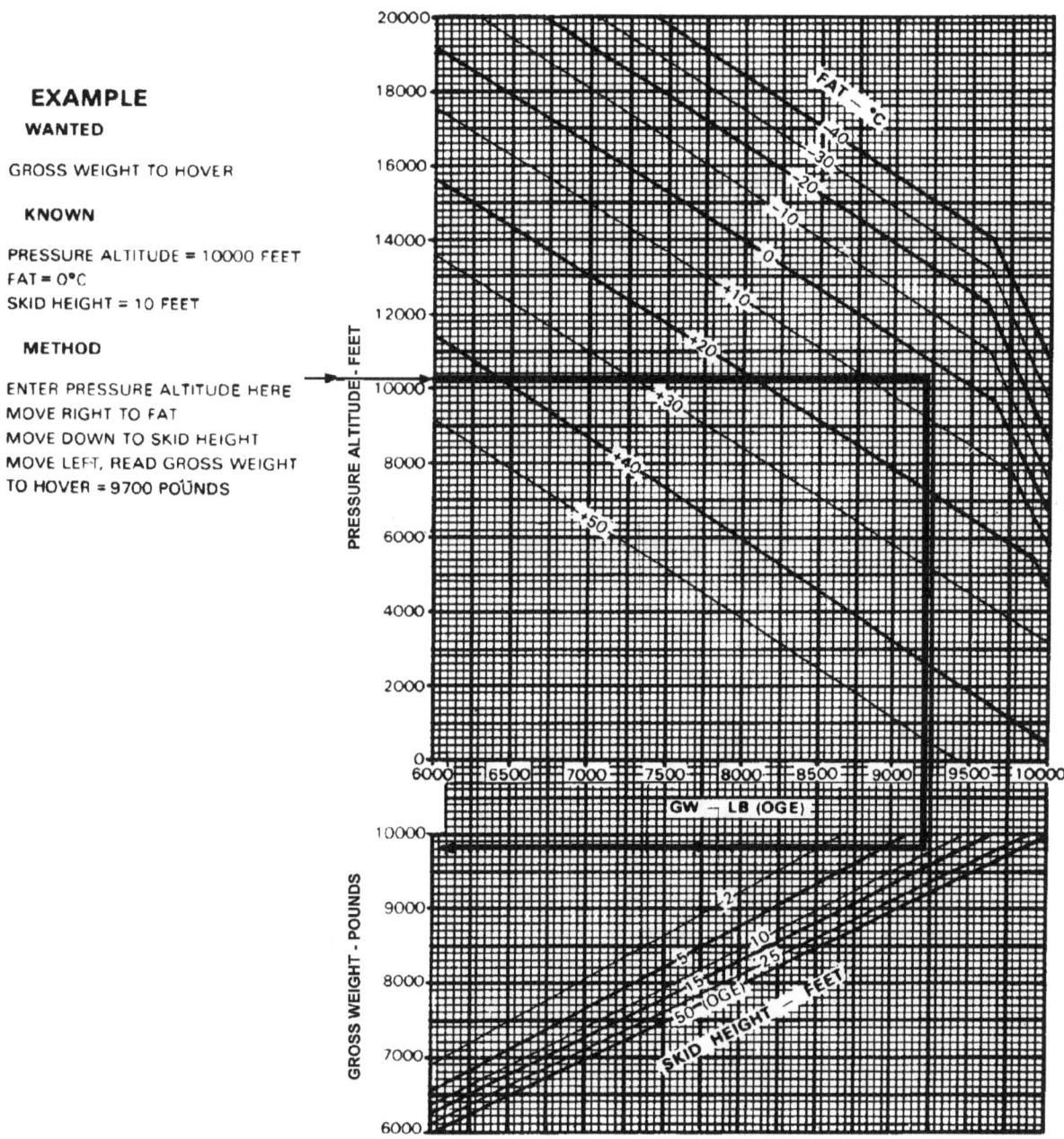

Figure 7-5. Hover (Ceiling) Chart (Sheet 1 of 3)

EXAMPLE B540

WANTED

MAXIMUM GROSS WEIGHT TO HOVER AT OGE   (USE WITH CHART ON SHEET 3)

KNOWN (REFERENCE EXAMPLE FOR FIGURE 7-2)

30 MINUTE CALIBRATED TORQUE AVAILABLE = 82% Q

PRESSURE ALTITUDE = 7000 FEET

FAT = +30°C

CALIBRATION FACTOR = 64

METHOD

ENTER PRESSURE ALTITUDE HERE

MOVE RIGHT AND INTERPOLATE FOR +30°C FAT

MOVE DOWN AND READ. DENSITY ALTITUDE = 10000 FEET

ENTER CALIBRATED TORQUE HERE

MORE UP TO INTERSECT OGE LINE

MOVE RIGHT TO INTERSECT THE VERTICAL

LINE FROM ❶ AND READ GROSS WEIGHT TO HOVER = 8500 POUNDS

B540 Figure 7-5. Hover (Ceiling) Chart (Sheet 2 of 3)

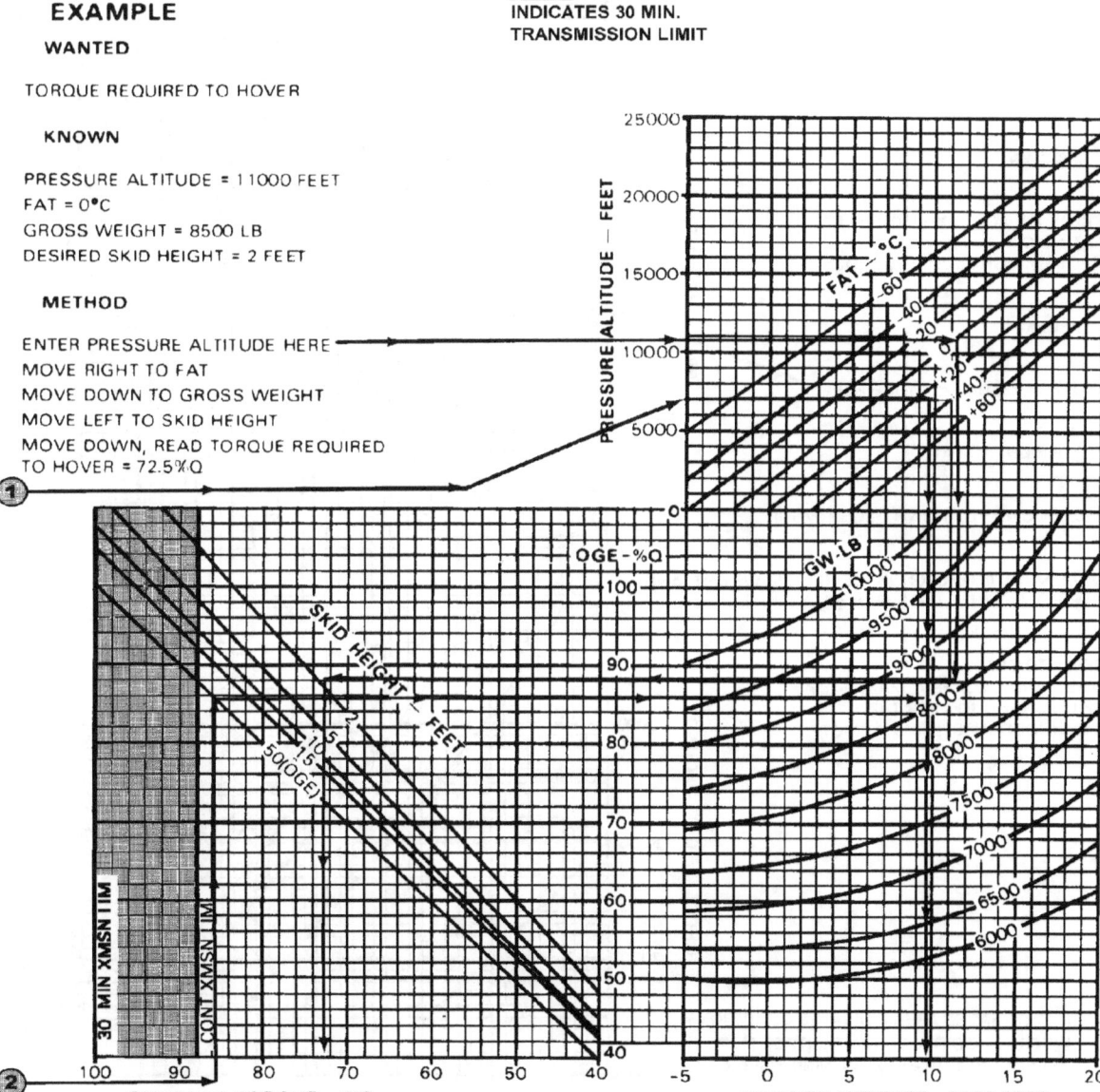

Figure 7-5. Hover (Ceiling) Chart (Sheet 3 of 3)

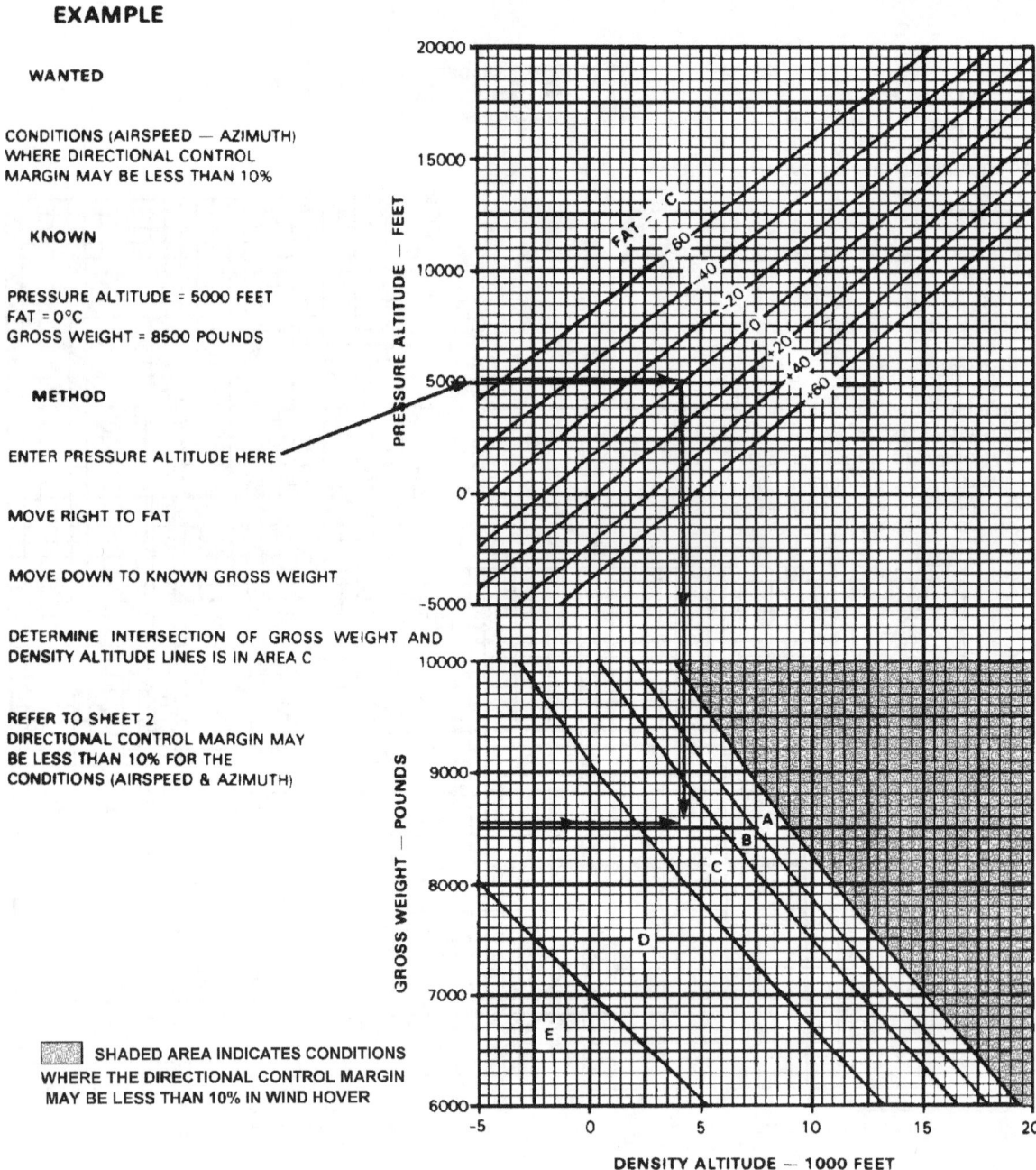

Figure 7-6. Directional Control Margin Chart (Sheet 1 of 2)

TM 1-1520-236-10

DIRECTIONAL CONTROL MARGIN

AREAS DERIVED FROM SHEET 1 OF 2

Wind speed in Knots (MAXIMUM WIND VELOCITY (Actual or Forecast))	A Starts at 0 KTS	B Starts at 10 KTS	C Starts at 13 KTS	D Starts at 16 KTS	E Starts at 20 KTS
0	30° - 140°				
5	30° - 140°				
10	30° - 140°				
15	30° - 140°	40° - 120°	60° - 120°		
20	30° - 140°	30° - 140°	30° - 140°	50° - 130°	
25	30° - 140°	40° - 140°	30° - 140°	50° - 140°	50° - 130°

Shaded area indicates areas where 10% tail rotor authority should be expected.

MS018548

Example

WANTED: AZIMUTH WHERE DIRECTIONAL CONTROL MARGIN MAY BE LESS THAN 10%.

KNOWN: 18 KNOT WINDS (FORECAST OR ACTUAL) ROUNDED UP TO 20 KNOTS, AREA "C" FROM SHEET 1 OF 2.

METHOD: FROM THE LEFT SIDE OF THE CHART LOCATE 20 KNOTS AND MOVE RIGHT, FROM THE TOP OF THE CHART LOCATE AREA "C" AND MOVE DOWN. WHERE THESE TWO POINTS INTERSECT IS THE AZIMUTHS TO AVOID, 30° - 140°.

NOTE 1: FORECAST OR ACTUAL WINDS SHOULD ALWAYS BE ROUNDED UP TO THE NEAREST 5 KNOTS.

NOTE 2: IN CALM WIND CONDITIONS, SIDEWARD FLIGHT TO THE RIGHT WILL INDUCE THE SAME EFFECT AS WINDS FROM THE RIGHT.

NOTE 3: 10% DIRECTIONAL CONTROL IS DEFINED AS 10% PEDAL TRAVEL REMAINING.

NOTE 4: REFER TO THE AH-1 AIRCREW TRAINING MANUAL FOR PREPARING THE PERFORMANCE PLANNING CARD (PPC).

Figure 7-6. Directional Control Margin Chart (Sheet 2 of 2)

SECTION V. CRUISE

7-21. DESCRIPTION.

The cruise charts (Figure 7-7, sheets 1 through 23) show the torque pressure and engine rpm required for level flight at various pressure altitudes, airspeed and gross weights. The cruise charts are presented for a clean drag configuration. However, any desired drag configuration (see Figure 7-8 for authorized armament configurations) can be solved by using a ratio between the $\Delta\%Q$ for the desired configuration (as shown in Figure 7-7, sheets 1 thru 23) and the $\Delta\%Q$ for the 8 TOW configuration. Add the calculated $\Delta\%Q$ of the desired configuration to the %Q of the clean configuration to solve for the total torque required for the desired configuration. Then read the fuel flow for the desired configuration.

Thus, the effects of added drag resulting from installed wing stores can be determined by applying the ΔF-SQ FT from the Drag Chart (Figure 7-8) to the cruise charts (Figure 7-7). Refer to Example B on Figure 7-7, sheet 1 for the method.

7-22. USE OF CHARTS.

The primary use of the charts is illustrated by the examples provided in Figure 7-7. The first step for chart use is to select the proper chart, pressure altitude and anticipated free air temperature; refer to chapter 7 index (paragraph 7-2). Normally, sufficient accuracy can be obtained by selecting the chart nearest to the planned cruising altitude and FAT, or the next higher altitude and FAT. If greater accuracy is required, interpolation between altitudes and/or temperatures will be required (see Figure 7-7, sheet 1, example A). You may enter the charts on any side; TAS, IAS, torque pressure, or fuel flow, and then move vertically or horizontally to the gross weight, then to the other three parameters. Maximum performance conditions are determined by entering the chart where the maximum range or maximum endurance and rate of climb lines intersect the appropriate gross weight; then read airspeed, fuel flow and torque pressure. For conservatism, use the gross weight at the beginning of cruise flight. For greater accuracy on long flights it is preferable to determine cruise information for several flight segments in order to allow for decreasing fuel weight (reduced gross weight). The following parameters contained in each chart are further explained as follows:

a. Airspeed. True and indicated airspeeds are presented at opposite sides of each chart. On any chart, indicated airspeed can be directly converted to true airspeed (or vice versa) by reading directly across the chart without regard for other chart information. Maximum permissible airspeed (VNE) limits appear as red lines on some charts. If no red line appears, VNE is above the limits of the chart.

b. Torque Pressure (%Q). Since pressure altitude and temperature are fixed for each chart, torque pressure required varies according to gross weight and air speed.

c. Fuel Flow. Fuel flow scales are provided opposite the torque pressure scales. On any chart, torque pressure may be converted directly to fuel flow without regard for other chart information. All fuel flow information is presented ECS off. Add 4 percent fuel flow for ECS on. With IR Suppressor installed, fuel flow will be increased by up to 4%.

d. Maximum Range. The maximum range lines indicate the combinations of weight and airspeed that will produce the greatest flight range per gallon of fuel under zero wind conditions. When a maximum range condition does not appear on a chart it is because the maximum range speed is beyond the maximum permissible speed (VNE); in such cases, use VNE cruising speed to obtain maximum range.

The maximum range line labeled "8 TOW" simply indicates the maximum range speed for a configuration with a Δ fe of five square feet more than the clean configuration. For all drag configurations other than clean, the delta torque required must be added to determine torque required and fuel flow. The maximum range lines for the clean configuration (Δ fe = 0) and 8 TOW (Δ fe = 5 sq ft) may be used as a guide to estimate maximum range speed for configurations with other drag values.

e. Maximum Endurance and Rate of Climb. The maximum endurance and rate of climb lines indicate the airspeed for minimum torque pressure required to maintain level flight for each gross weight, FAT and pressure altitude. Since minimum torque pressure will provide minimum fuel flow, maximum flight endurance will be obtained at the airspeed indicated.

7-23. CONDITIONS.

The cruise charts are based on operation at 100 percent rpm and ECS off.

CRUISE
PRESSURE ALTITUDE — SEA LEVEL
100% RPM, CLEAN CONFIGURATION, JP-4 FUEL

SHADED AREA INDICATES 30 MIN. TRANSMISSION LIMIT.

CRUISE
AH-1F
T53-L-703

FAT = -30°C

EXAMPLE A

WANTED

TORQUE REQUIRED FOR LEVEL FLIGHT, FUEL FLOW, INDICATED AIRSPEED

KNOWN

CLEAN CONFIGURATION, GROSS WEIGHT = 8000 LB, PRESSURE ALTITUDE = 1000 FEET, FAT = -30°C, DESIRED TRUE AIRSPEED = 110 KNOTS.

METHOD (INTERPOLATE)

ENTER TRUE AIRSPEED HERE
READ TORQUE, FUEL FLOW, AND IAS ON EACH ADJACENT ALTITUDE AND/OR FAT, THEN INTERPOLATE BETWEEN ALTITUDE AND FAT

SEE FIGURE 7-7 (SHT 2) ❶

ALTITUDE, FEET	SEA LEVEL	2000 FEET	1000 FEET
FAT, °C	-30	-30	-30
TORQUE, % Q	63.5	61.5	62.5
FUEL FLOW, LB/HR	600	570	585
IAS, KNOTS	124	119	121.5

EXAMPLE B

WANTED

ADDITIONAL TORQUE REQUIRED AND FUEL FLOW FOR ARMAMENT CONFIGURATION AND CONDITION IN EXAMPLE A

KNOWN

ARMAMENT CONFIGURATION FOR 2 19 TUBE ROCKET LAUNCHERS = 3.1 ΔF -SQ FT (FROM FIGURE 7-8).

METHOD

ENTER TRUE AIRSPEED AT 110 KNOTS AND MOVE RIGHT TO ΔF- SQ FT = 3.1 (BETWEEN 0.0 AND 5.0 ΔF - SQ FT). FROM THAT POINT MOVE UP TO READ 3.7% Q TORQUE. ADD 3.7% Q TORQUE TO THE TORQUE REQUIRED FOR LEVEL FLIGHT IN THE CLEAN CONFIGURATION AND THE CORRESPONDING INCREASE IN FUEL FLOW (APPROXIMATELY 18 POUNDS PER HOUR) TO THE CLEAN CONFIGURATION FUEL FLOW.

DATA BASIS: DERIVED FROM FLIGHT TEST

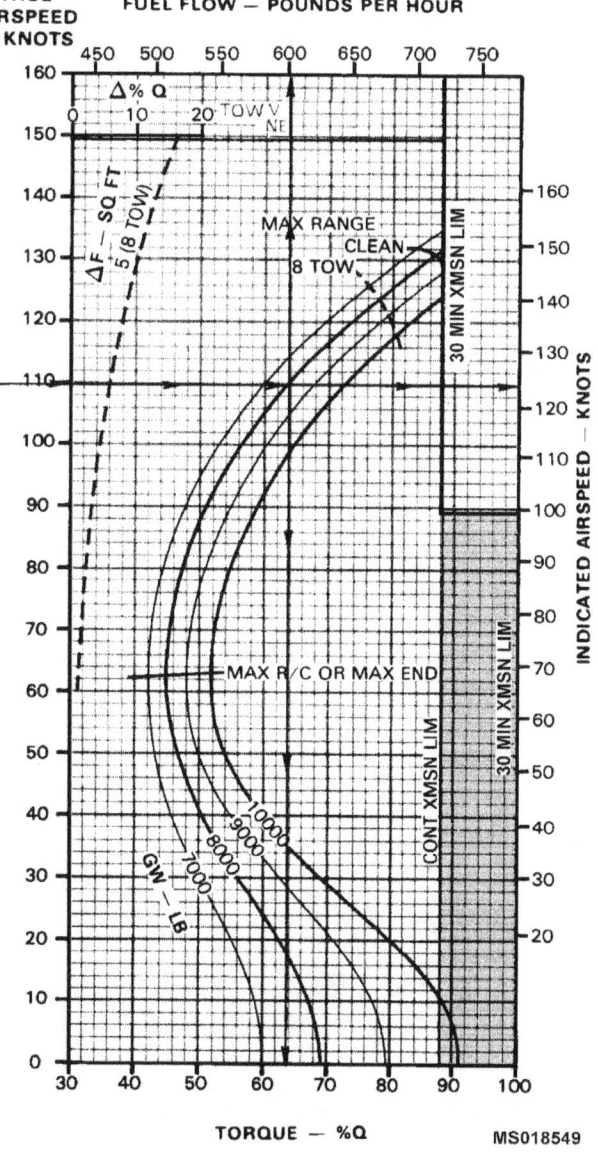

B540 Figure 7-7. Cruise Chart (Sheet 1 of 23)

TM 1-1520-236-10

CRUISE
PRESSURE ALTITUDE — 2000 FEET
100% RPM, CLEAN CONFIGURATION, JP-4 FUEL

CRUISE
AH-1F
T53-L-703

EXAMPLE

FAT = -30°C

WANTED

SPEED FOR MAXIMUM RANGE
TORQUE REQUIRED AND FUEL FLOW AT MAXIMUM RANGE SPEED FOR MAXIMUM ENDURANCE

KNOWN

CLEAN CONFIGURATION, FAT = -30°C,
PRESSURE ALTITUDE = 2000 FEET,
AND GROSS WEIGHT = 9000 POUNDS

METHOD

LOCATE (-30°C FAT, 2000 FEET) CHART
FIND INTERSECTION OF 9000 LB GROSS WEIGHT
LINE WITH THE MAXIMUM RANGE LINE
TO READ SPEED FOR MAXIMUM RANGE:
 MOVE LEFT, READ TAS = 129 KNOTS AND
 MOVE RIGHT, READ IAS = 141 KNOTS
TO READ FUEL FLOW REQUIRED:
 MOVE UP, READ DUEL FLOW = 695 LB/HR
TO READ TORQUE REQUIRED
 MOVE DOWN, READ TORQUE = 87% Q
FIND INTERSECTION OF 9000 LB GROSS WEIGHT
LINE WITH THE MAXIMUM ENDURANCE LINE
TO READ SPEED FOR MAXIMUM ENDURANCE:
 MOVE LEFT, READ TAS = 64 KNOTS AND
 MOVE RIGHT, READ IAS = 67 KNOTS

SEE FIGURE 7-7 (SHT 1) ❶

SHADED AREA INDICATES 30 MIN. TRANSMISSION LIMIT.

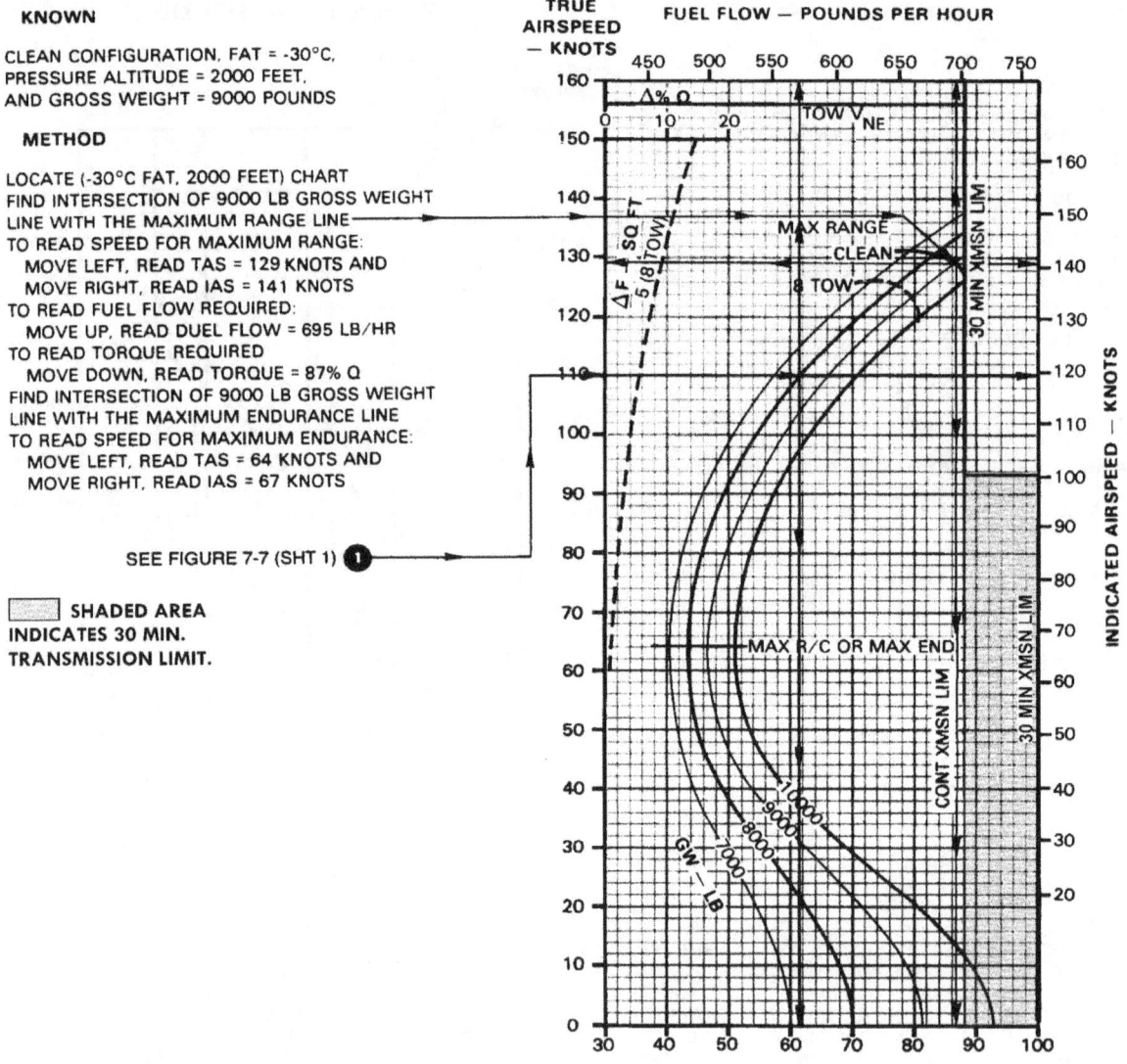

DATA BASIS: DERIVED FROM FLIGHT TEST

MS018550

B540 Figure 7-7. Cruise Chart (Sheet 2 of 23)

CRUISE
PRESSURE ALTITUDE — 4000 FEET TO 6000 FEET
100% RPM, CLEAN CONFIGURATION, JP-4 FUEL

CRUISE
AH-1F
T53-L-703

SHADED AREA INDICATES 30 MIN. TRANSMISSION LIMIT.

FAT = -30°C

DATA BASIS: DERIVED FROM FLIGHT TEST

MS018551

Figure 7-7. Cruise Chart (Sheet 3 of 23)

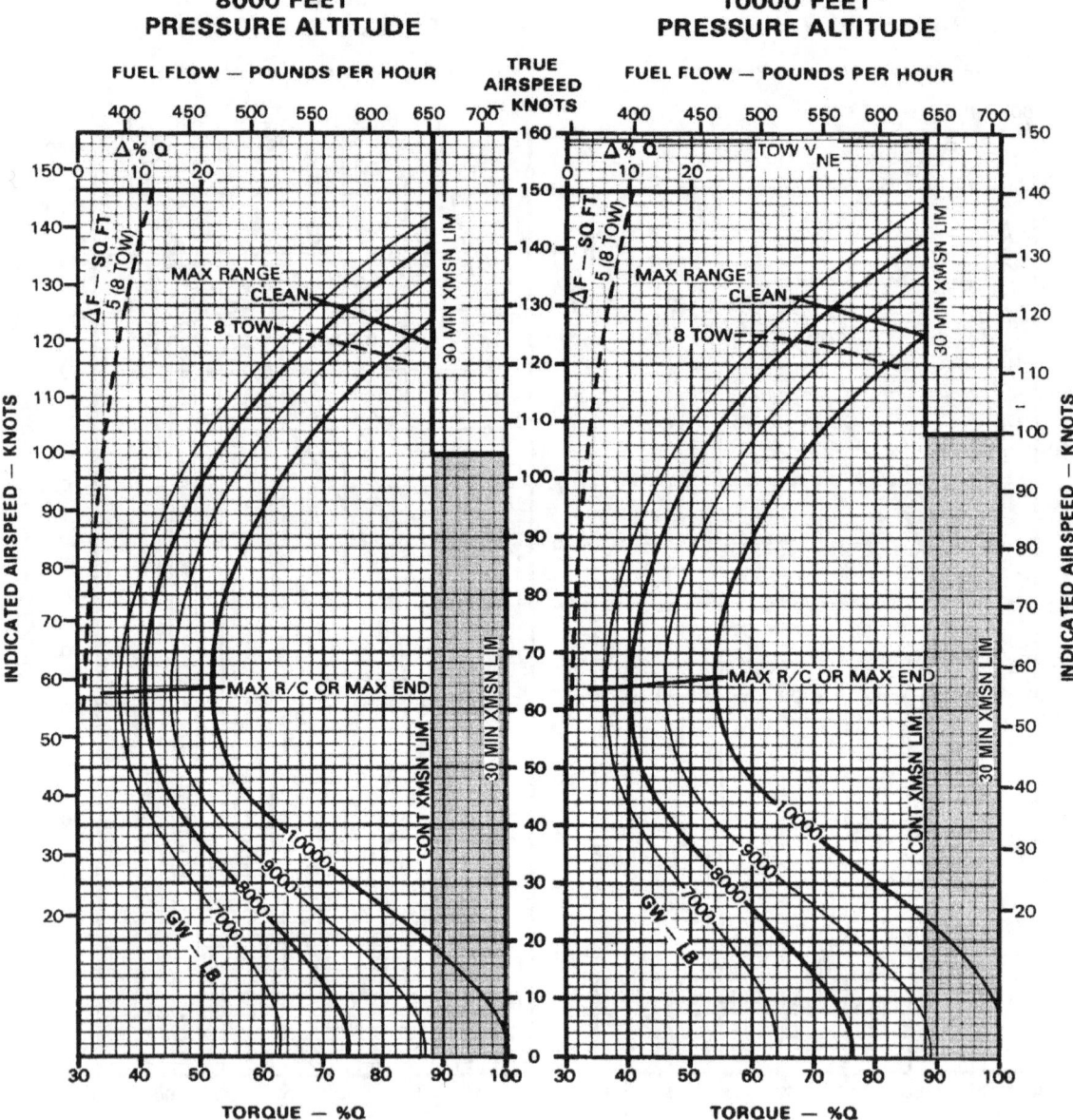

Figure 7-7. Cruise Chart (Sheet 4 of 23)

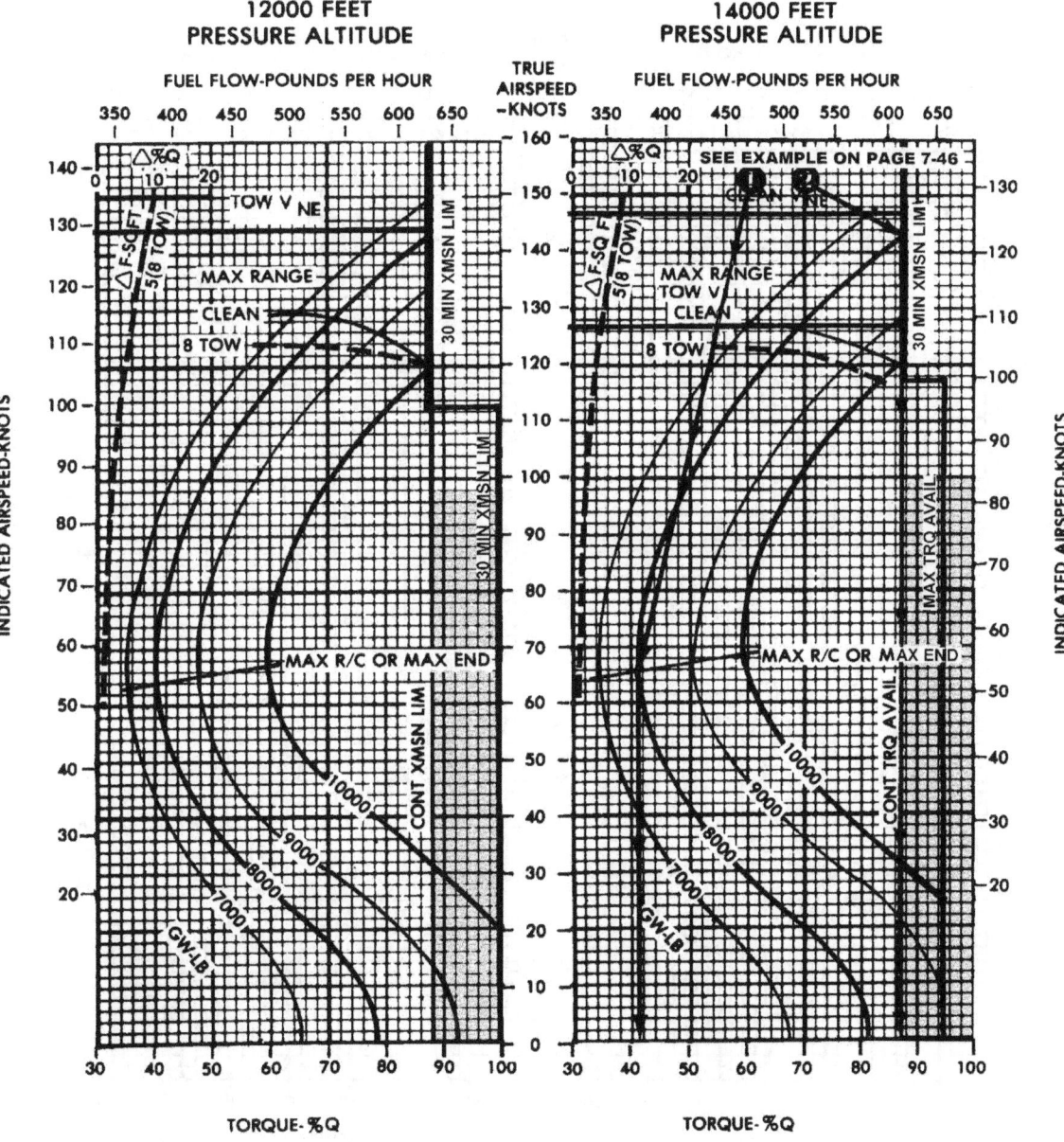

Figure 7-7. Cruise Chart (Sheet 5 of 23)

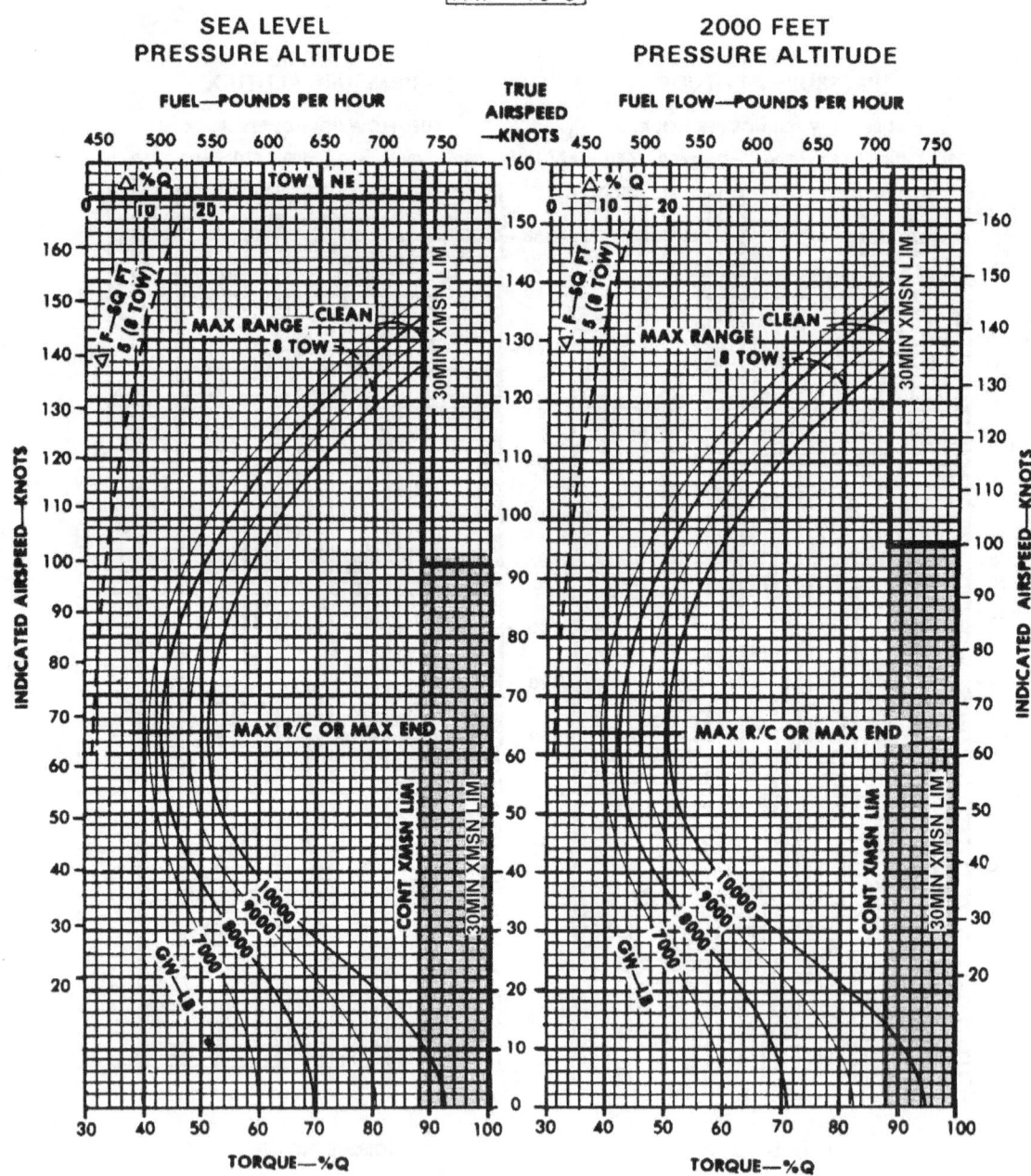

Figure 7-7. Cruise Chart (Sheet 6 of 23)

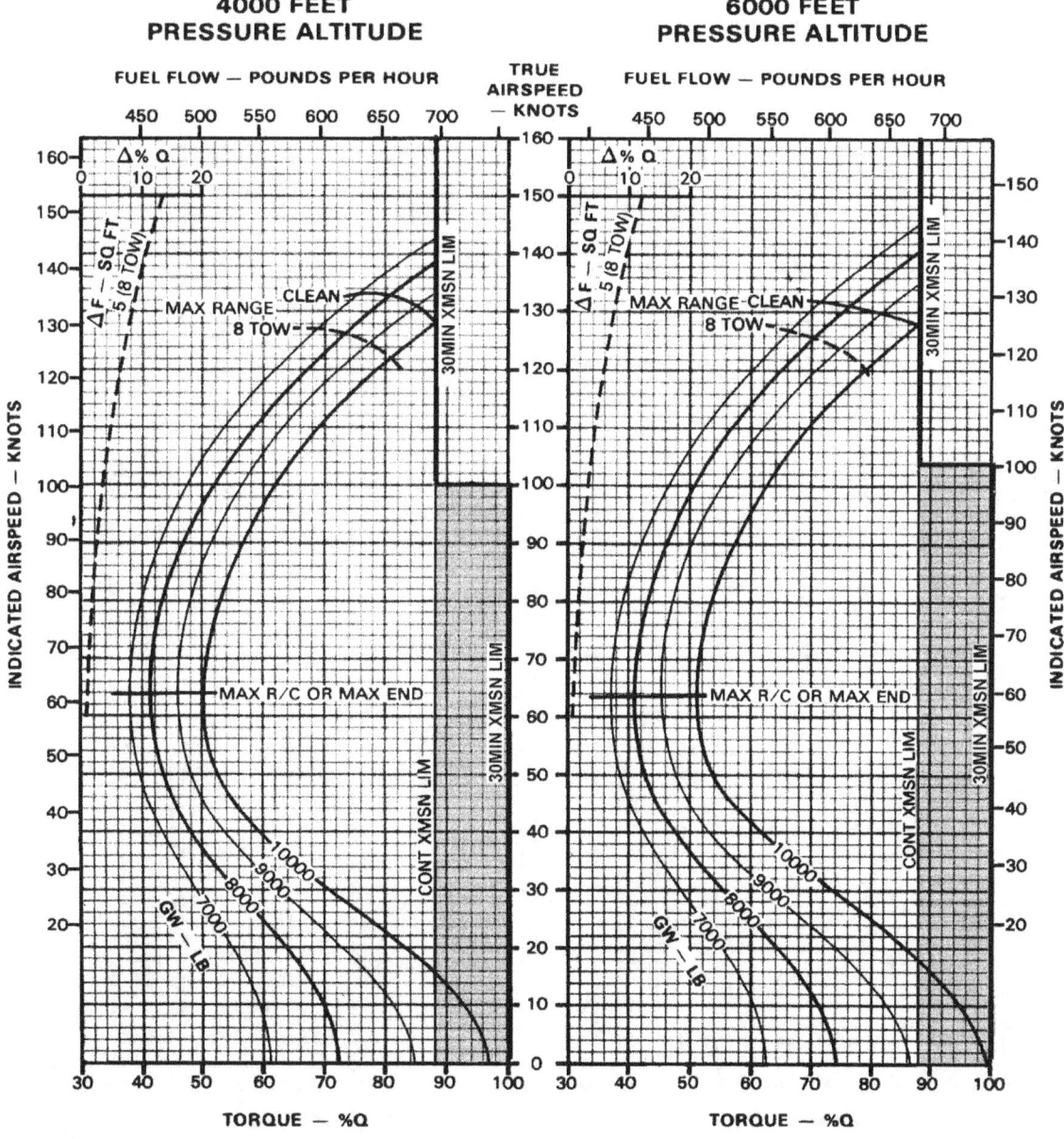

Figure 7-7. Cruise Chart (Sheet 7 of 23)

TM 1-1520-236-10

CRUISE
PRESSURE ALTITUDE — 8000 FEET TO 10000 FEET
100% RPM, CLEAN CONFIGURATION, JP-4 FUEL

CRUISE
AH-1F
T53-L-703

SHADED AREA INDICATES 30 MIN. TRANSMISSION LIMIT.

FAT = -15°C

DATA BASIS: DERIVED FROM FLIGHT TEST

MS018556

B540 Figure 7-7. Cruise Chart (Sheet 8 of 23)

7-26

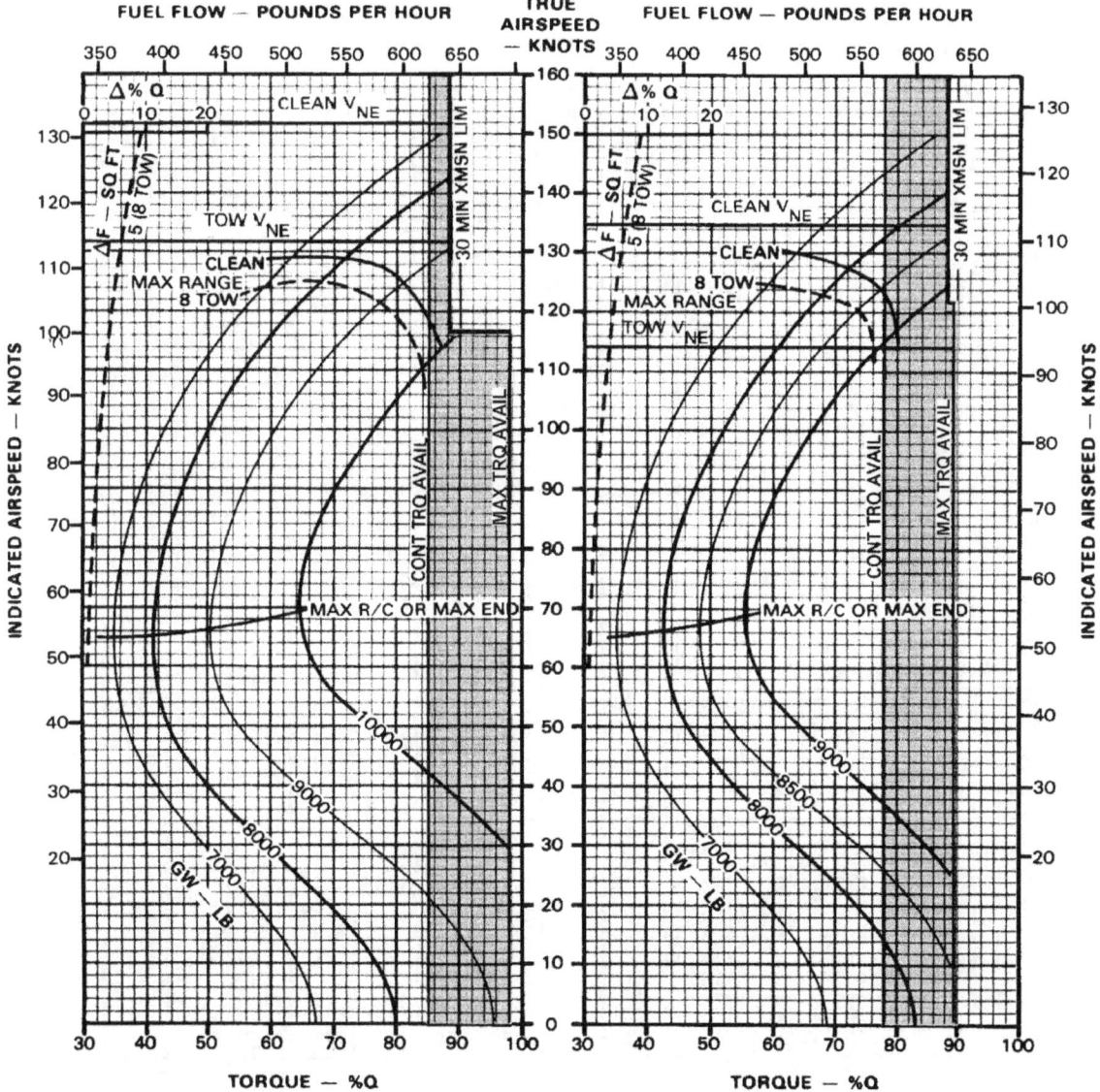

Figure 7-7. Cruise Chart (Sheet 9 of 23)

TM 1-1520-236-10

CRUISE
PRESSURE ALTITUDE — SEA LEVEL TO 2000 FEET
100% RPM, CLEAN CONFIGURATION, JP-4 FUEL

CRUISE
AH-1F
T53-L-703

SHADED AREA INDICATES 30 MIN. TRANSMISSION LIMIT.

FAT = 0°C

SEA LEVEL PRESSURE ALTITUDE

2000 FEET PRESSURE ALTITUDE

DATA BASIS: DERIVED FROM FLIGHT TEST

MS018558

B540 Figure 7-7. Cruise Chart (Sheet 10 of 23)

7-28

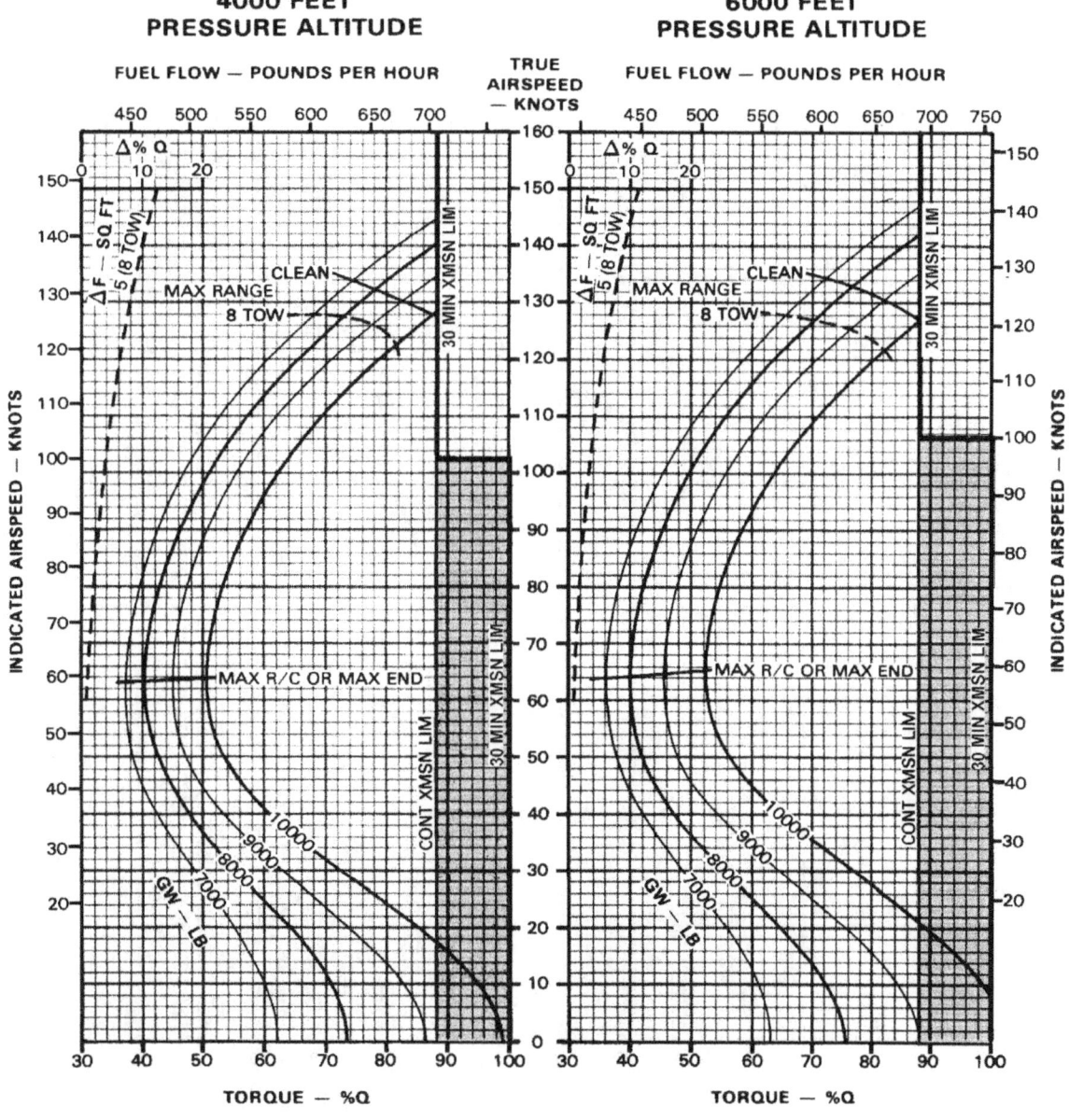

Figure 7-7. Cruise Chart (Sheet 11 of 23)

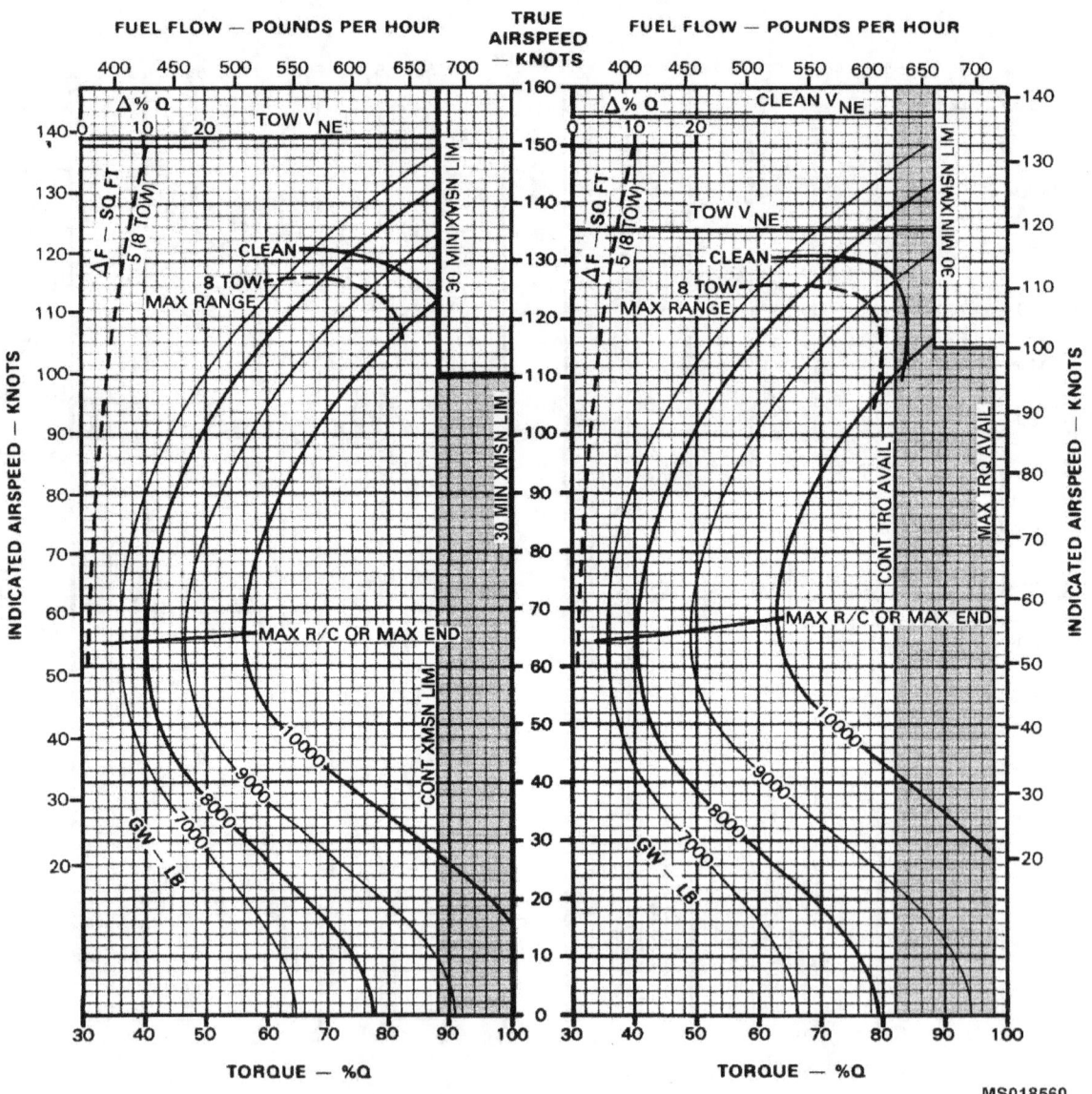

Figure 7-7. Cruise Chart (Sheet 12 of 23)

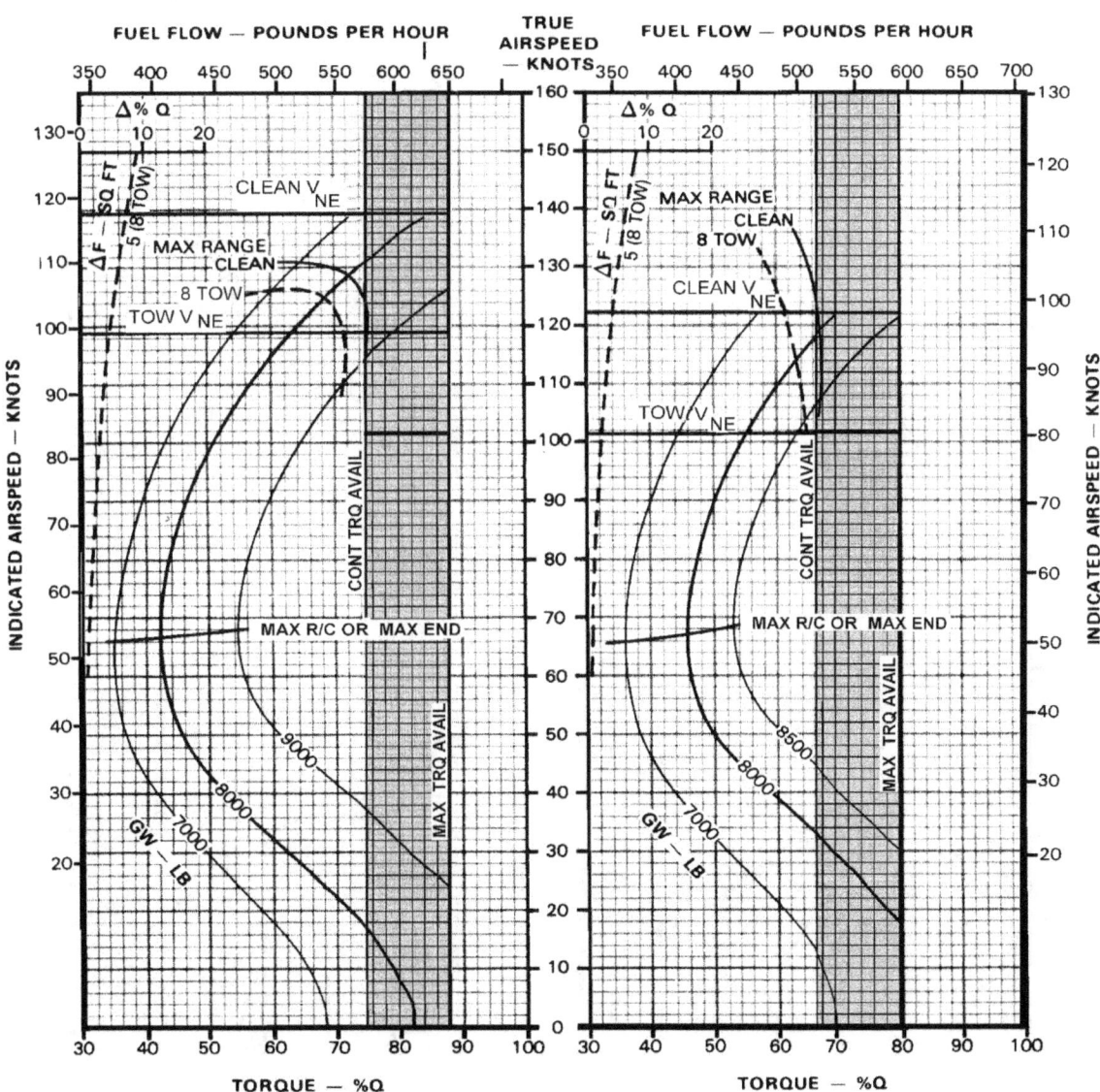

Figure 7-7. Cruise Chart (Sheet 13 of 23)

TM 1-1520-236-10

CRUISE
PRESSURE ALTITUDE - SEA LEVEL TO 2000 FEET
100% RPM, CLEAN CONFIGURATION, JP - 4 FUEL

CRUISE
AH-1F
T53-L-703

SHADED AREA INDICATES 30 MIN. TRANSMISSION LIMIT.

FAT = +15°C

SEA LEVEL PRESSURE ALTITUDE

2000 FEET PRESSURE ALTITUDE

DATA BASIS: DERIVED FROM FLIGHT TEST

MS018562

B540 Figure 7-7. Cruise Chart (Sheet 14 of 23)

CRUISE
PRESSURE ALTITUDE — 4000 FEET TO 6000 FEET
100% RPM, CLEAN CONFIGURATION, JP-4 FUEL

CRUISE
AH-1F
T53-L-703

SHADED AREA INDICATES 30 MIN. TRANSMISSION LIMIT.

FAT = +15°C

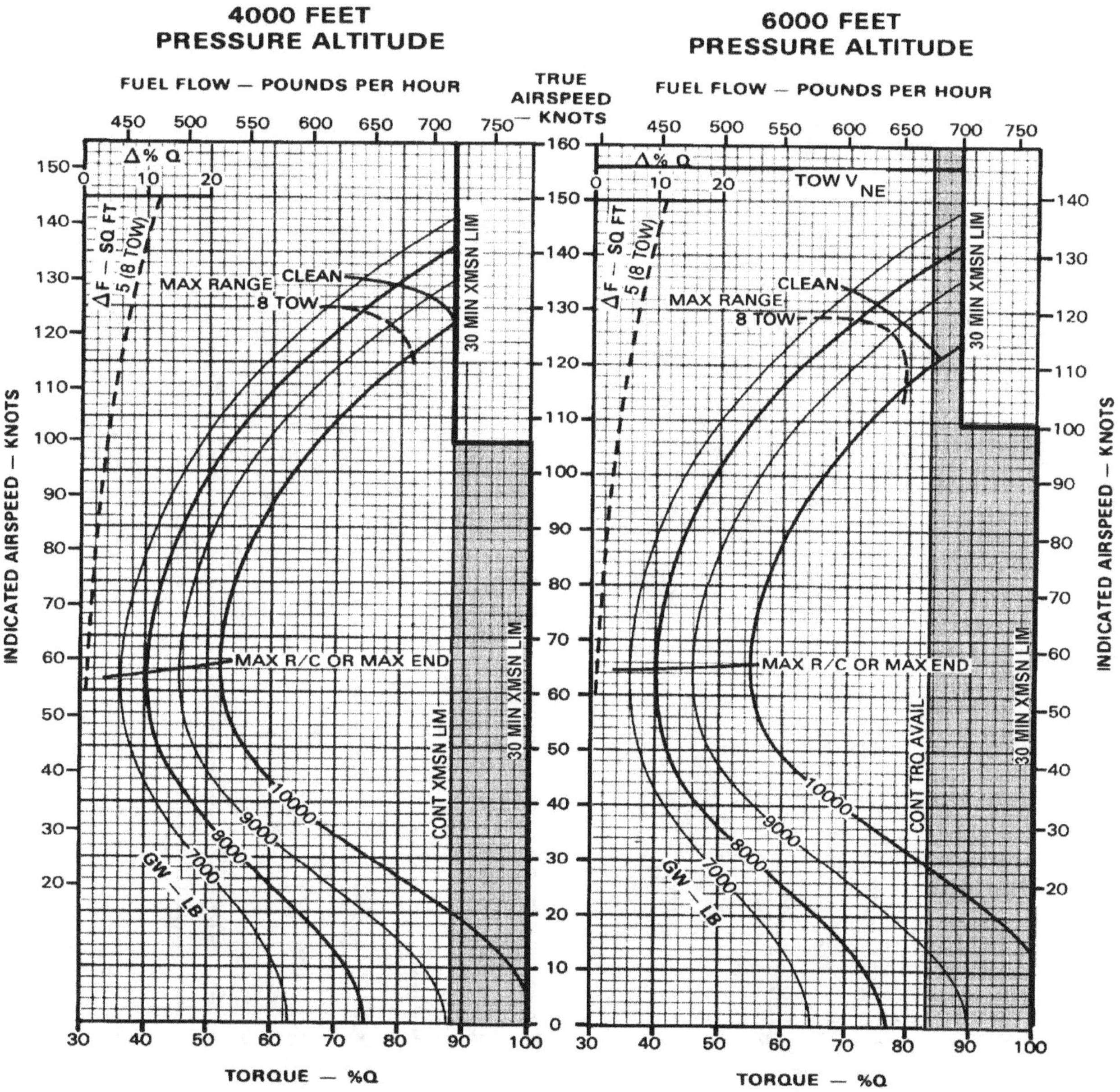

DATA BASIS: DERIVED FROM FLIGHT TEST

Figure 7-7. Cruise Chart (Sheet 15 of 23)

CRUISE

PRESSURE ALTITUDE — 8000 FEET TO 10000 FEET
100% RPM, CLEAN CONFIGURATION, JP-4 FUEL

CRUISE
AH-1F
T53-L-703

SHADED AREA INDICATES 30 MIN. TRANSMISSION LIMIT.

FAT = +15°C

Figure 7-7. Cruise Chart (Sheet 16 of 23)

DATA BASIS: DERIVED FROM FLIGHT TEST

MS018564

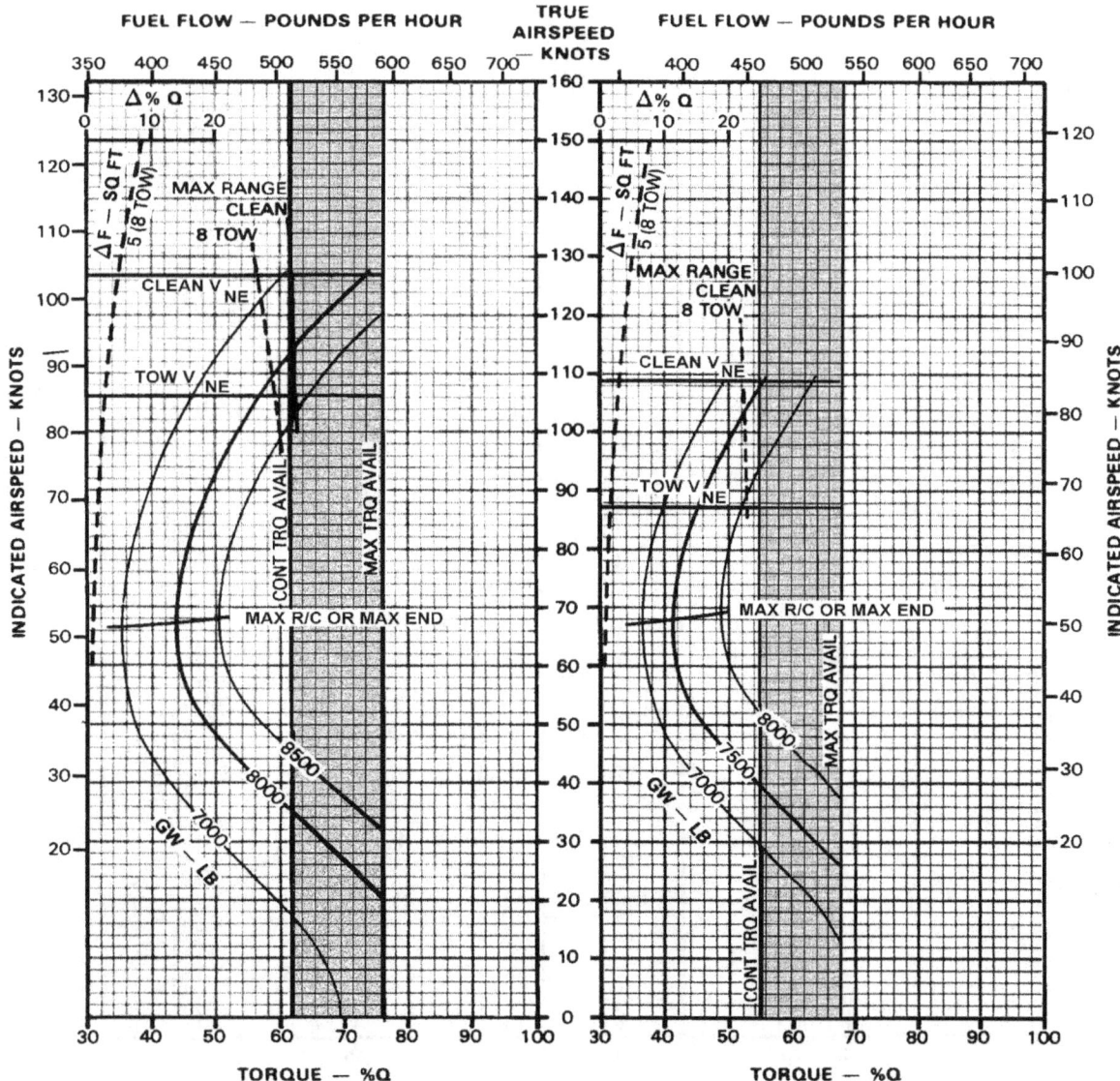

Figure 7-7. Cruise Chart (Sheet 17 of 23)

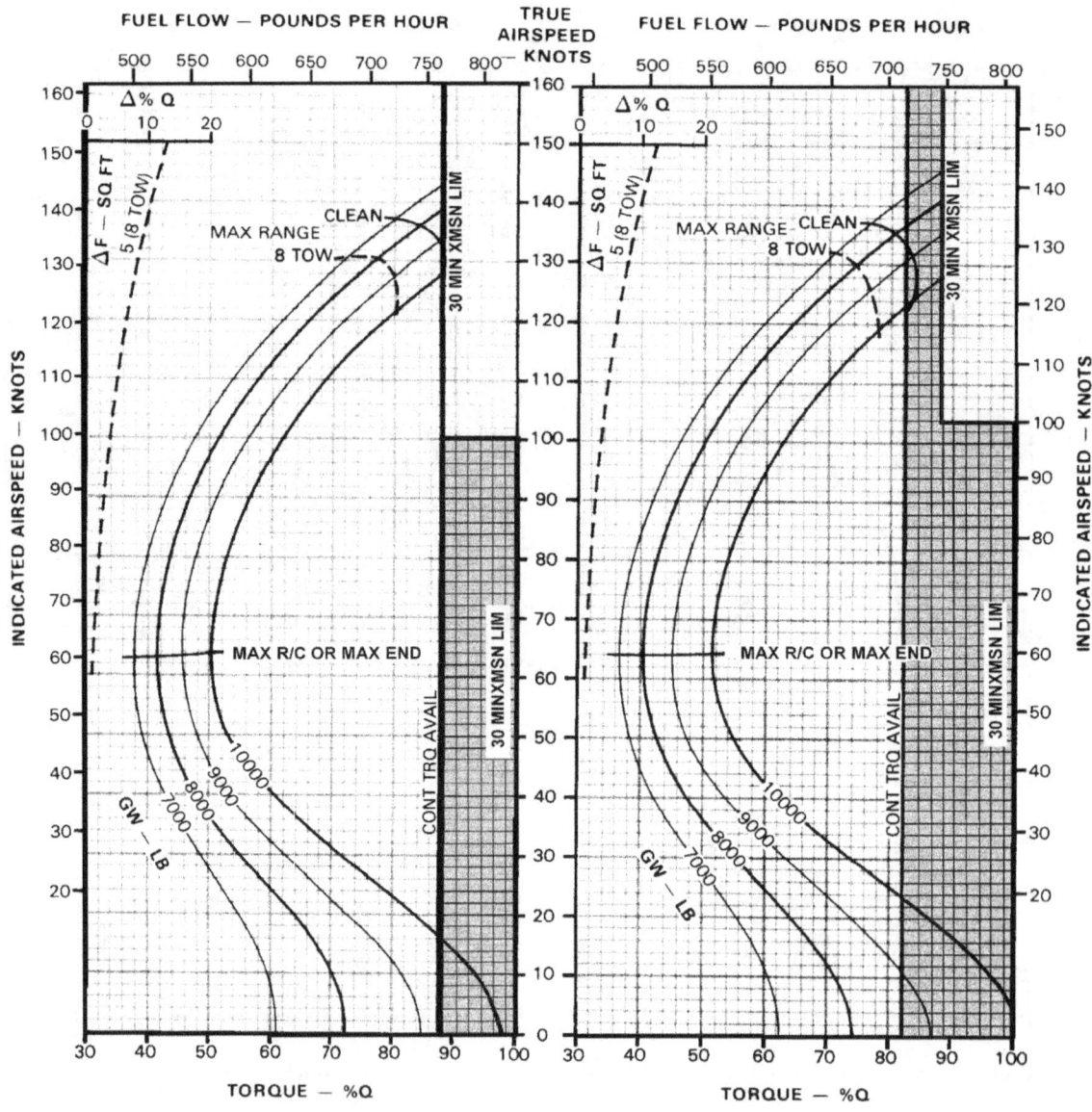

Figure 7-7. Cruise Chart (Sheet 18 of 23)

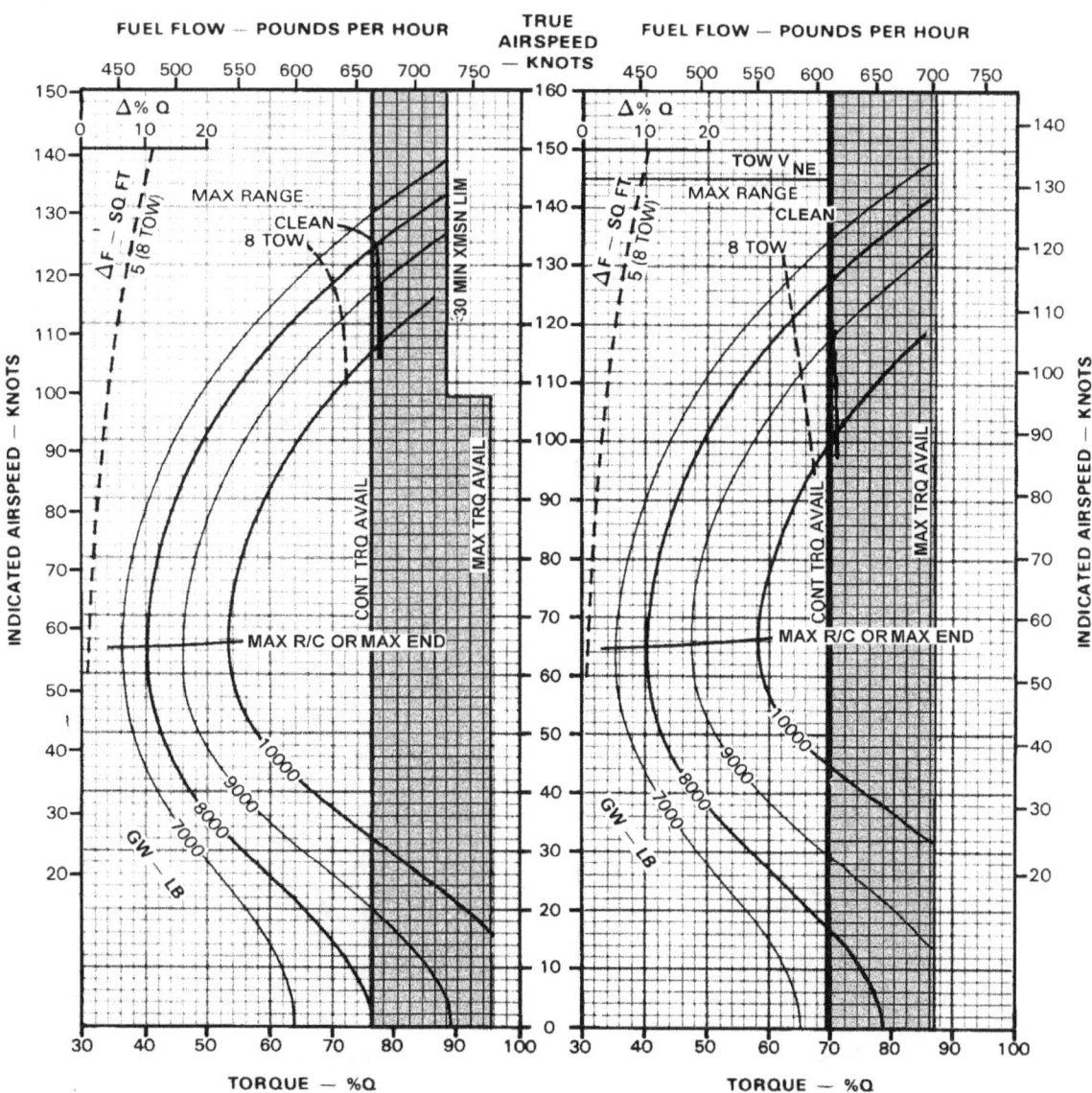

Figure 7-7. Cruise Chart (Sheet 19 of 23)

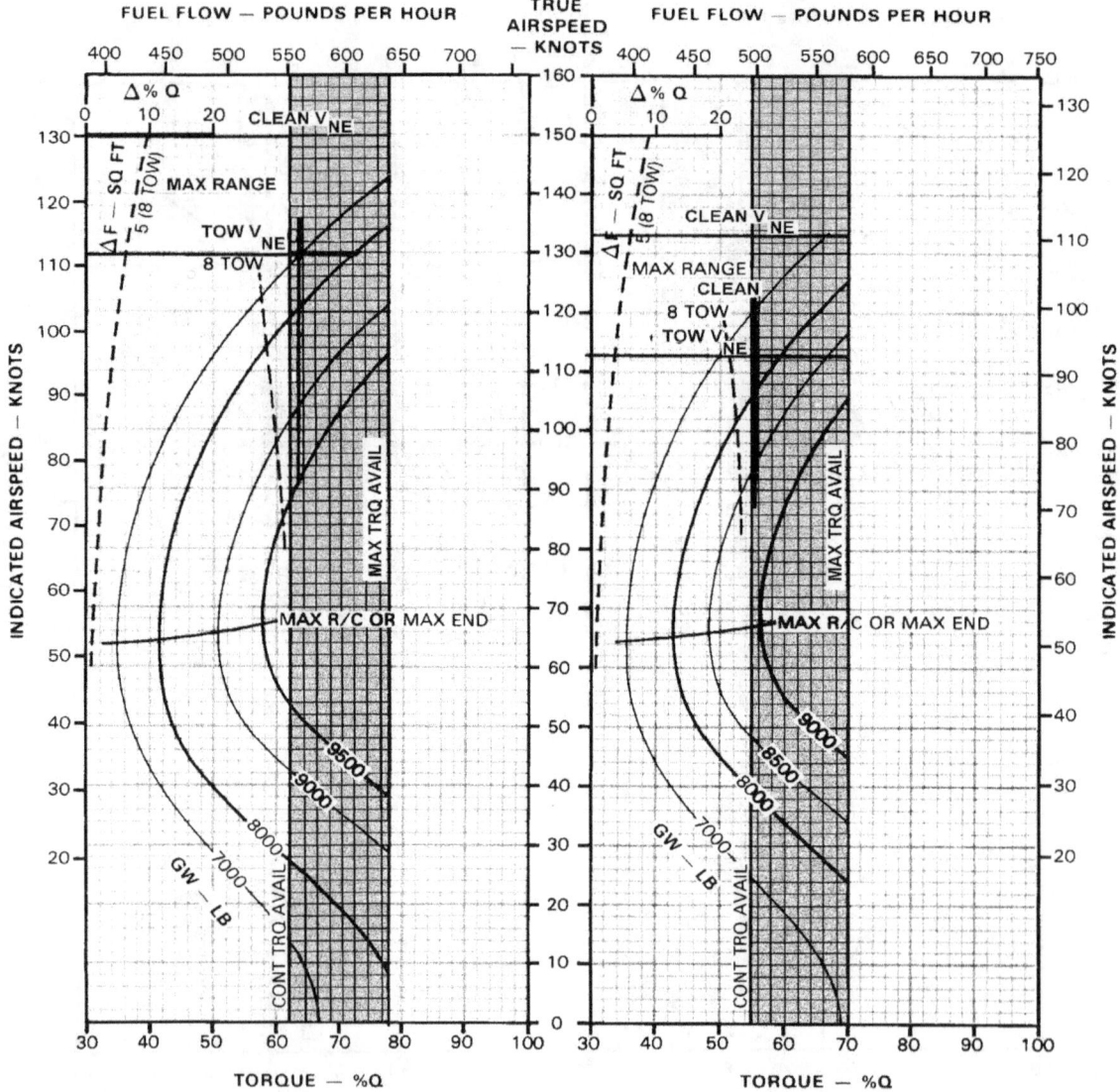

Figure 7-7. Cruise Chart (Sheet 20 of 23)

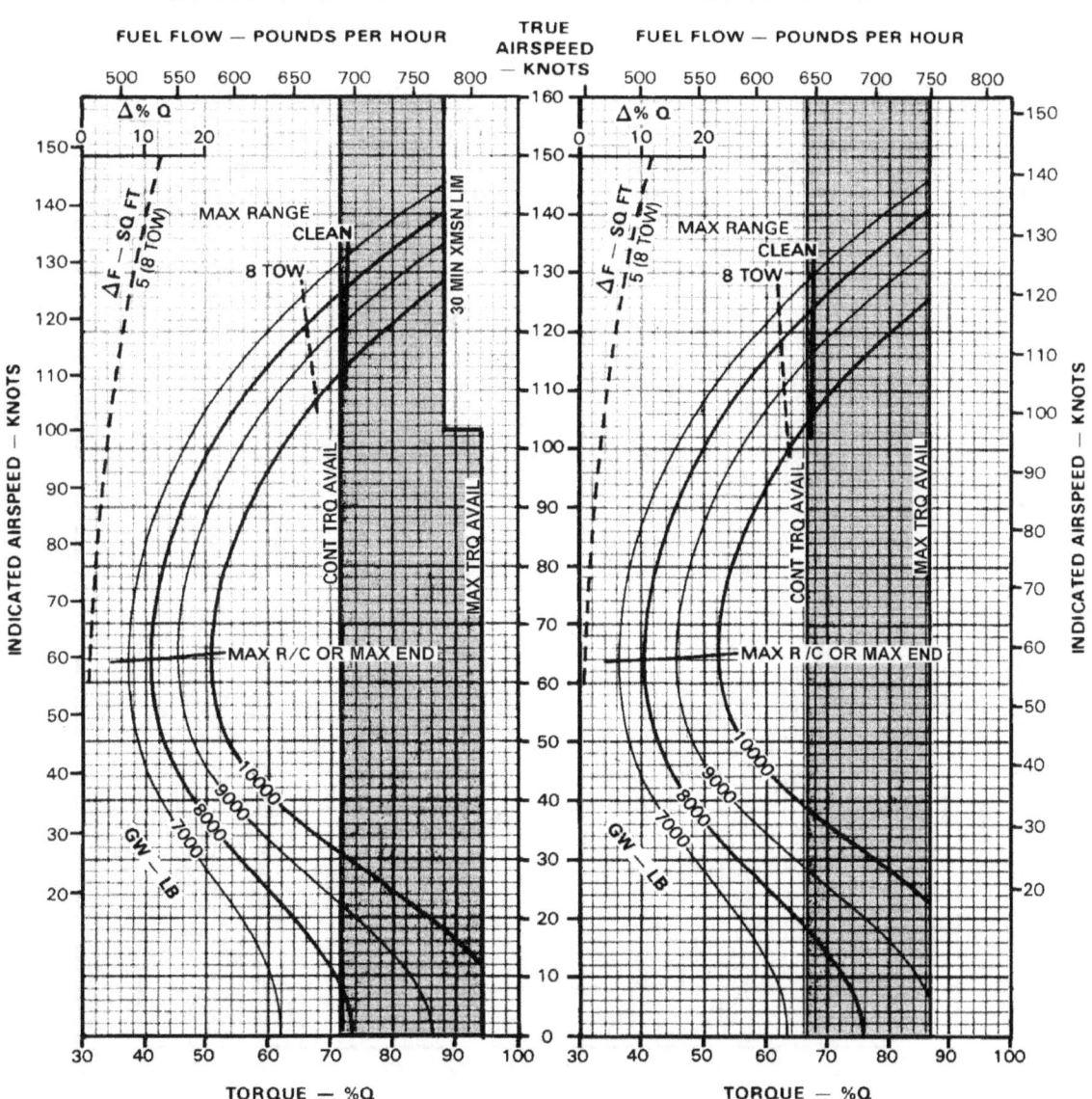

Figure 7-7. Cruise Chart (Sheet 21 of 23)

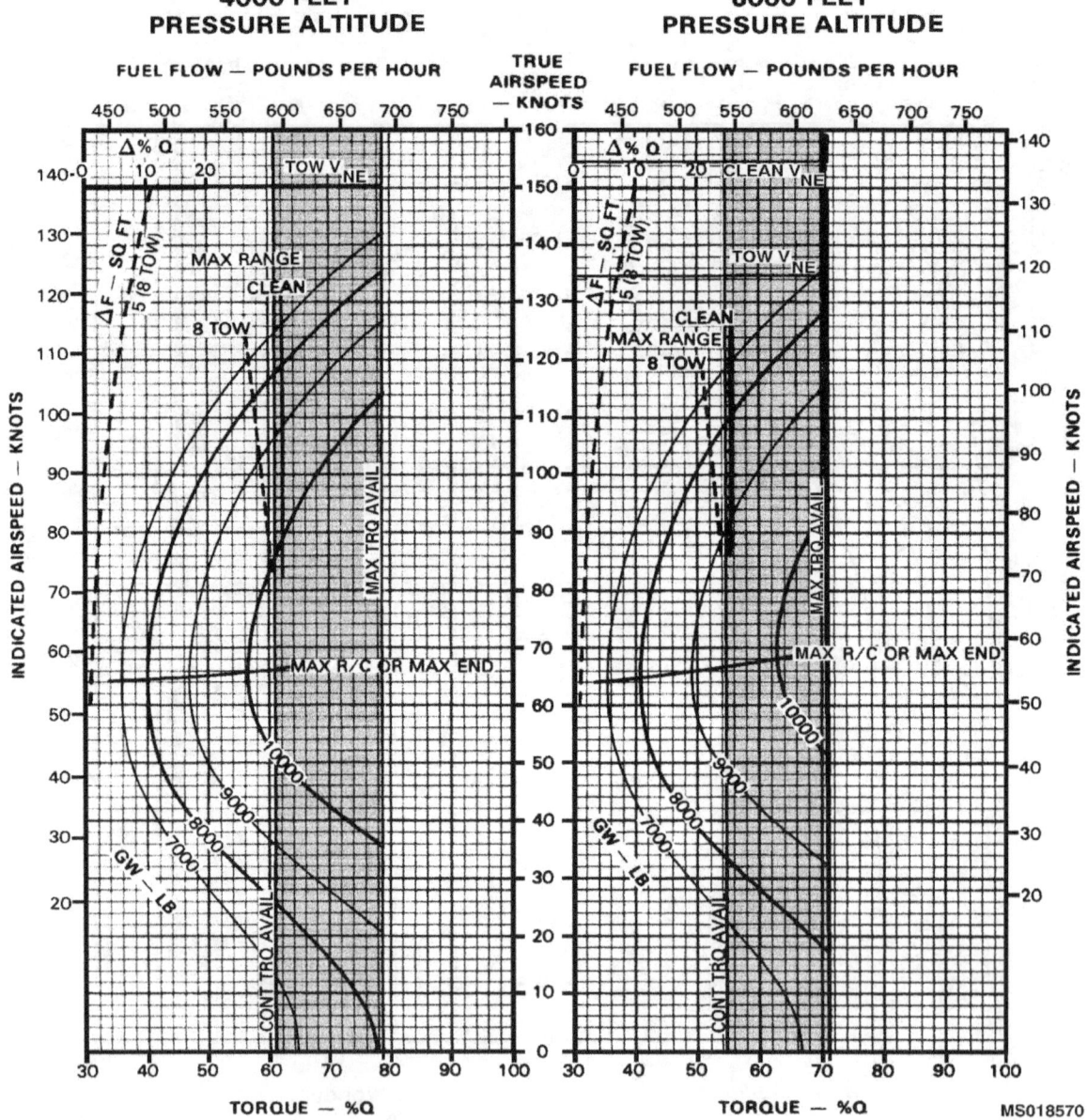

Figure 7-7. Cruise Chart (Sheet 22 of 23)

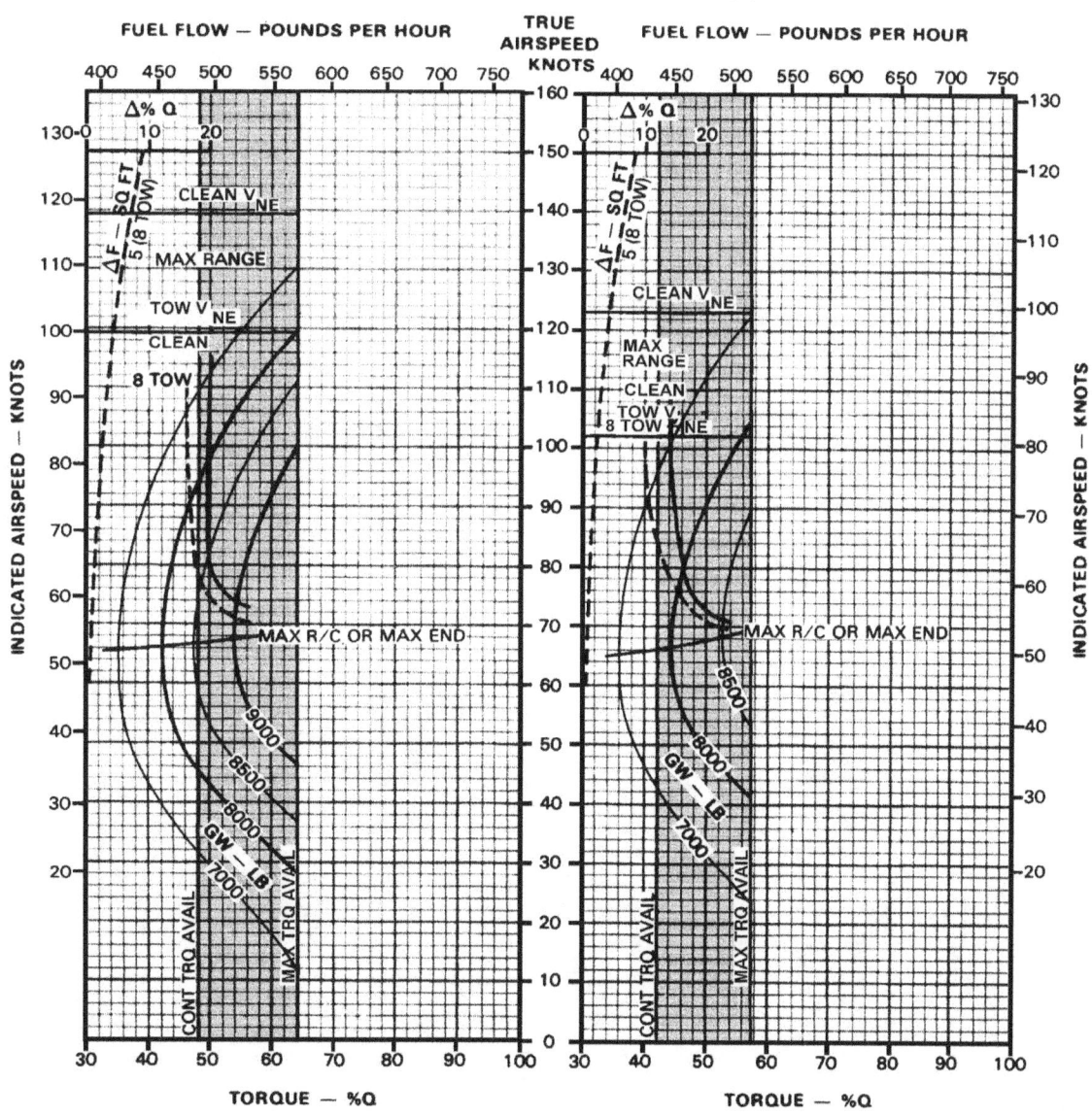

Figure 7-7. Cruise Chart (Sheet 23 of 23)

SECTION VI. DRAG

7-24. DESCRIPTION.

The drag chart (Figure 7-8) shows the equivalent flat plate drag area (ΔF) increment of all approved configurations.

7-25. USE OF CHART.

This chart is used to adjust the cruise charts (Figure 7-7) for the appropriate torque and fuel flow due to the equivalent flat plate drag area change (ΔF). Select a configuration from Figure 7-8 and read equivalent flat plate drag for that configuration. Proceed to Figure 7-7, example B for application of drag. With IR Suppressor installed, the equivalent flat plate drag area will be increased by 2 sq ft.

7-26. CONDITIONS.

The drag chart is based on 100 percent rpm.

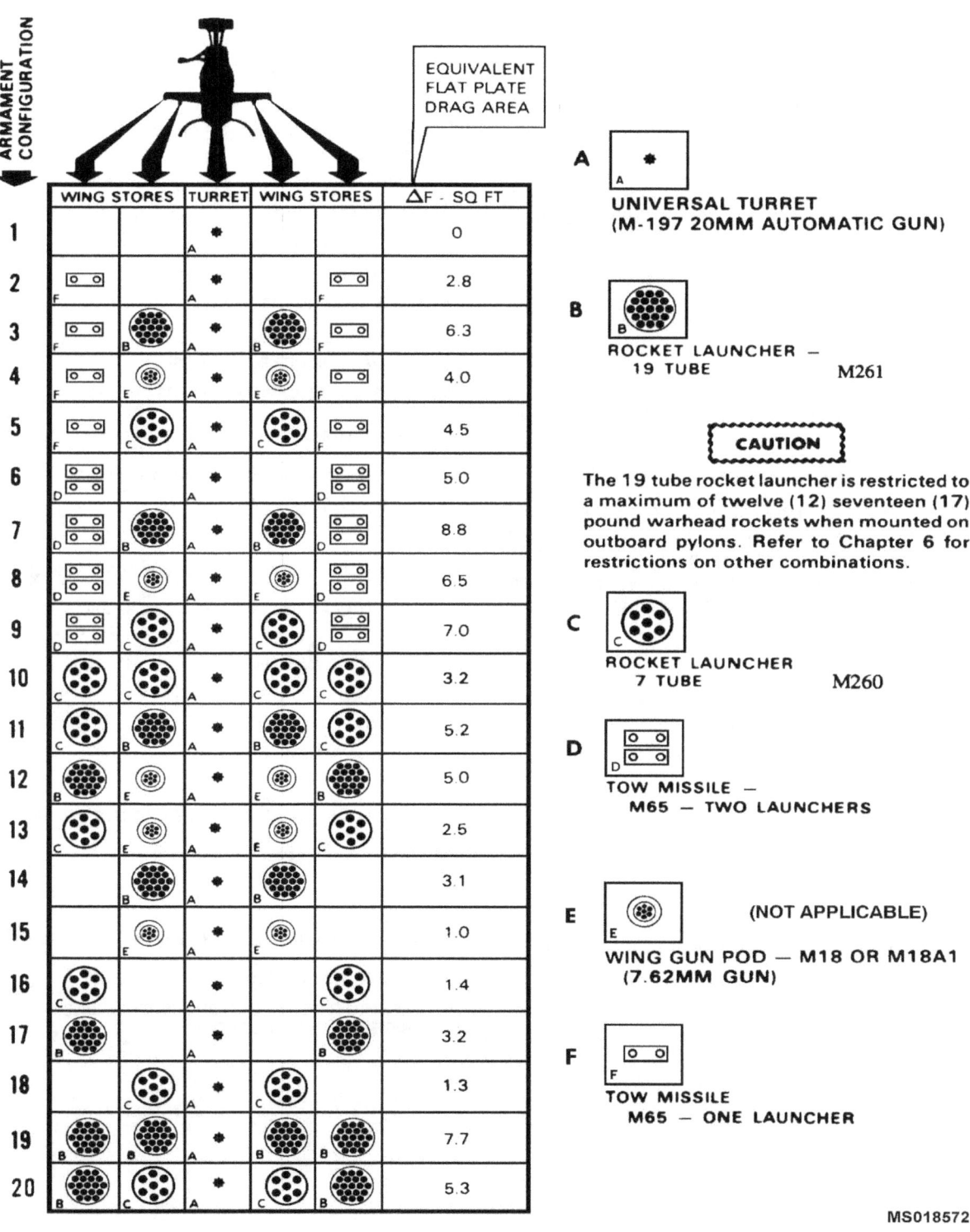

Figure 7-8. Drag Chart

SECTION VII. CLIMB – DESCENT

7-27. DESCRIPTION.

The upper grid of the climb descent chart (Figure 7-9) shows the change in torque (above or below torque required for level flight under the same gross weight and atmospheric conditions) to obtain a given rate of climb or descent.

7-28. USE OF CHART.

The primary uses of the chart are illustrated by the chart examples.

    a. The torque change obtained from the upper grid scale must be added to the torque required for level flight (for climb) - or subtracted from the torque required for level flight (for descent) - obtained from the appropriate cruise chart in order to obtain a total climb or descent torque.

    b. By entering the bottom of the upper grid with a known torque change, moving upward to the gross weight, and left to the corresponding rate of climb or descent may also be obtained.

7-29. CONDITIONS.

The climb-descent chart is based on the use of 100 percent rpm.

EXAMPLE B540

WANTED

EXCESS TORQUE AVAILABLE FOR CLIMB AT MAXIMUM CONTINUOUS POWER.

KNOWN

CLEAN CONFIGURATION

GROSS WEIGHT = 8000 LB

FAT = - 30° C

PRESSURE ALTITUDE = 14000 FEET

METHOD

LOCATE CHART (FIGURE 7-7, SHEET 5)

FIND INTERSECTION OF 8000 LB GROSS WEIGHT LINE WITH THE MAXIMUM RATE OF CLIMB LINE ⟶ ①

MOVE DOWN, READ TORQUE REQUIRED = 41.5% Q

FIND INTERSECTION OF 8000 LB GROSS WEIGHT LINE WITH THE CONTINUOUS TORQUE AVAILABLE LINE ⟶ ②

MOVE DOWN, READ TORQUE AVAILABLE = 87% Q

EXCESS TORQUE AVAILABLE = (87 - 41.5) = 45.5% Q

WANTED

RATE OF CLIMB AT 60 KIAS

MAXIMUM CONTINUOUS POWER

KNOWN

EXCESS TORQUE AVAILABLE (FROM EXAMPLE ON FIGURE 7-7. SHEET 5) = 45.5% Q

GROSS WEIGHT = 8000 LB

METHOD

ENTER CALIBRATED TORQUE SCALE HERE ⟶ ③

MOVE UP TO GROSS WEIGHT LINE

MOVE LEFT TO RATE OF CLIMB OR DESCENT SCALE.
READ RATE OF CLIMB = 1900 FT MIN

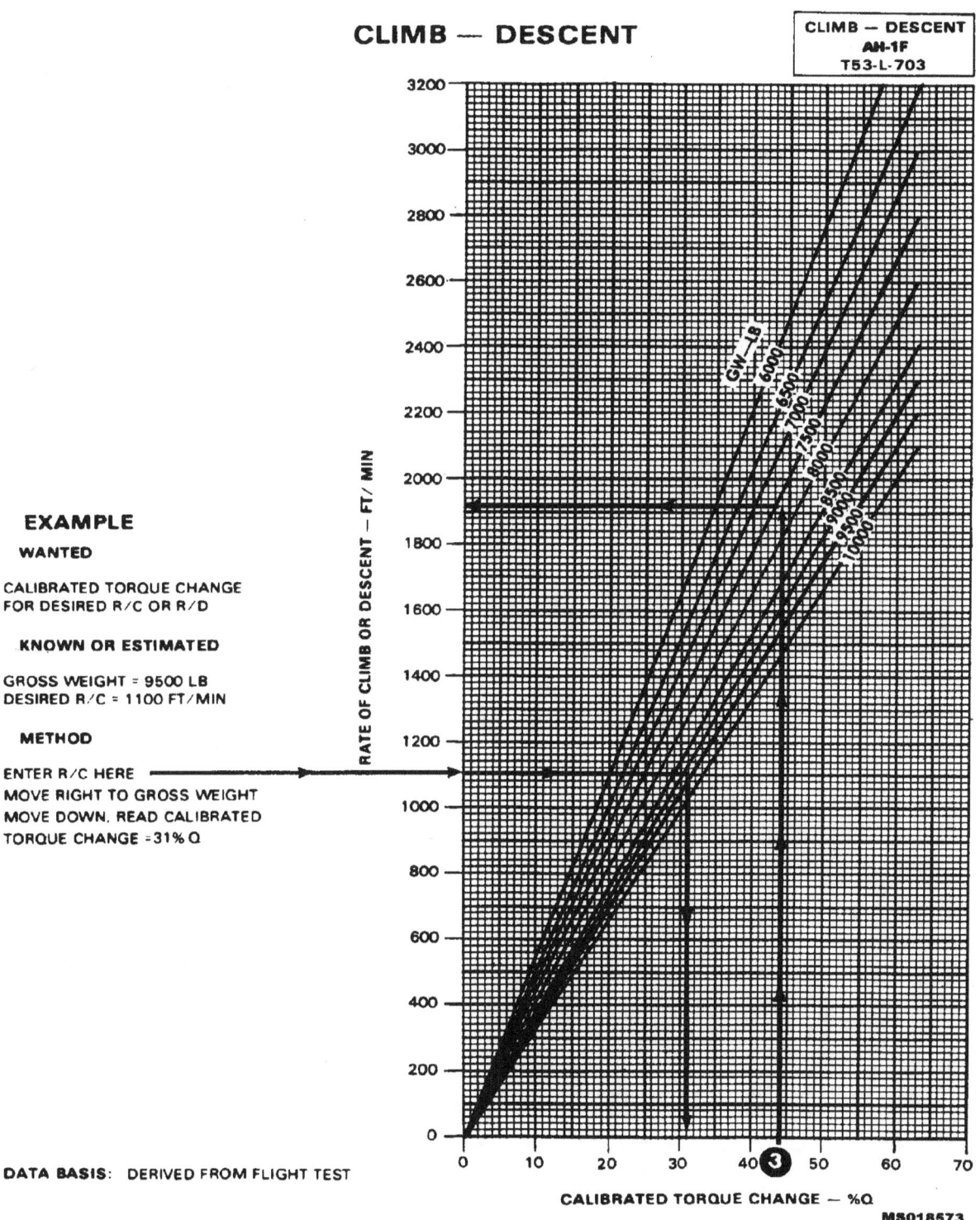

Figure 7-9. Climb - Descent Chart

SECTION VIII. IDLE FUEL FLOW

7-30. DESCRIPTION.

The idle fuel flow chart (Figure 7-10) shows the fuel flow at engine idle and at flat pitch with 100 percent rpm.

7-31. USE OF CHART.

The primary use of the chart is illustrated by the example. To determine the idle fuel flow, it is necessary to know the idle condition, pressure altitude, and free air temperature. Enter at the pressure altitude, move right to FAT in appropriate grid, then move down and read fuel flow on the scale corresponding to the condition. Refer to the cruise charts to obtain fuel flow for cruise power conditions.

7-32. CONDITIONS.

This chart is based on the use of JP-4 fuel.

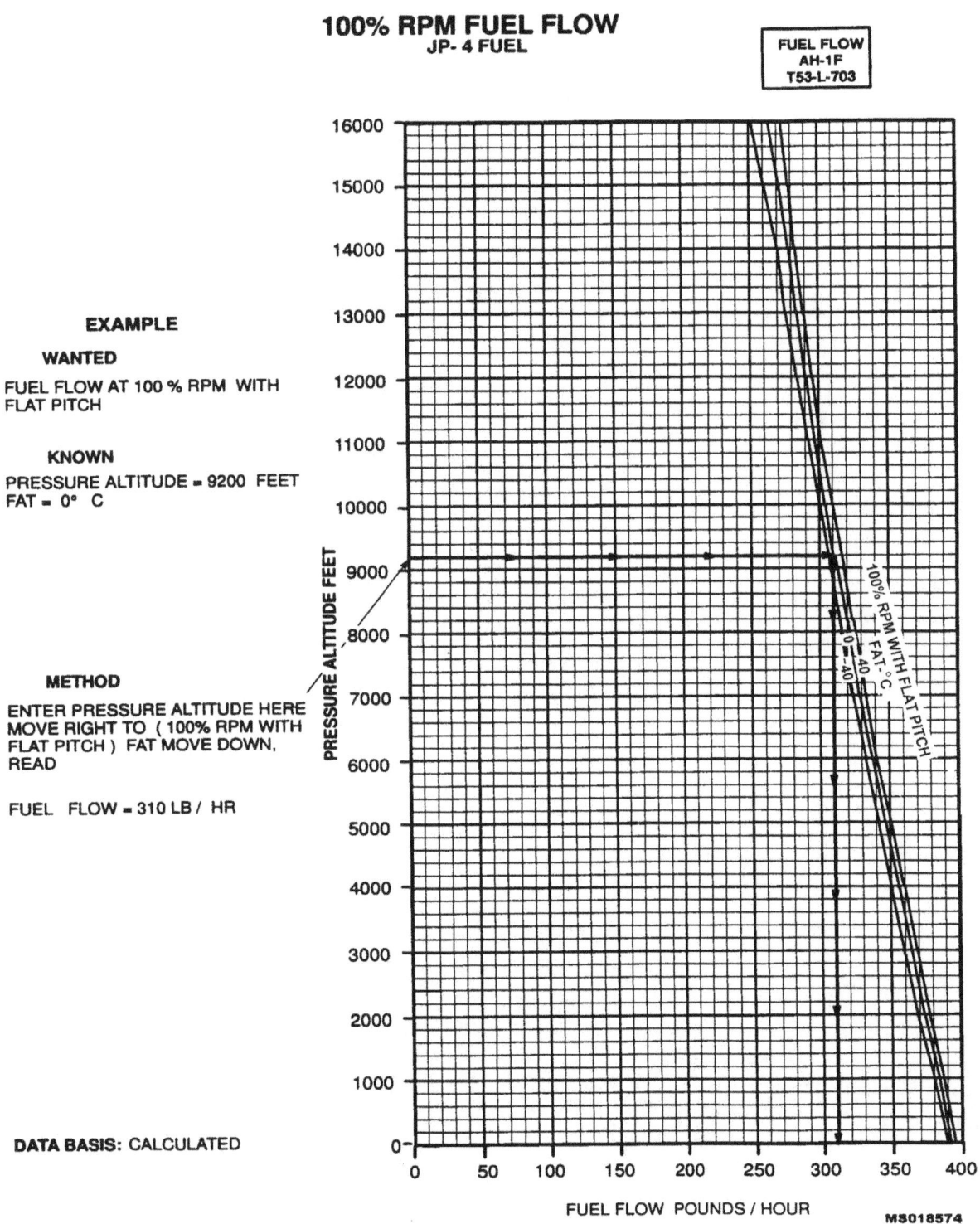

Figure 7-10. 100% RPM Fuel Flow Chart

TM 1-1520-236-10

CHAPTER 7.1

PERFORMANCE DATA K747

SECTION I. INTRODUCTION

NOTE

Chapter 7.1 provides information for the AH-1F equipped with the K747 main rotor blade.

Chapter 7 provides information for the AH-1F equipped with the B540 main rotor blade.

7.1-1. PURPOSE.

The purpose of this chapter is to provide the best available performance data for the AH-1F helicopter equipped with the K747 main rotor blade. Regular use of this information will enable you to receive maximum safe utilization from the aircraft. Although maximum performance is not always required, regular use of this chapter is recommended for the following reasons.

a. Knowledge of your performance margin will allow you to make better decisions when unexpected conditions or alternate missions are encountered.

b. Situations requiring maximum performance will be more readily recognized.

c. Familiarity with the data will allow performance to be computed more easily and quickly.

d. Experience will be gained in accurately estimating the effects of variables for which data are not presented.

NOTE

The information provided in this chapter is primarily intended for mission planning and is most useful when planning operations in unfamiliar areas or at extreme conditions. The data may also be used inflight, to establish unit or area standing operating procedures, and to inform ground commanders of performance/risk tradeoffs.

7.1-2. CHAPTER 7.1 INDEX.

The following index contains a list of the sections and their titles, the figure numbers, subjects and page numbers of each performance data chart contained in this chapter.

INDEX

SECTION		SUBJECT	PAGE NO.
I		INTRODUCTION	7.1-1
II		PERFORMANCE PLANNING	7.1-5
	Figure 7.1-1	Temperature Conversion Chart	7.1-6
III		TORQUE AVAILABLE	7.1-7
	Figure 7.1-2	Maximum Torque Available (30 Minute Operation) Chart	
		Engine Deice Off, ECS Off	7.1-8
	Figure 7.1-3	Torque Available (Continuous Operation) Chart	
	Sheet 1 of 2	Engine Deice Off, ECS Off	7.1-9
	Sheet 2 of 2	Engine Deice Off, ECS On	7.1-10
	Figure 7.1-4	Calibration Factor Conversion Chart	7.1-11

7.1-1

TM 1-1520-236-10

INDEX (Cont)

SECTION	SUBJECT	PAGE NO.
IV	HOVER	7.1-12
	Figure 7.1-5 Hover (Ceiling) Chart	
	Sheet 1 of 3 Maximum Torque Available (30 Minute Operation)	7.1-13
	Sheet 2 of 3 Example K747	7.1-14
	Sheet 3 of 3 All Configurations 100% RPM	7.1-15
	Figure 7.1-6 Directional Control Margin Chart	
	Sheet 1 of 2 Directional Control Margin Chart	7.1-16
	Sheet 2 of 2 Areas Derived From Sheet 1 of 2	7.1-17
V	CRUISE	7.1-18
	Figure 7.1-7 Cruise Chart	
	Sheet 1 of 23 FAT = -30°C, Pressure Altitude = Sea Level	7.1-19
	Sheet 2 of 23 FAT = -30°C, Pressure Altitude = 2000 Ft	7.1-20
	Sheet 3 of 23 FAT = -30°C, Pressure Altitude = 4000 Ft to 6000 Ft	7.1-21
	Sheet 4 of 23 FAT = -30°C, Pressure Altitude = 8000 Ft to 10000 Ft	7.1-22
	Sheet 5 of 23 FAT = -30°C, Pressure Altitude = 12000 Ft to 14000 Ft	7.1-23
	Sheet 6 of 23 FAT = 15°C Pressure Altitude = Sea Level to 2000 Ft	7.1-24
	Sheet 7 of 23 FAT = 15°C Pressure Altitude = 4000 Ft to 6000 Ft	7.1-25
	Sheet 8 of 23 FAT = 15°C Pressure Altitude = 8000 Ft to 10000 Ft	7.1-26
	Sheet 9 of 23 FAT = 15°C Pressure Altitude = 12000 Ft to 14000 Ft	7.1-27
	Sheet 10 of 23 FAT = 0°C Pressure Altitude = Sea Level to 2000 Ft	7.1-28
	Sheet 11 of 23 FAT = 0°C Pressure Altitude = 4000 Ft to 6000 Ft	7.1-29
	Sheet 12 of 23 FAT = 0°C Pressure Altitude = 8000 Ft to 10000 Ft	7.1-30
	Sheet 13 of 23 FAT = 0°C Pressure Altitude = 12000 Ft to 14000 Ft	7.1-31
	Sheet 14 of 23 FAT = 15°C Pressure Altitude = Sea Level to 2000 Ft	7.1-32
	Sheet 15 of 23 FAT = 15°C Pressure Altitude = 4000 Ft to 6000 Ft	7.1-33
	Sheet 16 of 23 FAT = 15°C Pressure Altitude = 8000 Ft to 10000 Ft	7.1-34
	Sheet 17 of 23 FAT = 15°C Pressure Altitude = 12000 Ft to 14000 Ft	7.1-35
	Sheet 18 of 23 FAT = 30°C Pressure Altitude = Sea Level to 2000 Ft	7.1-36
	Sheet 19 of 23 FAT = 30°C Pressure Altitude = 4000 Ft to 6000 Ft	7.1-37
	Sheet 20 of 23 FAT = 30°C Pressure Altitude = 8000 Ft to 10000 Ft	7.1-38
	Sheet 21 of 23 FAT = 45°C Pressure Altitude = Sea Level to 2000 Ft	7.1-39
	Sheet 22 of 23 FAT = 45°C Pressure Altitude = 4000 Ft to 6000 Ft	7.1-40
	Sheet 23 of 23 FAT = 45°C Pressure Altitude = 8000 Ft to 10000 Ft	7.1-41
VI	DRAG	7.1-42
	Figure 7.1-8 Drag Chart	7.1-43
VII	CLIMB – DESCENT	7.1-44
	Figure 7.1-9 Climb – Descent Chart	7.1-45
VIII	IDLE FUEL FLOW	7.1-46
	Figure 7.1-10 100% RPM Fuel Flow Chart	7.1-47

7.1-3. GENERAL.

The data presented covers the maximum range of conditions and performance that can reasonably be expected. In each area of performance, the effects of altitude, temperature, gross weight and other parameters relating to that phase of flight are presented. In addition to the presented data, your judgment and experience will be necessary to accurately obtain performance under a given set of circumstances. The conditions for the data are listed under the title of each chart. The effects of different conditions are discussed in the text accompanying each phase of performance. Where practical, data are presented at conservative conditions. However, NO GENERAL CONSERVATISM HAS BEEN APPLIED. All performance data presented are within the applicable limits of the aircraft.

7.1-4. LIMITS.

Applicable limits are shown on the charts as red lines. Performance generally deteriorates rapidly beyond limits. If limits are exceeded, minimize the amount and time. Enter the maximum value and time above limits on DA Form 2408-13-1 so proper maintenance action can be taken.

7.1-5. USE OF CHARTS.

a. Chart Explanation. The first page of each section describes the chart(s) and explains its uses.

b. Shading and Coding. Chart codes are used as follows:

(7) Example guidelines have arrows.

(8) Bold is used for limit lines, which are also labeled.

(9) Shading or patterns are used for precautionary or time-limited operation.

c. Reading the Charts. The primary use of each chart is given in an example and a green guideline is provided to help you follow the route through the chart. The use of a straight edge (ruler or page edge) and a hard fine point pencil is recommended to avoid cumulative errors. The majority of the charts provide a standard pattern for use as follows: enter first variable on top left scale, move right to the second variable, reflect down at right angles to the third variable, reflect left at right angles to the fourth variable, reflect down, etc. until the final variable is read out at the final scale. In addition to the primary use, other uses of each chart are explained in the text accompanying each set of performance charts.

NOTE
An example of an auxiliary use of the charts referenced above is as follows: Although the hover chart is primarily arranged to find torque required to hover, by entering torque available as torque required, maximum skid height for hover can also be found. In general, any single variable can be found if all others are known. Also, the tradeoffs between two variables can be found. For example, at a given pressure altitude, you can find the maximum gross weight capability as free air temperature changes.

7.1-6. DATA BASIS.

The type of data used is indicated at the bottom of each performance chart under DATA BASIS. The applicable report and date of the data are also given. The data provided generally is based on one of four categories:

a. Flight Test Data. Data obtained by flight test of the aircraft by experienced flight test personnel at precise conditions using sensitive calibrated instruments.

b. Derived From Flight Test. Flight test data obtained on a similar rather than the same aircraft and series. Generally small corrections will have been made.

c. Calculated Data. Data based on tests, but not on flight test of the complete aircraft.

d. Estimated Data. Data based on estimates having aerodynamic theory or other means but not verified by flight test.

7.1-7. SPECIFIC CONDITIONS.

The data presented are accurate only for specific conditions listed under the title of each chart. Variables for which data are not presented, but which may affect that phase of performance, are discussed in the text. Where data are available or reasonable estimates can be made, the amount that each variable affects performance will be given.

7.1-8. GENERAL CONDITIONS.

In addition to the specific conditions, the following general conditions are applicable to the performance data.

a. Rigging. All airframe and engine control are assumed to be rigged within allowable tolerances.

b. Pilot Technique. Normal pilot technique is assumed. Control movements should be smooth and continuous.

c. Aircraft Variation. Variations in performance between individual aircraft are known to exist; however, they are considered to be small and cannot be individually accounted for.

d. Instrument Variation. The data shown in the performance charts do not account for instrument inaccuracies or malfunctions.

e. Types Of Fuel. All flight performance data are based on JP-4 Fuel. The change in fuel flow and torque available, when using JP-5, JP-8, aviation gasoline or any other approved fuels, is insignificant.

7.1-9. PERFORMANCE DISCREPANCIES.

Regular use of this chapter will allow you to monitor instruments and other aircraft systems for malfunction, by comparing actual performance with planned performance. Knowledge will also be gained concerning the effects of variables for which data are not provided, thereby increasing the accuracy of performance predictions.

7.1-10. DEFINITIONS OF ABBREVIATIONS.

a. Unless otherwise indicated in Appendix B, abbreviations and symbols used in this manual conform to those established in Military Standard MIL-STD-12, which is periodically revised to reflect current changes in abbreviations usage. Accordingly, it may be noted that certain previously established definitions have been replaced by more current abbreviations and symbols.

b. Capitalization and punctuation of abbreviations varies, depending upon the context in which they are used. In general, lower case abbreviations are used in text material, whereas abbreviations used in charts and illustrations appear in full capital letters. Periods do not usually follow abbreviations; however, periods are used with abbreviations that could be mistaken for whole words if the period were omitted.

SECTION II. PERFORMANCE PLANNING

7.1-11. PERFORMANCE PLANNING.

Refer to AH-1 Aircrew Training Manual for preparing the performance planning card (PPC).

7.1-12. TEMPERATURE CONVERSION.

The temperature conversion chart (Figure 7.1-1) is arranged so that degrees Celsius can be converted quickly and easily by reading Celsius and looking directly across the chart for Fahrenheit equivalent and vice versa.

TM 1-1520-236-10

TEMPERATURE CONVERSION CHART

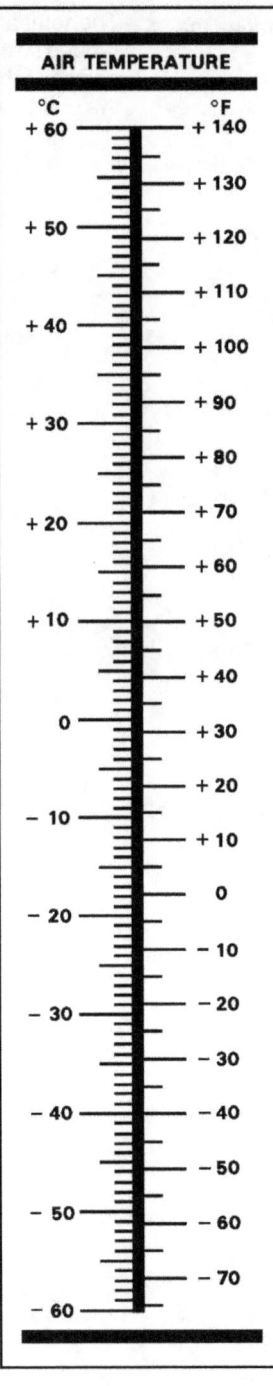

Figure 7.1-1. Temperature Conversion Chart

SECTION III. TORQUE AVAILABLE

7.1-13. DESCRIPTION.

The torque available charts show the effects of altitude and temperature on engine torque.

7.1-14. CHART DIFFERENCES.

Both pressure altitude and FAT affect engine power production. Figure 7.1-2 and Figure 7.1-3 show power available data at 30 minute power and maximum continuous power ratings in terms of the allowable torque as recorded by the torquemeter (%Q).

CAUTION

The power output capability of the T53-L-703 engine can exceed the transmission structural limit (100% Q) under certain conditions.

a. Figure 7.1-2 (sheet 1) is applicable for maximum power, engine deice off and ECS off, 30 minute Operation.

b. Figure 7.1-3 (sheet 1) is applicable for maximum continuous power, engine deice off, and ECS off.

c. Figure 7.1-3 (sheet 2) is applicable for maximum continuous power, engine deice off, and ECS on.

d. Prolonged IGE hover may increase engine inlet temperature as much as 10 degrees Celsius; therefore, a higher FAT must be used to correct for the increase under this condition.

7.1-15. USE OF CHARTS.

The primary use of the charts is illustrated by the examples. In general, to determine the maximum power available, it is necessary to know the pressure altitude, temperature and the aircraft calibration factor. By entering the upper left side of the chart at the known pressure altitude, moving right to the known temperature, then straight down to the calibrating factor line, then move left to the indicated torque scale and read an indicated torque available.

7.1-16. CONDITIONS.

Charts (Figure 7.1-2 and Figure 7.1-3) are based upon speeds at 100 percent rpm with grade JP-4 fuel. The use of aviation gasoline will not influence engine power. Fuel grade of JP-5 will yield the same nautical miles per pound of fuel and being 6.8 pounds per gallon will only result in increased fuel weight per gallon. Because JP-4 and JP-5 have the same energy value per pound, the JP-5 fuel will increase range by almost 5 percent per gallon of fuel.

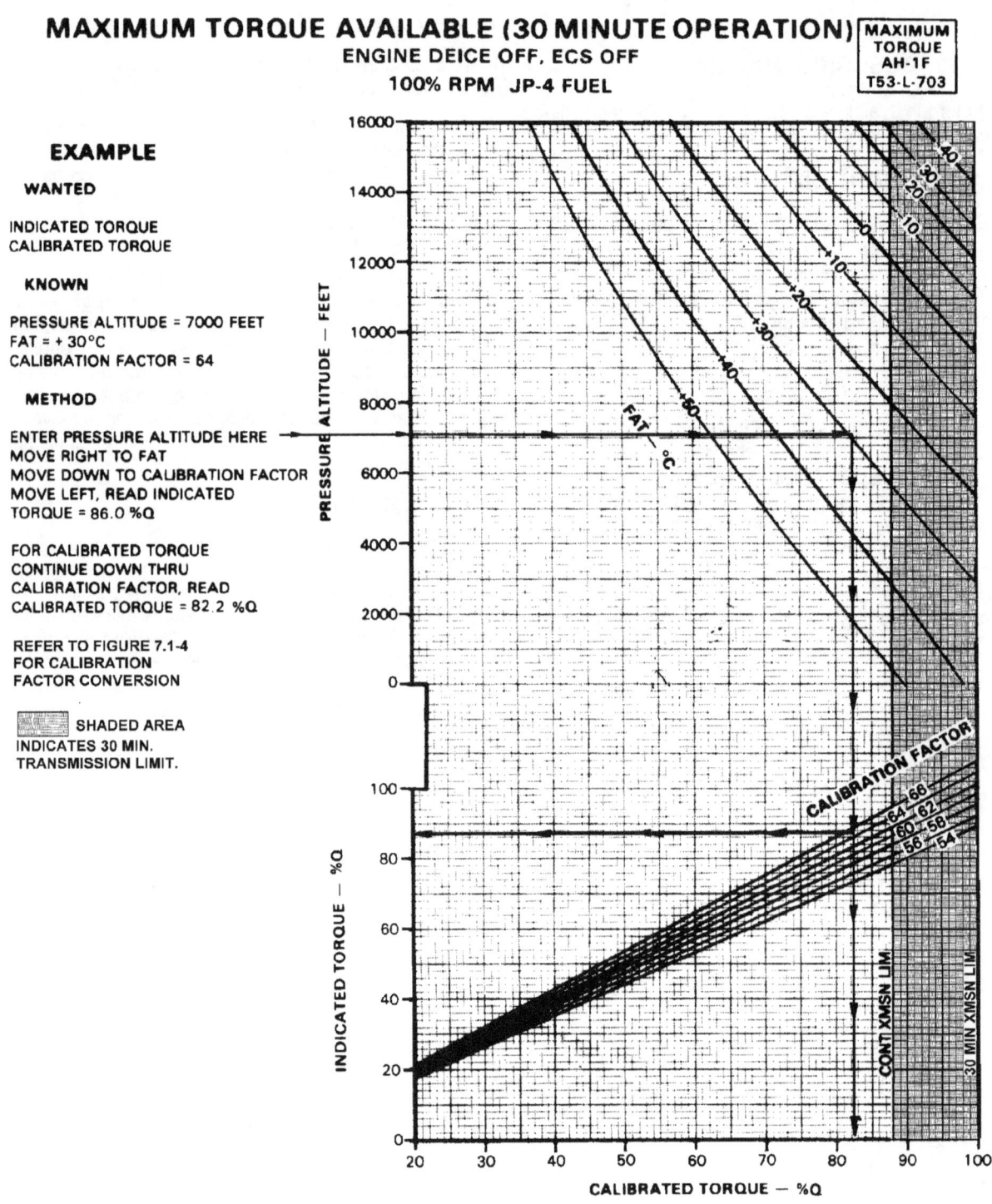

Figure 7.1-2. Maximum Torque Available (30-Minute Operation) Chart

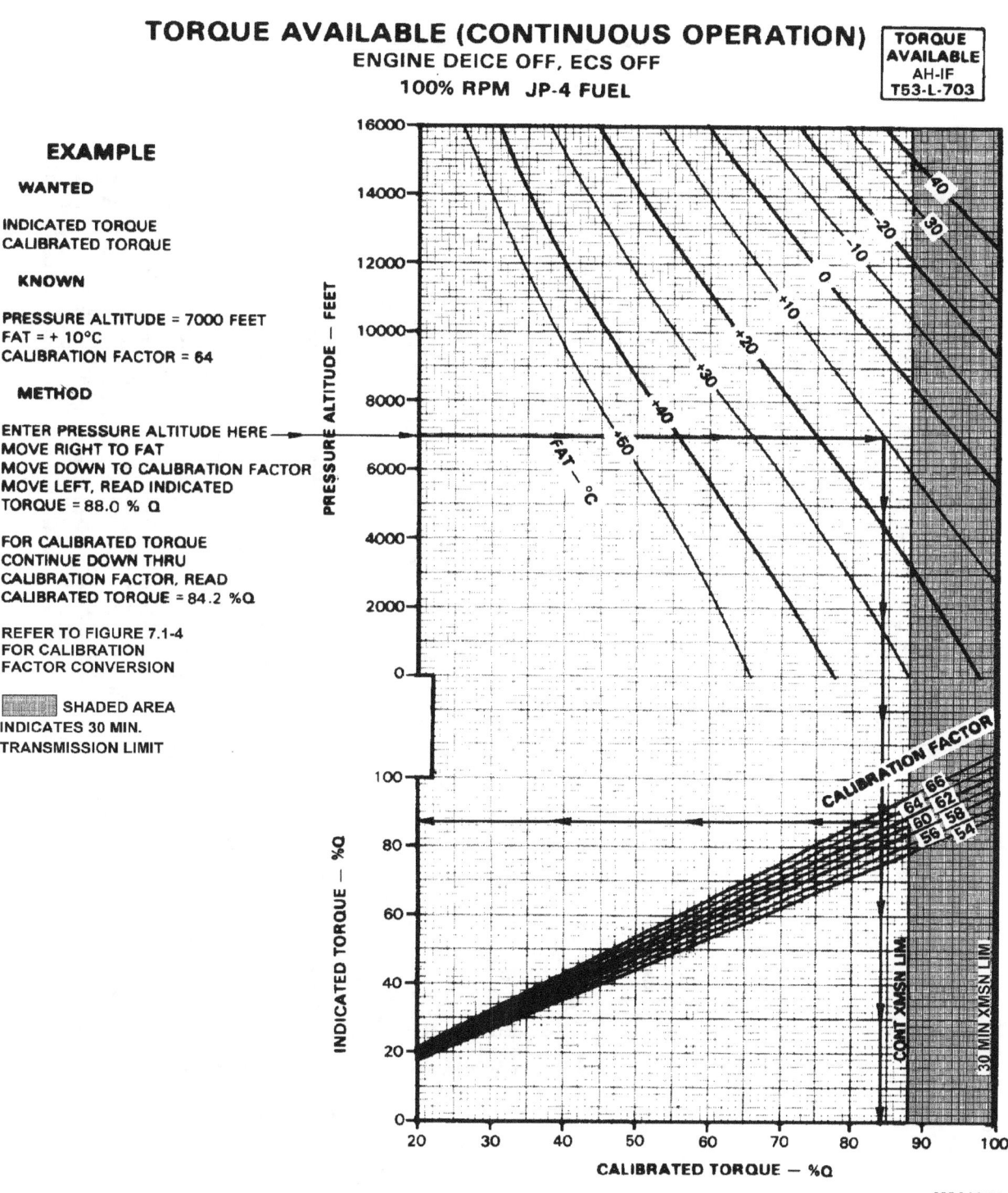

Figure 7.1-3. Torque Available (Continuous Operation) Chart (Sheet 1 of 2)

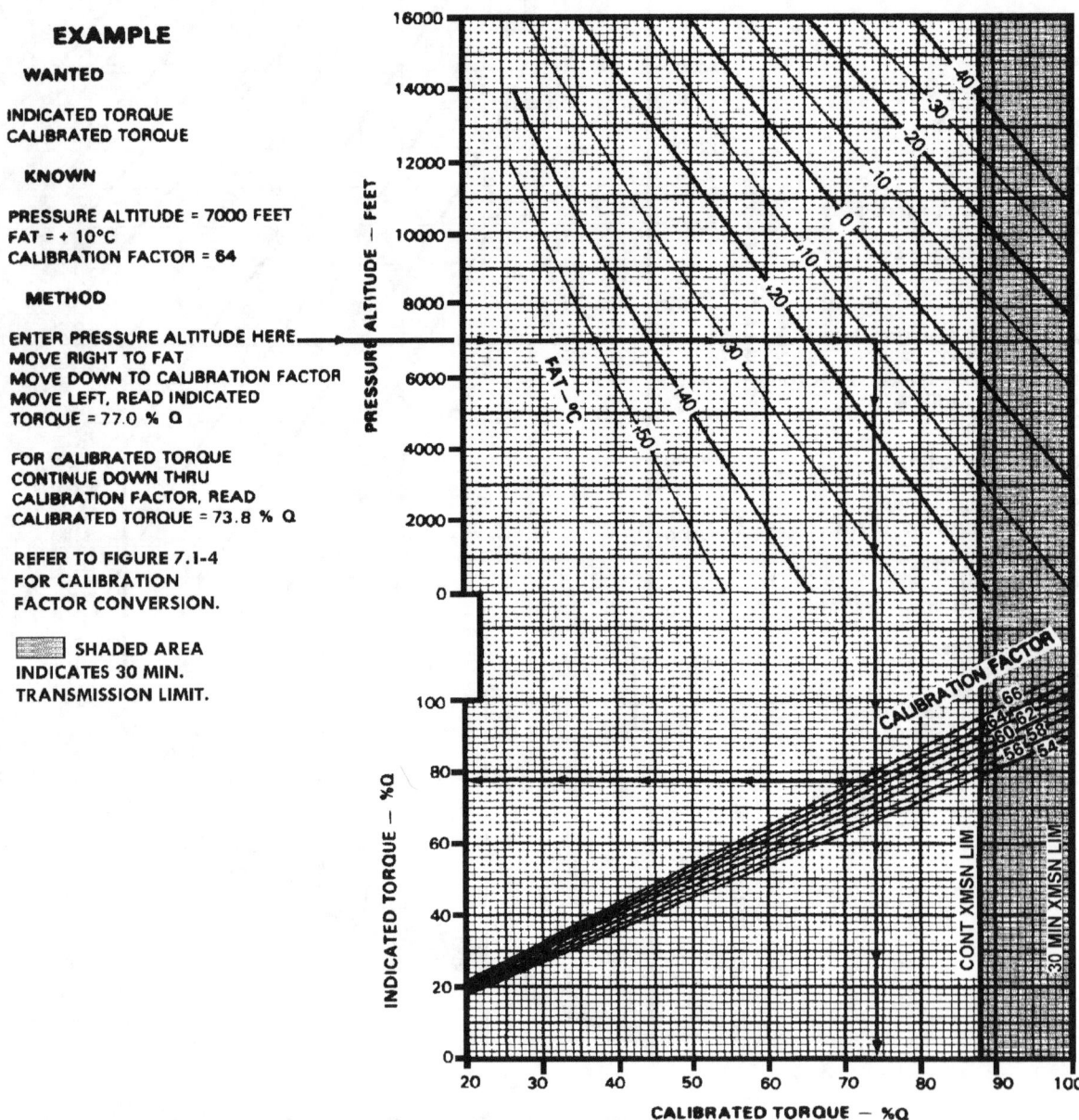

Figure 7.1-3. Torque Available (Continuous Operation) Chart (Sheet 2 of 2)

CALIBRATION FACTOR CONVERSION TABLE

CAL FACTOR CONVERSION TABLE									
64.0	63.9	63.8	63.7	63.6	63.5	63.4	63.3	63.2	63.1
4.2	4.1	4.0	3.8	3.7	3.6	3.5	3.4	3.3	3.2
63.0	62.9	62.8	62.7	62.6	62.5	62.4	62.3	62.2	62.1
3.1	2.9	2.7	2.5	2.2	2.0	1.8	1.6	1.4	1.2
62.0	61.9	61.8	61.7	61.6	61.5	61.4	61.3	61.2	61.1
1.0	0.9	0.8	0.7	0.6	0.5	0.4	0.3	0.2	0.1
61.0	60.9	60.8	60.7	60.6	60.5	60.4	60.3	60.2	60.1
0.0	-0.2	-0.4	-0.6	-0.8	-1.0	-1.2	-1.4	-1.6	-1.8
60.0	59.9	59.8	59.7	59.6	59.5	59.4	59.3	59.2	59.1
-2.0	-2.2	-2.3	-2.5	-2.7	-2.9	-3.1	-3.3	-3.5	-3.7
59.0	58.9	58.8	58.7	58.6	58.5	58.4	58.3	58.2	58.1
-3.8	-4.0	-4.2	-4.4	-4.6	-4.8	-4.9	-5.1	-5.3	-5.5

MS018543

EXAMPLE (UTILIZING TORQUE VALUE FROM FIGURES 7.1-2 OR 7.1-3)

WANTED

INDICATED TORQUE
CALIBRATED TORQUE

KNOWN

PRESSURE ALTITUDE = 7000 FEET
FAT = +30°C
CALIBRATION FACTOR = 64

METHOD

ENTER PRESSURE ALTITUDE
MOVE RIGHT TO FAT
FOR CALIBRATED TORQUE:
   CONTINUE DOWN THROUGH CALIBRATION FACTOR
   READ CALIBRATED TORQUE = 82.2%Q
FOR INDICATED TORQUE:
   ADD OR SUBTRACT CAL FACTOR CONVERSION TO CALIBRATED TORQUE
   FOR EXAMPLE: 4.2%Q + 82.2%Q = 86.4%Q INDICATED TORQUE

Figure 7.1-4. Calibration Factor Conversion Chart

SECTION IV. HOVER

7.1-17. DESCRIPTION.

The hover charts (Figure 7.1-5, sheets 1 through 3) show the hover ceiling and the torque required to hover respectively at various pressure altitudes, ambient temperatures, gross weights, and skid heights. Maximum skid height for hover can also be obtained by using the torque available from Figure 7.1-2.

7.1-18. USE OF CHART.

a. The primary use of the charts is illustrated by the charts examples. In general, to determine the hover ceiling or the torque required to hover, it is necessary to know the pressure altitude, temperature, gross weight and the desired skid height.

b. In addition to its primary use, the hover chart (sheet 2) can also be used to determine the predicted maximum hover height. To determine maximum hover height, proceed as follows:

(1) Enter chart at appropriate pressure altitude.

(2) Move right to FAT.

(3) Move down to gross weight.

(4) Move left to intersection with maximum power available (obtained from Figure 7.1-2).

(5) Read predicted maximum skid height. This height is the maximum hover height.

7.1-19. CONTROL MARGIN.

Ten percent pedal margin is considered adequate for safe directional control. Figure 7.1-5 (sheet 1) shows the combinations of relative wind velocity and azimuth which may result in marginal directional control. Figure 7.1-5 (sheet 1) shows the maximum right crosswind, in knots true airspeed, which one can achieve and still maintain 10 percent directional control margin for given gross weights and density altitudes. This figure has zone letters which are to be used in conjunction with Figure 7.1-5 (sheet 2). If, for example, your operating gross weight and density altitude are such that the point lies in zone C on sheet 1 then go to sheet 2. The zone identified by the letter C shows the wind velocity in knots that one can achieve while still maintaining a 10 percent directional control margin (e.g., if the wind were from 45 degrees you could have 18.5 knots of wind whereas, if from 60 degrees, only 15.4 knots). The left vertical zone lines on sheet 2 represent 10 percent control margin. As you move toward the right for that gross weight and density altitude, the control margin approaches zero.

7.1-20. CONDITIONS.

The hover charts are based upon calm wind conditions, a level ground surface, and the use of 100 percent rpm. In ground effect hover data is based upon hovering over a level surface. If the surface over which hovering will be conducted is known to be steep, uneven, covered with high vegetation, or if the type of terrain is unknown, the flight should be planned for out of ground effect hover capability.

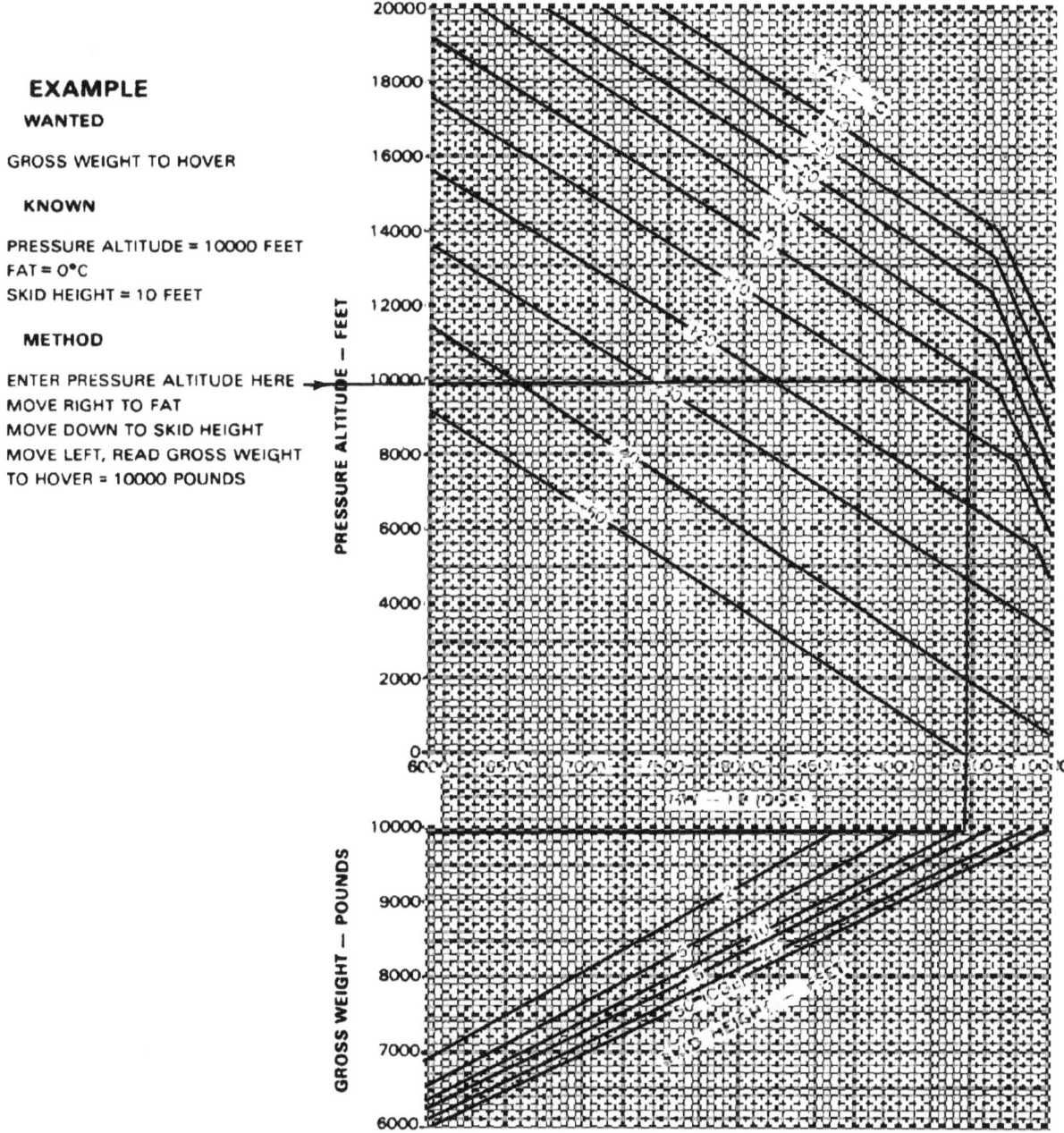

Figure 7.1-5. Hover (Ceiling) Chart (Sheet 1 of 3)

EXAMPLE K747

WANTED

MAXIMUM GROSS WEIGHT TO HOVER AT OGE   (USE WITH CHART ON SHEET 3)

KNOWN (REFERENCE EXAMPLE FOR FIGURE 7.1-2)

30 MINUTE CALIBRATED TORQUE AVAILABLE= 82% Q

PRESSURE ALTITUDE = 1000 FEET

FAT = +30 °C

CALIBRATION FACTOR = 64

METHOD

ENTER PRESSURE ALTITUDE HERE ⟶ ①

MOVE RIGHT AND INTERPOLATE FOR +30 °C FAT

MOVE DOWN AND READ DENSITY ALTITUDE = 10000 FEET

ENTER CALIBRATED TORQUE HERE ⟶ ②

MOVE UP TO INTERSECT OGE LINE

MOVE RIGHT TO INTERSECT THE VERTICAL

LINE FROM ① AND READ GROSS WEIGHT TO HOVER = 8700 POUNDS

K747 Figure 7.1-5. Hover (Ceiling) Chart (Sheet 2 of 3)

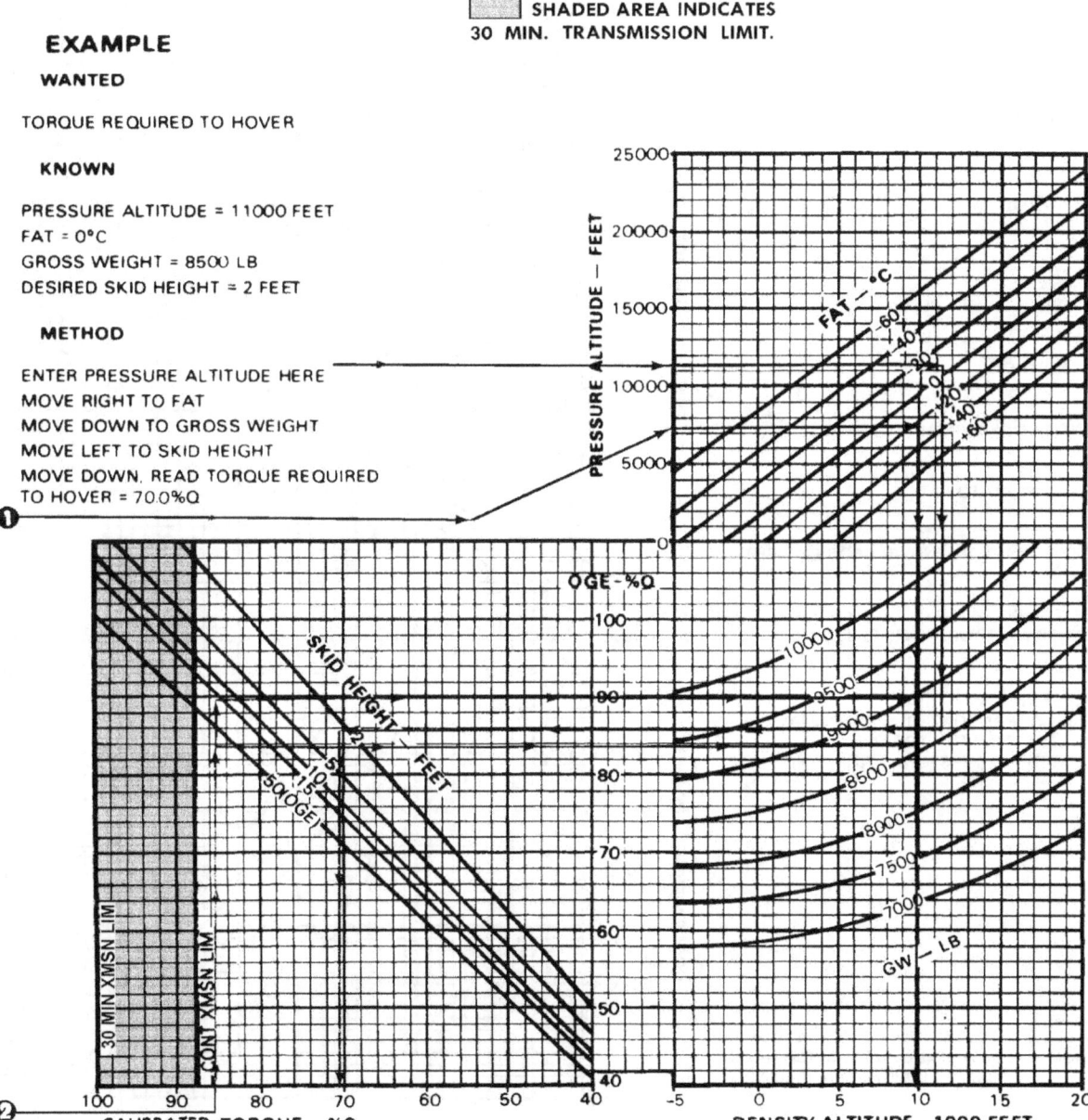

Figure 7.1-5. Hover (Ceiling) Chart (Sheet 3 of 3)

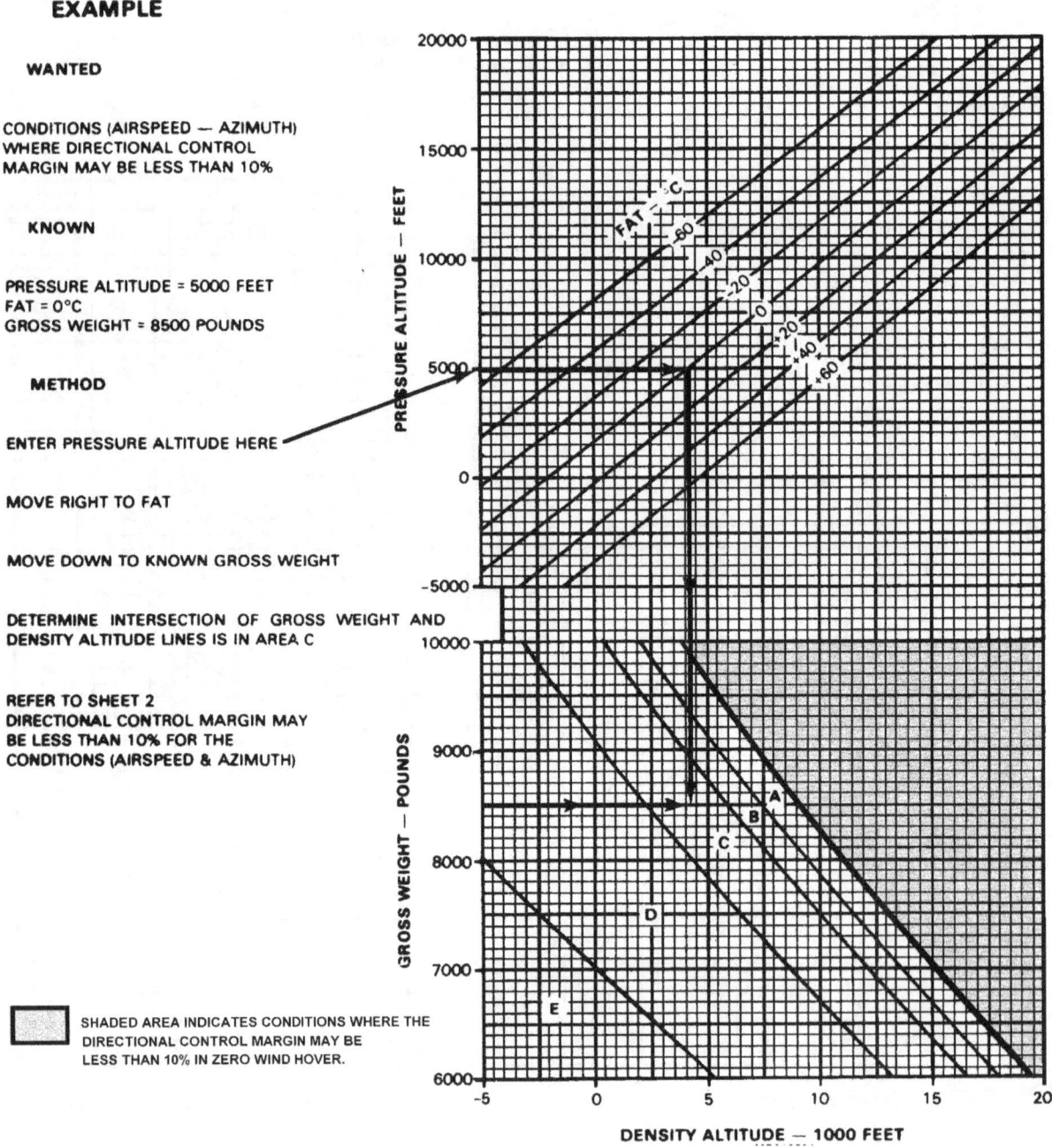

Figure 7.1-6. Directional Control Margin Chart (Sheet 1 of 2)

TM 1-1520-236-10

DIRECTIONAL CONTROL MARGIN

AREAS DERIVED FROM SHEET 1 OF 2

Wind speed in Knots	A Starts at 0 KTS	B Starts at 10 KTS	C Starts at 13 KTS	D Starts at 16 KTS	E Starts at 20 KTS
0	30° - 140°				
5	30° - 140°				
10	30° - 140°				
15	30° - 140°	40° - 120°	60° - 120°		
20	30° - 140°	30° - 140°	30° - 140°	50° - 130°	
25	30° - 140°	40° - 140°	30° - 140°	50° - 140°	50° - 130°

(MAXIMUM WIND VELOCITY (Actual or Forecast))

Shaded area indicates areas where 10% tail rotor authority should be expected.

MS018548

Example

WANTED: AZIMUTH WHERE DIRECTIONAL CONTROL MARGIN MAY BE LESS THAN 10%.

KNOWN: 18 KNOT WINDS (FORECAST OR ACTUAL) ROUNDED UP TO 20 KNOTS, AREA "C" FROM SHEET 1 OF 2.

METHOD: FROM THE LEFT SIDE OF THE CHART LOCATE 20 KNOTS AND MOVE RIGHT, FROM THE TOP OF THE CHART LOCATE AREA "C" AND MOVE DOWN. WHERE THESE TWO POINTS INTERSECT IS THE AZIMUTHS TO AVOID, 30° - 140°.

NOTE 1: FORECAST OR ACTUAL WINDS SHOULD ALWAYS BE ROUNDED UP TO THE NEAREST 5 KNOTS.

NOTE 2: IN CALM WIND CONDITIONS, SIDEWARD FLIGHT TO THE RIGHT WILL INDUCE THE SAME EFFECT AS WINDS FROM THE RIGHT.

NOTE 3: 10% DIRECTIONAL CONTROL IS DEFINED AS 10% PEDAL TRAVEL REMAINING.

NOTE 4: REFER TO THE AH-1 AIRCREW TRAINING MANUAL FOR PREPARING THE PERFORMANCE PLANNING CARD (PPC).

Figure 7.1-6. Directional Control Margin Chart (Sheet 2 of 2)

SECTION V. CRUISE

7.1-21. DESCRIPTION.

The cruise charts (Figure 7.1-7 sheets 1 through 23) show the torque pressure and engine rpm required for level flight at various pressure altitudes, airspeed and gross weights. The cruise charts are presented for a clean drag configuration. However, any desired drag configuration (see Figure 7.1-8 for authorized armament configurations) can be solved by using a ratio between the Δ%Q for the desired configuration (as shown in Figure 7.1-7, sheets 1 thru 23) and the Δ%Q for the 8 TOW configuration. Add the calculated Δ%Q of the desired configuration to the Δ%Q of the clean configuration to solve for the total torque required for the desired configuration. Then read the fuel flow for the desired configuration.

Thus, the effects of added drag resulting from installed wing stores can be determined by applying the ΔF-SQ FT from the Drag Chart (Figure 7.1-8) to the cruise charts (Figure 7.1-7). Refer to Example B on Figure 7.1-7, sheet 1 for the method.

7.1-22. USE OF CHARTS.

The primary use of the charts is illustrated by the examples provided in Figure 7.1-7. The first step for chart use is to select the proper chart, pressure altitude and anticipated free air temperature; refer to chapter 7.1 index (paragraph 7.1-2). Normally, sufficient accuracy can be obtained by selecting the chart nearest to the planned cruising altitude and FAT, or the next higher altitude and FAT. If greater accuracy is required, interpolation between altitudes and/or temperatures will be required (see Figure 7.1-7, sheet 1, example A). You may enter the charts on any side; TAS, IAS, torque pressure, or fuel flow, and then move vertically or horizontally to the gross weight, then to the other three parameters. Maximum performance conditions are determined by entering the chart where the maximum range or maximum endurance and rate of climb lines intersect the appropriate gross weight; then read airspeed, fuel flow and torque pressure. For conservatism, use the gross weight at the beginning of cruise flight. For greater accuracy on long flights it is preferable to determine cruise information for several flight segments in order to allow for decreasing fuel weight (reduced gross weight). The following parameters contained in each chart are further explained as follows:

a. Airspeed. True and indicated airspeeds are presented at opposite sides of each chart. On any chart, indicated airspeed can be directly converted to true airspeed (or vice versa) by reading directly across the chart without regard for other chart information. Maximum permissible airspeed (^{V}NE) limits appear as red lines on some charts. If no red line appears, (^{V}NE) is above the limits of the chart.

b. Torque Pressure (%Q). Since pressure altitude and temperature are fixed for each chart, torque pressure required varies according to gross weight and air speed.

c. Fuel flow. Fuel flow scales are provided opposite the torque pressure scales. On any chart, torque pressure may be converted directly to fuel flow without regard for other chart information. All fuel flow information is presented ECS off. Add 4 percent fuel flow for ECS on because of restricted exhaust flow.

d. Maximum Range. The maximum range lines indicate the combination of weight and airspeed that will produce the greatest flight range per gallon of fuel under zero wind conditions. When a maximum range condition does not appear on a chart it is because the maximum range speed is beyond the maximum permissible speed (VNE); in such cases, use VNE cruising speed to obtain maximum range.

e. Maximum Endurance and Rate of Climb. The maximum endurance and rate of climb line indicate the airspeed for minimum torque pressure required to maintain level flight for each gross weight, FAT and pressure altitude. Since minimum torque pressure will provide minimum fuel flow, maximum flight endurance will be obtained at the airspeeds indicated.

7.1-23. CONDITIONS.

The cruise charts are based on operation at 100 percent rpm and ECS off.

CRUISE
PRESSURE ALTITUDE — SEA LEVEL
100% RPM, CLEAN CONFIGURATION, JP-4 FUEL

CRUISE
AH-1F
T53-L-703

SHADED AREA INDICATES 30 MIN. TRANSMISSION LIMIT.

$FAT = -30°C$

EXAMPLE A

WANTED

TORQUE REQUIRED FOR LEVEL FLIGHT, FUEL FLOW, INDICATED AIRSPEED

KNOWN

CLEAN CONFIGURATION, GROSS WEIGHT = 8000 LB, PRESSURE ALTITUDE = 1000 FEET, FAT = -30°C, DESIRED TRUE AIRSPEED = 110 KNOTS.

METHOD (INTERPOLATE)

ENTER TRUE AIRSPEED HERE
READ TORQUE, FUEL FLOW, AND IAS ON EACH ADJACENT ALTITUDE AND/OR FAT, THEN INTERPOLATE BETWEEN ALTITUDE AND FAT

SEE FIGURE 7.1-7 (SHT 2) ❶

ALTITUDE, FEET	SEA LEVEL	2000 FEET	1000 FEET
FAT, °C	-30	-30	-30
TORQUE, % Q	66.2	63.0	64.6
FUEL FLOW, LB/HR	615	580	597.5
IAS, KNOTS	124	119	121.5

EXAMPLE B

WANTED

ADDITIONAL TORQUE REQUIRED AND FUEL FLOW FOR ARMAMENT CONFIGURATION AND CONDITION IN EXAMPLE A

KNOWN

ARMAMENT CONFIGURATION FOR 2 19 TUBE ROCKET LAUNCHERS = 3.1 ΔF-SQ FT (FROM FIGURE 7.1-8)

METHOD

ENTER TRUE AIRSPEED AT 110 KNOTS AND MOVE RIGHT TO ΔF-SQ FT = 3.1 (BETWEEN 0.0 AND 5.0 ΔF-SQ FT). FROM THAT POINT MOVE UP TO READ 3.7% Q TORQUE. ADD 3.7% Q TORQUE TO THE TORQUE REQUIRED FOR LEVEL FLIGHT IN THE CLEAN CONFIGURATION AND THE CORRESPONDING INCREASE IN FUEL FLOW (APPROXIMATELY 18 POUNDS PER HOUR) TO THE CLEAN CONFIGURATION FUEL FLOW.

DATA BASIS: DERIVED FROM FLIGHT TEST

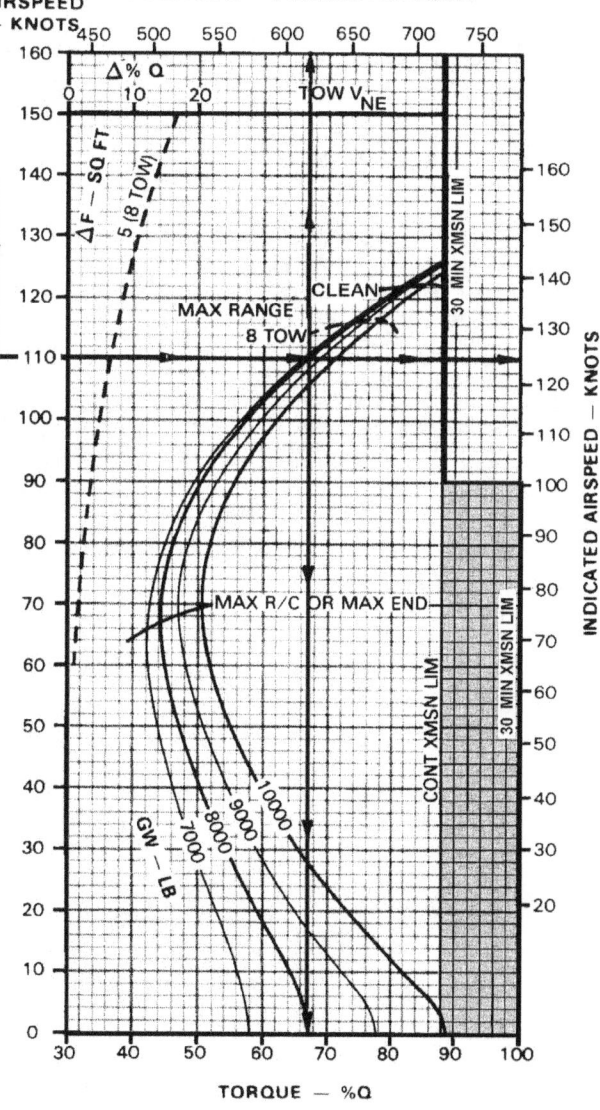

MS018582

K747 Figure 7.1-7. Cruise Chart (Sheet 1 of 23)

CRUISE
PRESSURE ALTITUDE — 2000 FEET
100% RPM, CLEAN CONFIGURATION, JP-4 FUEL

CRUISE
AH-1F
T53-L-703

EXAMPLE

FAT = -30°C

WANTED

SPEED FOR MAXIMUM RANGE
TORQUE REQUIRED AND FUEL FLOW AT MAXIMUM RANGE SPEED FOR MAXIMUM ENDURANCE

KNOWN

CLEAN CONFIGURATION, FAT = -30°C,
PRESSURE ALTITUDE = 2000 FEET,
AND GROSS WEIGHT = 9000 POUNDS

METHOD

LOCATE (-30°C FAT, 2000 FEET) CHART
FIND INTERSECTION OF 9000 LB GROSS WEIGHT LINE WITH THE MAXIMUM RANGE LINE
TO READ SPEED FOR MAXIMUM RANGE:
  MOVE LEFT, READ TAS = 128.5 KNOTS AND
  MOVE RIGHT, READ IAS = 140 KNOTS
TO READ FUEL FLOW REQUIRED:
  MOVE UP, READ DUEL FLOW = 700 LB/HR
TO READ TORQUE REQUIRED
  MOVE DOWN, READ TORQUE = 87.5% Q
FIND INTERSECTION OF 9000 LB GROSS WEIGHT LINE WITH THE MAXIMUM ENDURANCE LINE
TO READ SPEED FOR MAXIMUM ENDURANCE:
  MOVE LEFT, READ TAS = 70 KNOTS AND
  MOVE RIGHT, READ IAS = 74 KNOTS

SEE FIGURE 7.1-7 (SHT 1)

SHADED AREA INDICATES 30 MIN. TRANSMISSION LIMIT.

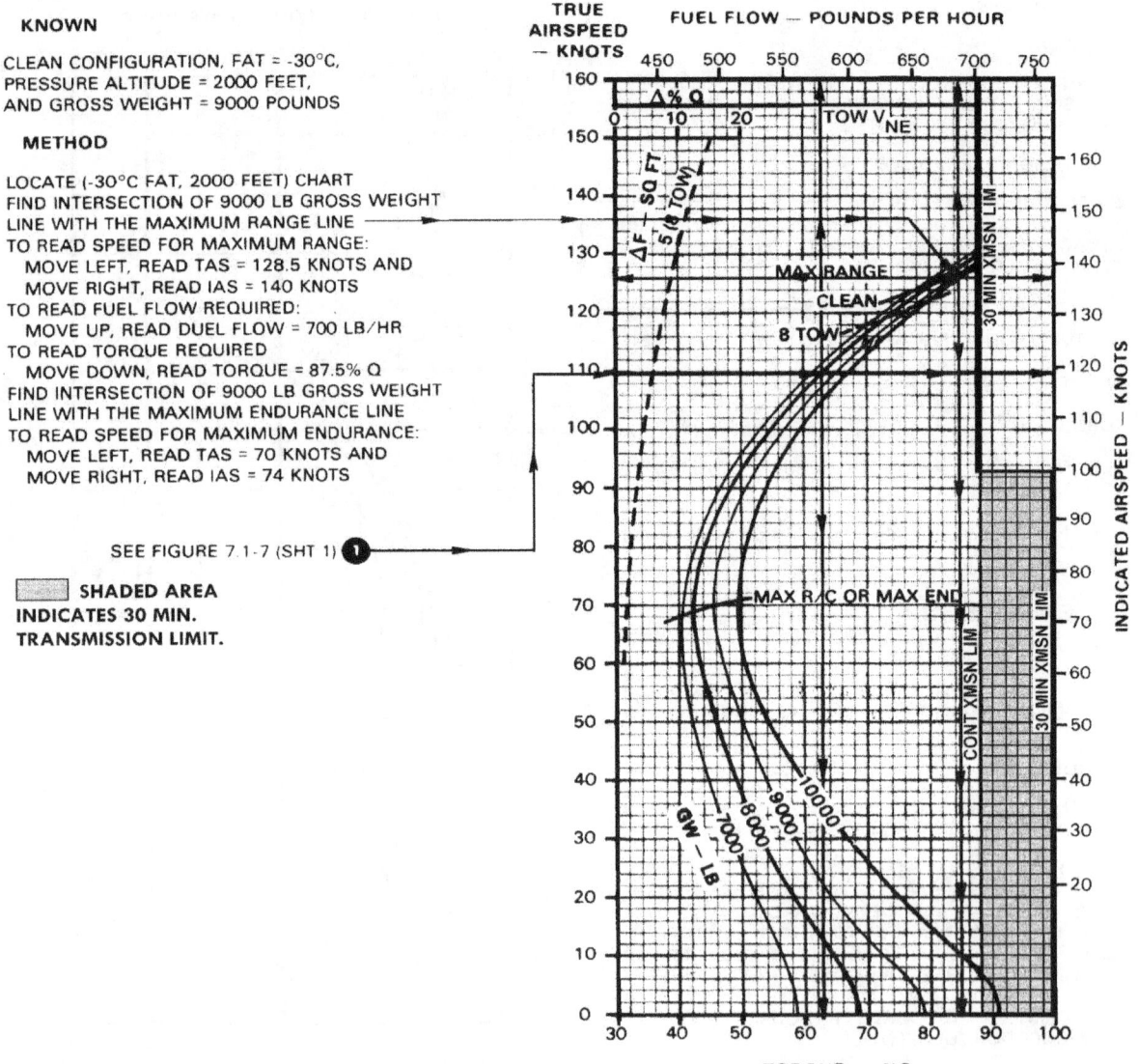

DATA BASIS: DERIVED FROM FLIGHT TEST

MS018583

K747 Figure 7.1-7. Cruise Chart (Sheet 2 of 23)

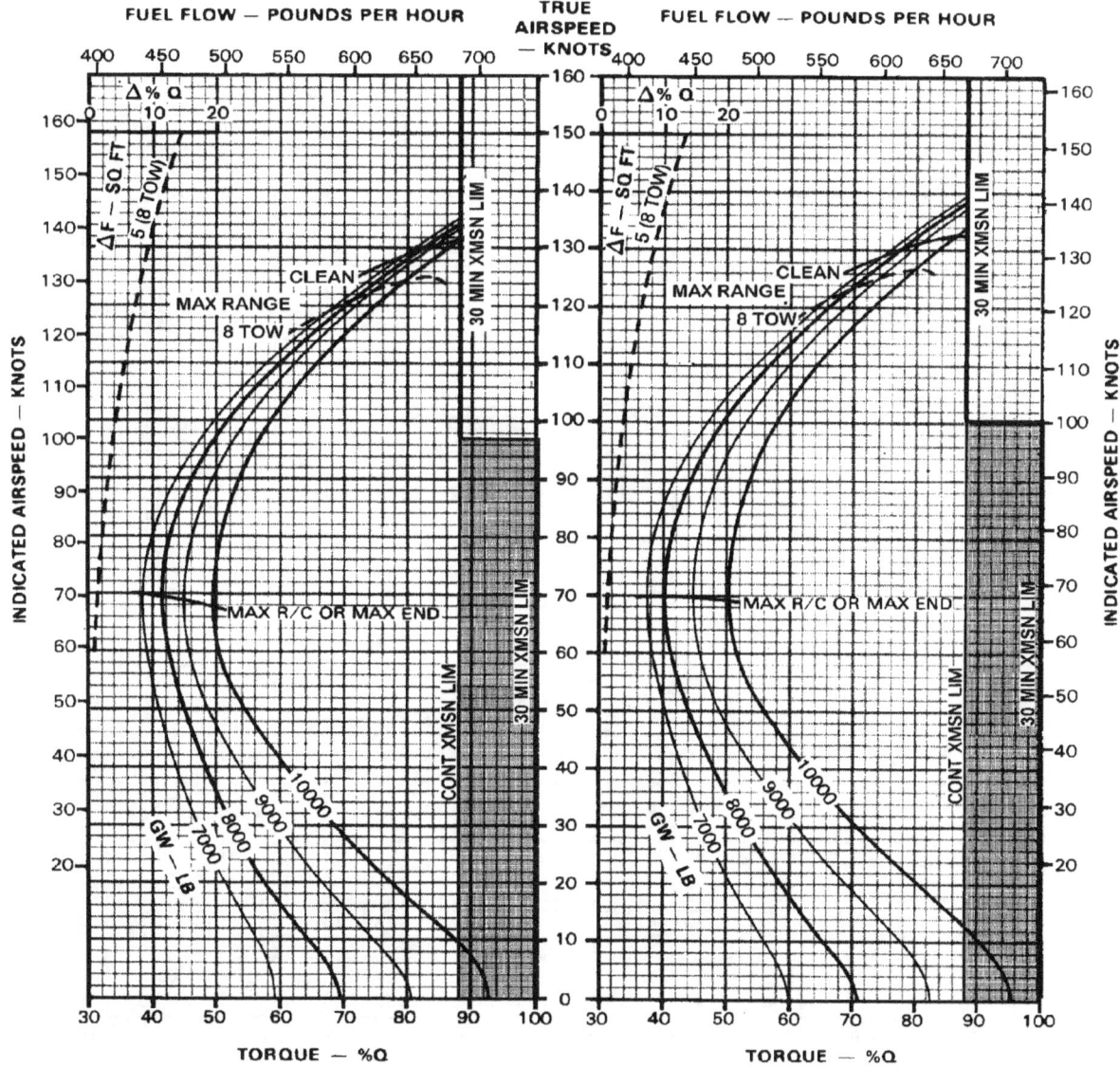

Figure 7.1-7. Cruise Chart (Sheet 3 of 23)

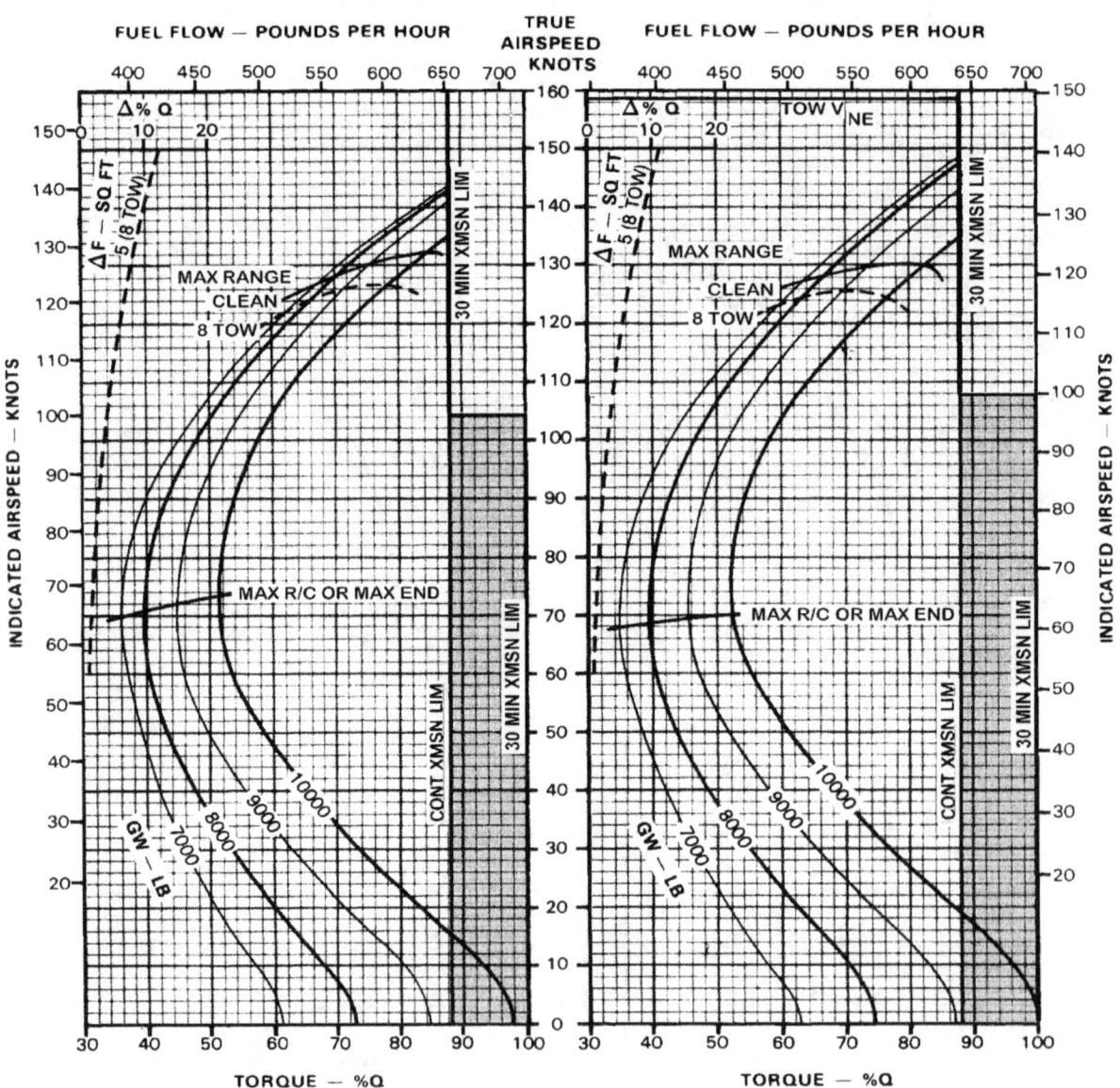

Figure 7.1-7. Cruise Chart (Sheet 4 of 23)

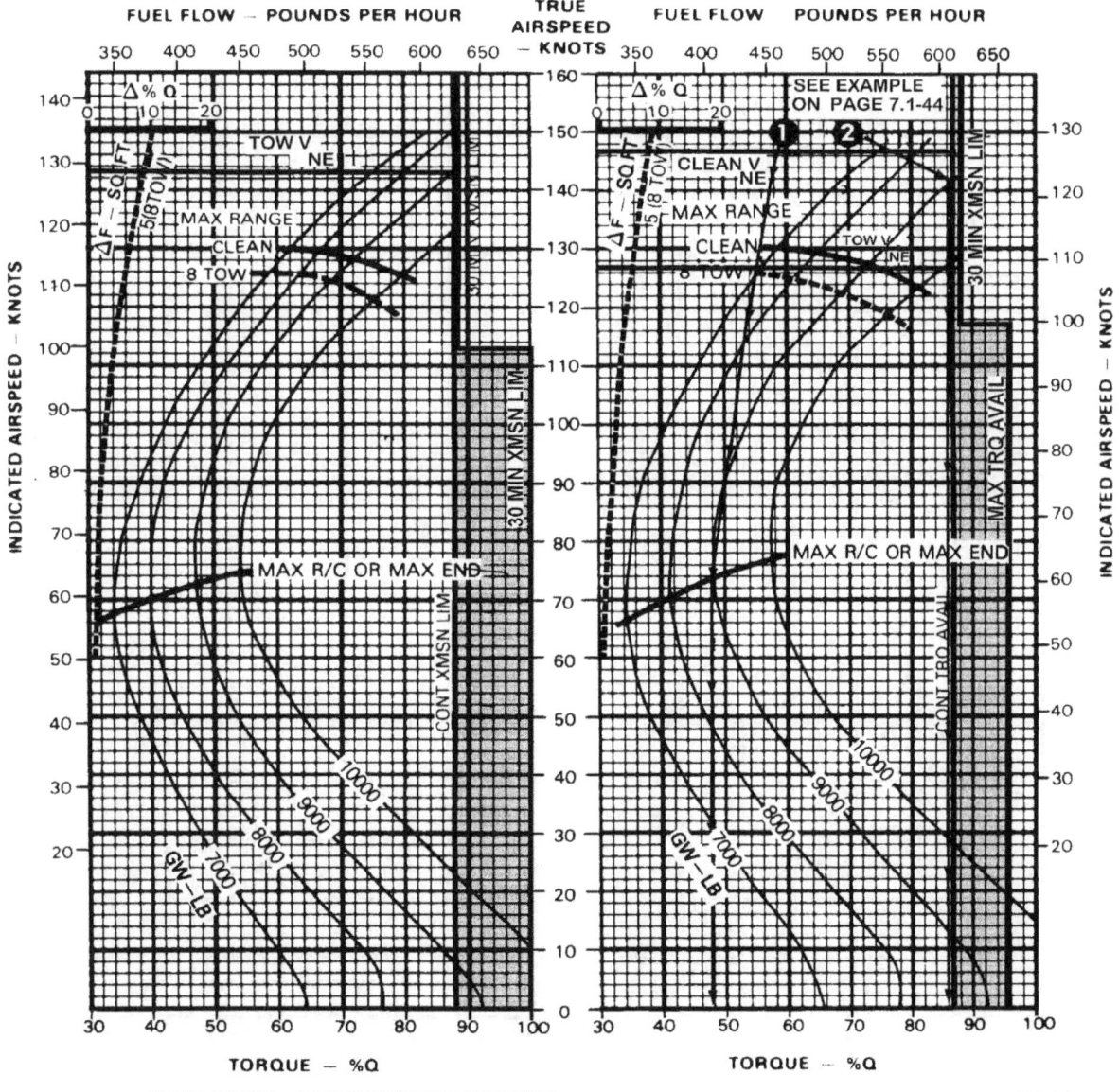

Figure 7.1-7. Cruise Chart (Sheet 5 of 23)

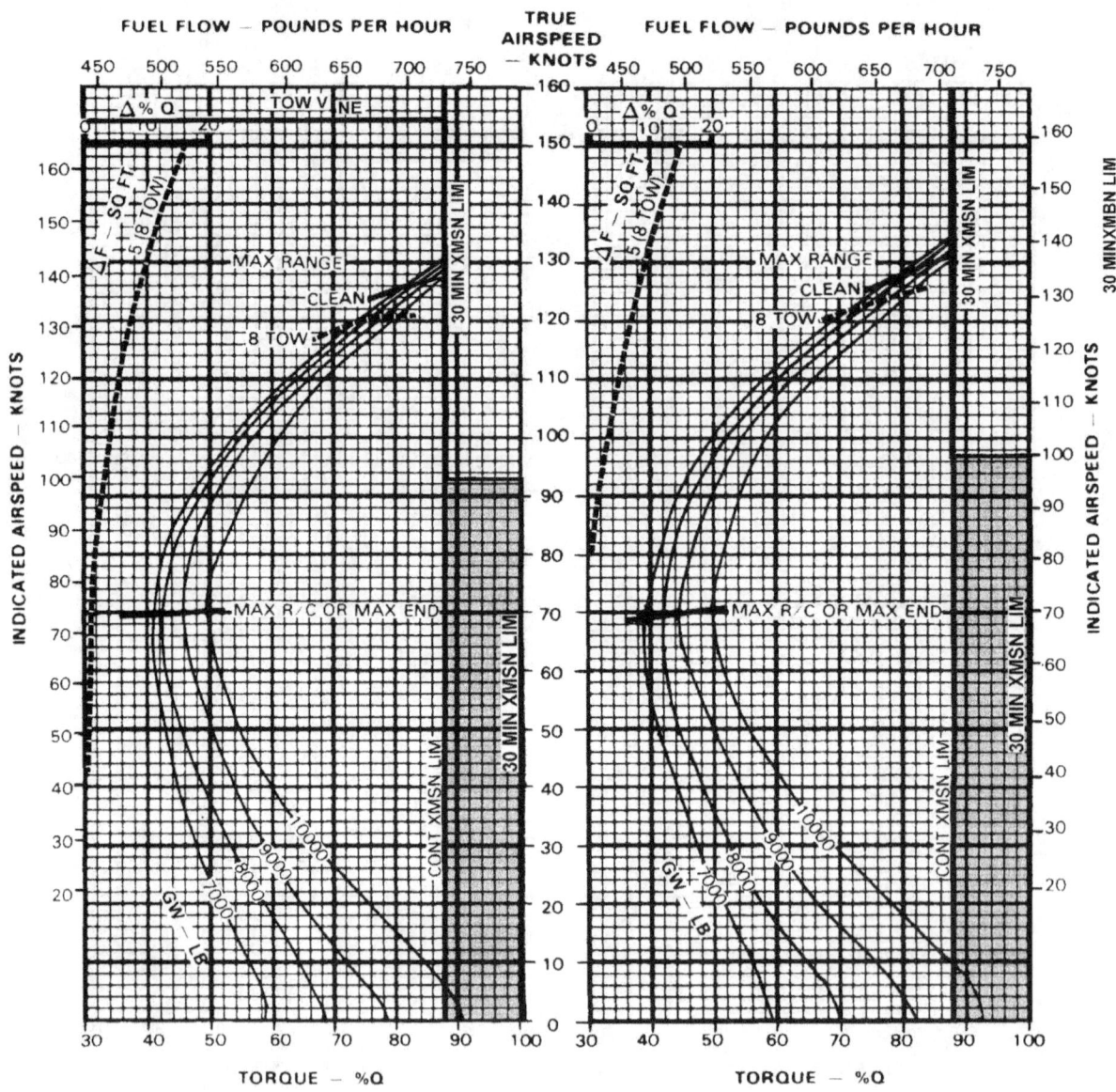

Figure 7.1-7. Cruise Chart (Sheet 6 of 23)

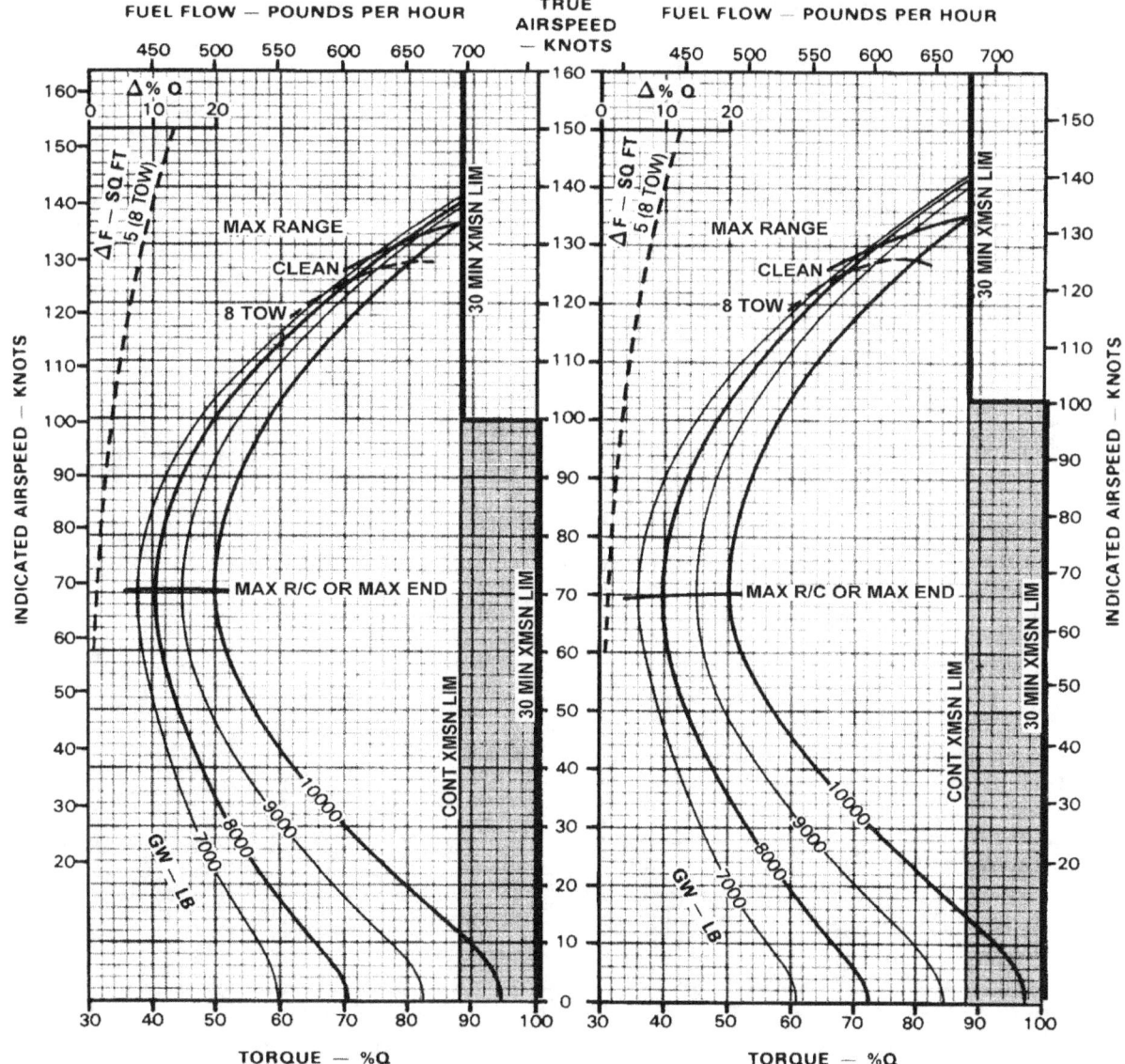

Figure 7.1-7. Cruise Chart (Sheet 7 of 23)

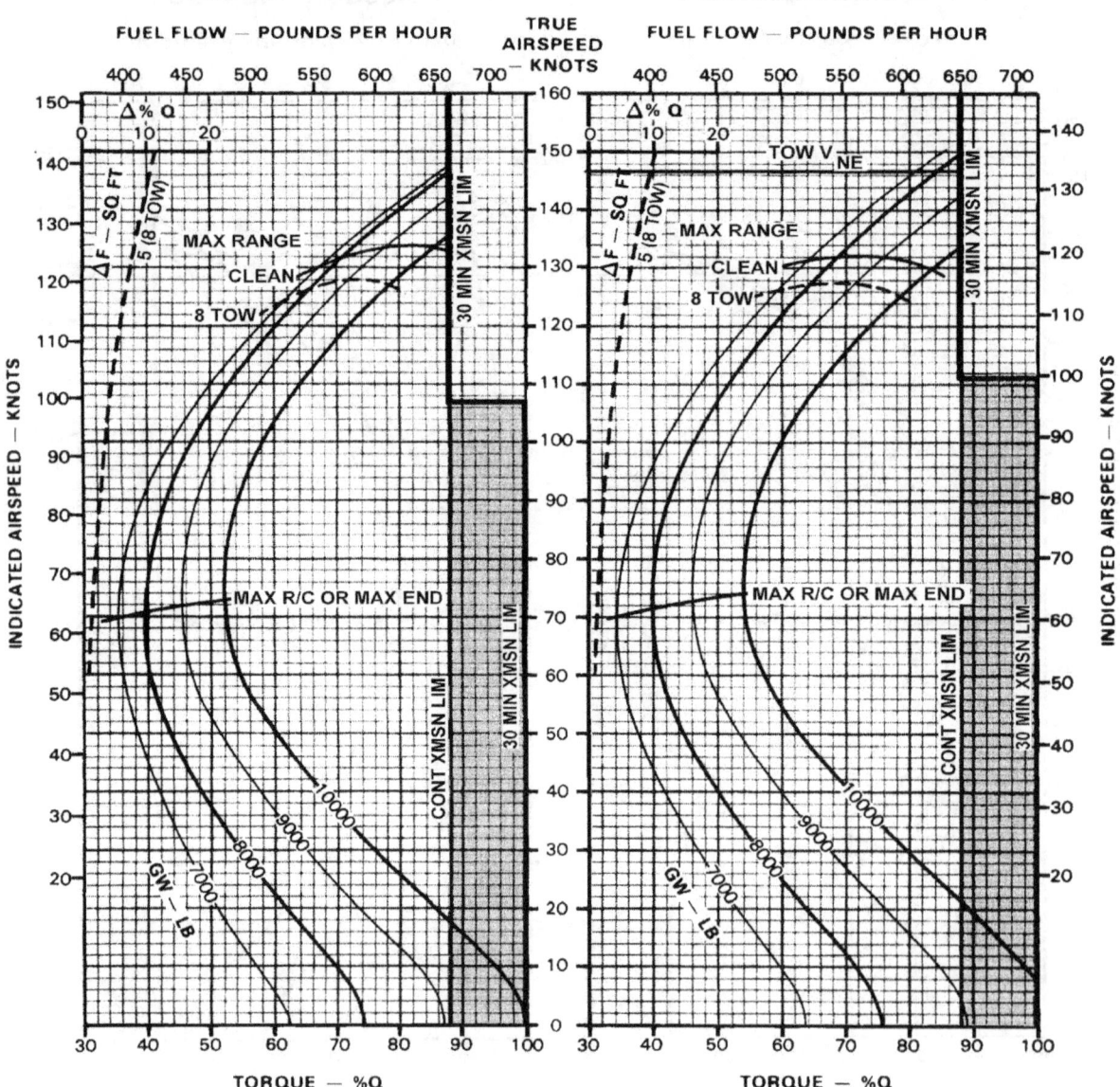

Figure 7.1-7. Cruise Chart (Sheet 8 of 23)

CRUISE
PRESSURE ALTITUDE — 12000 FEET TO 14000 FEET
100% RPM, CLEAN CONFIGURATION, JP-4 FUEL

CRUISE
AH-1F
T53-L-703

SHADED AREA INDICATES 30 MIN. TRANSMISSION LIMIT.

FAT = -15°C

12000 FEET PRESSURE ALTITUDE

14000 FEET PRESSURE ALTITUDE

DATA BASIS: DERIVED FROM FLIGHT TEST

MS018590

K747 Figure 7.1-7. Cruise Chart (Sheet 9 of 23)

7.1-27

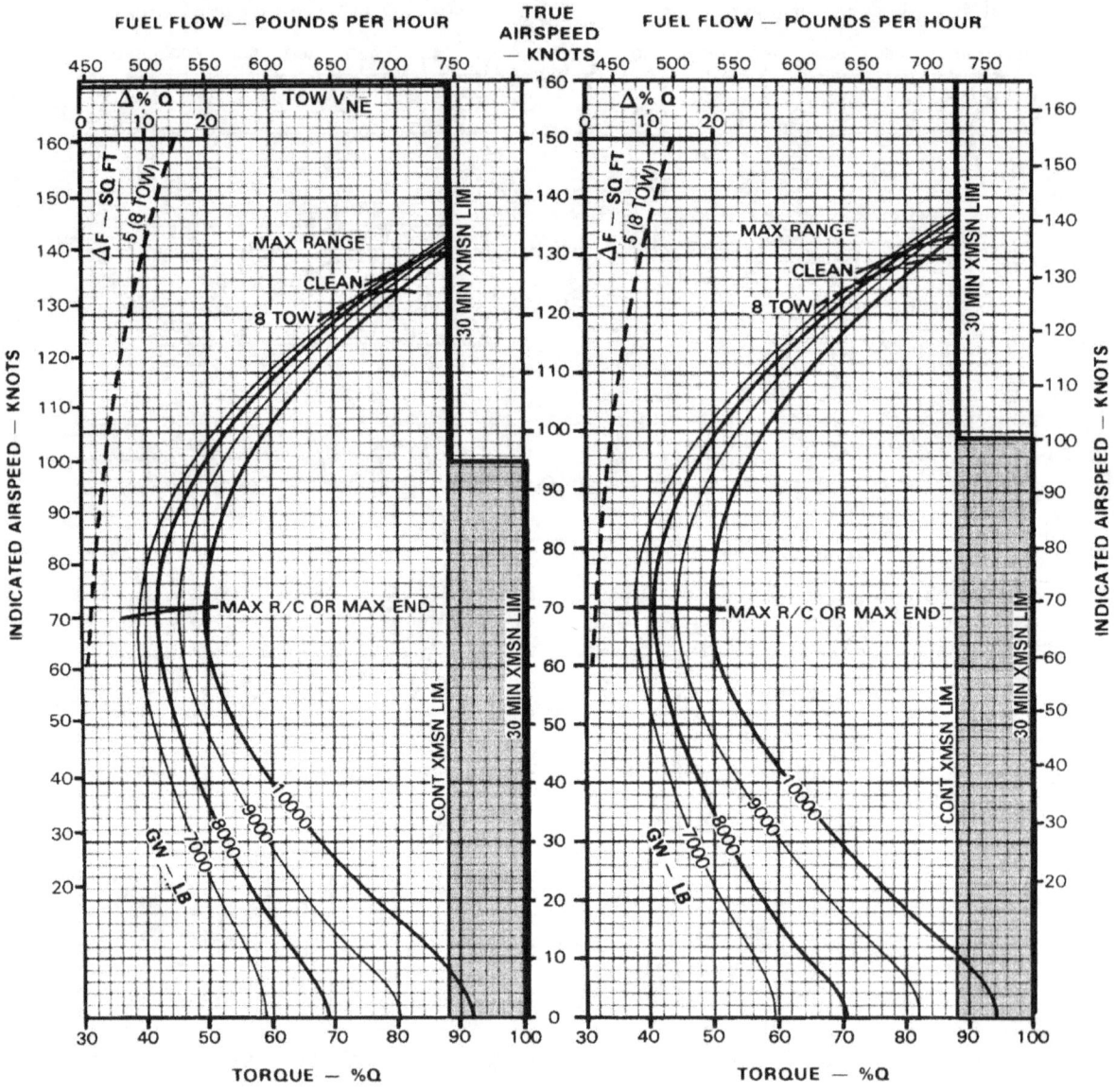

Figure 7.1-7. Cruise Chart (Sheet 10 of 23)

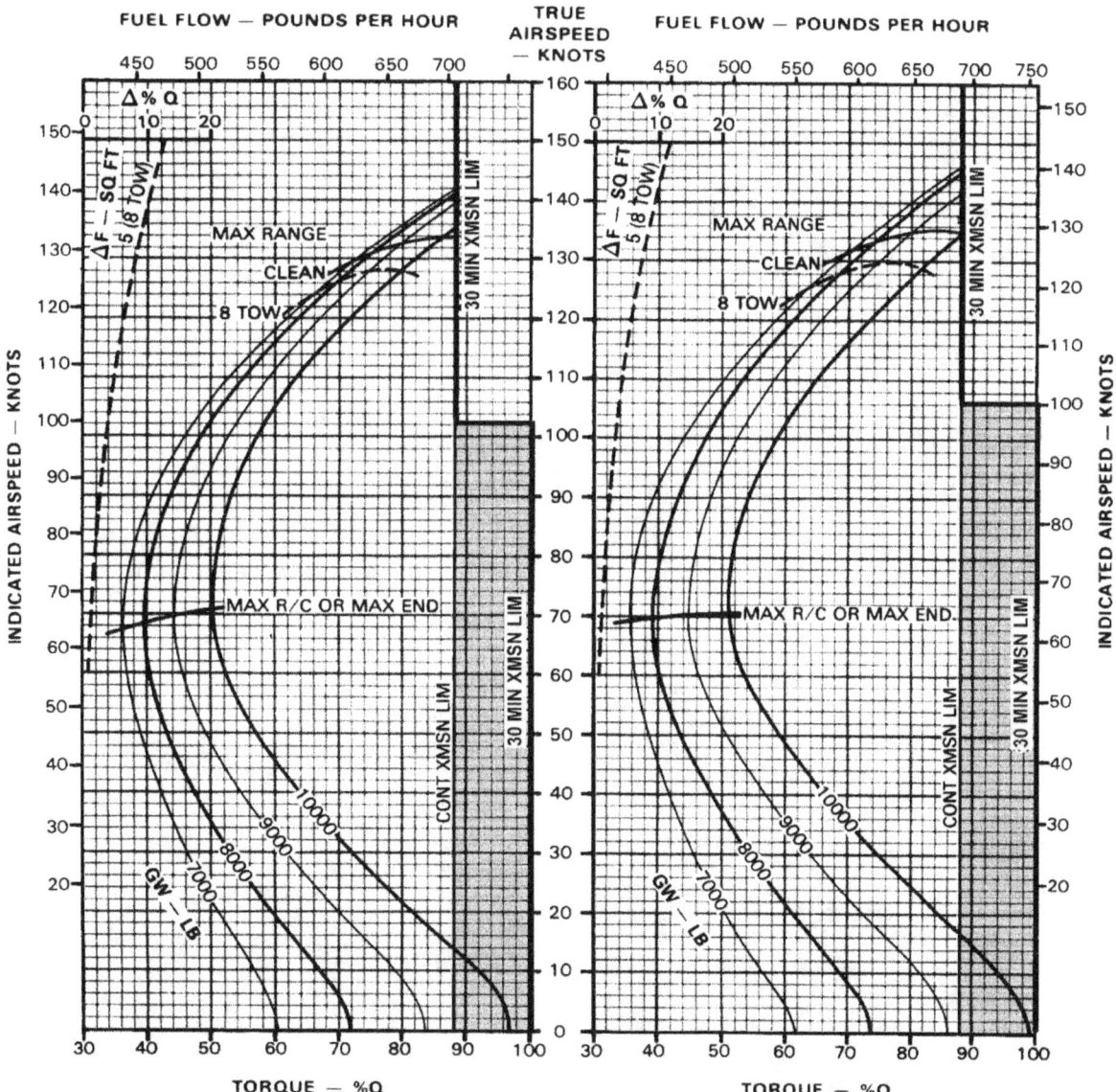

Figure 7.1-7 Cruise Chart (Sheet 11 of 23)

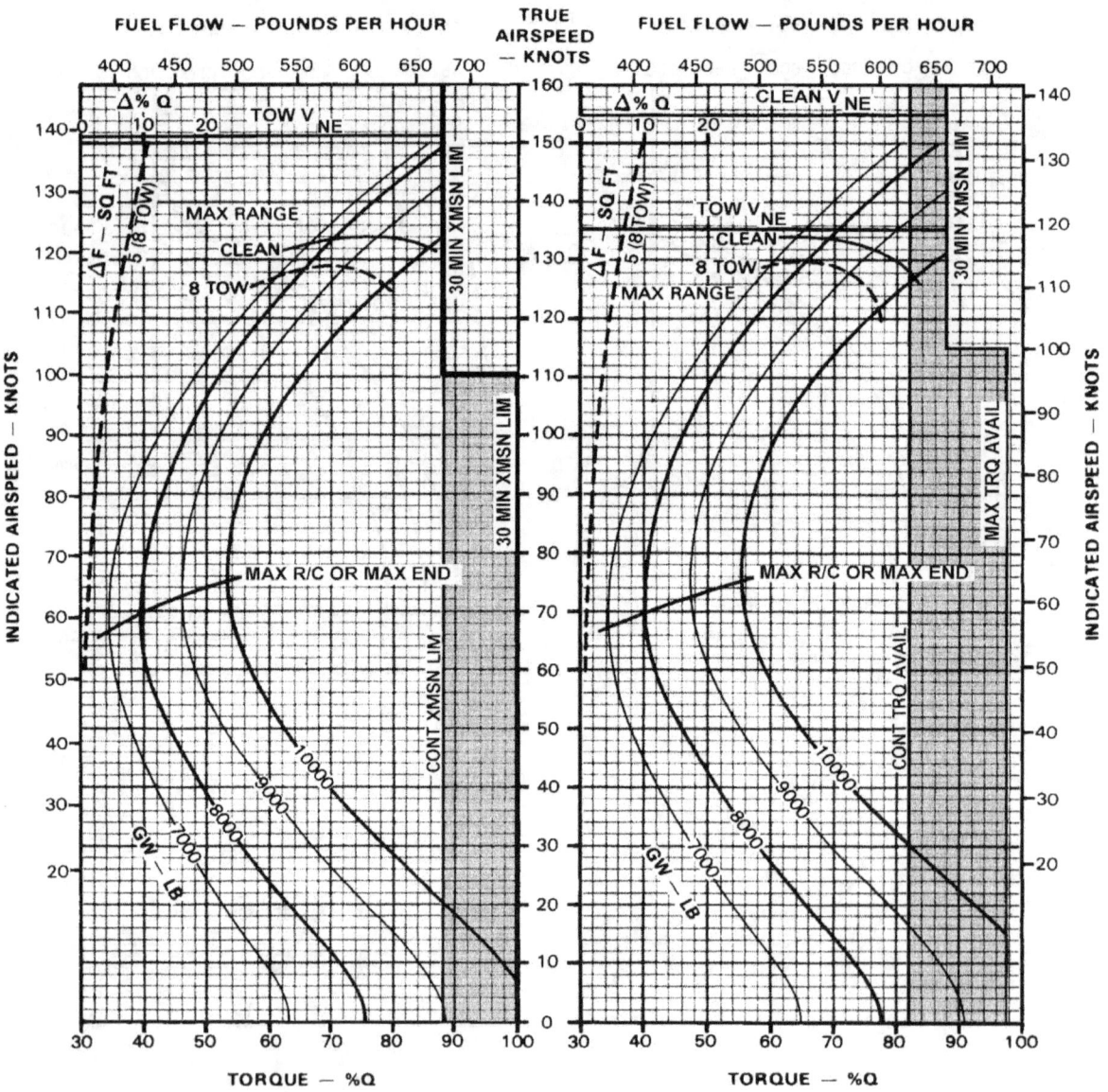

Figure 7.1-7. Cruise Chart (Sheet 12 of 23)

CRUISE
PRESSURE ALTITUDE — 12000 FEET TO 14000 FEET
100% RPM, CLEAN CONFIGURATION, JP-4 FUEL

CRUISE AH-1F T53-L-703

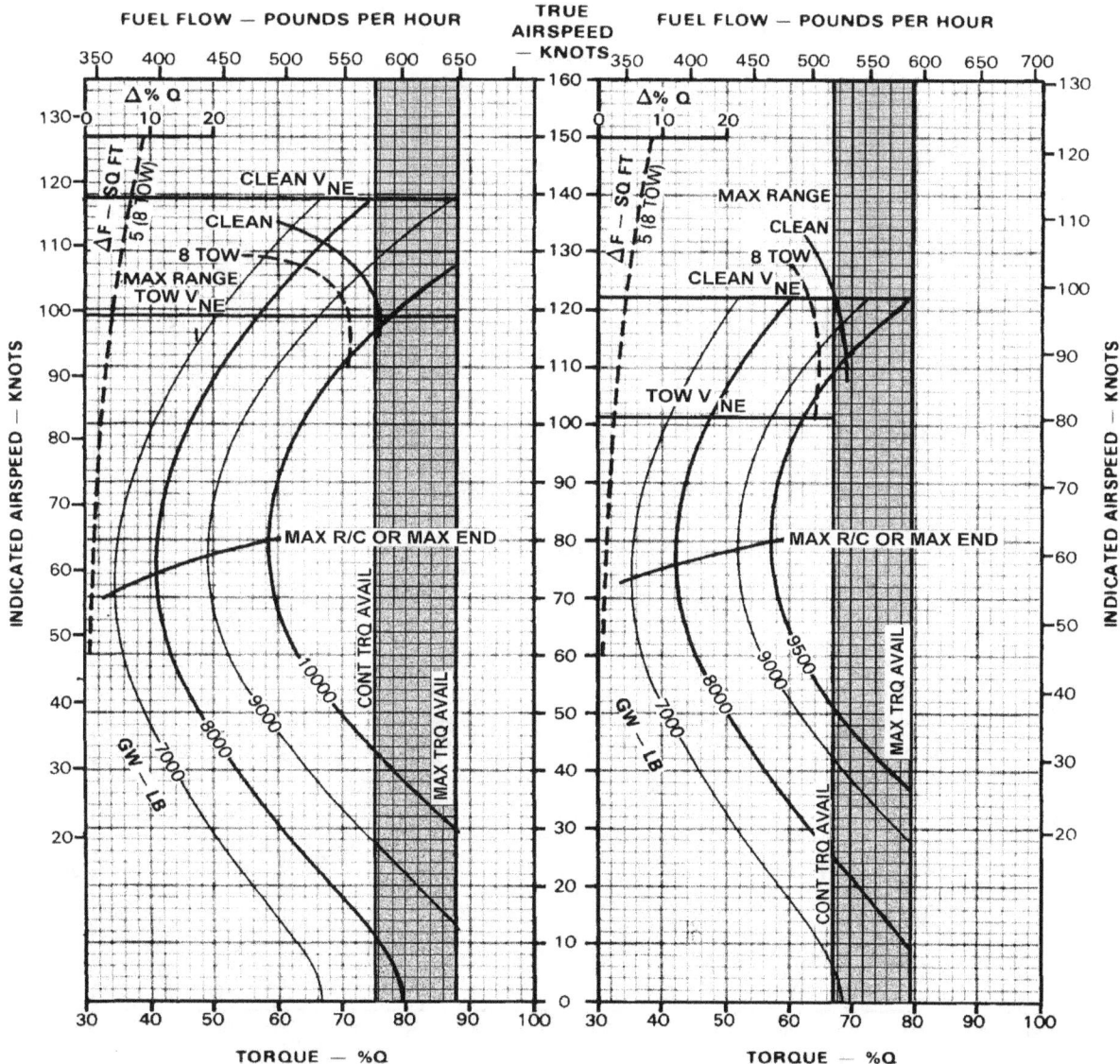

Figure 7.1-7. Cruise Chart (Sheet 13 of 23)

CRUISE
PRESSURE ALTITUDE — SEA LEVEL TO 2000 FEET
100% RPM, CLEAN CONFIGURATION, JP-4 FUEL

CRUISE
AH-1F
T53-L-703

SHADED AREA INDICATES 30 MIN. TRANSMISSION LIMIT.

FAT = +15°C

Figure 7.1-7. Cruise Chart (Sheet 14 of 23)

DATA BASIS: DERIVED FROM FLIGHT TEST

MS018595

TM 1-1520-236-10

CRUISE
PRESSURE ALTITUDE — 4000 FEET TO 6000 FEET
100% RPM, CLEAN CONFIGURATION, JP-4 FUEL

CRUISE
AH-1F
T53-L-703

SHADED AREA INDICATES 30 MIN. TRANSMISSION LIMIT.

FAT = +15°C

4000 FEET PRESSURE ALTITUDE

6000 FEET PRESSURE ALTITUDE

DATA BASIS: DERIVED FROM FLIGHT TEST

MS018596

K747 Figure 7.1-7. Cruise Chart (Sheet 15 of 23)

7.1-33

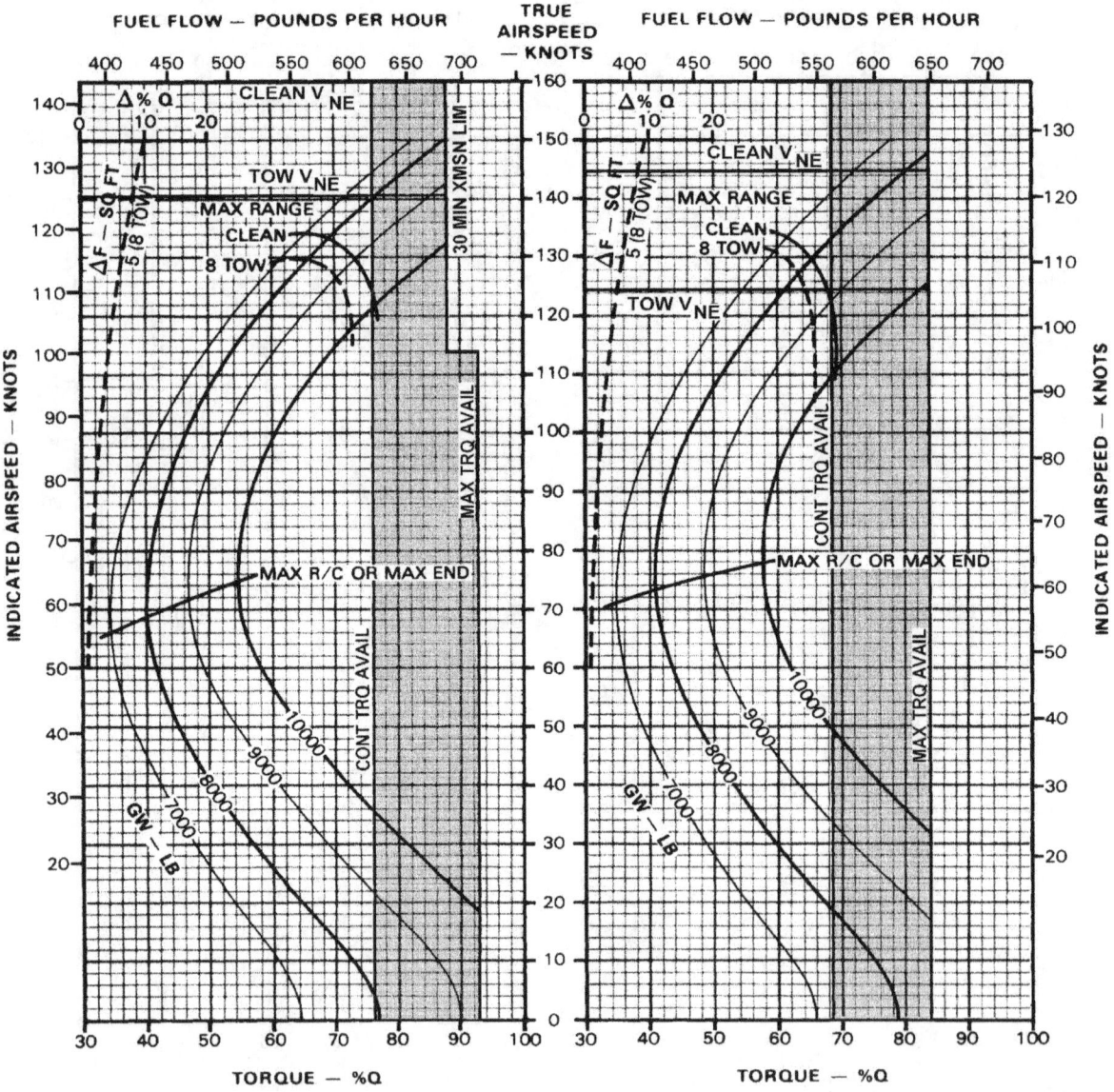

Figure 7.1-7. Cruise Chart (Sheet 16 of 23)

CRUISE
PRESSURE ALTITUDE — 12000 FEET TO 14000 FEET
100% RPM, CLEAN CONFIGURATION, JP-4 FUEL

CRUISE
AH-1F
T53-L-703

SHADED AREA INDICATES 30 MIN. TRANSMISSION LIMIT.

FAT = +15°C

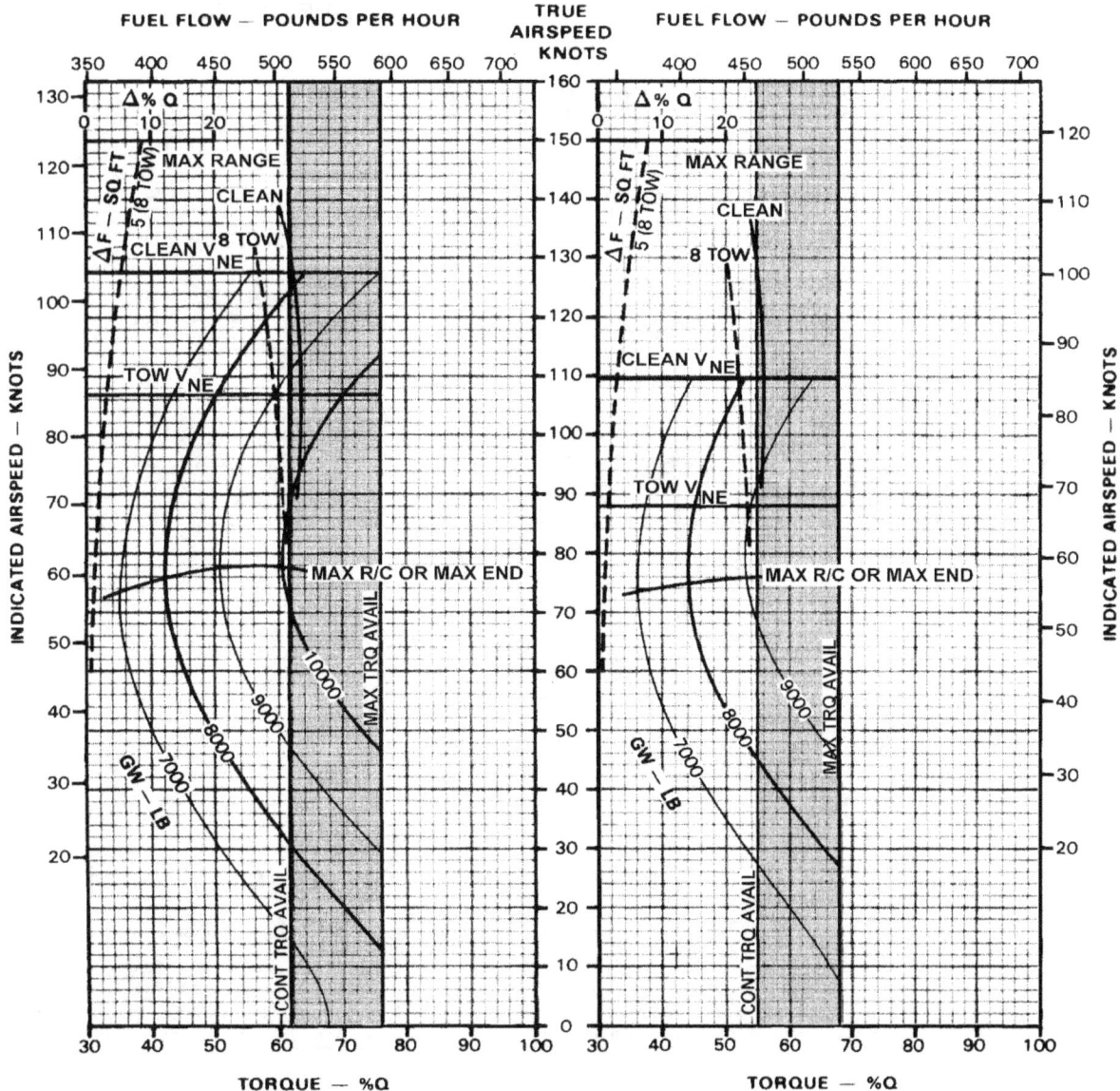

DATA BASIS: DERIVED FROM FLIGHT TEST

Figure 7.1-7. Cruise Chart (Sheet 17 of 23)

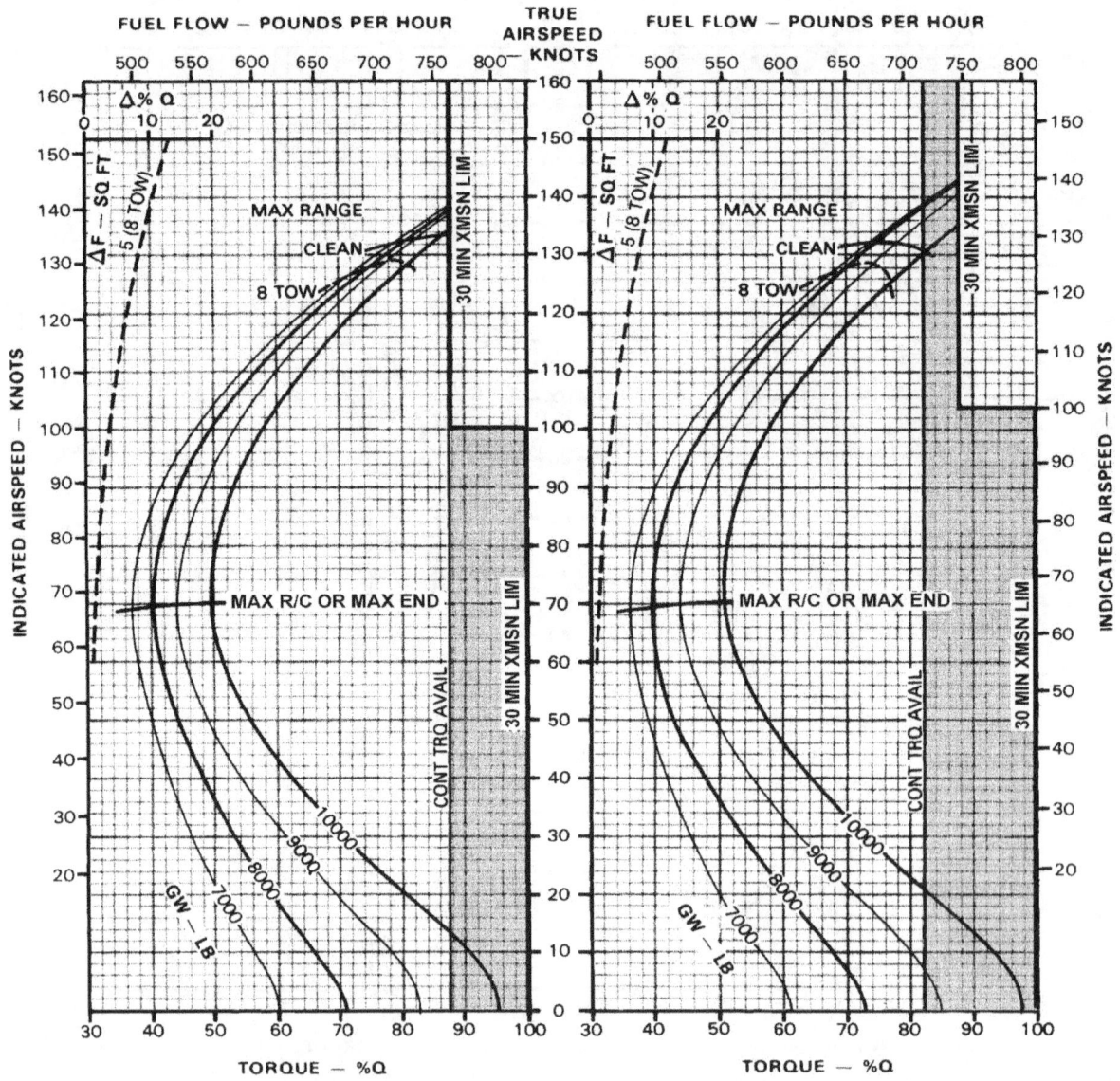

Figure 7.1-7. Cruise Chart (Sheet 18 of 23)

CRUISE
PRESSURE ALTITUDE — 4000 FEET TO 6000 FEET
100% RPM, CLEAN CONFIGURATION, JP-4 FUEL

CRUISE AH-1F T53-L-703

SHADED AREA INDICATES 30 MIN. TRANSMISSION LIMIT.

FAT = +30°C

DATA BASIS: DERIVED FROM FLIGHT TEST

Figure 7.1-7. Cruise Chart (Sheet 19 of 23)

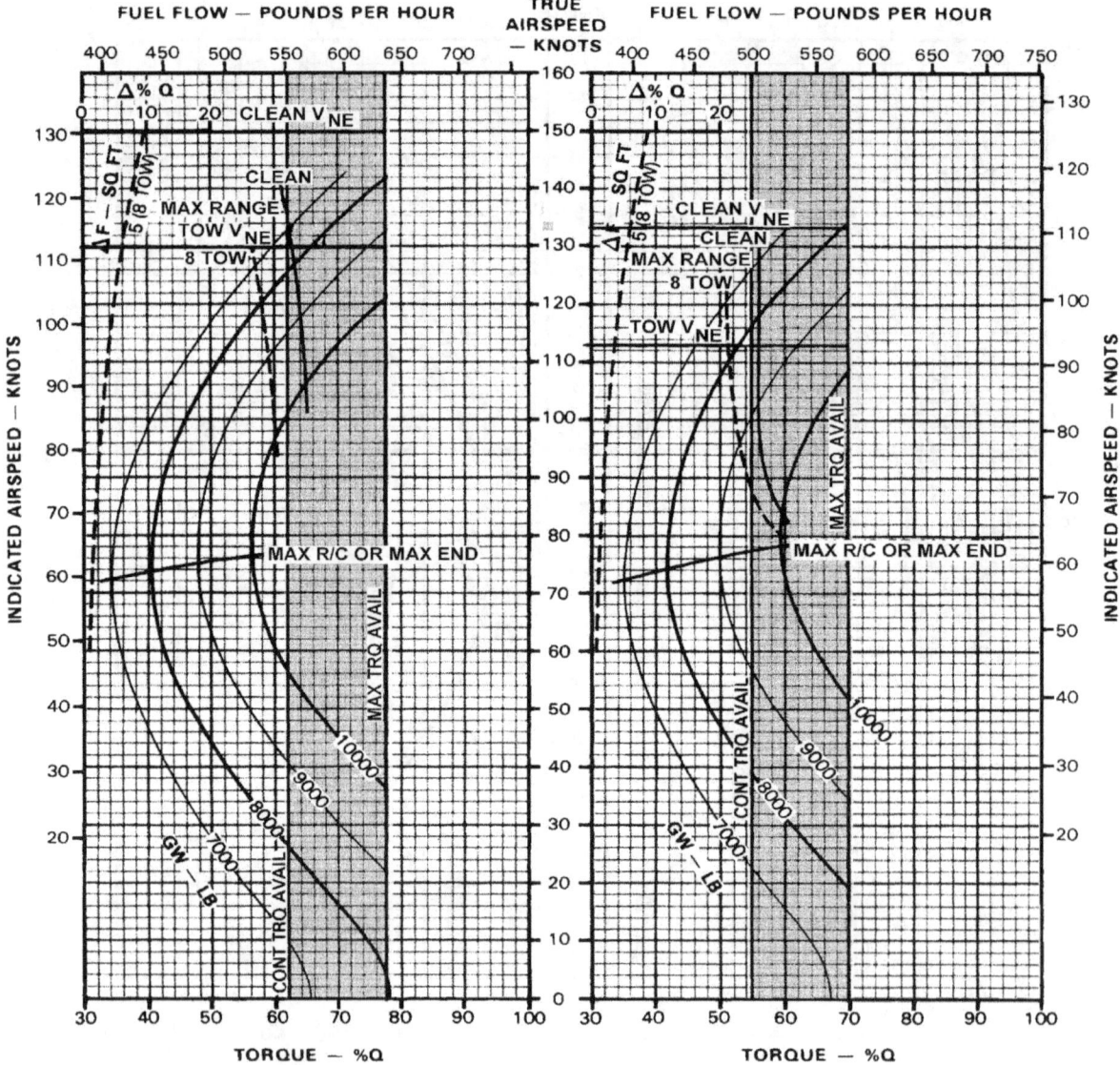

Figure 7.1-7. Cruise Chart (Sheet 20 of 23)

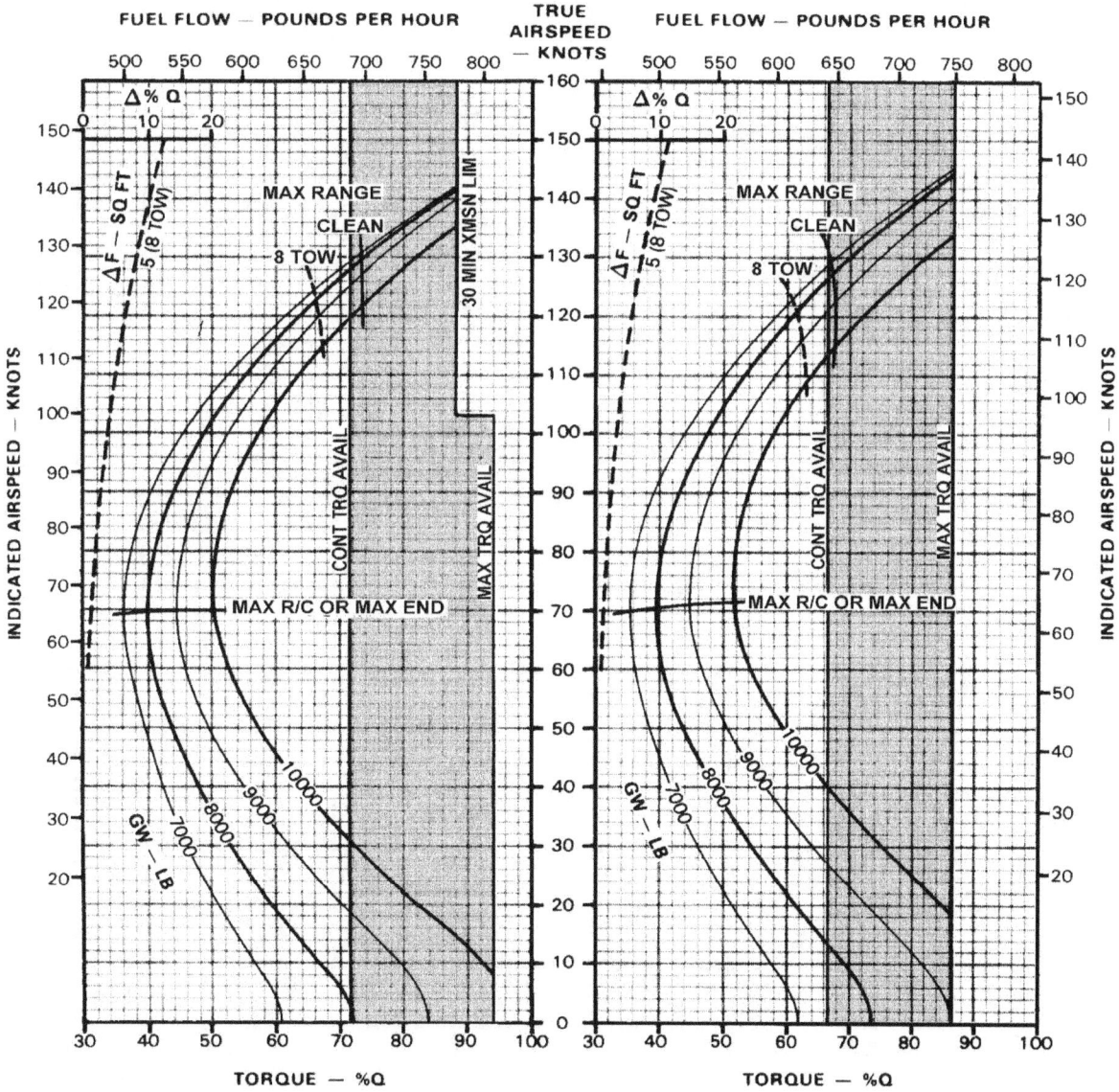

Figure 7.1-7. Cruise Chart (Sheet 21 of 23)

CRUISE
PRESSURE ALTITUDE — 4000 FEET TO 6000 FEET
100% RPM, CLEAN CONFIGURATION, JP-4 FUEL

CRUISE
AH-1F
T53-L-703

SHADED AREA INDICATES 30 MIN. TRANSMISSION LIMIT.

FAT = +45°C

4000 FEET PRESSURE ALTITUDE

6000 FEET PRESSURE ALTITUDE

DATA BASIS: DERIVED FROM FLIGHT TEST

MS018603

Figure 7.1-7. Cruise Chart (Sheet 22 of 23)

CRUISE

PRESSURE ALTITUDE — 8000 FEET TO 10000 FEET
100% RPM, CLEAN CONFIGURATION, JP-4 FUEL

CRUISE
AH-1F
T53-L-703

SHADED AREA INDICATES 30 MIN. TRANSMISSION LIMIT.

FAT = +45°C

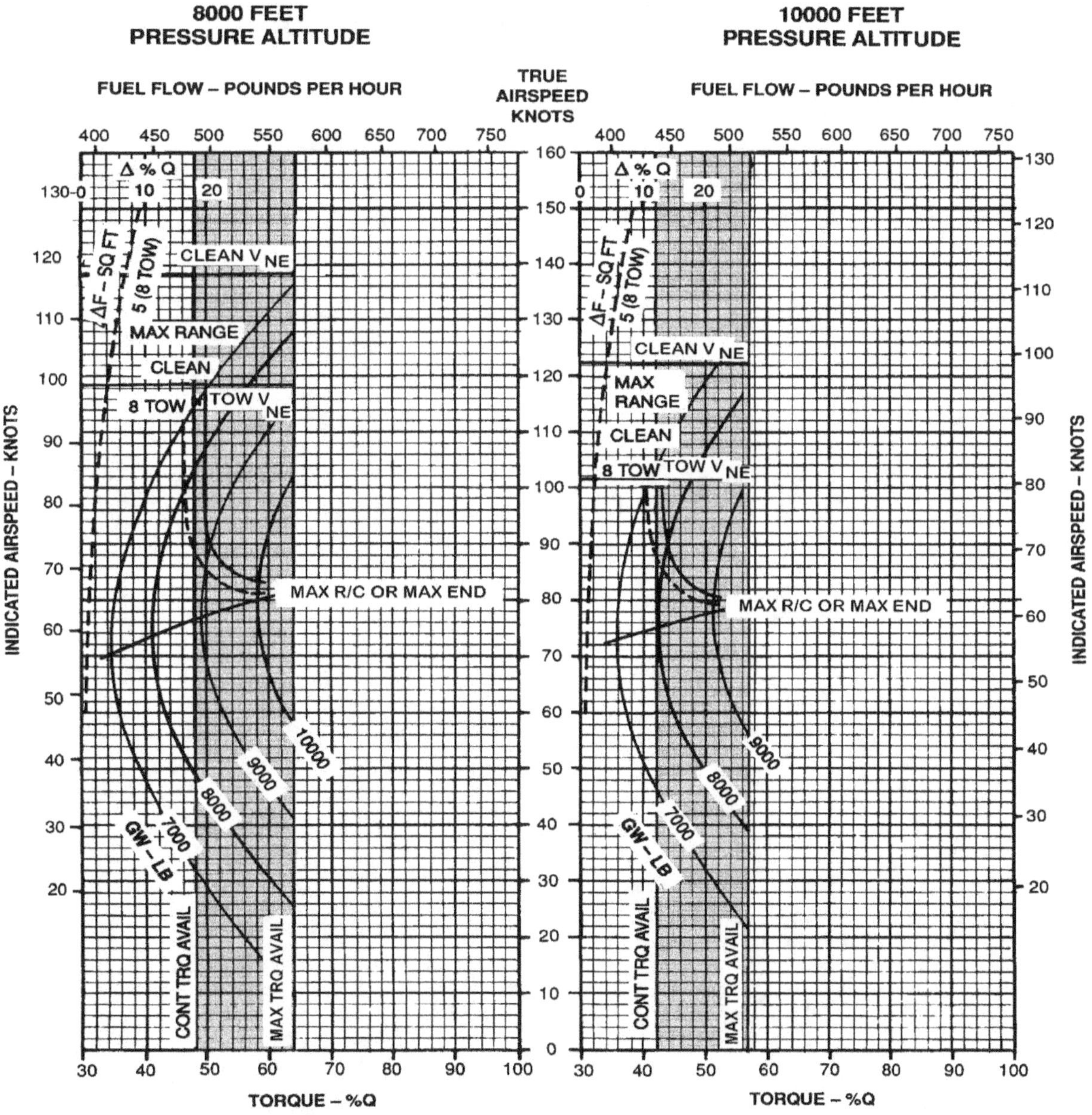

DATA BASIS: DERIVED FROM FLIGHT TEST

Figure 7.1-7. Cruise Chart (Sheet 23 of 23)

SECTION VI. DRAG

7.1-24. DESCRIPTION.

The drag chart (Figure 7.1-8) shows the equivalent flat plate drag area (ΔF) increment of all approved configurations.

7.1-25. USE OF CHART.

This chart is used to adjust the cruise charts (Figure 7.1-8) for the appropriate torque and fuel flow due to the equivalent flat plate drag area change (ΔF). Select a configuration from Figure 7.1-8 and read equivalent flat plate drag for the configuration. Proceed to Figure 7.1-8, example B for application of drag. With IR Suppressor installed, the equivalent flat plate drag area will be increased by 2 sq ft.

7.1-26. CONDITIONS. Not Applicable.

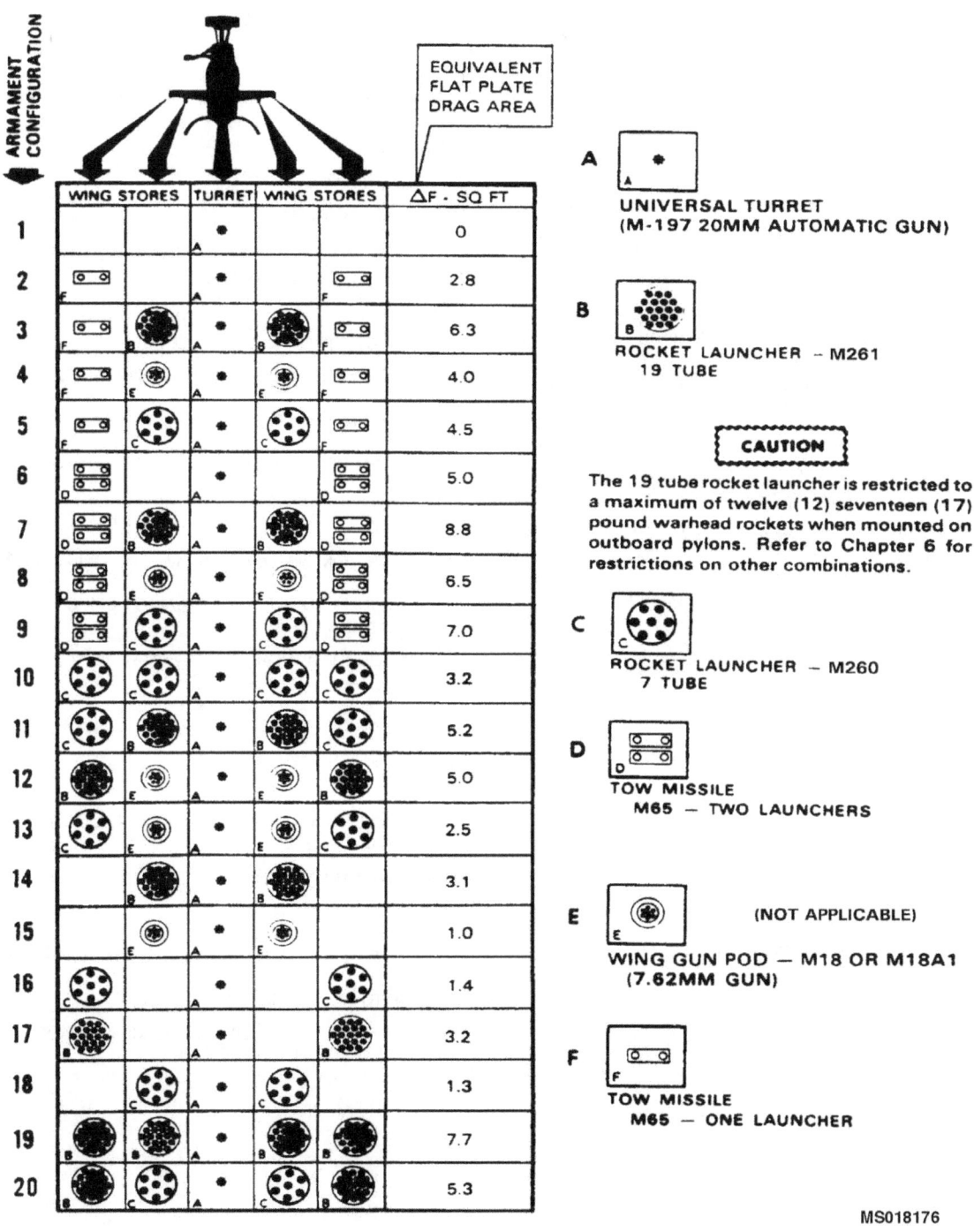

Figure 7.1-8. Drag Chart

SECTION VII. CLIMB – DESCENT

7.1-27. DESCRIPTION.

The upper grid of the climb descent chart (Figure 7.1-9) shows the change in torque (above or below torque required for level flight under the same gross weight and atmospheric conditions) to obtain a given rate of climb or descent.

7.1-28. USE OF CHART.

The primary uses of the chart are illustrated by the chart examples.

a. The torque change obtained from the upper grid scale must be added to the torque required for level flight (for climb) - or subtracted from the torque required for level flight (for descent) - obtained from the appropriate cruise chart in order to obtain a total climb or descent torque.

b. By entering the bottom of the upper grid with a known torque change, moving upward to the gross weight, and left to the corresponding rate of climb or descent may also be obtained.

7.1-29. CONDITIONS. Not applicable.

EXAMPLE K747

WANTED

EXCESS TORQUE AVAILABLE FOR CLIMB AT MAXIMUM CONTINUOUS POWER.

KNOWN

CLEAN CONFIGURATION

GROSS WEIGHT = 9000 LB

FAT = - 30°C

PRESSURE ALTITUDE = 14000 FEET

METHOD

LOCATE CHART (FIGURE 7.1-7, SHEET 5)

FIND INTERSECTION OF 9000 LB GROSS WEIGHT LINE WITH THE MAXIMUM RATE OF CLIMB LINE ──▶ ①

MOVE DOWN, READ TORQUE REQUIRED = 48.3% Q

FIND INTERSECTION OF 9000 LB GROSS WEIGHT LINE WITH THE CONTINUOUS TORQUE AVAILABLE LINE ──▶ ②

MOVE DOWN, READ TORQUE AVAILABLE = 87% Q

EXCESS TORQUE AVAILABLE = (87 - 48.3) = 38.7% Q

WANTED

RATE OF CLIMB AT 60 KIAS

MAXIMUM CONTINUOUS POWER

KNOWN

EXCESS TORQUE AVAILABLE (FROM EXAMPLE ON FIGURE 7.1-7. SHEET 5) = 38.7% Q

GROSS WEIGHT = 9000 LB

METHOD

ENTER CALIBRATED TORQUE SCALE HERE ──▶ ③

MOVE UP TO GROSS WEIGHT LINE

MOVE LEFT TO RATE OF CLIMB OR DESCENT SCALE. READ RATE OF CLIMB = 1440 FT MIN

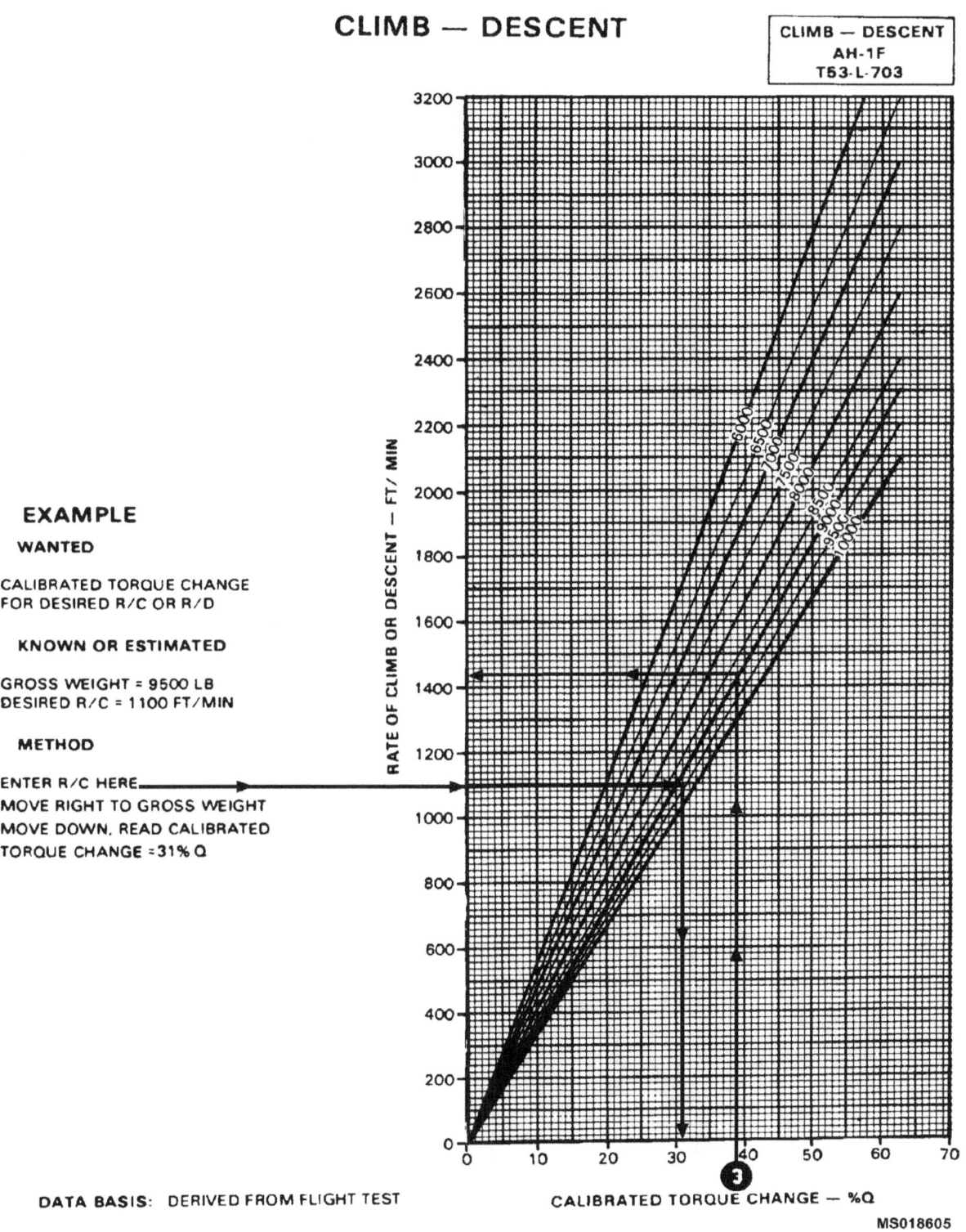

Figure 7.1-9. Climb - Descent Chart

SECTION VIII. IDLE FUEL FLOW

7.1-30. DESCRIPTION.

The idle fuel flow chart (Figure 7.1-10) shows the fuel flow at flat pitch with 100 percent rpm.

7.1-31. USE OF CHART.

The primary use of the chart is illustrated by the example. To determine the idle fuel flow, it is necessary to know the idle condition, pressure altitude, and free air temperature. Enter at the pressure altitude, then move right to FAT in appropriate grin, then move down and read fuel flow on the scale corresponding to the condition. Refer to the cruise charts to obtain fuel flow for cruise power conditions.

7.1-32. CONDITIONS.

This chart is based on the use of the JP-4 fuel. Fuel flow at engine ilde is approximately one half the flat pitch fuel flow.

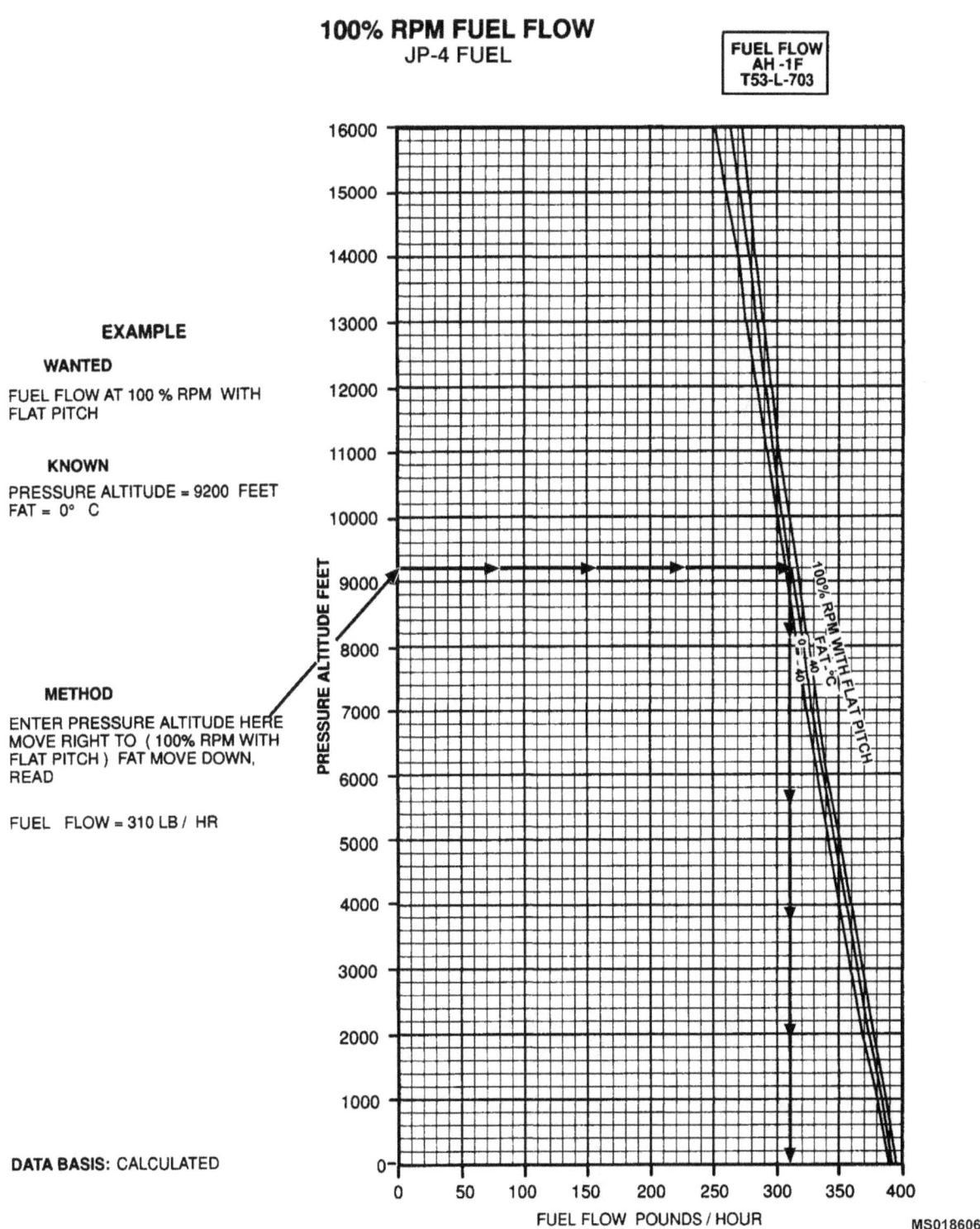

Figure 7.1-10. 100% RPM Fuel Flow Chart

CHAPTER 8
NORMAL PROCEDURES

SECTION I. CREW DUTIES

8-1. CREW DUTIES/RESPONSIBILITIES.

The minimum crew required to fly the helicopter is a pilot. Additional crewmembers, as required may be added at the discretion of the commander. The manner in which each crewmember performs his related duties is the responsibility of the pilot in command.

    a. **Pilot.** The pilot in command is responsible for all aspects of mission planning, preflight, and operations of the helicopter. He will assign duties and functions to all other crewmembers as required. Prior to or during preflight, the pilot will brief the crew on the mission, performance data, monitoring instruments, communications, emergency procedures, and armament procedures.

    b. **Gunner.** The gunner must be familiar with the pilot's duties. The gunner will assist the pilot as directed.

8-2. CREW BRIEF.

A crew briefing shall be conducted to ensure a thorough understanding of individual and crew responsibilities. The briefing should include, but not limited to, copilot, and ground crew responsibilities and the coordination necessary to complete the mission in the most efficient manner. A review of visual signals is desirable when ground guides do not have direct voice communications link with the crew.

8-3. CREW BRIEFING.

The following is a guide that should be used in accomplishing required crew briefing. Items that do not pertain to a specific mission may be omitted.

    a. Mission.

        (1) Mission brief.

        (2) NBC operations.

        (3) ASE equipmnt and use.

        (4) Actions on contact.

    b. Weather.

        Inadvertent IMC.

    c. Flight route.

        (1) Doppler.

        (2) Time enroute.

        (3) Altitude and techniques of movement.

    d. Performance data.

    e. Emergency actions.

        (1) Immediate action steps.

        (2) Mayday call.

        (3) Egress procedures.

        (4) Rendezvous points.

        (5) Emergency equipment.

    f. Crew duties and responsibilities.

        (1) Transfer of controls (normal and emergency).

        (2) Area of scan responsibilities.

    g. Pilot on the controls.

        (1) Positive aircraft control (Primary focus outside).

        (2) Avoid traffic and obstacles.

        (3) Announce all actions.

    h. Pilot not on the controls.

        (1) Announce traffic and obstacles.

        (2) Navigate.

        (3) Copy all required information.

        (4) Perform other duties as assigned.

        (5) Announce focusing "in and out of the cockpit".

        (6) Acknowledge intentions.

i. Both crewmembers.

    (1) Cross check instruments and systems.

    (2) Tune radios as required.

    (3) Most conservative action.

    (4) Two challenge rule.

j. Armament procedures.

    (1) Target priority.

    (2) Target handoff.

    (3) Ammo load.

k. NVG considerations.

l. Refuelling operations.

m. Required equipment.

n. Additional information/questions.

8-4. DANGER AREAS.

Refer to Figure 8-1.

8-5. MISSION PLANNING.

Mission planning begins when the mission is assigned and extends to the preflight check of the helicopter. It includes, but is not limited to, check of operating limits and restrictions; weight/balance and loading; performance; publications; flight plan; and crew briefings. The pilot in command shall ensure compliance with the contents of this manual that are applicable to the mission.

8-6. AVIATION LIFE SUPPORT EQUIPMENT (ALSE).

All aviation life support equipment required for mission (e.g., helmets, gloves, survival vests, survival kits, etc.) shall be checked.

TM 1-1520-236-10

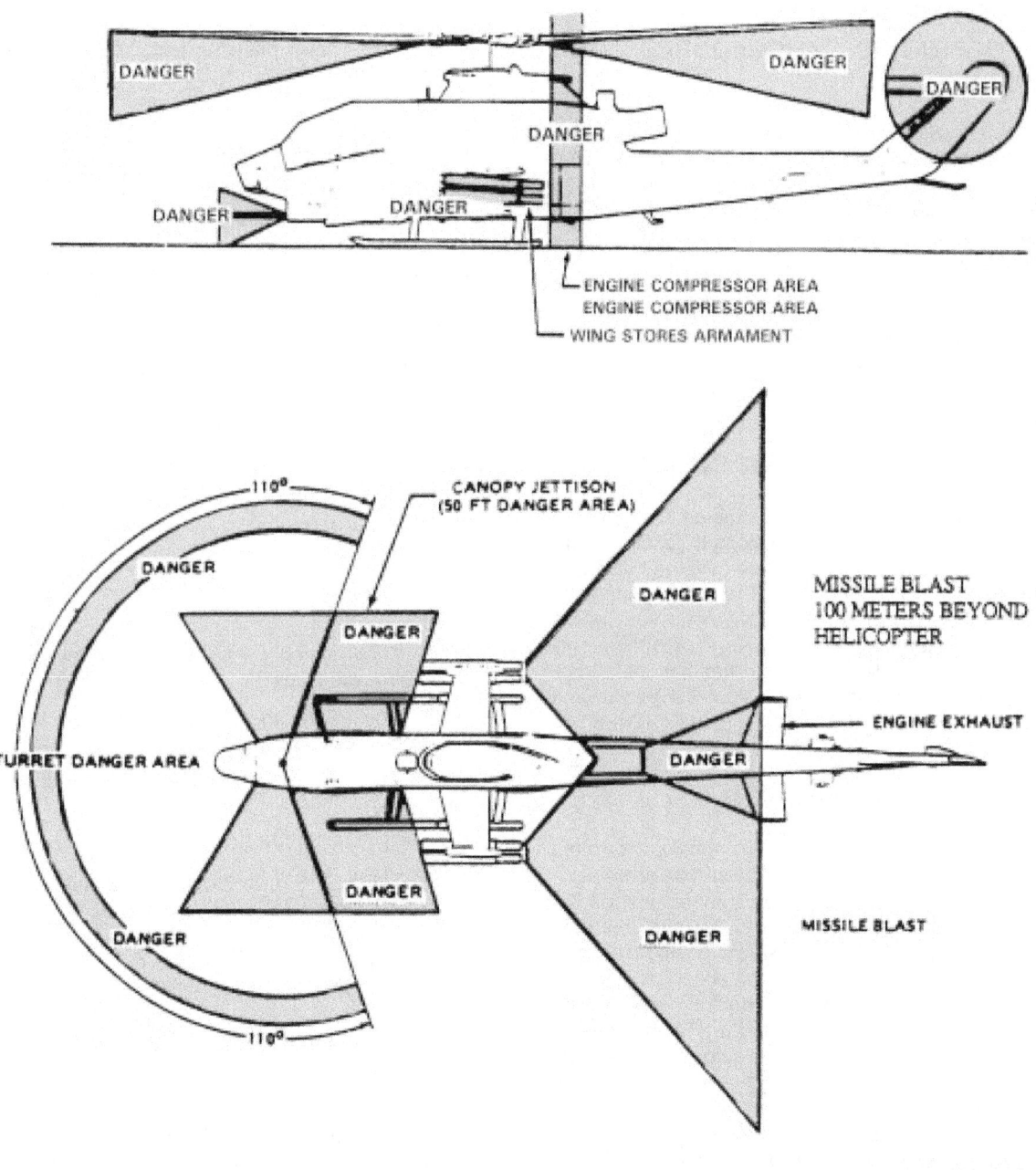

Figure 8-1. Danger Areas

SECTION II. OPERATING PROCEDURES AND MANEUVERS

8-7. OPERATING PROCEDURES AND MANEUVERS.

This section deals with normal procedures and includes all steps necessary to ensure safe and efficient operation of the helicopter from the time a preflight begins until the flight is completed and the helicopter is parked and secured. Unique feel, characteristics, and reaction of the helicopter during various phases of operation and the techniques and procedures used for hovering, takeoff, climb, etc., are described, including precautions to be observed. Your flying experience is recognized; therefore, basic flight principles are avoided. Only the duties of the minimum crew necessary for the actual operation of the helicopter are included.

8-8. MISSION EQUIPMENT CHECKS.

Mission equipment checks are contained in Chapter 4, MISSION EQUIPMENT. Descriptions of functions, operations, and effects of controls are covered in Section IV, FLIGHT CHARACTERISTICS, and are repeated in this section only when required for emphasis. Checks that must be performed under adverse environmental conditions, such as desert and cold weather operations, supplement normal procedure checks in this section and are covered in Section V, ADVERSE ENVIRONMENTAL CONDITIONS.

8-9. SYMBOLS DEFINITION.

The checklist includes items with annotative indicators immediately preceding the check to which they are pertinent. The "(O)" symbol indicates a requirement if the equipment is installed. The star "°" symbol indicates that a detailed procedure for the step is located in the performance section of the condensed checklist. When a helicopter is flown on a mission requiring intermediate stops, it is not necessary to perform all of the normal checks. The steps that are essential for safe helicopter operations on intermediate stops are designated as "thru-flight" checks. An asterisk "*" indicates that performance of steps is mandatory for all "thru-flights" when there has been no change in pilot-in-command. The asterisk applies only to checks performed prior to takeoff.

8-10. CHECKLIST.

Normal procedures are given primarily in checklist form and amplified as necessary in accompanying paragraph form when a detailed description of a procedure or maneuver is required. A condensed version of the amplified checklist, omitting all explanatory text, is contained in the Operators and Crewmembers Checklist, TM 1-1520-236-CL.

8-11. PREFLIGHT CHECK.

The pilot's walk-around and interior checks are outlined in the following procedures. The preflight check is not intended to be a detailed mechanical inspection. The steps that are essential for safe helicopter operation are included. The preflight may be made as comprehensive as conditions warrant at the discretion of the pilot.

8-12. BEFORE EXTERIOR CHECK.

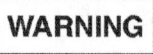

Do not preflight until armament systems are safe.

*1. Wing ejector rack – Jettison safety pins installed.

*2. TOW launcher – Missile arming levers up if TOW missiles are loaded.

*3. Rocket launchers – Igniter arms in contact with rockets if rockets are loaded.

*4. W2P1 – Disconnected if 20MM ammunition is loaded.

*5. JETTISON SELECT switches – OFF.

*6. TURRET STOW, ADS, FCC circuit breakers and TURRET DRIVE MOTOR switch – OUT/OFF.

(O) *7. CHAFF DISP CONT switch – SAFE.

*8. Canopy removal arming/firing mechanism safety pins – IN.

*9. Publications – Check in accordance with DA PAM 738-751 and any local required forms and publications.

10. BATTERY switch – START. A minimum of 22 volts indicate satisfactory condition to attempt battery start.

11. NON-ESNTL BUS switch – MANUAL.

12. Lights – Check if use is anticipated.

13. BATTERY switch – OFF.

14. Pilot's HSS linkage assembly – Check condition and stow.

15. Area behind pilot seat – Check as follows:

   a. First aid kit.

   b. HSS interface assembly.

   c. Electronic processing unit.

   d. N/ALQ 136.

   e. Sensor Amplifier Unit.

16. Both map lights – OFF.

17. Canopy – Check.

8-13. EXTERIOR CHECK (Fig 8-2).

8-14. AREA 1 – FUSELAGE AND MAIN ROTOR.

*1. Fuel – Check quantity and condition of grounding receptacle. Secure cap.

*2. Fuel sample – Check for contamination before first flight of the day. If the fuel sumps and filter have not been drained, drain and check as follows:

   a. Sumps – Drain

   b. BATTERY switch – START.

   c. FUEL switch – FUEL.

   d. Filter – Drain.

   e. FUEL switch – OFF.

   f. BATTERY Switch – OFF.

*3. Main Rotor Blade – Check.

4. Fuselage – Check as follows:

   a. Window Channel Assembly – Check.

   b. Static port – Check.

   c. Airspeed and directional sensor – Check.

*5. Ammunition bay (right side) – Check condition of door, and electrical wiring/connections. Check the following if installed.

(O) a. Ammunition box – Check condition, security, and quick-release pins.

(O) b. Ammunition chute – Check condition, security, and ammunition if loaded.

(O) c. Boost motor – Check.

*6. Hydraulic compartment – Check condition of lines, reservoir, cap, and ECS. Check electrical A connectors and filter buttons.

7. Landing gear – Check.

8. Area beneath transmission – Check condition of lines, controls, and electrical connectors. Check emergency hydraulic cap, fluid level and filter indicator button.

9. Wing – Check.

(O)° 10. TOW – Check as follows:

   a. Launcher mounting – Check upper launcher aft and forward bomb lugs secured to helicopter ejector rack. Swaybrace bolts firmly against launcher. Lower launcher aft and forward attaching points secure to upper launcher.

   b. Electrical connectors – Check upper and lower harnesses connected. Jettison quick disconnect lanyard attached and not twisted.

(O)° 11. Rocket launcher – Check as follows:

   a. Launcher mounting – Check launcher aft and forward bomb lugs secured. Swaybrace bolts firmly against launcher but not denting exterior.

   b. Electrical connectors – Check harnesses connected to launcher. Jettison quick disconnect lanyard attached.

   c. Launcher – Check launcher exterior and tube interiors for damage and corrosion.

12. Engine and transmission cowlings – Secure open.

*13. Transmission area – Check hydraulic pumps, lines, servo mounting bolts for slippage marks, servo, transmission oil level, filter buttons in and main drive shaft.

*14. Pylon area – Check laser assembly, engine oil reservoir, electrical connectors, and drive links for slippage marks.

*15. Swashplate and support – Check.

*16. Main rotor system/root end fitting inboard surface – Check.

*17. Particle separator and scavenge ejector – Check for FOD and check area beneath plenum.

18. Engine compartment – Check air intake, condition of fuel and oil lines, and fire detector sensing elements. Close cowlings.

19. Fuselage – Check.

TM 1-1520-236-10

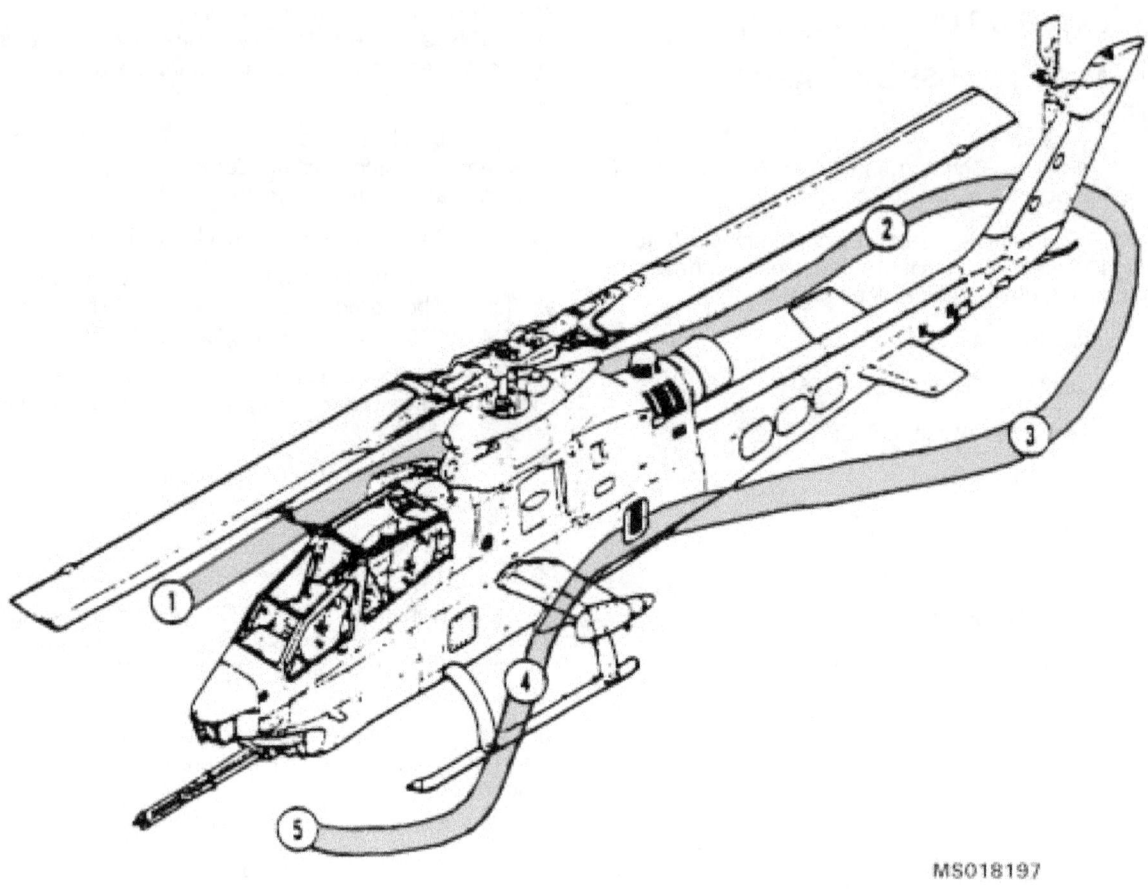

Figure 8-2. Exterior Check Diagram

8-15. AREA 2 – TAILSECTION – RIGHT SIDE.

1. Tailpipe/IR duct assembly – Check.

2. Electrical compartment – Check battery, vents, tailboom attaching bolts for slippage marks and circuit breakers in.

3. Right side tailboom – Check as follows:

    a. Air ejector area – Check.

    b. Skin – Check.

    c. Synchronized elevator – Check.

    d. Antennas – Check.

    e. Position light – Check.

    f. Tail skid – Check.

*4. 42 degree gearbox – Check oil level and cap secured.

*5. Main rotor blade – Check.

*6. Tail rotor – Check.

8-16. AREA 3 – TAIL SECTION – LEFT SIDE.

*1. 90 degree gearbox – Check oil level, cap secure.

2. Left side tailboom – Check as follows:

    a. Position light – Check.

    b. Tail rotor drive shaft – Check.

    c. Skin – Check.

    d. Antennas – Check.

    e. Synchronized elevator – Check.

    f. Air ejector area – Check.

3. Oil cooler compartment – Check.

8-17. AREA 4 – FUSELAGE – LEFT SIDE.

(O)° 1. Engine and transmission cowling – Secure open. Check engine air intake, condition of fuel and oil lines, fire detector sensing elements, and electrical connectors.

*2. Particle separator – Check for FOD and area beneath plenum.

3. Tail rotor drive shaft – Check.

4. Transmission area – Check lines, servo mounting bolts for slippage marks, servo, and lift link.

5. Swashplate and support – Check.

6. Drive links – Check for slippage marks.

7. Top of pylon – Check as follows:

    a. Anti-collision light – Check.

    b. Pitot tube – Check.

    c. FM antenna – Check.

    d. Upper cutter assembly – Check.

    e. Laser Sensor Assembly – Check.

8. Main rotor system – Check.

9. Engine and transmission cowling – Close.

10. Wing – Check.

(O)° 11. TOW – Check as follows:

    a. Launcher mounting – Check upper launcher aft and forward bomb lugs secure to helicopter ejector rack. Swaybrace bolts firmly against launcher. Lower launcher aft and forward attaching points secure to upper launcher.

    b. Electrical connectors – Check upper and lower harnesses connected. Jettison quick disconnect lanyard attached and not twisted.

(O)° 12. Rocket launcher – Check as follows:

    a. Launcher mounting – Check launcher aft and forward bomb lugs secured. Swaybrace bolts firmly against launcher but not denting exterior.

    b. Electrical connectors – Check harnesses connected to launcher. Jettison quick disconnect lanyard attached.

    c. Launcher – Check launcher exterior and tube interiors for damage and corrosion.

13. Area beneath transmission – Check controls and condition of hydraulic, oil, and fuel lines.

14. Landing gear – Check.

15. Lower fuselage – Check as follows:

    a. NVG lighting – Check.

    b. Searchlight – Check.

    c. Lower cutter assembly – Check.

*16. Hydraulic compartment – Check condition of lines, reservoir cap, electrical connectors, and ECS. Check fluid level and filter buttons in.

17. Canopy – Check (If single pilot – perform checks in paragraph 8-20).

18. Fire extinguisher – Check.

19. Gunner's HSS linkage assembly – Check condition and stow.

20. Map light – OFF.

21. Fuselage – Check.

22. Static port – Check.

*23. Ammunition bay (left side) – Check condition of door, electrical connections, and LCHR boresight switch – OFF. Check the following if installed:

(O)   a. Ammunition box – Check condition, security and quick release pins in.

(O)   b. Ammunition chute – Check condition, security and ammunition if loaded.

8-18. AREA 5 – NOSE SECTION.

° 1. Turret – Check as follows:

    a. Left side – Check recoil adapter, gun drive motor, and elevation drive motor.

    b. Gun mounting quick release pins – Secure.

    c. End and mid barrel clamps – Secure.

    d. Right side – Check AIM-1/EXL laser, slider assembly, feeder assembly, timing of feeder assembly to gun assembly, ammunition chute, and azimuth drive motor.

    e. Telescopic sight unit – Check.

2. Windshield and rain removal nozzles – Check.

*8-19. WALK AROUND CHECK.

1. Cowling, doors, and panels – Secure.

2. Covers, tiedowns, grounding cables, wing store safety pins, Chaff dispenser safety pin, and AIM-1/EXL warning flag – Remove and secure. Rotate main rotor 90 degrees.

(O) 3. TOW launchers missile arming levers – Check down.

(O) 4. W2P1 – Connect.

5. Crew briefing – Completed.

8-20. BEFORE STARTING ENGINE - GUNNERS STATION.

*1. ENG DE-ICE switch – OFF.

*2. GOV switch – AUTO.

*3. EMER HYDR PUMP switch – OFF.

*4. JTSN SEL – As desired.

*5. WING STORES JETTISON switch – Cover down and locked wired.

6. Avionics – As desired.

*7. Systems/flight instruments – Check condition, security and static indications.

*8. Attitude indicator – Caged and locked.

9. Standby compass – Full of fluid and deviation card current.

*10. PLT ORIDE switch – OFF.

*11. TUR SLEW switch – NORM.

*12. LASER SAFE/TURRET DEPR limit switch – DEPR limit.

*13. SHC ATS switch – STOW.

*14. TCP MODE SELECT switch – OFF.

*15. TCP TSU RTCL switch – OFF.

*16. Canopy removal arming/firing mechanism safety pin – Remove and stow (if occupied).

*17. Seat belt and shoulder harness – Check.

8-21. BEFORE STARTING ENGINE – PILOT STATION.

*1. IGNITION switch – ON.

2. FAT indicator – Check condition.

*3. Collective friction and lock – OFF.

NOTE

When rocket launchers are installed on outboard pylons, the SECU circuit breaker should be out to prevent pylon movement.

*4. AC circuit breaker panel – As desired.

*5. BATTERY switch – START.

*6. RPM SWITCH – OFF.

*7. GEN switch – OFF.

*8. ALTNR switch – OFF.

*9. NON ESNTL bus switch – As desired.

*10. FORCE TRIM switch – FORCE TRIM.

*11. HYD TEST switch – Centered.

*12. FUEL switch – ON (both boost pump caution lights out).

*13. ENG OIL BYP switch – AUTO.

*14. ENG DEICE switch – OFF.

*15. GOV switch – AUTO.

16. SCAS POWER – OFF.

17. CODE HOLD switch – OFF.

18. EMER HYDR PUMP switch – OFF.

*19. Systems/flight instrument – Check condition, security and static indications.

*20. MASTER CAUTION and RPM WARNING lights – Check illuminated.

*21. Caution panel lights – TEST. check overtorque light illuminated and RESET MASTER caution light.

*22. HUD – OFF; check condition.

23. FIRE DET TEST switch – TEST.

*24. Altimeter – Set.

*25. Radar altimeter – Off.

26. Clock – Set.

(O) 27. Low G Warning light – Press test.

28. HEAT/VENT AIR PULL knob – Out and vents adjusted.

*29. Avionics/mission equipment – OFF; set as desired.

30. COMPASS switch – MAG.

*31. LTS panel switches – Set as required.

*32. ECS panel switches – Set as required

*33. DC circuit breakers – In.

*34. Canopy removal arming/firing mechanism safety pin – Remove and stow.

*8-22. STARTING ENGINE.

WARNING

When helicopter is armed with rockets, make start with battery only, because it is hazardous to place GPU (or any electrical generating equipment) in close proximity due to danger of accidental firing of rockets.

1. GPU – Connect if GPU starting. A minimum of 22 volts is required for battery start.

2. Fireguard – Posted if available.

3. Rotor blades – Check clear and untied.

4. Throttle – Check and set for start.

° 5. Engine – Start as follows:

    a. Start switch – Press and hold (start time).

    b. DC voltmeter – Check indications. Battery start can be made provided the voltage is not below 14 volts when cranking through 10 percent N1 speed.

    c. Main rotor – Check turning as N1 reaches 15 percent. If not, abort the start.

    d. IGNITION SW – OFF, at 750 degrees C TGT.

    e. Starter switch – Release at 40 percent (N1) or after 35 seconds, whichever occurs first.

    f. Throttle – Slowly advance to 75 percent (N1). Check stop by attempting to roll throttle off.

    g. N1 – Check 68 percent to 72 percent. Hold a slight pressure against the idle stop during this check.

    h. IGNITION switch – ON after TGT has stabilized.

6. GEN switch – ON, check ammeter indication and DC GEN caution light out.

7. GPU – Disconnected (EXT PWR caution light off).

8. BATTERY switch – RUN.

TM 1-1520-236-10

> **CAUTION**
>
> Oil pressure may exceed maximum on low ambient temperature starts. Do not exceed engine idle until engine oil pressure is below 100 PSI.

9. Engine and transmission oil pressures – Check.

10. Caution lights – Check off (ALTNR and RECT lights are ON).

11. Ammeter – Check less than 200 amps.

> **CAUTION**
>
> Do not leave turret stow circuit breaker closed for more than 10 seconds, if turret fails to move to stow position. Damage to emergency stow control may occur.

12. Turret stowed check – Perform (not required for thru-flight).

° 13. Gunnery Checklist – Perform if applicable. Refer to Chapter 4, paragraph 4-25.

8-23. ENGINE RUNUP.

> **CAUTION**
>
> Minimize movement of the cyclic during ground runup to preclude damage to the input quill seal and the main driveshaft.

*1. Avionics/mission equipment – On as desired.

*2. SCAS POWER switch – POWER. Check NO–GO lights extinguish prior to 30 seconds.

NOTE

If the mechanically dimmable NO-GO lights are dimmed, a false indication could result in engagement of SCAS with an out-of-null condition.

NOTE

NO-GO lights may flicker slightly in the roll and yaw channels when the throttle is at flight idle. If lights do not extinguish, this is an indication of a SCAS deficiency.

*3. Ammo doors – Closed.

*4. Canopy doors – Secure.

*5. Throttle – 100%. As throttle is increased, the low rpm audio and warning light should reset at 94 ± 1% engine and rotor rpm. Throttle friction as desired.

*6. ALTNR switch – ON (ALTER and RECT lights out).

NOTE

Alternator should be left off during any maneuvers (emergency tasks) requiring multiple cycles through 91% RPM. Prior to turning the alternator switch off, TCP should be in the STBY TOW position.

*7. ENG DEICE switch – Check as required.

*8. Fuel quantity – Check and depress FUEL GAGE TEST switch.

*9. Engine and Transmission instruments – Check.

*10. DC voltmeter – Check approximately at 27.5 volts.

*11. Pitot heater – Check as required.

*12. SCAS – Check on first flight of day

   a. NO–GO lights – Check out.

   b. Engage PITCH, ROLL, and YAW channels one at a time and visually check around the helicopter. Have hand on the cyclic stick, and be prepared to immediately press the SAS REL switch if any abnormal tip path or control fluctuations are noted.

*13. TURRET DRIVE MOTOR switch – TURRET.

*14. ADS PWR circuit breaker – IN.

*15. FCC switch – FCC.

*16. RMS control panel – Set.

*17. MASTER ARM switch – STBY.

*18. WPNS CONTR switch – Gunner.

*19. RECOIL COMPEN switch – OFF (ON for live fire).

*20. HUD PWR switch – STBY.

*21. TCP switch – STBY TOW.

*22. **CN** FLIR control panel OFF/ON/BIT switch – ON.

*23. Avionics/mission equipment – Check and set as desired.

*24. Altimeters – Set current barometric pressure and radar altimeter.

*25. HSI heading – Set to correspond with standby compass.

*26. ADI – Set. Gunner attitude indicator uncage and set.

*27. HUD PWR switch – ON.

° 28. Armament–Systems – Check as follows: (Refer to Chapter 4, paragraph 4-24).

    a. TOW BIT – Check. (Performed only in STBY TOW).

    b. TSU tracking – Check.

    c. HSS BIT – Check.

    d. HSS to turret – Check.

    e. HSS to TSU and TSU to TURRET – Check.

    f. RMS BIT – Check.

(O)   g. HUD – Check.

(O)   h. ALT – Check.

    i. FLIR – Check.

29. Health Indicator Test (HIT) – Check. Perform as required. Refer to HIT/ENG log in helicopter log book. Check not required if utilizing In-Flight HIT check unless maintenance on engine has taken taken place since last return flight.

*8-24. BEFORE TAKE OFF CHECK.

1. TOW launchers – Missile arming levers down.

2. Wing ejector rack jettison safety pins – Removed.

3. RPM – 100 percent.

4. Systems – Check engine, transmission, electrical, and fuel systems indications.

5. TCP switch – TSU/GUN.

6. TURRET DRIVE MOTOR switch – TURRET.

NOTE

For multiple takeoffs and landings crewmembers may leave the TURRET DRIVE MOTOR switch in the OFF position (training only).

7. Avionics, armament and other mission equipment – Set as desired

*8-25. HOVER CHECK.

1. Flight controls – Check for correct position and response.

2. Engine and transmission instruments – Check.

3. Flight instruments – Check as required.

4. Hover power check – Perform. The power check is performed by comparing the indicated torque required to hover with the predicted values from performance charts.

8-26. BEFORE LANDING.

1. MASTER ARM switch – STBY. Verify STBY light is illuminated.

2. TURRET DRIVE MOTOR switch – OFF. Verify GUN ELEV STOWED light is illuminated.

NOTE

For multiple landings and takeoffs crewmembers may leave the TURRET DRIVE MOTOR switch in the OFF position (training only).

3. Avionics and mission equipment – Set as required.

8-27. ENGINE SHUTDOWN.

1. FORCE TRIM switch – FORCE TRIM.

2. TCP switch – OFF.

3. HUD night filter – DAY position.

4. HUD PWR switch – OFF.

5. FCC switch – OFF.

6. ADS PWR circuit breaker – Out.

7. TURRET STOW circuit breaker – Out.

8. Throttle – Reduce to idle. Allow TGT to stabilize for two minutes.

9. MASTER ARM switch – OFF.

10. TUR SLEW switch – GND TEST.

11. LASER SAFE/TURRET DEPR LIMIT switch – DEPR LIMIT.

12. HSS LINKAGE – STOW.

13. SCAS POWER switch – OFF

° 14. Gunnery checklist – Perform if applicable. Refer to Chapter 4, paragraph 4-26.

15. Engine, transmission, and electrical indications – Check.

16. Avionics and other missions equipment – OFF.
17. ECS panel switch – OFF.
18. Lights – Set as required.
19. Gunner's attitude indicator – Cage.

CAUTION

If a rapid rise in TGT is noted, ensure that the GEN switch is OFF. Press the starter switch to motor the engine (throttle closed) stabilizing temperature within limits.

20. Throttle – Off.
21. FUEL switch – OFF.
22. ALTNR switch – OFF RESET.
23. GEN switch – OFF.
24. BATTERY switch – START.
25. IGNITION switch – As required.
26. Canopy removal arming/firing mechanism safety pins – In.
27. Collective friction and lock – ON.
28. BATTERY switch – OFF.

8-28. BEFORE LEAVING HELICOPTER.

WARNING

When helicopter is to be parked where ambient temperature equals or exceeds 32 degrees C, the fire extinguisher shall be removed until the next mission.

1. Walk around – Check for damage, fluid levels and any leaks.
2. Mission equipment – Secure.
3. Wing ejector rack jettison safety pins – Installed.
4. TOW missile arming lever – Up (if missiles are installed).

WARNING

Rocket igniter arms must remain in contact with rockets to reduce possibility of ignition from EMI (electromagnetic interference).

5. Rocker igniter arms – In contact with rockets.
6. Chaff dispenser system safety pin – Insert.
7. AIM-1/EXL aiming light protective covering/warning flag – Installed.
8. Forms and Records – Make entries on DA Form 2408-13-1 if any of the following conditions were experienced:

    a. Flown in a loose grass environment.

    b. Operated within 10 nautical miles of salt water.

    c. Operated within 200 nautical miles of volcanic activity.

    d. Exposed to radioactivity.

9. Helicopter – Secure.

SECTION III. INSTRUMENT FLIGHT

8-29. INSTRUMENT FLIGHT PROCEDURES.

This helicopter is not certified for operation under instrument meteorological conditions although adequate navigation and communications equipment installed for instrument flight. Flight characteristics and range are the same during instrument flight conditions as operations in visual flight conditions. Refer to FM 1-240, FM 1-300, AR 95-1, and FAR Part 91 for instrument flight rules and weather information.

SECTION IV. FLIGHT CHARACTERISTICS

8-30. OPERATING CHARACTERISTICS.

The flight characteristics of this helicopter, in general, are similar to other single rotor helicopters.

8-31. ROLLOVER CHARACTERISTICS.

Refer to FM 1-203, Fundamentals of Flight.

8-32. BLADE STALL.

a. **General.** In forward flight, some portions of the rotor disk swept by the retreating blade are always stalled. How this stalled area affects the performance and flying qualities depends on the size of the stalled area. The size of the stalled area increases with increases of gross weight, airspeed, density altitude, "g" loading, or with a decrease in rpm. The rolling and pitching motion which is often associated with rotor stall will not occur.

b. **Stall Recognition.** The pilot will notice a progressive increase in vertical vibration level, mostly at 2 per rev, as more of the rotor disk becomes stalled. An increase in any of the above stall-inducing factors will result in higher 2 per rev vibration, and eventually the onset of control force feedback. Both the 2 per rev vibration and feedback forces will be progressively greater as blade stall affects more of the rotor area. Because of the progressive nature of blade stall with this rotor system, there is no abrupt threshold or onset of rotor stall, and therefore no meaningful "stall limit" exists.

c. **Stall Reduction.**

(1) The amount of stall and associated vibration encountered may be reduced by reducing collective.

(2) Reducing the g loading of the maneuver may be accomplished by applying:

(a) Forward cyclic.

(b) Reducing airspeed.

(c) Increasing operating rpm.

(d) Reducing altitude.

8-33. CONTROL FEEDBACK.

a. Feedback in the cyclic stick or collective stick is caused by high loads in the control system. These loads are generated during severe maneuvers and can be of sufficient magnitude to overpower or feed through the main boost cylinders and into the cyclic and/or collective stick. The pilot will feed this feedback as an oscillatory "shaking" of the controls even though he may not be making control inputs after the maneuver is established. This type of feedback will normally vary with the severity of the maneuver. The pilot should regard it as a cue that high control system loads are occurring and should immediately reduce the severity of the maneuver.

b. The gunner station side arm flight controls are designed for emergency conditions and have a reduced mechanical advantage. Because of this reduced mechanical advantage of the gunner's cyclic and collective control, severe maneuvers should be avoided while flying from the gunner station.

8-34. DIVING FLIGHT.

a. Diving flight presents no particular problems in the helicopter; however, the pilot should have a good understanding of such things as rates of descent versus airspeed, rate of closure, and rates of descent versus power. The helicopter gains airspeed quite rapidly in a dive and it is fairly easy to exceed VNE. Rates of descent of 3500 ft./min. to 4800 ft./min. are not uncommon during high-speed dives. High rates of descent coupled with high flight path speeds require that the pilot monitor both rate of closure and terrain features very closely and plan his dive recovery in time to avoid having to make an abrupt recovery.

> **WARNING**
>
> **If an abrupt recovery is attempted at speeds near VNE, "mushing" of the helicopter can occur. If mushing is experienced, do not increase collective, as this will aggravate the condition. Figure 8-3 depicts the altitude lost during a pullout rate of descent for various G loadings.**

b. Mushing occurs when the aircraft is flying in a partly stalled condition with controls ineffective to regain altitude. It is a transient condition that results in an increased loss of altitude in dive recoveries or in an increased turning radius. Sometimes it may be difficult to differentiate between settling due to the inertia created at higher rates of descent or settling due to mushing.

c. To avoid mushing, entry into any G maneuver must be a progressive and smooth entry to effect a quicker and more efficient recovery. Enough time must be allowed for the recovery by avoiding target fixation in dives or in excessive turns. A good understanding of blade stall and stall reduction is required.

8-35. POWER DIVES.

At speeds above the maximum level flight speed, the rate of descent will increase approximately 1000 ft./min. for every 10 knots increase in airspeed for the full power condition.

8-36. PITCH CONE COUPLING.

a. Pitch cone coupling is the characteristic of the rotor to inherently reduce blade pitch with increasing coning under loading which aids to maintain rpm and retard blade stall. With severe rotor loading, the rotor rpm may overspeed above the red line unless collective pitch is increased.

b. When g load is placed upon the rotor system through steep turns, dive recoveries, or other high stress maneuvers, the rotor blades cone upward. Most of the inherent bending action is absorbed by the flexible yoke assembly. As the hub bends, the pitch change horns exert a downward pressure on the pitch control tubes. The control tubes, however, are fixed through the control system and are unable to move. As pressure continues to be applied, the leading edge of the blade begins to rotate downward via the feather bearing. This directly reduces pitch in the blades which in turn acts to increase rotor rpm. As the rotor rpm begins to increase, the N2 governor senses the change and begins to decrease engine power, resulting in a corresponding decrease in torque and N1. When performing g maneuvers, maintaining a constant torque setting is of prime importance in preventing overspeeding of the rotor.

8-37. TRANSIENT TORQUE.

a. Transient torque, although evident in all semirigid single-rotor system helicopters, is a phenomenon which is quite pronounced in the AH-1F. With a rapid application of left lateral cyclic, a rapid torque increase followed by a decrease will be evidenced. This condition occurs as a result of temporary increased induced drag being placed on the rotor system by the additional pitch in the advancing blade.

b. With a rapid application of right lateral cyclic, a rapid torque decrease followed by an increase will be evidenced. This condition occurs as a result of drag being reduced in the rotor system due to the reducing of pitch in the advancing blade, which temporarily decreases the blade's resistance to the airflow. Increasing and decreasing rotor system drag will produce corresponding torque changes due to the fact that the rotor system's requirement for an increase or decrease in power is sensed and subsequently supplied by the fuel control system. As airspeed and severity of the maneuver are increased, the transient torque effect is also increased. The pilot should become familiar with this characteristic and form a natural tendency to compensate with collective control to avoid exceeding the helicopter torque and rotor rpm limitations.

TM 1-1520-236-10

DIVE RECOVERY DISTANCE

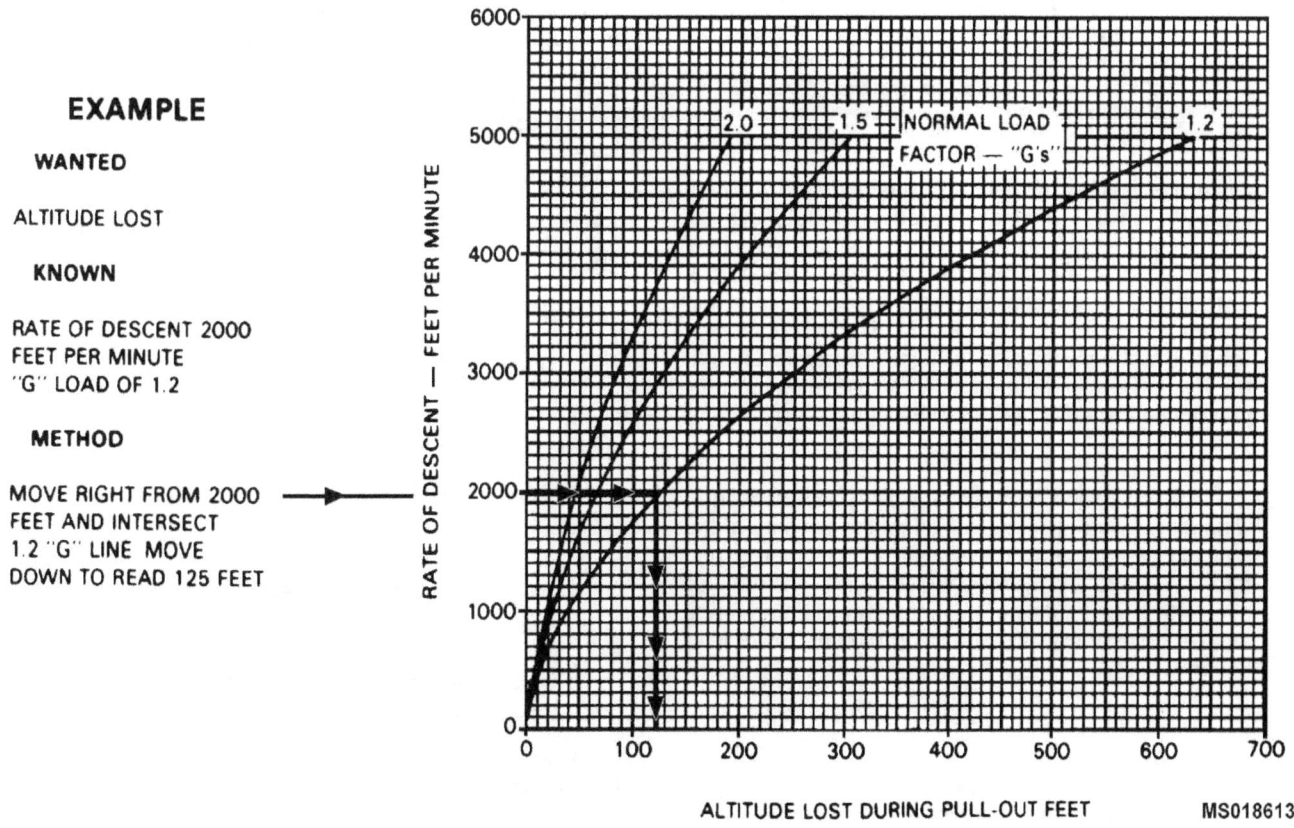

Figure 8-3. Dive Recovery Distances

8-15

8-38. MANEUVERING FLIGHT.

During left rolling maneuvers or high power dives, torque increases occur. To prevent main transmission overtorque, care must be exercised in monitoring torque pressure to enable the pilot to reduce power as required to prevent overtorque.

8-39. LOW G MANEUVERS.

WARNING

Intentional flight below +0.5g is prohibited. Abrupt inputs of the flight controls cause excessive main rotor flapping, which may result in mast bumping and must be avoided. If an abrupt right roll should occur when rapidly lowering the nose, PULL IN AFT CYCLIC to stop the rate and effect recovery. Left lateral cyclic WILL NOT effect recovery from a well-developed right roll during flight at less than one g, and it may cause severe main rotor flapping. DO NOT move collective or directional controls or disengage the SCAS during recovery.

a. Because of mission requirements, it may be necessary to rapidly lower the nose of the helicopter in order to (1) acquire a target; (2) stay on target; or (3) recover from a pullup. At moderate to high airspeeds, it becomes increasingly easy to approach zero or negative load factors by abrupt forward cyclic inputs. The helicopter may exhibit a tendency to roll to the right simultaneously with the forward cyclic input; this characteristic being most pronounced when roll SCAS is disengaged.

b. Such things as sideslip, weight and location of wing stores and airspeed will affect the severity of the right roll. Variances in gross weight, longitudinal cg, and rotor rpm may affect the roll characteristics. The right roll occurs throughout the normal operating airspeed range and becomes more violent at progressively lower load factors.

NOTE

When it is necessary to rapidly lower the nose of the helicopter, it is essential that the pilot monitor changes in roll attitude as the cyclic is moved forward.

8-40. ROTOR RPM – POWER OFF.

The following steps list the factors which affect power-off rotor rpm.

a. **Airspeed.** In autorotation, rotor rpm varies with airspeed. Maximum rotor rpm is achieved at a steady state of 60 to 80 knots (Figure 8-4). Rotor rpm decreases at stabilized airspeeds above or below 60- to 80-knot range. When changing airspeeds, cyclic movement will produce a rotor rpm other than that produced under steady-state conditions as follows:

(1) From low airspeed. Example: From a stabilized 30-knot autorotative condition, a positive forward cyclic movement to increase airspeed will cause the rotor rpm to decrease initially and then increase when the helicopter is stabilized at the higher speed.

(2) From high airspeed. Example: From a stabilized 120 KIAS autorotative condition, a positive aft cyclic movement to decrease airspeed will cause the rotor rpm to increase initially and then decrease when the helicopter is stabilized at the lower speed.

b. **Gross Weight.** The power-off rotor rpm varies significantly with gross weight. A low gross weight will produce a low rotor rpm. A high gross weight will produce a high rotor rpm. With the collective system correctly rigged to a minimum blade angle (full down collective stick), the pilot must manually control rpm with the collective stick in order to prevent overspeed of the rotor when at high gross weight.

8-41. AUTOROTATION CHARACTERISTICS.

a. The K747 main rotor blades have a greater tendency to overspeed in autorotation than the B540 main rotor blades.

b. Refer to FM 1-203, Fundamentals of Flight, Section IV, Autorotation.

8-42. MAST BUMPING.

WARNING

Abrupt inputs of the flight controls cause excessive main rotor flapping, which may result in mast bumping and must be avoided.

a. Mast bumping (flapping-stop contact) is the main rotor yoke contacting the mast. It may occur during slope landings, rotor start-up/coast-down, or when the approved flight envelope is exceeded. If mast bumping is encountered in flight, land as soon as possible.

(1) If mast bumping occurs during a slope landing, reposition the cyclic control to stop the bumping and re-establish a hover.

(2) If mast bumping occurs during start-up or shut-down, move cyclic to minimize or eliminate bumping.

(3) If mast bumping occurs during rearward or sideward flight, move cyclic slightly toward center position and apply pedal to bring the nose into a relative wind.

b. Because of mission requirement, it may be necessary to rapidly lower the nose of the helicopter with cyclic input or make a rapid collective reduction. At moderate to high airspeeds, it becomes increasingly easy to approach less than +0.5g by abrupt forward cyclic inputs. Variance in such things as sideslip, airspeed, gross weight, density altitude, center of gravity, and rotor speed may increase main rotor flapping and increase the probability of mast bumping. Rotor flapping is a normal part of maneuvering and excessive flapping can occur at greater than 1g flight; but, flapping becomes more excessive for many given maneuvers at progressively lower load factors.

(1) In the event of loss of all engine power at high speed, aft cyclic must be applied to maintain rotor rpm and to avoid mast bumping during autorotation entry.

(2) If the flight envelop is inadvertently exceeded by low g flight (below +0.5g), move the cyclic aft to regain positive thrust on the rotor before correcting rolling tendencies.

TM 1-1520-236-10

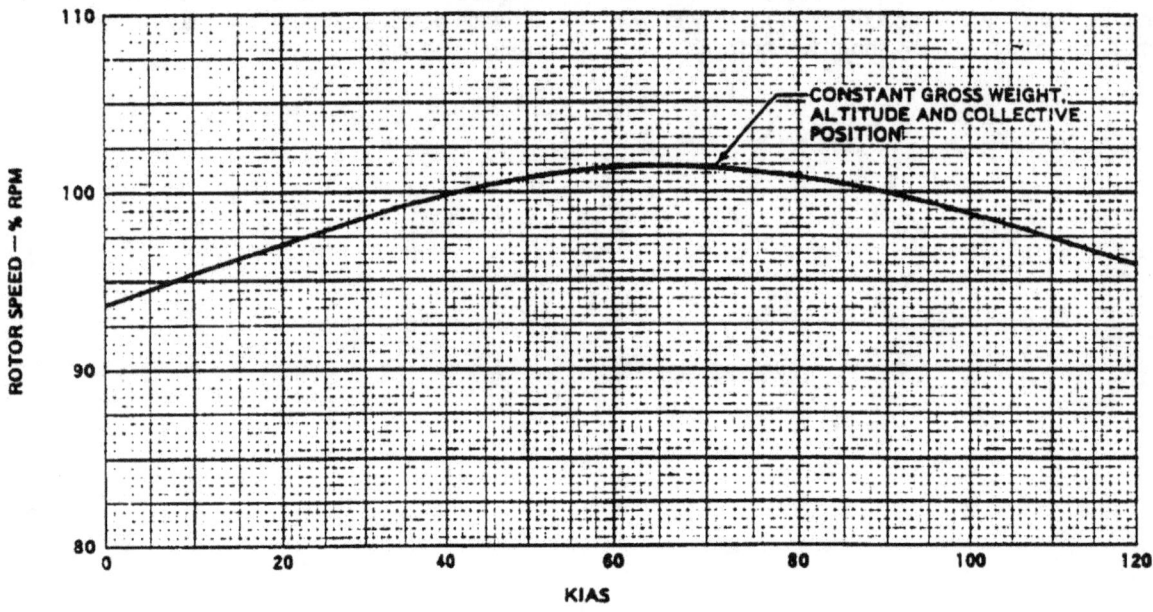

Figure 8-4. Main Rotor RPM Versus Airspeed (Power Off)

TM 1-1520-236-10

SECTION V. ADVERSE ENVIRONMENTAL CONDITIONS

8-43. GENERAL.

This section provides information relative to operation under adverse environmental conditions (snow, ice and rain, turbulent air, extreme cold and hot weather, desert operations, mountainous and altitude operation) at maximum gross weight.

8-44. TEMPERATURE LIMITATION (HUB MOMENT SPRING AIRCRAFT ONLY).

Remove elastomeric spring prior to operating aircraft when OAT is below -25 degrees Fahrenheit or if this temperature is anticipated to occur during flight. If however, sub -25 degrees Fahrenheit temperatures are encountered during flight with the elastomeric springs installed, change altitude in an attempt to find warmer OAT. Elastomeric springs shall be reinstalled when the OAT is expected to remain above -25 degrees Fahrenheit or the threat of sub -25 degrees Fahrenheit temperatures no longer exists.

8-45. COLD WEATHER OPERATIONS.

Operation of the helicopter in cold weather or an arctic environment presents no unusual problems if the operators are aware of those changes that do take place and conditions that may exist because of the lower temperatures and freezing moisture.

a. **Inspection.** The pilot must be more thorough in the walk-around check when temperatures have been at or below 0 degrees C (32 degrees F). Water and snow may have entered many parts during operations or in periods when the helicopter was parked unsheltered. This moisture often remains to form ice which will immobilize moving parts or damage structure by expansion and will occasionally foul electric circuitry. Protection covers afford majority protection against rain, freezing rain, sleet, and snow when installed on a dry helicopter prior to precipitation. Since it is not practical to completely cover an unsheltered helicopter, those parts not protected by covers and those adjacent to cover overlap and joints require closer attention, especially after a blowing snow or freezing rain. Accumulation of snow and ice should be removed prior to flight. Failure to do so can result in hazardous flight due to aerodynamic and center of gravity disturbances as well as the introduction of snow, water, and ice into internal moving parts and electrical systems. The pilot should be particularly attentive to the main and tail rotor systems and their exposed control linkages.

> **CAUTION**
>
> At temperatures of -35 degrees C (-31 degrees F) and lower, the grease in the spherical couplings of the main and tail rotor transmission driveshafts and tail-rotor driveshaft coupling may congeal to a point that the couplings cannot operate properly. If temperature is -44 degrees C (-47 degrees F) or below, the pilot must be particularly careful to monitor engine instruments for high oil pressure.

b. **Transmission.** Check for proper operation by turning the main rotor opposite to the direction while an observer watches the driveshaft to see that there is no tendency for the transmission to "wobble" while the driveshaft is turning. If found frozen, apply heat (do not use open flame and avoid overheating boot) to thaw the spherical couplings before attempting to start engine.

c. **Checks.**

(1) Before exterior check 0 degrees C (32 degrees F) and lower. Perform check as specified in Section II.

(2) Exterior check 0 degrees C (32 degrees F) to -54 degrees C (-65 degrees F). Perform exterior check as outlined in Section II, plus the following checks.

(a) Surfaces and controls – Check free of ice and snow. Deicing fluid or heat should be used to remove ice.

(b) Fluid levels – Check contraction of the fluids in the helicopter system at extreme low temperature causing indication of low levels. A check made just after the previous shutdown and carried forward to the walk-around check is satisfactory if no leaks are in evidence. Filling when the system is cold-soaked will reveal an over-full condition immediately after flight, with the possibility of forced leaks at seals.

(c) Engine Air Inlet – Remove all loose snow that could be pulled into and block the engine intake during starting.

(3) Interior check – All flights 0 degrees C (32 degrees F) to -54 degrees C (-65 degrees F). Perform check as specified in Section II.

(4) Interior check – Night flights 0 degrees C (32 degrees F) to -54 degrees C (-65 degrees F). Perform checks as specified in Section II.

8-19

(5) Engine starting check -0 degrees C (32 degrees F) to -54 degrees C (-65 degrees F).

> **CAUTION**
>
> As the engine cools to an ambient temperature below 0 degrees C (32 degrees F) after engine shutdown, condensed moisture may freeze engine seals. Ducting hot air from an external source through the air Inlet housing will free a frozen rotor. Perform check as outlined in Section II. During cold weather, starting the engine, oil pressure gage will indicate maximum (100 psi). The engine should be warmed up at engine idle until the engine oil pressure indication is below 100 psi.

(6) Hydraulic filter indicators – Reset if popped out.

(7) Engine runup check. Perform the check as outlined in Section II.

> **WARNING**
>
> Control system checks should be performed with extreme caution when helicopter is parked on snow and ice. There is reduction as ground friction holding the helicopter stationary, controls are sensitive and response is immediate.

d. **Engine Starting without External Power Supply.** If a battery start must be attempted when the helicopter and battery have been cold-soaked at temperatures between -26 degrees C to -37 degrees C (-15 degrees F to -35 degrees F), preheat the engine and battery if equipment is available and time permits. Preheating will result in a faster starter cranking speed which tends to reduce hot start hazard by assisting the engine to reach a self-sustaining speed (40 percent N1) in the least possible time.

8-46. SNOW.

Refer to FM 1-202, Environmental Flight.

8-47. DESERT AND HOT WEATHER OPERATION.

Refer to FM 1-202, Environmental Flight.

8-48. TURBULENCE AND THUNDERSTORMS.

Flight in thunderstorms and heavy rain which accompanies thunderstorms should be avoided. If turbulence and thunderstorms are encountered inadvertently, use the following procedures:

a. Check that safety belts and harnessers are tightened.

b. PITOT HTR – ON.

c. Power – Adjust to maintain a penetration speed of 100 KIAS or VNE whichever is slower.

d. Radios – Turn volume down on any radio equipment badly affected by static.

e. At night – Turn interior lights to full bright to minimize blinding effect of lightning.

f. Maintain a level attitude and constant power setting. Airspeed fluctuations should be expected and disregarded.

g. Maintain the original heading, turning only when necessary.

h. The altimeter is unreliable due to differential barometric pressures within the storm. An indicated gain or loss of several hundred feet is not uncommon and should be allowed for in determining minimum safe altitude.

8-49. ICING CONDITIONS.

> **WARNING**
>
> Intentional flight into known icing condition is prohibited. If icing conditions are encountered during flight, every effort should be made to vacate the icing environment.
>
> Firing of aircraft weapons in icing conditions is prohibited. The weapons covered are: TOW missile, 2.75 inch FFAR, and 20 MM gun. A very serious safety hazard exists if aircraft weapons are fired in icing weather conditions. The TOW missile warhead can detonate in close proximity to aircraft. The warhead fuse is damaged as missile is launched through ice in missile launcher. Gun barrels and breeches can rupture if gun muzzles are clogged with ice. The FFAR are held captive in the launcher tubes by the frozen ice.

CAUTION

When operating at FAT of 5°C (40°F) or below, icing of the engine air particle separator and FOD screens can be expected. Continued accumulation of ice will result in partial or complete power loss.

Continuous flight in light icing conditions is not recommended because the ice shedding induces rotor blade vibrations, adding greatly to the pilot's work load.

a. If icing conditions become unavoidable, the pilot should turn the PITOT HTR/ADS, ECS HTR and ENG DEICE switches on.

b. During icing conditions one or all of the following can be expected to occur:

(1) Obscured forward field of view due to ice accumulation on the canopy. If the ECS fails to keep the canopy clear of ice, the side windows may be used for visual reference during landing.

(2) One-per-rotor-revolution vibrations ranging from mild to severe caused by asymmetrical ice shedding from the main rotor system. The severity of the vibration will depend upon the temperatures and the amount of ice accumulations on the blades when the ice shed occurs. The possibility of an asymmetric ice shed occurring increases as the outside air temperature decreases. Severe vibrations may occur as a result of main rotor asymmetrical ice shedding. If icing conditions are encountered while in flight, land as soon as practicable. All ice should be removed from the rotor system before attempting further flight.

(3) An increase in torque required to maintain a constant airspeed and altitude due to ice accumulation on the rotor system.

(4) Possible degradation of the ability to maintain autorotational rotor speed within operating limits.

(5) Inability to increase torque due to blockage of the improved particle separator.

c. Control activity cannot be depended upon to remove ice from the main rotor system. Vigorous control movements should not be made in an attempt to reduce low-frequency vibrations caused by asymmetrical shedding of ice from the main rotor blades. These movements may induce a more asymmetrical shedding of ice, further aggravating helicopter vibration levels.

d. If a 9-percent (or greater) torque pressure increase is required above the cruise torque setting used prior to entering icing conditions, it may not be possible to maintain autorotational rotor speed within operational limits, should engine failure occur.

WARNING

Ice shed from the rotor blades and/or rotating components presents a hazard to personnel during landing and shutdown. Ground personnel should remain well clear of the helicopter during landing and shutdown. Passengers/crew/members should not exit the aircraft until the rotor has stopped turning.

8-50. RAIN.

Rain removal system does not remove rain In flight.

TM 1-1520-236-10

CHAPTER 9
EMERGENCY PROCEDURES

SECTION I. HELICOPTER SYSTEMS.

9-1. HELICOPTER SYSTEMS.

This section describes the helicopter systems emergencies that may reasonably be expected to occur and presents the procedures to be followed. Emergency operation of mission equipment is contained in this chapter insofar as its use affects safety of flight. Emergency procedures are given in checklist form when applicable. A condensed version of these procedures is contained in the condensed checklist, TM 1-1520-236-CL.

9-2. IMMEDIATE ACTION EMERGENCY STEPS.

WARNING

To obtain maximum protection from the restraint system during an emergency landing, each crewmember should place their shoulders against the seat back, manually lock the shoulder harness, and keep back straight.

NOTE

The urgency of certain emergencies requires immediate and instinctive action by the pilot. The most important single consideration is helicopter control. All procedures are subordinate to this requirement. The MASTER CAUTION should be reset after a malfunction to allow systems to respond to subsequent malfunctions. If time permits during a critical emergency, transmit a MAY DAY CALL, set transponder to emergency, jettison external stores (if appropriate), and lock shoulder harnesses. Those steps that must be performed immediately in an emergency situation are underlined. These steps must be committed to memory and performed without reference to the checklist. Emergency situations with non-underlined steps may be accomplished with use of the checklist.

9-3. DEFINITION OF EMERGENCY TERMS.

For the purpose of standardization, these definitions shall apply.

a. The term "<u>LAND AS SOON AS POSSIBLE</u>" is defined as landing at the nearest suitable landing area (e.g., open field) without delay. (The primary consideration is to ensure the survival of occupants.)

b. The term "LAND AS SOON AS PRACTICABLE" is defined as landing at a suitable landing area. (The primary consideration is the urgency of the emergency.)

c. The term "<u>AUTOROTATE</u>" is defined as adjusting the flight controls as necessary to establish an autorotational descent and landing.

    1. <u>Collective – Adjust</u> as required to maintain rotor RPM.

    2. <u>Pedals – Adjust</u> as required.

    3. <u>Throttle – Adjust</u> as required.

    4. <u>Airspeed – Adjust</u> as required.

(O) 5. Wing stores – Jettison as appropriate

d. The term "<u>EMER SHUTDOWN</u>" is defined - as engine shutdown without delay.

    1. <u>Throttle – Off.</u>

    2. <u>FUEL switch – OFF.</u>

    3. <u>BATTERY switch – OFF.</u>

e. The term "<u>EMER GOV OPNS</u>" is defined as manual control of the engine RPM with the GOV AUTO/EMER switch in the EMER position. Because automatic acceleration, deceleration and overspeed control are not provided with the GOV switch in the EMER position throttle and collective coordinated control movements must be smooth to prevent compressor stall, overspeed, overtemperature, or engine failure.

9-1

CAUTION

No more than 78% torque is available in the EMER position due to limited fuel flow and may be significantly reduced based on ambient conditions.

1. GOV switch – EMER.

2. Throttle – Adjust as necessary to control RPM.

3. LAND AS SOON AS POSSIBLE.

    f. The term "JETTISON CANOPY" is defined as activation of the linear explosive canopy removal system to remove windows and separate doors from the helicopter. Emergency exits are shown in Figure 9-1.

WARNING

Activation of the canopy removal systems when combustible fuel vapors are present can result in an explosion/fire. Crew members survival knife may be used as an alternate means of egress.

WARNING

Canopy removal system handle must be pulled completely out of the arm/fire mechanism or the canopy removal system will not function.

1. Arming/firing mechanism handle – Turn 90°.

2. Arming/firing mechanism handle – Pull.

WARNING

Simultaneous or near simultaneous pulling of both the pilot's and gunner's arming/firing mechanism handle may result in injury to one or both of the crewmemebers. The pilot must coordinate with the gunner prior to system firing.

9-4. AFTER EMERGENCY ACTION.

After a malfunction of equipment has occured, appropriate emergency actions have been taken and the helicopter is on the ground, an entry shall be made in the Remarks Section of DA Form 2408-13-1 describing the malfunction. Ground and flight operations shall be discontinued until corrective action has been taken.

9-5. EMERGENCY ENTRANCE.

Crew removal is accomplished through the crew doors or through the windows with crash rescue equipment.

9-6. EMERGENCY EQUIPMENT.

Emergency equipment consists of a fire extinguisher, first aid kit, and linear explosive canopy removal system (Refer to Figure 9-1). Wing store jettison capability is provided by explosive cartridges installed at each wing store pylon.

9-7. MINIMUM RATE OF DESCENT.

The speed for minimum rate of descent is **60 KIAS**.

9-8. MAXIMUM GLIDE DISTANCE.

The speed for best glide distance is **100 KIAS** (clean configuration) and **90 KIAS** (wing stores).

9-9. ENGINE.

9-10. ENGINE MALFUNCTION – PARTIAL OR COMPLETE POWER LOSS.

    a. The indications of an engine malfunction, either a partial or a complete power loss are left yaw, drop in engine rpm, drop in rotor rpm, drop in N1, low rpm audio alarm, illumination of rpm warning light, change in engine noise.

WARNING

Do not respond to the rpm audio and/or warning light illumination without first confirming engine malfunction by one or more of the other indications. Normal indications signify the engine is functioning properly and that there is a tachometer generator failure or an open circuit to the warning system, rather than an actual engine malfunction.

TM 1-1520-236-10

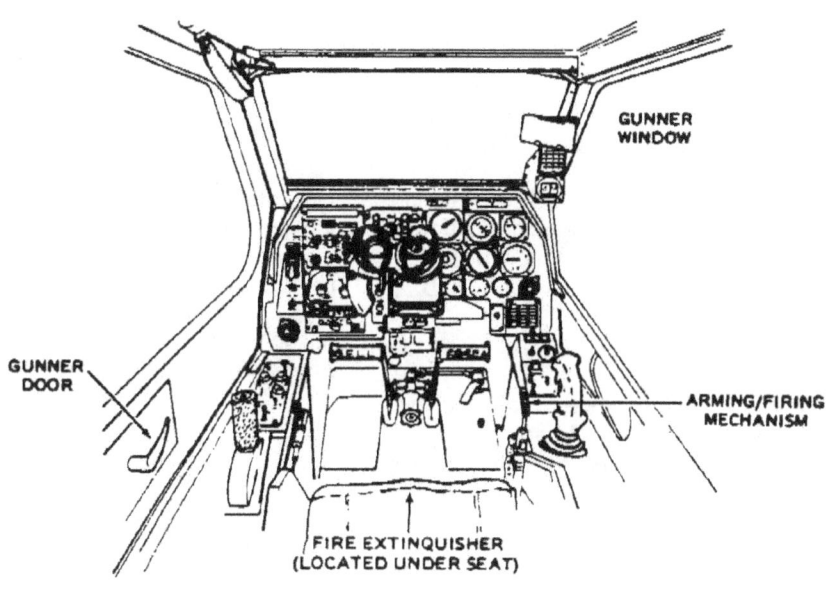

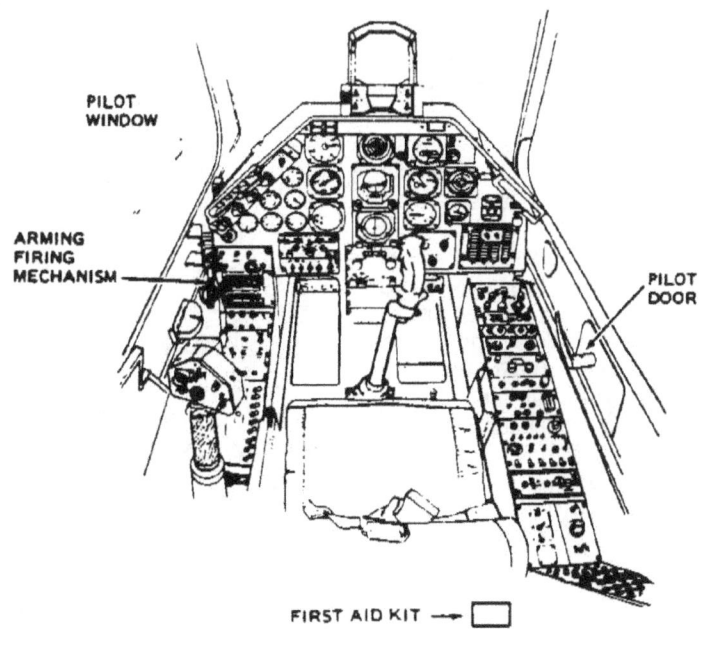

Figure 9-1. Emergency Exits and Equipment (Typical)

b. **Partial power loss.** Under partial power conditions, the engine may operate relatively smoothly at reduced power or it may operate erratically with intermittent surges of power. A stabilization of the N1 should indicate a partial power condition. In instances where a power loss is experienced without accompanying power surging, the helicopter may sometimes be flown at reduced power to a favorable landing area. Under these conditions, the pilot should always be prepared for a complete power loss. In the event a partial power condition is accompanied by erratic engine operation or power surging, and flight is to be continued, perform EMER GOV OPNS. If continued flight is not possible, AUTOROTATE (throttle off).

c. **Complete power loss.**

(1) Under a complete power loss condition, delay in recognition of the malfunction, improper technique or excessive maneuvering to reach a suitable landing area reduces the probability of a safe autorotational landing. Flight conducted within the caution area of the height-velocity chart (Figure 9-2) exposes the helicopter to a high probability of damage despite the best efforts of the pilot.

(2) From conditions of low airspeed and low altitude, the deceleration capability is limited, and caution should be used to avoid striking the ground with the tail rotor. Initial collective reduction will vary after an engine malfunction dependent upon the altitude and airspeed at the time of the occurrence. For example, collective pitch must not be decreased when an engine failure occurs at zero airspeed and approximately 15 feet; whereas, during cruise flight conditions, altitude and airspeed are sufficient for a significant reduction in collective pitch, thereby, allowing rotor rpm to be maintained in the safe operating range during autorotational descent. At high gross weights, the rotor may tend to overspeed and require collective pitch application to maintain the rpm below the upper limit. Collective pitch should never be applied to reduce rpm below normal limits for extending glide distance because of the reduction in rpm available for use during autorotational landing.

(3) Through a speed range of 120 to 190 KIAS, an engine failure will cause the nose of the helicopter to pitch up as a result of its aerodynamic qualities. The SCAS system detects this airframe movement and will attempt to correct with a forward cyclic control input, thereby causing serious rotor flapping and possible mast bumping. To prevent SCAS from making this correction there must be pilot input. In a nose-low attitude or level flight, the input should be aft cyclic movement. In a nose-high attitude, such as dive pullout, the input should be a forward cyclic movement. During the recovery from a high-speed engine failure, the important point to remember is to maintain the necessary rotor rpm and movement to keep the rotor system loaded. Speed should be reduced to successfully reach the intended landing area. After entering autorotation, follow standard autorotation procedures. Do not exceed 120 KIAS in sustained autorotation.

CAUTION

Engine failure at 150 KIAS and greater requires a pilot recognition and reaction time of less than one second to place the aircraft in a trim condition and to preclude unacceptable high left roll rates (greater then 28 degrees/sec). Heavy buffeting of the tailboom and vertical fin and heavy control feedback during recovery are associated with engine failure at high speed and high power conditions.

9-11. ENGINE MALFUNCTION – HOVER.

AUTOROTATE.

9-12. ENGINE MALFUNCTION – LOW ALTITUDE/LOW AIRSPEED OR CRUISE.

1. AUTOROTATE.
2. EMER GOV OPNS.

9-13. ENGINE MALFUNCTION – 120 KIAS AND ABOVE.

1. CYCLIC – Adjust.
2. AUTOROTATE.
3. EMER GOV OPNS.

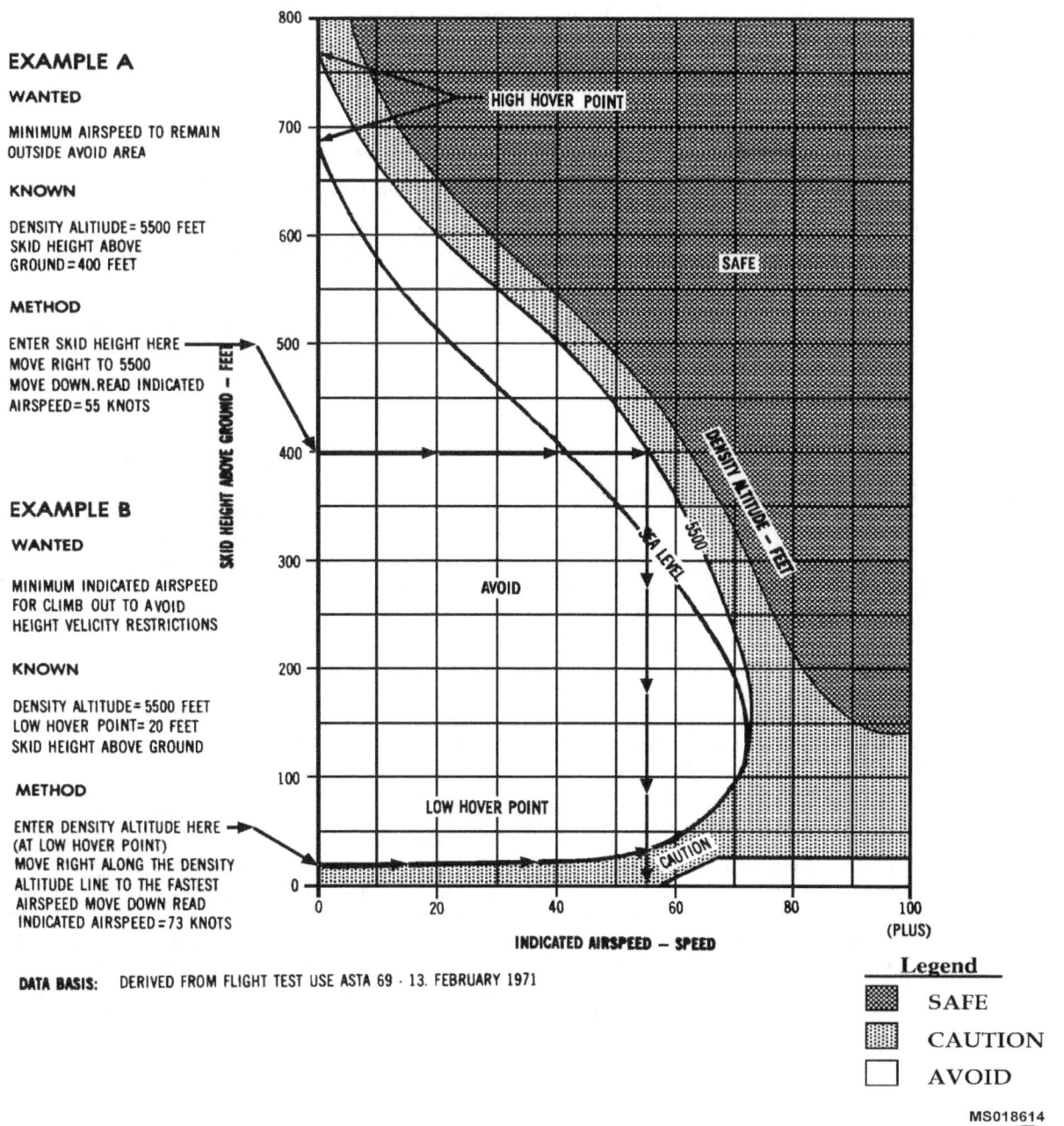

Figure 9-2. Height Velocity Diagram

9-14. DROOP COMPENSATOR FAILURE.

Droop compensator failure will be indicated when engine rpm is no longer controlled by application of collective pitch. The engine will tend to overspeed as collective pitch is decreased and will underspeed as collective pitch is increased. If the droop compensator fails, make minimum collective movements and execute a shallow approach to the landing area. If unable to maintain the operating RPM within limits:

EMER GOV OPNS.

9-15. ENGINE COMPRESSOR STALL.

Engine compressor stall (surge) is characterized by a sharp rumble or loud sharp reports, severe engine vibration, and rapid rise in turbine gas temperature, depending on the severity of the surge. Maneuvers requiring rapid or maximum power applications should be avoided. Should this occur:

1. Collective – Reduce.

2. All bleed air – OFF.

3. LAND AS SOON AS POSSIBLE.

9-16. INLET GUIDE VANE ACTUATOR FAILURE.

a. If the guide vanes fail in the closed position, a maximum of 35-44 percent of torque will be available. Although N1 may indicate normal, power applications above 35-44 percent will result in deterioration of N2 and rotor rpm while increasing N1. Placing the GOV switch in the EMER position will not provide any increased power capability and increases the possibility of an N1 overspeed and an engine overtemperature. Should a failure occur, LAND AS SOON AS PRACTICABLE to an area that will permit a run-on landing with minimum power applications.

b. If the inlet guide vanes fail in the open position during normal flight, it is likely that no indications will be experienced. As power applications are made from increasingly lower N1 settings, acceleration times will correspondingly increase, and the possibility of a compressor stall is likely. Should this failure occur, LAND AS SOON AS PRACTICABLE to an area that will permit a run-on landing.

9-17. ENGINE OVERSPEED.

Engine overspeed will be indicated by a right yaw, rapid increase in both rotor and engine rpm, rpm warning light illuminated, and an increase in engine noise. An engine overspeed may be caused by a malfunctioning N2 governor or fuel control. If an overspeed is experienced:

1. Collective – Increase to load the rotor in an attempt to maintain rpm below the maximum operating limit.

2. Throttle – Reduce to normal operating rpm. If rpm cannot be controlled:

3. EMER GOV OPNS.

9-18. ENGINE OIL TEMPERATURE HIGH.

If the engine oil temperature exceeds the operating limits as specified in Chapter 5, LAND AS SOON AS POSSIBLE.

9-19. ROTORS, TRANSMISSION, AND DRIVE SYSTEMS.

9-20. TAIL ROTOR FAILURE – FLIGHT.

Because of the many different malfunctions that can occur, it is not possible to provide a solution for every emergency. The success in coping with the emergency depends on quick analysis of the condition and selection of the proper emergency procedure. The following is a discussion of some types of malfunctions, probable effects, and corrective actions.

a. **Complete Loss of Thrust Components.**

(1) **Complete Loss of Tail Rotor Thrust.** This is a situation involving a break in the drive system, such as a severed driveshaft, wherein the tail rotor stops turning and no thrust is delivered by the tail rotor. A failure of this type in powered flight will usually result in the nose of the helicopter swinging to the right (left side slip) and usually a roll of the fuselage. Nose down tucking will also be present. If powered flight is possible, continue to a suitable landing area and AUTOROTATE (throttle off), and coordinate the resulting maneuver with cyclic control. The most advisable procedure, if further flight is not possible, is to immediately AUTOROTATE (throttle off). The pilot should expect that some rotation will be present until touchdown. Touchdown should be in as level an attitude as possible and ground speed as low as possible to minimize turnover.

(2) **Loss of Tail Rotor Components.** Except for a more severe nose tuck due to the forward cg shift, this situation would be quite similiar to a complete loss of thrust as discussed above. When a loss of components is suspected, AUTOROTATE (throttle off).

b. **Fixed Pitch Failure.**

(1) **General.** Failures of this type (wedged control, jammed slider, etc.) are characterized by either a lack of directional response when a pedal is pushed or the pedals will be in a locked position. At approximately 100 KIAS and above, the cambered vertical fin will begin to become more effective and as a result, a left yaw condition will increase and conversely, a right yaw will decrease. To aid in directional control, the rpm may be decreased with the throttle until rpm is controlled manually. Increasing the throttle and/or collective will move the nose to the right, decreasing the throttle and/or collective will move the nose to the left.

WARNING

If the pedals cannot be moved with a moderate amount of force, do not attempt a maximum effort since a more serious malfunction and set of circumstances could result.

(2) **Left fixed pitch.** If it has been determined the tail rotor pitch is fixed in a left pedal applied position, an autorotative landing should not be attempted. The pilot should use only that power necessary to produce a controllable degree of side slip and continue to the nearest suitable landing area. To accomplish a landing, establish a powered approach with an airspeed that will allow a desirable rate of descent without producing an uncomfortable left yaw attitude and right sideslip condition. Just prior to landing, adjust throttle and collective as necessary to align the helicopter with touchdown.

(3) **Right fixed pitch.** If the tail rotor becomes fixed during cruise flight or a reduced-power situation, the helicopter will yaw to the right when power is increased. For either of these situations, a running type landing can be performed. If the right yaw becomes excessive when adding power at touchdown, reduce the throttle and cushion the landing with collective. The greatest problem is the compromise that may have to be made between rate of descent and yaw attitude since the collective is the primary control for both of these parameters.

9-21. TAIL ROTOR FAILURE – HOVER.

a. If the tail rotor pitch is fixed in a left pedal position, simultaneously reduce throttle and gradually increase collective pitch to land the helicopter.

b. If total loss of tail rotor thrust/fixed right pedal is experienced:

1. Throttle – Reduce.
2. AUTOROTATE.

9-22. MAIN DRIVESHAFT FAILURE.

A failure of the main driveshaft will be indicated by a left yaw (this is caused by the drop in torque applied to the main rotor), increase in engine rpm, decrease in rotor rpm, low rpm audio alarm, and/or illumination of the rpm warning light. This condition will result in complete loss of power to the rotor and a possible engine overspeed. If a failure occurs:

1. AUTOROTATE.
2. Throttle – Off.

9-23. TRANSMISSION SPRAG CLUTCH MALFUNCTION.

9-24. CLUTCH FAILS TO DISENGAGE.

A clutch failing to disengage in flight will he indicated by the rotor rpm decaying with engine rpm as the throttle is reduced to the engine idle position when entering autorotational descent. This condition results in total loss of autorotational capability. If a failure occurs, do the following:

1. Throttle – On.
2. LAND AS SOON AS POSSIBLE.

9-25. CLUTCH FAILS TO RE-ENGAGE.

During recovery from autorotational descent, clutch malfunction may occur and will be indicated by a reverse needle split (engine rpm higher than rotor rpm).

1. AUTOROTATE.
2. Throttle – Off.

9-26. FIRE.

The safety of the helicopter occupants is the primary consideration when a fire occurs. On the ground, it is essential that the engine be shut down, crew evacuated and fire fighting begun immediately. If the helicopter is airborne when a fire occurs, the most important single action that can be taken by the pilot is to land the helicopter.

9-27. FIRE – ENGINE START.

The following procedure is applicable during engine starting if TGT limits are exceeded, or if it becomes apparent that they will be exceeded. Flames emitting from the tailpipe are acceptable if the limits are not exceeded.

1. Starter switch – Press until TGT is in the normal operating range.

2. Throttle – Off.

3. FUEL switch – OFF.

9-28. FIRE – GROUND.

a. **Pilot's Station.**

EMER SHUTDOWN.

b. **Gunner's station.**

(1) IDLE STOP – RELEASE and hold.

(2) Throttle – Off.

(3) EMER ELEC PWR switch – EMERG OFF.

9-29. FIRE – FLIGHT.

If the fire light illuminates and/or fire is observed during flight, prevailing circumstances (such as VFR, IMC, night, altitude, and landing areas available), must be considered in order to determine whether to execute a power-on (max Vne), or a power-off landing (max - 120 KIAS).

a. **Power-On**

1. LAND AS SOON AS POSSIBLE.

2. EMER SHUTDOWN.

b. **Power-Off.**

1. AUTOROTATE.

2. EMER SHUTDOWN.

9-30. ELECTRICAL FIRE – FLIGHT.

Prior to shutting off all electrical power, the pilot must consider the equipment that is essential to a particular flight environment that will be encountered; e.g., flight instruments and fuel boost pumps. In the event of electrical fire or suspected electrical fire in flight:

1. BATTERY switch – START.

2. Electrical switches – OFF.

3. NON-ESNTL BUS switch – NORMAL.

4. LAND AS SOON AS POSSIBLE.

5. EMER SHUTDOWN.

If landing cannot be made as soon as possible and flight must be continued, the defective circuits may be identified and isolated. Electrical switches should be turned ON one at a time in the priority required. When malfunctioning circuit is identified, turn switch off.

9-31. FUMES FROM ECS.

If fumes are emitted in the cockpit from the ECS System:

1. ECU switch – OFF.

If fumes continue:

2. LAND AS SOON AS POSSIBLE.

9-32. SMOKE AND FUME ELIMINATION.

1. Vents – Open.

2. LAND AS SOON AS POSSIBLE.

9-33. FUEL.

9-34. SINGLE OR DUAL FUEL BOOST PUMP FAILURE.

Continued flight below 6000 feet or less pressure altitude is permitted.

Single or dual pump failure.

1. FUEL switch – ON.

2. FUEL BOOST circuit breaker(s) – OUT.

3. LAND AS SOON AS PRACTICABLE.

CAUTION

Nose-down attitudes greater than 15 degrees should he avoided because engine failure may occur due to fuel starvation when the forward fuel boost pump is inoperable and with less than 320 pounds of fuel remaining.

9-35. ELECTRICAL SYSTEM.

9-36. DC GENERATOR FAILURE – DC CAUTION LIGHT ILLUMINATION.

> **NOTE**
>
> As battery voltage is depleted there is a possibility of activation of the RPM warning light and RPM audio systems.

1. GEN BUS RESET/GEN FIELD circuit breakers – IN.

2. GEN switch – Move to RESET then to GEN position.

If generator is not restored, continue as follows:

3. GEN switch – OFF.

9-37. ALTERNATOR FAILURE – ALTER AND RECT CAUTION LIGHT ILLUMINATION.

1. <u>ALTNR switch – OFF RESET, then ON.</u>

If alternator is not restored:

2. <u>ALTNR – OFF RESET.</u>

3. <u>LAND AS SOON AS POSSIBLE.</u>

9-38. TRANSFORMER RECTIFIER UNIT (TRU) FAILURE – RECT CAUTION LIGHT ILLUMINATION.

1. ALTNR switch – OFF RESET.

2. ALTNR switch – ON.

9-39. OVERHEATED BATTERY.

If overheated battery is suspected or detected proceed as follows:

1. <u>BATTERY switch – OFF.</u>

2. <u>LAND AS SOON AS POSSIBLE.</u>

3. <u>EMER SHUTDOWN.</u>

> **WARNING**
>
> Do not open battery compartment and attempt to disconnect or remove overheated battery, fluid will cause thermal burns and may explode.

9-40. HYDRAULIC SYSTEM FAILURE.

If a hydraulic malfunction should occur below an air speed of 40 KIAS, the pilot should turn on the emergency hydraulic pump (as appropriate) and land the aircraft as soon as possible. If terrain does not permit a landing, accelerate the aircraft to the best controllable airspeed above 40 KIAS and comply with the appropriate failure that has occurred.

> **WARNING**
>
> **The ability to increase collective (torque) may be limited during a single system failure and will be limited during a dual system failure. Collective once lowered may not be able to be raised again; if altitude cannot be maintained, jettison wing stores as appropriate.**
>
> **Generator and alternator/rectifier failure combined with hydraulic failure will allow not more than five minutes of operating time of the emergency hydraulic pump.**
>
> **During a single system failure, do not move hydraulic test switch to failed system position. Hydraulic pressure to good system will be interrupted.**

9-41. HYDRAULIC FAILURE – SINGLE SYSTEM.

Loss of system No.1 will result in loss of tail rotor servo and the yaw SCAS actuator. Loss of No. 2 hydraulic system will result in loss of pitch and roll SCAS actuators. Cyclic and collective control feedback may be evident during abrupt maneuvers.

1. <u>EMER HYDR PUMP switch – OFF</u> (pilot and gunner).

2. <u>HYD CONTR circuit breaker – In.</u>

3. <u>EMER HYD PUMP circuit breaker – In.</u>

4. <u>SCAS – Disengage appropriate channels.</u>

   a. No. 1 system – Yaw channel.

   b. No. 2 system – Pitch and roll channels.

5. <u>MASTER ARM switch – OFF.</u>

6. LAND AS SOON AS PRACTICABLE. A run-on landing at a speed of **50 KIAS** or above is recommended.

7. EMER HYDR PUMP switch - EMER HYDR PUMP (final approach).

9-42. HYDRAULIC FAILURE – DUAL SYSTEM.

Loss of both hydraulic systems will result in loss of hydraulic pressure to the SCAS actuators, cyclic, collective, and tail rotor servos.

WARNING

During power application above 60 percent, roll oscillations may become unmanageable. If oscillations become severe, reduce collective until oscillations are manageable. Below 40 KIAS cycle feedback forces become unmanageable.

1. EMER HYDR PUMP switch – OFF (pilot and gunner).

2. HYD CONTR and circuit breaker – In.

3. EMER HYD PUMP circuit breaker – In.

4. SCAS – Disengage all channels.

5. MASTER ARM switch – OFF.

6. LAND AS SOON AS PRACTICABLE. A run-on landing at a speed of **50 KIAS** or above is recommended.

7. EMER HYDR PUMP switch – EMER HYDR PUMP (final approach).

NOTE

When the collective pitch creeps down, turn the EMER HYDR PUMP switch on and increase collective as required; then, turn the system off. This procedure can be repeated as required. During emergency hydraulic pump operation, collective movement may be slower than normal.

9-43. LANDING AND DITCHING.

9-44. LANDING IN TREES.

A landing in trees should be made when no other landing area is available. Select a landing area containing the least number of trees of minimum height. Decelerate to zero ground speed at tree-top level and descend into the trees vertically, applying collective pitch as necessary for minimum rate of descent. Prior to the main rotor blades entering the tree, ensure throttle is off and apply all of the remaining collective pitch.

9-45. DITCHING – POWER ON.

If it becomes necessary to ditch the helicopter, accomplish an approach to an approximate 3-foot hover above the water and proceed as follows:

1. MASTER ARM – OFF.

2. PLT ORIDE – OFF.

3. JETTISON CANOPY.

4. Gunner – Exit.

NOTE

Correct for cg shift of 2.5 to 4.0 inches when gunner exits helicopter.

5. Hover – Clear of gunner.

WARNING

Life preserver should not be inflated until clear of helicopter.

6. AUTOROTATE (Throttle – Off). Apply full collective pitch prior to the main rotor blades entering the water. Maintain a level attitude as the helicopter sinks and until it begins to roll, then apply cyclic in direction of the roll. Pilot should exit when main rotor stops.

9-46. DITCHING – POWER OFF.

If ditching is imminent, accomplish engine malfunction emergency procedures. Decelerate to zero forward speed, level helicopter and jettison canopy just prior to entering the water. Apply collective pitch as the helicopter sinks and until it begins to roll, then apply cyclic in the direction of the roll. Exit when the main rotor is stopped.

NOTE

There may be a tendency to decelerate too high over water due to depth perception.

9-47. FLIGHT CONTROL/MAIN ROTOR SYSTEM MALFUNCTIONS.

a. Failure of components within the flight control system may be indicated through varying degrees of feedback, binding, resistance, or sloppiness. These conditions should not be mistaken for hydraulic power failure.

b. Imminent failure of main rotor components may be indicated by a sudden increase in main rotor vibration and/or unusual noise. Severe changes in lift characteristics and/or balance condition can occur due to blade strikes, skin separation, shift or loss of balance weights or other material. Malfunctions may result in severe main rotor flapping. In the event of a main rotor system malfunction, proceed as follows:

WARNING

Danger exists that the main rotor system could collapse or separate from the aircraft after landing. A decision must be made whether occupant egress occurs before or after the rotor has stopped.

1. LAND AS SOON AS POSSIBLE.

2. EMER SHUTDOWN.

9-48. LOW G WARNING.

1. Cyclic – Aft to return rotor to positive thrust condition.
2. Reduce severity of maneuver.

9-49. MAST BUMPING.

If mast bumping occurs:

1. Reduce severity of maneuver.
2. LAND AS SOON AS POSSIBLE.

9-50. STABILITY AND CONTROL AUGMENTATION SYSTEM (SCAS) FAILURE.

A failure of the SCAS will be evident by an abrupt change in pitch, roll, and/or yaw attitude which, when corrected by the pilot, will result in an abnormal cyclic or pedal position. When SCAS is disengaged, a second correction may be required by the pilot to return level flight. Mast bumping may occur. SCAS off flight is limited to 100 KIAS MAXIMUM. Additionally, power settings above 60% should be avoided when operating at airspeeds between 60 and 100 KIAS with inoperative roll and yaw SCAS channel because of instability. If a failure occurs, proceed as follows:

1. SAS REL button – Press.

If condition persists:

2. SCAS POWER switch – OFF.

3. Unaffected SCAS channels – Re-engage only if power switch has not been turned off.

4. LAND AS SOON AS PRACTICABLE.

SECTION II. MISSION EQUIPMENT

9-51. WING STORES EMERGENCY JETTISON.

a. **Pilot Wing Stores Jettison Procedures.**

1. JETTISON SELECT switches – As required.
2. JETTISON switch – Press.

b. **Gunner Wing Stores Jettison Procedures.**

1. JTSN SEL switch – As required.
2. WING STORES JETTISON switch – Up.

9-52. TOW MISSILE EMERGENCY PROCEDURES.

a. **Hangfire/Misfire.**

1. Pedals – Maintain trim.
2. Wing stores – Check for fire.
3. LAND AS SOON AS POSSIBLE – Ensure weapons are pointed at safe area.
4. Armament switches – OFF.
5. EMER SHUTDOWN.
6. Helicopter – Exit 90 degrees from line of fire.

b. **Emergency Wire Cut.** Should a power loss occur to the TOW system which causes the M65 to momentarily shut down, the system will automatically return to a ready-to-fire mode. If the TCP MODE SELECT switch is in ARMED MAN, then the gunner must press his WIRE CUT to sever the wires to the missile. If the TCP MODE SELECT switch is in ARMED AUTO, the gunner must reset the TCP MODE SELECT switch to manual and turn the MISSILE SELECT switch just fired and then press the WIRE CUT switch to sever wires to the missile just fired. If wire fails to cut, fly helicopter in a crab away from the wire. Approach and landing should be made in a crab to prevent entangling wire with helicopter.

WIRE CUT switch – Press.

c. **TOW Missile Flight Motor Failure.**

WIRE CUT switch – Press.

d. **TOW Missile Erratic in Flight.**

1. Attempt to keep missile down range.

2. Emergency wire – Cut if needed.

9-53. RUNAWAY GUN.

1. MASTER ARM switch – OFF.

2. PLT ORIDE switch – OFF.

Table 9-1. Emergency Procedures for Caution Segments (Pilot and Gunner Caution Panels)

Light	Corrective Action
MASTER CAUTION	(No segment light) LAND AS SOON AS POSSIBLE.
ENG/ENGINE OIL PRESS	LAND AS SOON AS POSSIBLE.
XMSN/TRANS OIL PRESS	LAND AS SOON AS POSSIBLE.
ENG OIL BYPASS	LAND AS SOON AS POSSIBLE.
TRANS OIL BYPASS	LAND AS SOON AS POSSIBLE.
TRANS OIL HOT	LAND AS SOON AS POSSIBLE.
ENG FUEL PUMP	LAND AS SOON AS POSSIBLE.
ENG CHIP	LAND AS SOON AS POSSIBLE.
TRANS, 42°, 90° CHIP	LAND AS SOON AS POSSIBLE.
CHIP DETECTOR	LAND AS SOON AS POSSIBLE.
FWD FUEL BOOST	Refer to emergency procedure.
FUEL FILTER	LAND AS SOON AS POSSIBLE.
FUEL LOW	Information/system status.
AFT FUEL BOOST	Refer to emergency procedure.
DC GEN	Refer to emergency procedure.
RECT	Information/system status.
ALTER	Refer to emergency procedure.
EXT PWR	Close door.
GOV EMERG	Information/system status.
IFF CODE HOLD	Information/system status.
IFF CAUTION	Information/system status.
#1 HYD PRESS	Refer to emergency procedure.
EMERG HYD PUMP ON	Information/system status.
#2 HYD PRESS	Refer to emergency procedure.
SPARE	LAND AS SOON AS POSSIBLE.
GUN ELEV STOWED	Information/system status.
HUD INOP	Information/system status.
FCC INOP	Information/system status.
LASER ARMED	Information/system status.
IRCM INOP	Information/system status.

APPENDIX A
REFERENCES

AR 70-50	Designating and Naming Military Aircraft, Rockets, and Guided Missiles
AR 95-1	Army Aviation General Provisions and Flight Regulations
AR 95-16	Weight and Balance – Army Aircraft
AR 385-40	Accident Reporting and Records
DA Pamphlet 738-751	The Army Maintenance Management System – Aviation (TAMMS-A)
FC 1-213	Aircrew Training Manual
FM 1-202	Environmental Flight
FM 1-203	Fundamentals of Flight
FM 1-204	Night Flight Techniques and Procedures
FM 1-230	Meteorology for Army Aviation
FM 1-240	Instrument Flying and Navigation for Army Aviations
FM 10-68	Aircraft Refueling
TB MED 501	Noise and Conservation of Hearing
TM 9-1005-257-12	Operator and Organizational Maintenance; Armament Pod, Aircraft 7.62MM Machine gun: M18 and M18A1
TM 9-1055-460-14	Operator, Organizational, Direct Support, General Support Maintenance: 2.75 Inch Aircraft Rocket Launcher M158A1, M200, and M200A1
TM 9-1090-203-12	Operator and Organizational Maintenance: Armament Subsystem, Helicopter, 7.62MM Machine Gun - 40MM Grenade Launcher, M28 and M28E1
TM 9-1090-203-12-2	Operator and Organizational Maintenance: Armament Subsystem, Helicopter, 7.62MM Machine Gun - 40MM Grenade Launcher M28E1E2
TM 9-1090-206-20-1	Aviation Unit Maintenance Manual for Armament Subsystem, Helicopter 20MM Automatic Gun: XM97E1
TM 9-1090-206-30	DS & GS Maintenance, Armament Subsystem XM97E1

TM 9-1090-207-13 & P	Aviation Unit and Intermediate Maintenance Manual with Repair Parts and Special Tools List (RPSTL) (Including Depot Maintenance Repair Parts and Special Tools) for Stores Management.
TM 9-1095-206-23 & P	Operator's Aviation Unit Maintenance & Aviation Intermediate Maintenance Manual (Including Repair Parts and Special Tool Lists) M-130 CHAFF Dispenser System.
TM 9-1270-212-14	Operator, Organizational, and Direct Support Maintenance Manual for XM128 and XM136 Helmet Sight Subsystem (HSS)
TM 9-1270-212-14 & P	Operator, Organizational, DS & GS Maintenance Manual & Repair Parts & Special Tools List, Fire Control Subsystems, Helmet Detected M128/M136
TM 9-1270-218-13 & P	Aviation Unit & Intermediate Maintenance Manual & Repair Parts & Special Tools List, Fire Control Computer XM22
TM 9-1270-219-13 & P	Aviation Unit & Intermediate Maintenance Manual & Repair Parts & Special Tools List, Fire & Flight Air Data Subsystem XM143
TM 9-1270-220-13 & P	Aviation Unit & Intermediate Maintenance Manual & Repair Parts & Special Tools List, Heads up Display XM76
TM 9-1425-473-20	Organizational Maintenance Instructions Armament Subsystem, Helicopter, TOW Guided Missile XM65
TM 9-1425-473-34	DS & GS Maintenance Manual, Armament Subsystem, Helicopter, TOW Missile M65
TM 9-4931-363-14 & P	Operator, Organizational, DS & GS Maintenance Manual & Repair Parts & Special Tools List, Fire Control Subsystem, M128 M136 Test Set AN/GSM-249
TM 9-4931-375-13 & P	Aviation Unit & Intermediate Maintenance Manual & Repair Parts & Special Tools List, Fire Control Subsystem, XM141 Computer Test Set
TM 9-4931-376-13 & P	Aviation Unit & Intermediate Maintenance Manual & Repair Parts & Special Tools List, Boresight Controller XM34
TM 9-4931-377-13 & P	Aviation Unit & Intermediate Maintenance Manual & Repair Parts & Special Tools List, Fire Control Subsystem, Test Set XM34
TM 9-4931-378-13 & P	Aviation Unit & Intermediate Maintenance Manual & Repair Parts & Special Tools List, Fire & Flight Air Data Subsystem, Test Set XM142
TM 9-4931-583-23 & P	Aviation Unit & Intermediate Maintenance Manual & Repair Parts & Special Tools List, Boresight Device (AH-1S)
TM 9-4933-224-13 & P	Electronic Test Set XM137
TM 9-4933-227-13 & P	DS & GS Maintenance Manual & Repair Parts & Special Tools List, RMS Test Set XM135

TM 9-4935-473-14-1	Operator, DS, & GS Maintenance Manual Test Set, Guided Missile (TSGM) (TOW Airborne System) includes C1-4
TM 9-4935-473-14-2	Theory & Troubleshooting Maintenance Manual, Test Set, Guided Missile (TSGM) (TOW Airborne System) includes C1-4
TM 11-1520-236-20	Organizational Maintenance Manual, Electronic Equipment Configuration, Army Model AH-2S Helicopters
TM 11-1520-236-34	DS & GS Maintenance Manual, Electronic Equipment Configurations, Army Model AH-1S Helicopters
TM 11-4920-209-15-1	Operator's Organizational, DS, GS, & Depot Maintenance, including Repair Parts & Special Tools List, Table, Tilting, Gyro Instrument Testing MX-4042A/ASW-12
TM 11-5821-259-20	Organizational Maintenance Manual, Radio Sets AN/ARC-114 & AN/ARC-114A, Network Impedance Matching CU 1794/ARC-114; Network Impedance Matching Quadrature Hybrid CU-1796/ARC-114
TM 11-5821-259-35	DS, GS & Depot Maintenance Manual, Radio Sets AN/ARC-114 & AN/ARC-114A
TM 11-5821-260-12-1	Operator's & Organizational Maintenance Manual, Radio Set AN/ARC-115A(V)1
TM 11-5821-260-20	Organizational Maintenance Manual, Radio Set AN/ARC-115
TM 11-5821-260-34-1	DS & GS Maintenance Manual, Radio Set AN/ARC-115A(V)1
TM 11-5821-260-35	DS, GS & Depot Maintenance Manual, Radio Set AN/ARC-115
TM 55-1520-236-CL	Operators and Crewmembers Checklist – AH-1P/E/F Helicopter
TM 750-244-1-5	Procedures for the Destruction of Aircraft and Associated Equipment to Prevent Enemy Use
DOD FLIP	DOD Flight Information Publication (Enroute)
FAR Part 91	Flight Air Regulation Part 91

APPENDIX A
ABBREVIATIONS

AADS	Airspeed and Direction Sensor
ACQ	Acquire
ADF	Automatic Direction Finder
ADI	Attitude Direction Indicator
ADS	Air Data Subsystem, Fire and Flight
AGL	Above Ground Level
ALT	Airborne Laser Tracker
ALT	Altitude
AM	Amplitude Modulation
ANT	Antenna
AVAIL	Available
BAT	Battery
BFO	Beat Frequency Oscillator
BIT	Built-In-Test
BRG PTR	Bearing Pointer
C	Celsius
CAS	Calibrated Airspeed
CARR	Carrier
CCW	Counter Clockwise
CG	Center of Gravity
CHAN	Channel
CL	Centerline
CONFIG	Configuration

CONT	Continuous
CONT	Control
CW	Clockwise
DEC	Decrement
DECR	Decrease
DELTA Δ	Incremental Change
DG	Directional Gyro
DSCRM	Discriminator
ECAS	Enhanced Cobra Armament System
ECS	Environmental Control System
EIA	Electronic Interface Assembly
EID	Emitter Identification Data
EMER	Emergency
END	Endurance
F	Fahrenheit
FAT	Free Air Temperature
FCC	Fire Control Computer
FCP	FLIR Control Panel
FFAR	Folding Fin Aerial Rocket
FIX	Position Fix
FLIR	Forward Looking Infrared
FLT	Flight
FM	Frequency Modulation
FOD	Foreign Object Damage
FPS	Feet Per Second
FT	Foot

FT/MIN	Feet Per Minute
FWD	Forward
ΔF	Increment of Equivalent Flat Plate Drag Area
GACP	Gunner Accuracy Control Panel
GAL	Gallon
GAL/HR	Gallon Per Hour
GD	Guard
GHS	Gunner Helmet Sight
GND	Ground
GNR	Gunner
GPS	Global Positioning System
GRWT	Gross Weight
GW	Gross Weight
GYRO	Gyroscope
HDG	Heading
HP	Horsepower
HR	Hour
HSI	Horizontal Situation Indicator
HSS	Helmet Sight Subsystem
HTR	Heater
HUD	Heads Up Display
HVY HOG	Heavy Hog
HYDR	Hydraulic
Hz	Hertz
IAS	Indicated Airspeed
ICDU	Integrated Control and Display Unit

ICS	Interphone Control Station
IFF	Identification Friend or Foe
IGE	In Ground Effect
IN	Inch
INC	Increment
INCR	Increase
IND	Indication
IN HG	Inches of Mercury
INV	Inverter
IR	Infrared
JTSN	Jettison
KCAS	Knots Calibrated Airspeed
KIAS	Knots Indicated Airspeed
KM	Kilometer
KTAS	Knots True Airspeed
KN	Knots
KVA	Kilovolt-Ampere
L	Left
LB	Pounds
LAI	Low Airspeed Indicator
LB/HR	Pounds Per Hour
LDS	Laser Detecting Set
LHG	Left Hand Grip
LIM	Limit
LOS	Line of Sight
LRF	Laser Range Finder
LTG	Lights

M	Modernized Cobra
MAG	Magnetic
MAN	Manual
MAX	Maximum
MHF	Medium - High Frequency
MHz	Megahertz
MIC	Microphone
MIN	Minimum
MIN	Minute
MM	Millimeter
MOD	Modified
MSI	Missile Status Indicator
NAV	Navigation
NO	Number
NM	Nautical Mile
NORM	Normal
NVG	Night Vision Goggles
N1	Gas Turbine Speed
N2	Power Turbine Speed
OFP	Operational Flight Program
OGE	Out of Ground Effort
OPS	Operations
ORIDE	Override
OVRD	Override
PHS	Pilot Helmet Sight
PLT	Pilot
POS	Position

PRESS	Pressure
PSI	Pounds Per Square Inch
PSI	Pilot Steering Indicator
PVT	Private
PWR	Power
%Q	Percent Torque
R	Right
R + A	Range and Azimuth
R/C	Rate of Climb
RCVR	Receiver
R/D	Rate of Descent
RMI	Radio Magnetic Indicator
RPM	Revolutions Per Minute
RKT	Rocket
RMS	Rocket Management Subsystem
RSDS	Radar Signal Detecting Set
RTCL	Reticle
SAS	Stability Augmentation System
SCAS	Stability and Control Augmentation System
SECU	Servo Electronic Control Unit
SEL	Select
SIF	Selected Identification Features
SHC	Sight Hand Control
SPEC	Specification
SQ	Squelch
STA	Station
STBY	Standby

STS	Status and Setup
SQ FT	Square Feet
TAS	True Airspeed
TCP	TOW Control Panel
TGT	Turbine Gas Temperature
TML	TOW Missile Launcher
TMS	TOW Missile System
TOW	Tube-Launched, Optically-Tracked, Wire Command Link
T/R	Transmit-Receive
TRK	Track
TRQ	Torque
TSU	Telescopic Sight Unit
UHF	Ultra-High Frequency
USAASTA	United States Army Aviation Systems Test Activity
VAC	Volts, Alternating Current
VCR	Video Cassette Recorder
VDC	Volts, Direct Current
VHF	Very High Frequency
VIGV	Variable Inlet Guide Vane
VOL	Volume
VOR	VHF Omnidirectional Range
V_{NE}	Velocity, Never Exceed (Airspeed Limitation)
VSI	Vertical Speed Indicator
WG STA	Wing Station
WPN	Weapon
WPT	Waypoint

XMTR   Transmitter

XMSN   Transmission

XPDR   Transponder

INDEX

| Subject | Paragraph, Figure, Table Number | Subject | Paragraph, Figure, Table Number |

Numbers

100% RPM Fuel Flow Chart .... F 7.1-10,
 7.1-30
100% RPM Fuel Flow Chart .... F 7-10, 7-30
2.75 Inch Rocket Launcher Moment Chart
 F 6-3, 6-7
2.75 Rockets/19 Round Pods Outboard Wing Stations
 6-8

A

AC Power Indicators and Controls 2-62
After Emergency Action 9-4
AH-1 Aircraft with Miles/Ages Installed Per
 TM 9-1270-223-10 Have The Following
 Restrictions 5-15
Air Induction System 2-19
Airborne Laser Tracker (ALT) 4-23
Airspeed Indicators 2-69
Airspeed Limitations 5-11
Airspeed Operating Limits Chart .... F 5-3, 5-11
ALT - Inflight Procedures 4-27
ALT Control Panel .... F 4-22, 4-10, 4-23
ALT Major Components - Helicopter Locations
 F 4-23, 4-23
Alternator 2-57
Alternator Failure Alter and Rect Caution Light
 Illumination 9-37
Ammunition Moment Table .... F 6-7, 6-7
Antenna Locations .... F 3-2, 3-2
Anti-Collision Light 2-64
Appendix A. References 1-4
Appendix B. Abbreviations and Terms 1-5
Approved Commercial Fluids - Equivalents
 for MIL-H-5606 .... F 2-28, 2-86
Approved Commercial Fuels - Equivalents for
 JP-4, JP-5 and JP-8 .... F 2-26, 2-61
Approved Commercial Fuels - Equivalents for
 JP-4, JP-5, and JP-8 .... F 2-26, 2-86, 2-88

Index 1

Subject	Paragraph, Figure, Table Number
Approved Commercial Fuels, Oils, and Fluids	2-86
Approved Commercial Oils - Equivalents for MIL-L7808 and MIL-L23699 Oils	F 2-27, 2-86
Approved Military Fuels, Oils, Fluids and Unit Capacities	F 2-25, 2-85, 2-88
Area 1 - Fuselage and Main Rotor	8-14
Area 2 - Tailsection - Right Side	8-15
Area 3 - Tail section - Left Side	8-16
Area 4 - Fuselage - Left Side	8-17
Area 5 - Nose Section	8-18
Armament Description	4-12
Armament Firing Modes	4-8
Armament Firing Modes	F 4-4, 4-8, 4-10, 4-11
Armament Hydraulic System	2-44
Armament-Systems Check	4-24
Army Aviation Safety Program	1-7
Authorized Armament Configuration	F 4-2, 4-6
Authorized Armament Configurations	4-6
Autorotation Characteristics	8-41
Aviation Life Support Equipment (ALSE)	8-6

B

Subject	Paragraph, Figure, Table Number
Battery	2-55
Before Exterior Check	8-12
Before Landing	8-26
Before Leaving Helicopter	8-28
Before Starting Engine - Gunners Station	8-20
Before Starting Engine - Pilot Station	8-21
Before Take Off Check	8-24
Blade Stall	8-32

C

Subject	Paragraph, Figure, Table Number
Canopy	2-9
Canopy Defrosting Deicing and Rain Removal Systems	2-52
Canopy Door Limitations	5-12
Canopy Removal System	2-15

Center of Gravity Limitations	5-8
Chaff Dispenser	M-130, 4-31
Chapter 7 Index	7-2
Chapter 7.1 Index	7.1-2
Chart Differences	7-14, 7.1-14
Checklist	8-10
Circuit Breaker Panels	F 2-20, 4-3
Circuit Breaker Panels	F 2-20, 2-62, 2-63, 2-65
Circuit Breaker Panels	F 2-20, 2-61
Circuit Breaker Panels	F 2-20, 4-12
Classification of Helicopter	6-2
Climb - Descent Chart	F 7-9, 7-27
Climb Descent Chart	F 7.1-9, 7.1-27
Clutch Fails To Disengage	9-24
Clutch Fails To Re-Engage	9-25
Cockpit Utility Lights	2-66
Cold Weather Operations	8-45
Collective Control System	2-31
Combination of Light and Heavy 2.75 Rockets on Outboard Wing Stations (19 Round Pod) 6-4, 6-7, 6-8	F
Communication and Associated Electronics Equipment	F 3-1, 3-2
Compass Control Panel C-6347( )ASN–43 F 3-13, 3-51	
Conditions 7-16, 7-20, 7-23, 7-26, 7-29, 7-32, 7.1-16, 7.1-20, 7.1-23, 7.1-32	
Conditions. Not applicable	7.1-26, 7.1-29
Control AN/ARC-186(V)	F 3-9, 3-35
Control Components In Relationship To Armament Subsystems	F 4-3, 4-7, 4-10, 4-11
Control Feedback	8-33
Control Margin	7-19, 7.1-19
Controls and Functions - Direction Finder Set 3-47	
Controls and Functions - Gyromagnetic Compass	3-51
Controls and Functions - Horizontal Situation Indicator (HSI)	3-43
Controls and Functions - Laser Detecting Set	3-82
Controls and Functions - Radio Set AN/ARC-186(V)	3-35
Controls and Functions - Transponder Set	3-68
Controls and Functions - VHF/AM Radio Set	3-26

Controls and Functions - VHF/FM Radio 3-9
Controls and Functions - VOR/LOG/GS/MB System 3-55
Controls and Functions GPS Trimpack 3-64
Controls and Functions Infrared - Countermeasures Set 4-2
Controls and Functions Interphone Control 3-5
Controls and Functions Radar Warning Set 3-74, 3-78
Controls and Functions UHF/AM Radio Set 3-30
Controls and Functions VHF/FM Radio Set 3-13
Controls and Functions Voice Security Equipment TSEC/KY-58 3-17
Controls and Indicators 2-28
Course Indicator (RMI) Gunner .... F 3-15, 3-50
Course Indicator (RMI) Gunner F-15, 3-54
Crew Brief 8-2
Crew Briefing 8-3
Crew Compartment Diagrams 2-6
Crew Duties/Responsibilities 8-1
Cruise Chart .... F 7.1-7, 7.1-21, 7.1-22
Cruise Chart .... F 7-7, 7-21, 7-22, 7-25
Cyclic Control System 2-30

D

Danger Areas 8-4
Danger Areas .... F 8-1, 8-4
Data Basis 7-6, 7.1-6
DC and AC Power Distribution 2-54
DC and AC Power Distribution Schematic .... F 2-18, 4-3
DC and AC Power Distribution Schematic .... F 2-18, 2-54, 2-55, 2-63 2-65

Subject	Paragraph, Figure, Table Number
DC Generator Failure DC Caution Light Illumination	9-36
Definition of Emergency Terms	9-3
Definitions of Abbreviations	7-10, 7.1-10
Description	1-3, 2-29, 2-35, 7-13, 7-17, 7-21, 7-24, 7-27, 7-30, 7.1-13, 7.1-17, 7.1-21, 7.1-24, 7.1-27, 7.1-30
Description - Direction Finder Set	3-46
Description - GPS Trimpack	3-63
Description - Gyromagnetic Compass	3-50
Description - Horizontal Situation Indicator (HSI)	3-42
Description - Infrared Countermeasure Set AN/ALQ-144	4-1
Description - Laser Detecting Set	3-81
Description - Radar Jammer Set AN/ALQ-136	4-3
Description - Radar Warning Set	3-73, 3-77
Description - Radio Set AN/ARC-186(V)	3-34
Description - Transponder Set	3-67
Description - UHF/AM Radio Set	3-29
Description - VHF/AM Radio Set	3-25
Description - Voice Security Equipment TSEC/KY-58	3-16
Description - VOR/LOC/GS/MB System	3-54
Description - Interphone Control	3-4
Description of Dispenser, General Purpose M-130,	4-29
Description - VHF/FM Radio Set	3-8, 3-12
Descriptionn - Doppler Navigation Set	3-58
Desert and Hot Weather Operation	8-47
Destruction of Army Material to Prevent Enemy Use	1-8
Direction Finder Set	3-45
Direction Finder Set AN/ARN-89	F 3-12, 3-47
Directional Control Margin Chart	F 7-6, 7-19
Dispenser Sub-Systems	4-30
Ditching - Power Off	9-46
Ditching - Power On	9-45
Diving Flight	8-34
Doppler Navigation Set	3-57

Doppler Navigation System .... F 3-17, 2-68
Doppler Navigation System .... F 3-17, 3-60
Drag Chart .... F 7.1-8, 7.1-21, 7.1-24
Drag Chart .... F 7-8, 7-21, 7-24, 7-25
Driveshafts 2-47
Droop Compensator Failure 9-14
Droop Compersator 2-24

E

ECS Controls .... F 2-17, 2-51, 2-53
Electrical Circuit 2-42
Electrical Fire-Flight 9-30
Electrical System 9-35
Electronic Equipment Configuration 3-2
Emergency Entrance 9-5
Emergency Equipment 9-6
Emergency Exits and Equipment (Typical) .... F 9-1, 2-12,
   2-13, 2-15, 9-3, 9-6
Emergency Hydraulic System 2-43
Emergency Operation 3-32
Emergency Operation Transponder Set 3-70
Emergency Procedures for Caution Segments
   T 9-1, 9-53
Engine 2-17, 9-9
Engine Compressor Stall 9-15
Engine Fire Detection System 2-81
Engine Fuel Control System 2-21
Engine Inlet Anti-Icing/Deicing System 2-20
Engine Instruments and Indicators 2-26
Engine Limitations (Figure 5-1) 5-7
Engine Malfunction - 120 KIAS and Above 9-13
Engine Malfunction - Hover 9-11
Engine Malfunction - Low Altitude/Low
   Airspeed or Cruise 9-12

Subject	Paragraph, Figure, Table Number
Engine Malfunction-Partial or Complete Power Loss	9-10
Engine Oil Supply System	2-25
Engine Overspeed	9-17
Engine Protection	2-18
Engine Runup	8-23
Engine Shutdown	8-27
Engine-Oil Temperature High	9-18
Environmental Control System (ECS)	2-53
Environmental Restrictions	5-14
Exceeding Operational Limits	5-3
Explanation of Change Symbols	1-10
Exterior Check (Fig 8-2)	8-13
External Power Receptacle	2-59

F

Subject	Paragraph, Figure, Table Number
Filter Indicators	2-40
Fire	9-26
Fire-Engine Start	9-27
Fire-Flight	9-29
Fire-Ground	9-28
First Aid Kit	2-13
Flight Control/Main Rotor System Malfunctions	9-47
FLIR Control Panel (FCP)	F 4-10, 4-11
Folding Fin Aerial Rocket (2.75 inch) Launcher	F 4-18, 4-18
Folding Fin Aerial Rocket Moment Chart	F 6-5, 6-7
Folding Fin Aerial Rocket Moment Chart	F 6-6, 6-7
Force Trim System	2-33
Forms and Records	1-9
Free Air Temperature (FAT) Indicator	2-73
Fuel	9-33
Fuel Data	6-9
Fuel Moment Chart	F 6-10, 6-9
Fuel Supply System	2-27
Fuel System Servicing	2-88

Index 7

Fumes From ECS 9-31

G

Gear Boxes 2-46
General 1-1, 3-1, 5-2, 6-1, 7-3, 7.1-3, 8-43
General Arrangement 2-2
General Arrangement (Typical) .... F 2-1, 2-63
General Arrangement .... F 2-1, 2-2, 2-30, 2-46, 2-51, 2-59, 2-65, 2-69, 4-12
General Conditions 7-8, 7.1-8
General Description 2-1
GPS Trimpack 3-62
GPS Trimpack .... F 3-18, 3-64
Gunner Armament Control Panel .... F 4-13, 4-11
Gunner Electrical Power Control 2-60
Gunner Instrument and Control Panel
.... F 2-7, 2-8, 2-26, 2-43, 2-49, 2-67, 2-68, 2-69, 2-71, 2-72, 2-74
Gunner Map Case 2-83
Gunner Miscellaneous Control Panel (Typical) .... F 2-12, 2-26
Gunner Miscellaneous Control Panel .... F 2-11, 2-21, 2-23, 2-68
Gunner Miscellaneous Control Panel .... F 2-12, 2-20, 2-21, 2-23, 2-60, 2-68, 2-76
Gunner Sight Hand Control (SHC) ...... F 4-14, 4-11
Gunner Station Diagram .... F 2-5, 2-6, 2-68
Gunner Station Lighting 2-68
Gunner Switches and Indicators 4-11
Gunner Telescopic Sight Unit (TSU) With FLIR ....
F 4-9, 4-11
Gunner TOW Control Panel (TCP) .... F 4-7, 4-11
Gunnery Checklist - Engine Run-Up Procedure
.... 4-25
Gunnery Checklist - Engine Shutdown Hot/Cold Arming Procedures ....
4-26
Gyromagnetic Compass Set 3-49

Subject	Paragraph, Figure, Table Number

H

Subject	Paragraph, Figure, Table Number
Heads Up Display (HUD)	4-13
Heads Up Display	F 4-5, 4-10
Height Velocity Diagram	F 9-2, 9-10
Helicopter Designation System	1-11
Helicopter Station Diagram	6-3
Helicopter Station Diagram (Typical)	F 6-1, 6-3
Helicopter Systems	9-1
Helmet Sight Subsystem (HSS)	F 4-6, 4-10, 4-11
Helmet Sight Subsystem (HSS)	4-14
Horizontal Situation Indicator (HSI)	F 3-10, 3-42, 3-43, 3-50
Horizontal Situation Indicator (HSI)	3-41
Hover (Ceiling) Chart	F 7.1-5, 7.1-17
Hover (Ceiling) Chart	F 7-5, 7-17
Hover Ceiling Chart	F 7.1-5, 7.1-19
Hover Check	8-25
HSI Display Control Panel	F 3-11, 3-42, 3-43
Hydraulic Failure - Dual System	9-42
Hydraulic Failure - Single System	9-41
Hydraulic System Failure	9-40
Hydraulic System No. 1	2-36
Hydraulic System No. 2	2-37

I

Icing Conditions	8-49
Ignition - Starter System	2-22
Immediate Action Emergency Steps	9-2
Index	1-6
Indicators and Caution Lights	2-48
Inlet Guide Vane Actuator Failure	9-16
Instrument Flight Procedures	8-29
Instrument Markings (Figure 5-1)	5-5
Instrument Markings	F 5-1, 5-6, 5-7
Instruments and Controls, Pilot Instrument Panel Gunner Instrument Panel	2-8

Integrated Armament Functional Description 4-9
Interphone Control 3-3
Interphone Control Panel C-6533/( )/ARC
   F 3-3, 3-5
Interrelation of Armament 4-7

J

K

KY - 58 Audio Tones - Normal and Equipment
   Malfunction 3-23

L

Landing and Ditching 9-43
Landing Gear 2-7
Landing In Trees 9-44
Laser Detecting Set 3-80
Laser Range Finder Control Panel .... F 4-15, 4-11
Laser Range Finder Firing Is Accommplished As
   Follows 4-16
Limits 7-4, 7.1-4
Loading Charts 6-4
Low Airspeed Indicator (LAI) 2-70
Low Airspeed Indicator (LAI) ..... F 2-22, 2-70, 4-12
Low G Maneuvers 8-39
Low G Warning 9-48
Low G Warning System 2-78
Low Pressure Caution Lights 2-41

M

M 130 Chaff Moment Chart .... F 6-9, 6-4
M147 Rocket Management Subsystem (RMS) Display Unit .... F 4-16, 4-10
M147 Rocket Management System
   F 4-17, 2-67, 2-68

Subject	Paragraph, Figure, Table Number
Magnetic (Standby) Compass	2-74
Main Differences	2-5
Main Driveshaft Failure	9-22
Main Rotor	2-49
Maneuvering Flight	8-38
Mast Bumping	8-42, 9-49
Master Caution System	2-76
Maximum Glide Distance	9-8
Maximum Torque Available (30 Minute Operation) Chart	F 7-2, 7-14, 7-16, 7-17
Maximum Torque Available (30-Minute Operation) Chart	F 7.1-2, 7.1-14, 7.1-16,
Maximum Torque Available (30-Minute Operation) Chart	F 7.1-2, 7.1-17, 7.1-18
Miles/Ages	4-5
Minimum Crew Requirements	5-4
Minimum Rate of Descent	9-7
Mission Equipment Checks	8-8
Mission Planning	8-5
Mode 4 Operation (APX-100)	3-71

N

Subject	Paragraph, Figure, Table Number
Night Vision Goggle (NVG) Bags	2-84

O

Subject	Paragraph, Figure, Table Number
Oil Data	6-10
Oil Debris Detection System (ODDS)	2-79
Operating Characteristics	8-30
Operating Procedures - Automatic Remote Keying	3-21
Operating Procedures - Clear Voice	3-19
Operating Procedures - Manual Remote Keying	3-22
Operating Procedures - Radio set AN/ARC - 186	3-40
Operating Procedures - Zeroing	3-20
Operating Procedures and Maneuvers	8-7
Operating Procedures Secure Voice	3-18

Operation - AM Emergency (EMER AM) Mode . 3-38
Operation - Control (Mode) Settings 3-36
Operation - Direction Finder Set 3-48
Operation - Doppler Navigation Set
.... 3-60, 3-61
Operation - FM Emergency (EMER FM) Mode
3-39
Operation - GPS Trimpack 3-65
Operation - Gyromagnetic Compass 3-52
Operation - Horizontal Situation Indicator (HSI)
3-44
Operation - Laser Detecting Set (AN/APR-39(V)1
and AN/APR-39A(V) Family) 3-83
Operation - Radar Warning System 3-75, 3-79
Operation - Transponder Set 3-69
Operation - UHF/AM Radio Set 3-31
Operation - VHF/AM Radio Set 3-27
Operation - VOR/LOC/GS/MB System 3-56
Operation - Interphone Control 3-6
Operation - Transmit/Receive (TR) Mode 3-37
Operation VHF/FM Radio Set 3-14
Operation - Radar Countermeasures Set 4-4
Operation - VHF/FM Radio Set 3-10
Over Torque Caution Light 2-80
Overheated Battery 9-39

P

Performance Discrepancies 7-9, 7.1-9
Performance Planning 7-11, 7.1-11
Personnel Moment Chart .... F 6-2, 6-6
Personnel Doors 2-10
Personnel Moments 6-6
Pilot and Gunner Caution Panels
2-61, 2-62, 2-76
Pilot and Gunner Caution Panels ...... F 2-23, 2-28
Pilot and Gunner Cyclic Control Stick
F 2-14, 2-33, 2-34, 4-11
Pilot and Gunner Cyclic Control Stick
2-67, 2-68
Pilot Armament Circuit Breakers .... F 4-24, 4-10

Subject	Paragraph, Figure, Table Number	Subject	Paragraph, Figure, Table Number
Pilot Armament Control Panel	F 4-12, 4-10		
Pilot Checklist Holder	2-82		
Pilot Collective Control Stick	2-65		F 2-15, 2-21, 2-22, 2-31,
Pilot DC Power Indicators and Controls	2-61		
Pilot Electrical Power Panel	F 2-19, 2-61, 2-62		
Pilot Engine Control Panel	2-26, 2-28, 2-33, 2-77		F 2-10, 2-20, 2-22, 2-25,
Pilot Instrument and Control Panel	2-67, 2-69, 2-71, 2-72, 2-73, 2-77, 2-78, 2-80, 2-81		F 2-6, 2-8, 2-22, 2-26, 2-28, 2-48, 2-49,
Pilot Instrument and Control Panel	F 2-6, 4-3		
Pilot Instrument and Control Panel	F2-6, 2-67		
Pilot Light Control Panel	F 2-21, 2-64		
Pilot Light Control Panel	2-64, 2-67, 2-76		F 2-21, 2-63,
Pilot Miscellaneous Control Panel	2-43		F 2-13, 2-28,
Pilot SCAS Control Panel	F 2-16, 2-34		
Pilot Seat Installation	F 2-8, 2-11		
Pilot Station Diagram (Typical)	F 2-4, 4-20		
Pilot Station Diagram	F 2-4, 2-6, 2-65		
Pilot Station Lighting	2-67		
Pilot Switches and Indicators	4-10		
Pitch Cone Coupling	8-36		
Pitot Tube/Air Data System Heater	2-51		
Portable Fire Extinguisher	2-12		
Position Lights	2-63		
Power Dives	8-35		
Power Plant Installation	F 2-9, 2-17		
Preflight Check	8-11		
Pressure Altimeters	2-71		
Principal Dimensions	2-3		
Principal Dimensions	F 2-2, 2-3		
Prohibited Maneuvers	5-13		
Purpose	5-1, 7-1, 7.1-1		

R

Radar Countermeasures Set Control Indicator F 4-1, 4-4

Radar-Warning Indicator and Control AN/APR-39 F 3-20, 2-67 ....

Radar Warning Indicator and Control AN/APR-39 F 3-20, 3-74 ....

Radar Warning Indicator and Control AN/APR-39 F 3-20, 3-82 ....

Radar Warning Indicator and Control AN/APR-39A(V)1 3-82 .... F 3-22, 3-78,

Radar Warning Indicator Self-Test Displays AN/APR-39(V)1 .... F 3-21, 3-75

Radar Warning Indicator Self-Test Displays AN/APR-39A(V)1 .... F 3-22, 3-78

Radar Warning Set 3-72, 3-76

Radio Aids To Navigation 2-75

Radio Set AN/ARC-186 (V) 3-33

Rain 8-50

Reservoir Fluid Sight Gasses 2-39

Restriction - Doppler Navigation Set 3-59

Rocket Operation - Inflight Procedures 4-19

Rockets 4-18

Rollover Characteristics 8-31

Rotor Limitations 5-6

Rotor RPM - Power Off 8-40

Rotors, Transmission, and Drive Systems 9-19

RPM High - Low Limit Warning System 2-77

RPM Increase-Decrease (Incr-decr) Switches 2-23 ....

Runaway Gun 9-53

Subject	Paragraph, Figure, Table Number

S

Subject	Ref
Search Light/Landing Light	2-65
Seats	2-11
Series and Effectivity Codes	1-12
Servicing	2-85
Servicing Diagram	F 2-24, 2-85, 2-88
Single or Dual Fuel Boost Pump Failure	9-34
Smoke and Fume Elimination	9-31, 9-32
Snow	8-46
Specific Conditions	7-7, 7.1-7
Stability and Control Augmentation System (SCAS)	2-34
Stability and Control Augmentation System(SCAS) Failure	9-50
Starter - Generator	2-56
Starting Engine	8-22
Survival Kit	2-14
Symbols Definition	8-9

T

Subject	Ref
Tail Rotor	2-50
Tail Rotor Control System	2-32
Tail Rotor Failure - Flight	9-20
Tail Rotor Failure - Hover	9-21
Telescopic Sight Unit (TSU)	F 4-8, 4-11
Temperature Conversion	7-12, 7.1-12
Temperature Conversion Chart	F 7.1-1, 7.1-12
Temperature Conversion Chart	F 7-1, 7-12
Temperature Limitation (Hub Moment Spring Aircraft Only)	8-44
Test Switch	2-38
Torque Available (Continuous Operation) Chart	7.1-14, 7.1-16
Torque Available (Continuous Operation) Chart	F 7-3, 7-16
Torque Available (Continuous Operation) Chart	F 7-3, 7-14

F 7.1-3,

TOW Missile 4-15
Tow Missile Emergency Procedures 9-52
TOW Missile Launcher .... F 4-11, 2-67, 4-15
TOW Missile Moment Chart .... F 6-8, 6-7, 6-9
Tow Operation - Inflight Procedures 4-17
Transformer Rectifier Unit (TRU) 2-58
Transformer Rectifier Unit (TRU) Failure – Rect Caution Light Illumination 9-38
Transient Torque 8-37
Transmission 2-45
Transmission Sprag Clutch Malfunction 9-23
Transponder Set 3-66
Transponder Set (AN/APX-100) Control Panel F 3-19, 3-68
Turbulence and Thunderstorms 8-48
Turbulence Restrictions 5-9
Turning Radius 2-4
Turning Radius .... F 2-3, 2-4
Turret Operation - Inflight Procedures 4-21
Types and Uses of Fuels Oils and Fluids 2-87

U

UHF/AM Radio Set 3-28
Universal Turret 4-20
Universal Turret Components F 4-20, 4-11, 4-20
Use of Chart 7-18, 7-25, 7-28, 7-31, 7.1-18, 7.1-25, 7.1-28, 7.1-31
Use of Charts 7-5, 7-15, 7-22, 7.1-5, 7.1-15, 7.1-22
Use of Shall, Will, Should, and May 1-13

Subject	Paragraph, Figure, Table Number

V

Subject	Paragraph, Figure, Table Number
Vertical Speed Indicator	2-72
VHF/AM Radio Set	3-24
VHF/AM Radio Set AN/ARC-115	F 3-7, 3-26
VHF/FM Radio (AN/ARC-201)	3-11
VHF/FM Radio Set	3-7
VHF/FM Radio Set AN/ARC-114A	F 3-4, 3-9
VHF/FM Radio Set AN/ARC-201	F 3-5, 3-13
Voice Security Equipment T/SEC KY-58	F 3 - 6: 3-17
Voice Security Equipment T/SEC KY-58	F 3-6, 3-15
VOR/LOC/GS/MB Control Panel C-10048/ARN-123	F 3-16, 3-55
VOR/LOC/GS/MB System	3-53

W

Subject	Paragraph, Figure, Table Number
Walk Around Check	8-19
Warning, Cautions, and Notes Definition	1-2
Weight and Balance Loading Data	6-7
Weight and Balance Records	6-5
Weight Limitations	5-10
Wing Stores Emergency Jettison	9-51
Wing Stores Jettison	2-16, 4-22
Wing Stores Jettison	F 4-21, 4-10
Wire Strike Protection System	4-28
Wire Strike Protection System	F 4-25, 4-28

X Y Z

©2011 Periscope Film LLC
ISBN #978-1-935700-64-7
www.PeriscopeFilm.com

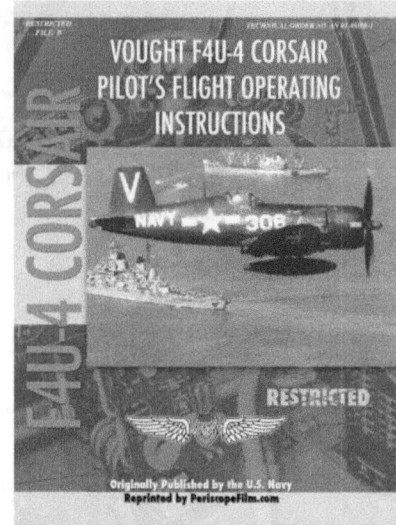
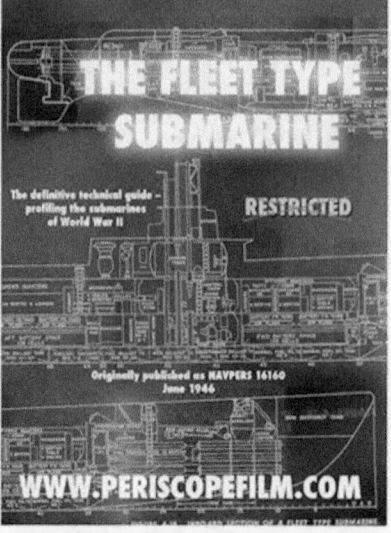
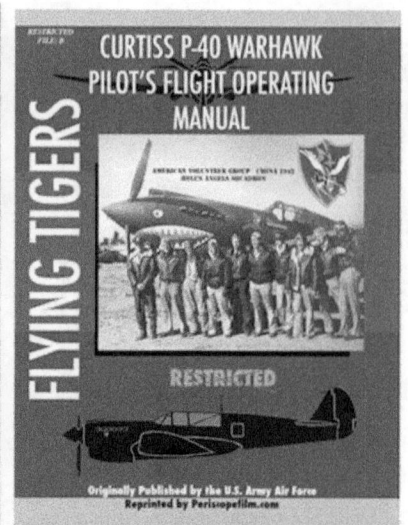

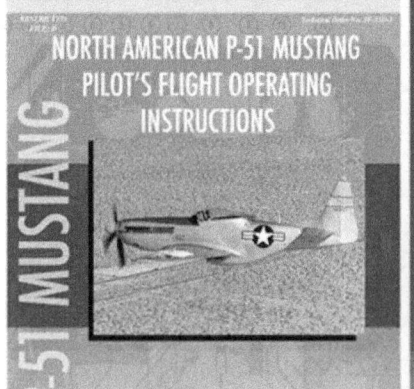

ALSO NOW AVAILABLE
FROM PERISCOPEFILM.COM